AF477311

Praise for *The Flight of Kurrawurra*

This is lovely work. You've connected very well the artwork and the inspiration you feel directly from. Readers can feel how close to your heart this is. Thank you.

—Professor Liz Stephens, author of Days Are Gods

That is a beautiful painting of a mother and her child. Your relationship with your mother must have been very special.

—Judith Dickson

What an epic experience. It seems a lifetime is lived in such a few short years.

—Dionne Sincere

Bravo on a strong, engaging, heartfelt piece.

—Leah Erickson

Thank you for sharing your lovely story! It is like a painting.

—Sahar Kashi

5 stars Reviews. Readers Favorite.
The Flight of Kurrawurra will leave readers enriched and connected, to experience joy and beauty of just having lived on the earth.

—Mamta Madhavan

5 star review from Readers Favorite.
Pertinent to spirituality and especially the current issues facing humanity, we journey with the author in an edification that is sure to open many eyes and ears to new perspectives.

—K.C.Finn

THE FLIGHT OF KURRAWURRA

THE **FLIGHT** OF KURRAWURRA

AN AUSTRALIAN ODYSSEY

LYNDON PATRICK BERCHY

The Flight of Kurrawurra. An Australian Odyssey.

For information about this title or to order other books and/or electronic media, contact the publisher:

Wedgetailbooks Publishing

Norra Ringvagen 8
Kristinehamn 681 34
Varmlands
Sweden
www.wedgetailbooks.com

ISBNs:
978-91-986372-0-5 Hardcover Print Version
978-91-986372-1-2 Softcover Print Version
978-91-986372-2-9 eBook Version

Printed in the United States of America

Library of Congress Control Number: 1-8848899461

Cover and Interior design and Book Trailer: 1106 Design

Visit the author's web site at www.wedgetailbooks.com

And to Him forever be the glory,
the Giver of all gifts and blessings.

For my mother and father.
My sons, Sean and Joshua—a stolen generation.
My daughters, Caitlin, Faye, and Elaine.
For my native people of Australia.

To those who judge the degree of a culture by the degree of its technological sophistication, the fact that the Australian natives live in the same fashion now as they did thousands of years ago may imply that they are uncivilised or uncultured. However, I would suggest that if a civilization be defined by the degree of polishing of an individual's mind and the building of his or her character, and if that culture reflects the measure of our self-discipline as well as our level of consciousness, then the Australian Aboriginals are actually one of the most civilised and highly cultured peoples in the world today.

~ THE VENERABLE E. NANDISVARA
Nayake Thero, PhD

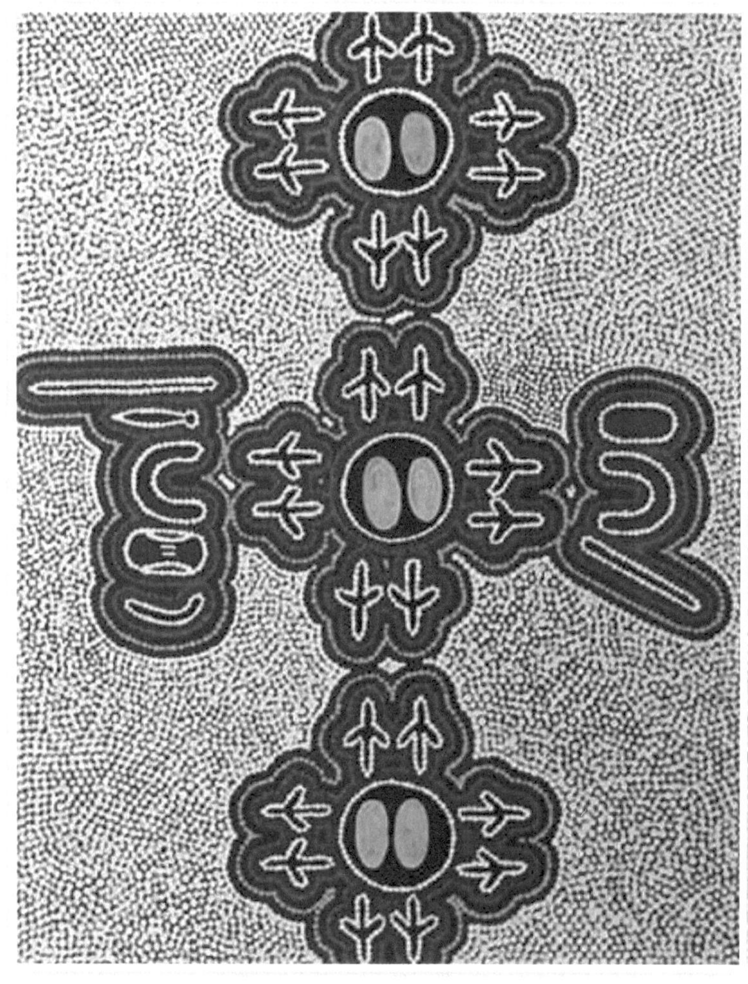

Wedgetail Eagle, *a native Australian painting by Linda Walker Napurrula.*

"A meandering dream to meet me there,

a place and time—a memory to hold.

Go ahead on, mate, don't ponder where

An old man is waiting for a story to be told

A smile and Mirriwa to meet and greet (Mirriwa is a frilled lizard)
A grey-haired man to help you walk with your feet.

Can you now find water in a hole? Out in the desert sand I am told?

Look for footprints of birds and beast converging close
or be lost wandering and die of thirst"

Oh, my soul! You have carried me to the wise and old.

~ Lyndon Patrick Berchy

CONTENTS

PART ONE

PART TWO

PART THREE

THE FLIGHT OF KURRAWURRA

The Flight of Kurrawurra is a novel of an incredible adventure, awesome storytelling, a pilgrimage of a moral purpose, considering a genuine, uncommon story of the existence of an Anglo-Indian youngster transforming into a man through human adversity.

In the late 1980s, the author set out on a journey from India to the land of his dreams—Australia. Relinquishing a cherishing family for an enterprise of a fantasy, he lives as an illicit migrant; embracing the Aussie culture, he escapes into the outback to live with native Aboriginal people. In the endlessness of the red land, he finds a people and culture that enamor his spirit. Intrinsically woven into its magic, the torments of a lost era, a stolen generation, a people so extraordinarily wronged by this nation, he is held together as one of their own.

In a franticness and aching to see his parents, whom he lovingly cherished, he unlawfully changes his name and gets an Australian nationality with an alternate identity.

Fortified with this freedom to leave and return to Australian shores, he sets out on a reroute journey that discovers him in Europe. He gets hitched and becomes a father of two children; he then confronts the ethical issue of separation and divorce, torn from his children and sold out by the woman he cherished. His children, now a stolen generation of a civilised society, were reliving an ancient Aboriginal pain once again.

Through prospects of incarceration and an awful battle to see his kids, he is educated of European injustice, embarking on a course like climbing Mount Everest without oxygen, on the road to the "court of human wrongs." His is a remarkably awakening, spiritual journey—a liberation of truth, love, and a revelation of the Word of God, restoration of his soul.

Unfathomably, this story is a noteworthy tribute to his resolve that will enthral your heart. This is an eye-gouging enterprise, an affectionate adventure, yet delicately, an expressive, fugitive vision.

This book will abandon you with mind-boggling quality to recognise what is conceivable when you accept and walk in soul and not in substance to overcome this human life. This is not a fluke; this is a memoir of a powerful spiritual journey, a pilgrimage of grace, revelation, and faith with works.

Phenomenally clear, a colossally stunning, gritty bona fide adventure of human endeavour to caress your soul.

PREFACE

To envision that I am as yet alive composing this book is a supernatural occurrence. I lived through hazardous circumstances, ventured to the far corners of the planet, and headed out to faraway goals that the vast majority would not have envisioned. I met such a significant number of individuals en route. The human condition has moved me. Maybe, of all the difficulties I have seen and suffered, I think understanding the Gospel might be our most prominent test yet. It is the human condition that exists in a fallen state as far back as when Adam and Eve were ousted from the Garden of Eden. What is striking about that terrible event is that God sewed clothes and covered the naked bodies that had become sinful. That condition of man and woman still prevails in the world even today. I had this vision of a father watching his children leave from the east of the Garden. I wondered how God felt to see them go. It must have been painful because He is the God who loves us.

Today the world may appear to be more befuddled than it was at any point, and understanding the Gospel might be more puzzling than it was at any point.

As we are inundated by a host of media, it would require a nonadherent superhuman exertion to envision an existence where no media existed by any means.

In my journey in Israel, hiking through the Golan trail, walking in this ancient land, it was hard to imagine that at the time of the

Gospel, information and communication were happening in a world where no technology existed; communication was done through the spoken word. I was asked by a Jewish companion an essential inquiry: What did God do before He made the world? I had come unravelled by the question to which I had no response to give the man. He grinned at me and urged me to think progressively significant. However, regardless, I couldn't find the understanding into the solution to this inquiry. He set his arm around my shoulder and stated, "I see you have an extraordinary hunger for the Word." At that point, it came as a fortune revelation. The Lord God made the Word, the letters to speak the Word. Blessed be his holy name. Yvhv. Of course, it struck me: the Word was made. My joy was so full the moment I understood. I was excited and my joy contagious.

"Yes, indeed," added my Jewish friend. "Let's go to the beginning, shall we?" Then we opened the Bible and read Genesis 1:1–3.

1. In the beginning, God created the heaven and the earth.
2. And the ground was without form and void, and darkness was upon the face of the deep. And the Spirit of God moved upon the front of the waters.
3. And God said, let there be light: and there was light.

We paused and realised that the Word was created first. Because it had to be spoken, and as the scriptures read, the spirit of the Lord moved upon the faces of the water; and when God spoke the Word, the Spirit carried out the commandment. So, the Spirit and the Word are one, and they are together. And so, as it also is written in the Gospel of John 1:1–5,

1. In the beginning, was the Word, and the Word was with God, and the Word was God.
2. The same was at the beginning with God.
3. All things were made by him, and without him was not anything made that was made.
4. In him was life, and the life was the light of men.
5. And the light shineth in darkness; and the darkness comprehended it not.

And for this reason, Yeshua HaMashiach, Jesus Christ, spoke the Word.

> 5. Jesus answered, Verily, verily, I say unto thee, Except a man be born of water and the Spirit, he cannot enter into the kingdom of God.
> 6. That which is born of the flesh is flesh, and that which is born of the Spirit is Spirit. (John 3:5–6)

Glory, hallelujah.

In the times of Jesus, people were not educated. Henceforth, the spoken word was a dominant part of individuals' communication, and they may have been uneducated or scarcely proficient; they didn't have a clue about any language other than the one verbally expressed by their folks. They wedded among their various factions and carried on with the existence of working the land and getting fish from the sea of Galilee. Vast numbers of them lived and died in their little towns, rarely venturing far away from the region of the zones where they were born.

What is more, at the hour of Jesus, there were no streets, and none of the advanced educational institutions, frameworks, and administrations—which we so underestimate now. Such offices were not present; just the trade-exchange places existed for individuals to carry their produce to exchange. Housing, nourishment, sanctuary, and clean water were the obligations of the families and networks. The state gave, strikingly, none of these administrations, but the individuals were abused by the rulers, and even the commonplace representative exhausted the populace brutally.

I sat on the edge above the valley of Galilee, close to Mount Hattan. I looked at the ancient in modern times. I understood that we are living in a similar condition on the Earth as they did back then. Our governments cruelly abuse our lives, and labour frameworks are made to persecute and oppress individuals and their lives.

LIFE IN ANCIENT TIMES

The Roman-Greco times that managed the world at that point had establishments that we would today consider a repulsive idea, for example, human slavery; perhaps we are made to accept that we are at more freedom today than those individuals were. However, I see the world and understand it's most likely more awful now than it was in those days. We are, on the whole, still held in subjugation one way or the other by the institutions we have established in Europe, America, or any place else on the planet. In the ancient world, tax collectors were people to be feared. Everything served the delights of Rome. Indeed, even till this day, most governments are of the Roman style in one manner or the other. We as a whole serve the wants of our governments. We are still, from numerous points of view, living in comparative models of the past.

In old times, there was an unmistakable chain of distinctive hierarchy: at the top was the ruler—in actuality, a human lord. Beneath this lay a thin layer of the nobility, aristocrats, who owed their riches and status to the support of the king. Religious leadership and control went to the strict sanctuary, and the high priest was additionally connected to the Roman governor who nominated him.

In this way, numerous Jews accepted that these men served the Roman magistrates' offering. After the strict gentry came the expert class; these well-prepped, instructed, prepared laypeople were to breed and to hold positions in a nearby organization. Vast numbers of these men were Pharisees and scribes of significant strict groups.

Below them were the majority of the populace; labourers, the jobless, the weak, and the debilitated made up a large portion of the masses. I saw *ants* in the word *peasants*. How pertinent! The truth was that these individuals drudged like ants in the provinces to encourage the extravagant existence of the privileged.

Jesus came to a world and a general public fundamentally the same as the one we live in today, as much as we are persuaded that we have made noteworthy progressions as people in the cutting-edge world. We are all together still caught in the social orders we live in. Having encompassed our lives with perpetual material greed, we have come to decimate the planet Earth all the while. In a period on the planet when there is such massive accentuation of environmental change and radical developments of dissent, I feel disheartened to discover that not one of these fights raise the issue of profound spiritual change. I have made this adventure of life this far, and in my human condition, I have discovered a voyage that drove me forward, my childhood love, Jesus Christ. I am a born-again Christian and a Hebrew. I made the hybrid from natural life to living in the spirit of Christ Jesus.

Jesus Christ is the same yesterday, today, and until the end of time (Hebrews 13:8.).

I have employed some credible information from other authors as I researched more about the history of India, the Anglo-Indians, the wedge-tailed eagle, and the native Australian Aboriginal people. I give credit to this information that has helped me to deliver a book that gives credibility to the facts as I experienced in real life. My greatest inspiration to writing this book is the Holy Bible and the inner voice of the Holy Spirit. I do not believe in human accolades or earthly glory. I am a born-again child of the Most High, true Almighty Father, the Holy God of Israel. As I walked through the wilderness with Jesus by my side, I found myself alone with him, and as my heart poured out, I lay in a pool of tears at night, alone in the wilderness as I walked the Jesus trail. I went to find restoration to my spirit and soul and never to be lost again in the world I live in.

In addition to all of this, I want to give thanks to many of the Jewish people—the scholars, the rabbis, the students on long bus journeys to Eilat, Israel—and for the discussions with them on why I believed that Jesus was the Holy Messiah. Along the way, I met many ordinary people and several evangelists, with both of whom I had deep conversations of the Torah and the Word of God. I'd like to mention Dr. Jack Leitner, from Framingham, Massachusetts, for giving me a blessing of a Jewish name in Israel. It was one of the many blessings I received, and I felt this supernatural blessing like Jacob, who received his blessing when God called him "Israel."

I could not possibly write all the names of the Jewish people, yet I want to acknowledge the strangers I met along the way, the couple who appeared near the stream and offered me refreshing grapes to quench my thirst. They gave me words of blessings, saying, "You shall find salvation at the end of your journey," only for me to look back and find them disappeared. A stranger in Jerusalem with a friendly face who was sitting on the wall as I walked toward the central bus station greeted me and, in our conversation, told me where I was going and what I should do in the forest that led me to Elijah's cave. I won't ever forget the man in sackcloth at Jaffa gate, telling me about his vision.

Here is my human story, and I trust it motivates you and leads you to traverse and go to the opposite side of the stream and become a crossover. Indeed, a unique restoration and spiritual change is required on the planet in this moment. We are as yet living in old oppressions under Roman-style governments. The world is, however, experiencing a remedy, and man can't fix it; what man *can* do is disguise it, make it look better, endeavour to make it seem more attractive to the populaces of the world. The old-fashioned isn't far in truth from present-day times.

For me, everything has transformed. I have made the voyage crosswise over to the opposite side of the waterway, and I am anchored in Christ Jesus. In the entirety of my disappointments, my stupid acts, and my defective life, the Lord has been steadfast, and I live in the undeserved kindness and elegance of Christ Jesus, Yeshua HaMashiach.

INTRODUCTION

We had driven in my Holden Statesman from Kalgoorlie in Western Australia across miles of empty, desolate roads, heading into the great Nullarbor Plain in South Australia. The longest road trains in the world are a spectacle that will be encountered and experienced only in this sprawling red land. I was petrified driving my car, passing one of these monsters in either direction, on the world's longest straightest road. It is a scary proposition until you get inured to it. The red dust embraced travellers, transforming them into little specks of dust in the vastness of its desert sands.

Peter Stone was a tall, red-haired young man, from the mining town of Kalgoorlie. He was about five feet ten. He had thick, sunburnt skin that had freckles all over. It looked dehydrated, beer-inculcated, tobacco-engrossed, smoke-roasted, sun-baked, and marijuana-mangled, and it occasionally turned even redder when it was fed more "rocket fuel, evil spirit"—cocktail toxins available in any pub across this vastness. Peter Stone's breath was filled with alcohol, and he had a tongue that packed a volume of profanity—it was the thickness of his tongue, I think. When he rolled up a joint and smoked it and added more alcohol, the demon of aggression was amplified like a Stratocaster belting out an evil tune, and it would appear out of nowhere. He would occasionally spit at you while talking to your face; he never apologised. There was a volatility in him that made me aware of a possibly hidden violent nature—it's all an image in the end. I was doing him a favour driving across this vast land from Perth to Melbourne in this fantastic continent I still dotingly call home.

I was an immigrant who'd entered the country legally. I just did not want to leave this red land; it was not illegal to have a dream—this was my childhood dream, so I just stayed. Well, I guess that made me an illegal Aussie with a nice car, a wandering star. I had a legal Australian driver's license and a tax-file number. I paid taxes and worked in the mining sector. I was more Aussie than Aussie. Melbourne was a city filled with three hundred of my cousins from my mother's *and* father's sides of the family, all living in this city. I did not know all of them, but I had so much extended family in this country that it was a part of me in a big way. Now, driving across this land on an endless journey of everywhere and nowhere, I was hoping to make it across with Mr. Aggressive. I was hoping the car did not break down along the way. If Mr. Aggressive took aggressiveness to another level and died of aggressive binge-drinking alcohol and toxin abuse out here in the desert sands, leaving me with a dead body on my hands, such attention was not something I was looking forward to.

Peter was going to Melbourne to meet his grandfather that he had never known or ever seen. Grandad was an Anzac veteran, still going strong but fragile nevertheless; Peter said he wanted to meet the old bugger before he carked it. I was a wandering star with no orbit, and every place or town along the way was a home to me. I had no one but myself. Everyone I deeply loved was far away from me across a vast ocean. This was my adventure and my story in the making.

We had camped in sleeping bags out in the desert sands, and the southern sky lit up in the blackness, in a grandeur that I cannot express in words. Peter was drunk, stoned, and dead to the world, five to six metres away from me, lying like a corpse in the desert. I lay in my sleeping bag, looking at the universe, all alone, like a speck of dust embraced by the desert sands and the greatness of these southern skies. My eyes were transfixed at the millions and billions of stars, the galaxies, and the endless spaces. I lay there feeling so tiny, so small, so insignificant, so minuscule, and yet I knew there was a great love in the heavens. I was a man on the planet Earth resting on a desert floor. I felt unique and knew in my spirit there was an awesome God out there, with the grandeur of this creation. Suddenly, the sky changed before my very eyes: shooting stars, a meteorite bonanza—they were falling like raindrops. Out of their orbits, they were burning up like lost souls and fading into the darkness in a spectacular show of endings, coming to an end, burning up forever. I thought about the Earth and wondered if this could happen to us. I reassured myself that the ground was in its orbit and that it was most unlikely that one of these out-of-orbit meteorites, this medley of heavenly bodies of flashing light in the vastness of this fantastic phantasmagoria, would come crashing on us; we would not be spinning out of control in this vastness before my very eyes. Something of high power kept the Earth in its orbit, and I was on it. I was mystified by my thoughts.

I lay there for hours in silence at the most beautiful sky my eyes and soul had ever seen. I was twenty-one years old, emotionally intact. I had no heartaches, no heartbreaks, no grief. I was not involved in a rat race. I was not broken and bore no marks of disfigurement. I had no drugs, alcohol abuse, no dehydrated condition, beer-treated, smoke-roasted, sun-baked skin. I had not passed out in a drunken stupor across the most beautiful desert floor and a night sky that touched the deepest thoughts of my soul. I was in orbit with the creation that night. Only love filled my heart with a warm appreciation for all those people in my life, for this fantastic creator, whose spectacular art of expression of amazing love filled the sky; like a holy hand out of the beauty, it touched my soul as tears expressed appreciation across my wet cheeks, while lying there across this desert floor. My heart and soul were in orbit within me, and I was not afraid of this world. I trusted this feeling in my soul, and it was faith. Next to me, sleeping on the desert sand, was an image of a shooting star out of orbit in the night sky, burning up forever into the vastness of oblivion. Drunk, drugged, stoned, lying dead on the desert floor was Peter Stone—he missed it all. The chapters of Australia will tell you this story as it unfolds in this memoir.

I came back here today to this place in my spirit for you. Thus, here is my story now, and I hope you can walk with me through this time when I was in orbit with creation. I have made this journey of life, with all of its remarkable experiences. I hope they will edify you in some way. I hope in many ways, for this is the purpose of the book, to help us understand our function in our orbits and not be blown away and die like a bright shooting star, although it *does* look beautiful in the sky. In its beauty, it is disappearing into the darkness of the creation of the universe forevermore. All stories have a beginning, so let me take you to India to start mine.

PART ONE

CHAPTER 1

HOME

I was born in a small town on the eastern coast of India. I was not born in India because I made that choice, but I was born to an Anglo-Indian family who was explicitly known as the leftovers of the great British Empire. I am a part of that legacy. Our parents had five children, and I was the fourth born among three sisters and a brother. The town was called Waltair; this was the old British name given to the city, which eventually changed over time. Don't ask me to pronounce the Indian name of this town; it is so complicated that it requires me to twist my tongue in every direction trying to pronounce the darn thing.

Here, try it: Vishakhapatnam. You see what I mean? To me, it was always *Waltair*. Now I would encounter Aboriginal names in Australia that required the same twisting of the tongue. India, as I knew it as a child, was the most racist country in the world, with all its castes and creeds, discrimination, and the law of untouchables. I felt different; we were discriminated against for being mixed Anglo descendants. There was particular umbrage that remained against the British, and I suppose we did face some of its hostility towards us.

I embarked on this book-writing expedition with a lot of personal examination in my thoughts, in the most profound emotions in my spiritual thought process, bearing in mind the value I would bring to you reading this book. As the author, I contemplated this question to myself: Why would anybody want to read my story? I hope you will feel all of my life through these pages. When you come to the end of it, I entreat that you will feel connected and be enriched by the account of my life.

Often I would sit at a place, a busy street, drinking a cup of tea, just watching people walking by; it is a fantastic thing, unobtrusive research, to let the world transit in front of you while you observe the fascinating faces of the lives of people passing you by. I wondered if they realised that there was a book in them. We all have stories, but few of us take the time or make an effort to tell them. I decided that this would not happen to me.

I would like to think that I have lived a fascinating life. A journey through the pages of this book may reveal this to you, but I will let you be the judge of that. In my heart, I want to give you my story and hope something deeply profound and meaningful will come to you; it's my legacy to the world I lived in. Everything that is born must die, and everyone, I believe, should leave a legacy for those who are still left on the Earth—an anecdote of hope and joy that it's just beautiful to have lived on Earth.

ANGLO-INDIANS

When people ask you your ethnic background, there are many choices available, depending on what your ethnicity is. Many of you have filled out an online job application, and I am sure it was a lot of detailed work getting through it.

I always had a choice of two or more races that fit the bill when it comes to describing my ethnic background. You see, I am an Anglo-Indian. Some people look at me strangely when I specifically say that I am not an Indian but an Anglo-Indian by birth, Australian by nature, and Dutch by passport.

The Anglo part came from my European grandmothers. My mother's mother was Adaline De La Croix, and my father's mother was Innocenza Berchy.

Several British soldiers served the *Nizam* of Hyderabad, including my grandmother Innocenza. Most people are unaware of the history of Hyderabad. I intend to illuminate you on this journey of the Anglo-Indian culture.

We were consequently mixed British, and with every other European colonisation, English was our primary language; it was strange when individuals suggested that we spoke excellent English. I knew they didn't recognise an Anglo-Indian.

After the independence of India in 1947, the British left the "jewel in the crown" in a hasty retreat, as they did in most countries they colonised. With this sudden demise of the British, the Anglo-Indian community was left behind, with no land of their own.

As I researched these questions as a teenager with several Anglo-Indian elders, they responded by telling me that they lived in India like kings; they had good jobs, living in prosperity under the patronage and ruling *Nizam* of Hyderabad.

This was all to change when the emperor, the *Nizam*, lost power in Hyderabad. It was the beginning of the end; the subsequent collapse of Anglo-Indian society soon followed. When the privileges and opportunities were detached, the Anglo-Indian community, who thrived under the *Nizam*, were now under threat of extinction. The pompous British were too embarrassed to accept us as citizens even though they were the ones who left us there without any choice.

Many of the Anglo-Indians who did have British passports did not want to go to England, for many reasons. The weather was one, as was lack of certain privileges of having servants and maids in England, privileges they had in India. They feared that life would not be so privileged anymore, and the sense of community and unity would be lost. The joy among them in India was perhaps greater at that time, and they may have not seen any need to start new lives elsewhere. The "comfort zone" syndrome may have been a prime reason they remained in India. This was certainly the case with my father. He would say that old persons in the West are left lonely and alone, and he did not want to end up in a home, old and lonely. My dad did not sugarcoat his words about the West and its lonely old people in homes.

Many of them feared their children would go astray as family values deteriorated; the richness of the Anglo-Indian culture was their commitment to marriages and family. Divorces were a sporadic occurrence in this community, a close-knit society who kept these strong values. Marriage breakups were very rare among them. Moving to the West was a fearful proposition for some of them. For all the good reasons they had, some of these fears did come true for the families who moved overseas to a new Western life.

October Coup: A Memoir of the Struggle for Hyderabad by Mohammed Hyder was written about the struggle for this city where my parents were born.

My dad, Edward (Eddy), was born on November 20, 1933; it was the same year the Ford Rheinland, an automobile built by Ford of Germany, was launched, while Billie Holiday, "Lady Day," released her second song and first hit, "Riffin' the Scotch." My dad was born to become a great fan of her music.

Three years later, on May 6, 1936, my mother, Valarie Philomena, was born in the same city of Hyderabad, India. My mother shared the same day and year of birth with the American tennis player Darlene Hard. That year, Jesse Owens sprinted to win the one-hundred-metre gold medal in Olympics, an historical event for a black man, debunking Hitler's claim that his Aryan race was a superior class of human being. Amid all these events across the globe, my mother came into this world.

Both my parents were born at a time and place in India in the city of Hyderabad under the rule of the *Nizam*, the richest man in the world in the 1940s. Anglo-Indians were a product of the British Empire, with a mixture of Western and Indian names, customs, and complexions. My dad had the whiter side, while my mother came from the darker side of the mix of Anglo-Indian ethnicity.

> The definition of "Anglo-Indian" has become more unshackled in recent decades. It can now denote any mixed British-Indian parentage, but, for many, its primary meaning refers to people of longstanding mixed lineage, dating back up to 300 years into the sub-continent's colonial past.
>
> In the 18th century, the British East India Company followed previous Dutch and Portuguese settlers in encouraging employees to marry native women and plant roots. The company would even pay a sum for every child born of these cross-cultural unions.
>
> When the British finally departed in 1947, they left behind a Westernised mixed-race sub-population about 300,000 strong who weren't necessarily glad to see the British leave.
>
> "The Anglo-Indians, now left in a twilight zone of uncertainty, felt a sharp sense of betrayal, with dismay at the fact that Britain made no effort to offer the people an opportunity to return to the land of their forefathers."

Most of the Anglo-Indians were more "Anglo" than "Indian." Only darker complexions betrayed their origins. Otherwise, they dressed like the British, their mother tongue was English with an accentual twang of Indian, and they were predominantly Christians.

Soon they began leaving in droves in the 1950s and 1960s, dispersing throughout the Commonwealth countries of Canada, Australia, and New Zealand, as well as their "motherland," the UK.

The Anglo-Indians also had a distinctive cuisine—*jalfrezi* was a popular household staple, Indian-Chinese food that includes browning marinated bits of meat, fish or vegetables in oil and savours to create a dry, thick sauce. As the dish incorporates green chillies, a *jalfrezi* can range in warmth from medium to exceptionally hot; it was unlike anything on Indian-restaurant menus. Then there was pepper water, a bowl of thin, spicy soup ladled on to the rice. Other typical dishes include Country Captain Chicken and Railway Lamb Curry—a throwback to the subcontinent's railways, on which many Anglo-Indians worked. Now, this unique hybrid culture overarching Anglo-Indian identity is expiring, diluted through intermarriage.

"I'm a piece of that culture now quickly vanishing as the more-youthful eras consolidate—as they ought to—into the standard of their embraced nations. Other than nostalgic memories of a more established era, their Indian past has all but blurred into insensibility."

ANGLO-INDIAN OR NOT?

Merle Oberon: The star of *The Scarlet Pimpernel* and *Wuthering Heights* claimed she was born in Tasmania, although relatives said her birth certificate proves she was born in Mumbai.

Sir Cliff Richard: Born in Lucknow, northeast India, he denied his mother was Anglo-Indian but told BBC Radio 4's *Woman's Hour* his step-sisters were.

Alistair McGowan: Born in Worcestershire, the comedian discovered his father's Indian nationality when appearing on the BBC show *Who Do You Think You Are?*

It's uncertain how many Anglo-Indians stayed in India, uncounted since a 1941 census. But the estimated 125,000, living mostly in Calcutta and Madras, are re-enacting the same assimilation—marrying Indians and adopting their culture. They are becoming indistinguishable.

"Previously, the community was too Anglicised—clinging to English traditions and customs," explains Philomena Eaton, convenor of the Calcutta Anglo-Indian Service Society. "But today it's visible that they are much more integrated into society in customs, language, clothing, and social interactions. Many more Anglos today can easily converse in Hindi and Bengali than they did in 1947. It's a significant turnaround for the community in India, which rarely married Indians before 1947. After that date, they saw employment opportunities diminished by their inability to speak local languages.

—(*Anglo-Indians: Is Their Culture Dying out?* BBC News. [BBC, January 4, 2013.])

In other words, if you did not integrate into Indian society, your survival as an Anglo-Indian in India was going to become impossible.

When I was at school, most Anglo-Indian children struggled to get past the alphabets and weird symbols of the Indian language; according to the ethnologic lists, there are 438 languages in use and fourteen not in use. There is a total of twenty-two official languages in India.

As an Anglo-Indian youngster, I refused to learn the Indian language. I believed that Indians should be glad the British gave them a speech that brought this diverse country together. Hence, I thought that they all should learn English, and I certainly did not need to acquire an Indian language that was not going to be beneficial to me in any way.

With this attitude in mind, I never learned the language properly, and the highest grade or marks I ever got was a zero. I recall my Hindi exams in school. When the teacher handed me the question paper,

I could not make heads or tails of it. I sat there meticulously writing all the weird symbols and alphabets of the question paper on the answer sheet. As I handed her the answer sheet, my teacher looked at me, shaking her head and informing me that my grade was going to be an oval-shaped egg. Secretly (she never knew), I did not give a rat's butt about the class. In my little mind, I bloody could not care less. I replied, "I know about the zero, but my handwriting is good; you should give me a mark for that." I was a cheeky bugger, and as guilty as charged, she gave me a zero and took away the one target I asked her for—the excellent handwriting; she told me that I was an arrogant Anglo-Indian boy who deserved nothing more than a zero. I still bloody could not care less. There was a little pompous British in me somewhere, and my Indian teacher got a dose of it. I was not going to live in India; I was going to go to Australia to become an Aussie.

To have a clearer understanding of my unique culture, it is necessary to know some history and background of the *Nizam* of Hyderabad. Many British expats worked for the *Nizam*, including members of my family.

HISTORY OF THE CITY OF HYDERABAD AND THE RULING *NIZAM*, 1911 TO 1948

According to the research offered on the fall of this city of the *Nizam*, one of the all-time wealthiest listed in *Forbes* Magazine 2008, a detailed article depicts the history of this ruler.

THE FALL OF THE CITY OF HYDERABAD

The last *Nizam* of the Princely State of Hyderabad and Berar, Fath Jang Nawab Mir Osman Ali Khan Asaf Jah VII, was "The Richest Man in the 1940s," having a fortune estimated at $2 billion. He ruled Hyderabad between 1911 and 1948 until it was made part of India because of Operation Polo, launched by the Indian Government.

The *Nizam* of Hyderabad was even featured on the cover of *TIME* magazine. While rulers of other big states like Kashmir, Jodhpur, Bikaner, Indore, and Bhopal were given the title of

"His Excellency" (H.E.), the *Nizam* of Hyderabad alone had the title of "His Exalted Highness" (H.E.H.).

During the rule of Aurangzeb's great-grandson Muhammad Shah (1719–1748), the governor of Deccan was one Nizam-ul-Mulk. In 1723, he decided to carve himself a kingdom. Another Mughal functionary, Mubariz Khan, had created a near-independent state in Hyderabad, which was attacked by the *Nizam* in 1724. After forsaking his capital in Aurangabad, the *Nizam* moved to Hyderabad and founded the most influential independent Muslim state of the South.

Later *Nizams* were played as puppet pawns in the hands of the British and the French of Pondicherry. After the French were defeated by the British, the *Nizam* of Hyderabad switched his allegiance to the British and ruled till the independence of India under British protection.

When India attained her independence, and Sardar Patel was in the process of integrating India's princely states, Jammu and Kashmir, Junagadh and Hyderabad decided to seek accession with Pakistan or declare independence. Hyderabad was the largest of the sovereign states and included parts of present-day Andhra Pradesh, Karnataka, and Maharashtra states. Its ruler, the *Nizam* Osman Ali Khan, was a Muslim, although more than 80 percent of its people were Hindu. The *Nizam* of Hyderabad kept on changing his position, and Patel could take no more.

Patel asked for the Indian Army to incorporate Hyderabad (in his ability as Acting Prime Minister) when Nehru was visiting Europe. The activity was named "Operation Polo," in which a considerable number of Razakar powers were executed. However, Hyderabad was serenely secured into the Indian Union.

Post Operation Polo, the *Nizam* of Hyderabad had lost every one of its forces and was simply a stylised head of the state.

Hyderabad, through the span of seven eras of *Nizams*, had turned into the wealthiest state in the world. In any case, the world related most to its seventh ruler, Mir Osman Ali Khan, who is acclaimed for his quirks and riches. He consulted with the Portuguese in the 1940s to purchase Goa from them. He possessed the world's vainglorious fortunes yet lived like a sick person, smoked modest *bidis*, and wore worn-out garments.

His gathering of pearls alone could top off an Olympic-sized swimming pool. He picked up the renowned Jacob Diamond—the 400-carat precious stone, twofold the measure of the Kohinoor and world's fifth-biggest, through a well-known "Jewel Suit" in 1892. The Jacob Diamond was later bought by the Government of India in 1995, following a skirmish of 24 years with the *Nizam*'s trust for an expected $13 million alongside different jewels of the *Nizams*, currently held at the Reserve Bank of India, Mumbai. The estimation of the Jacob Diamond alone is 100 million pounds. The seventh and last *Nizam* found the duck-egg-sized precious stone concealed in his dad's shoes and used it as a paperweight.

The *Times* covered the story of his riches on February 22, 1937; his gems have an expected estimation of $150 million; he had $250 million in gold bars and his capital sums amounting to $1.4 billion, not to mention the "Mines of Golconda."

The *Nizam*'s jewels, esteemed at $250–$350 million by Sotheby's and Christie's, go back to the mid-18th century to the mid-20th century. Created in gold and silver and adorned with enamelling, the gems are set with Colombian emeralds, precious stones from the Golconda mines, Burmese rubies, spinels, and pearls from Basra and the Gulf of Mannar.

According to history, Osman Ali Khan nominated not his son, but grandson Mukarram Jah (born in France from a Turkish mother), to be the next (and last) titled *Nizam* of Hyderabad. Mukarram Jah could not endure the battles over his grandfather's wealth and escaped to Australia, where, despite having the best education money could buy (Harrow, Cambridge, LSE, Sandhurst), he operated bulldozers, married, and divorced five times, one of his wives being a former Miss Turkey. Now he lives in a two-room apartment in Istanbul, Turkey.

The *Nizam* of Hyderabad is reported to have impregnated 86 of his mistresses, siring more than 100 illegitimate children and a sea of rival claimants.

—(*Nizam of Hyderabad: Fifth on the Forbes "All-Time Wealthiest" HelloJi*, April 12, 2008.)

Hyderabad, the largest princely state at the time of Indian independence, was caught in a complex web, partly of its own making. Bred on the delusion of "born to rule," always protected by the British and egged on by the Razakar, a volunteer militia, the seventh *Nizam*, Mir Osman Ali Khan, was pitching for an independent sovereign state. Often susceptible to wrong advice, the *Nizam* took the "dispute" of Hyderabad's future to the U.N. Security Council, even while preposterously considering the option of merging Hyderabad with newly carved-out Pakistan. On the other hand, India was furiously pursuing Hyderabad to join the Indian Union, adopting a carrot-and-stick policy authored by Sardar Vallabbhai Patel.

Patel was gearing up to launch a military operation euphemistically called a "Police Action." Congress, Arya Samajis, and Communists were running freedom movements both for the liberation of Hyderabad from the *Nizam*'s rule and an end to feudalism. The period preceding the liberation of Hyderabad State on September 17, 1948, a full 13 months after Indian independence, was turbulent, to say the least. In his memoir, Mohammed Hyder brings alive all these aspects, lucidly weaving facts of history with his annotations based on interactions with some of the most powerful state and non-state actors of the time who shaped the destiny of Hyderabad.

Using to full effect his situation as the man at ground zero during that critical transition period, the Hyderabad Civil Service officer came up with a balanced narrative shorn of exaggerations. As Collector of Osmanabad (now part of the State of Maharashtra), a large politically sensitive border district of Hyderabad State, he had several unenviable tasks. The most challenging was tackling "violent raids" by the Congress from Indian territory "to cripple civil administration and provoke annexation" and reining in the armed Razakars, floated by Majlis-e-Ittehadul-Muslimeen, who took upon themselves the task of protecting Muslims and Muslim rule.

The book is an edited version of Hyder's tenure in Osmanabad written by him in jail in July and August of 1949. He was in prison after the new Hyderabad government suspended and arrested him and slapped 23 cases on him, including 14 murders, arson, and looting—an ordeal undergone by several officers of the time.

The Hyderabad question, he observes, had become a major unresolved issue at the beginning of 1947, no less worrying than Kashmir. In a dispassionate dissection of the unfolding situation, he presents the causes, the differing perceptions and perspectives of the turmoil, and the *Nizam*'s as well as the Muslims' dilemma. At the level of popular politics, there was one overwhelming fact, he explains: "Hyderabad was predominantly Hindu, with Muslims representing some 20 percent of the population. From one perspective, its political arrangements were self-evidently undemocratic, with an autocratic Muslim ruler at the head of the system and a small, apparently reactionary Muslim ruling class dominating its administration and political life."

Expectedly, he finds a contrasting perception inside the ruling system: "Hyderabad was viewed as a state blessed with a remarkably secular outlook, enjoying communal harmony, with a benevolent ruler concerned with the advancement of the poor and the protection of the oppressed, an excellent administration … and a heterogeneous ruling elite…" of which Anglo-Indians were a part of the protection force aligned with the British.

TURNING POINT

Probing political and social processes, the author considers the massive demonstration in Hyderabad city by Razakars led by the Majlis' leader, Syed Qasim Razvi, in October 1947 against the administration's decision to sign a "Standstill Agreement" as a "turning point." The agreement between Hyderabad and the Indian Union spoke of maintaining the status quo of the princely state pending accession.

It was this demonstration in front of the houses of the Prime Minister, Nawab of Chattari, advisor, Sir Walter Monckton, and Minister, Nawab Ali Nawaz Jung, the chief negotiators, the author says, that forced them to call off their Delhi visit to sign the agreement. It was treated as "a triumph for Qasim Razvi over the rule, the government, and the people of Hyderabad" and perceived as the "October Coup."

In a chapter devoted to Razvi and his phenomenal rise from a small-time lawyer in Lathur to a larger-than-life Majlis leader, Hyder lays threadbare his persona and philosophy, based on a marathon conversation. Questions he posed and the responses he got provide insights into Razvi, often reviled by a section as the man who sowed the seeds of a communal divide in Hyderabad with his infamous mission. How could a Muslim minority, headed by a Muslim ruler, continue to dominate a vast and politically conscious Hindu majority in Hyderabad? To Hyder's query, Razvi's responses were sharp: "The *Nizams* have ruled Hyderabad for more than 200 years in an unbroken line... The system must have some good in it if it has lasted 200 years. Do you agree?

"...We Muslims rule because we are more fit to rule... We rule, and they [Hindus] own! It is a good arrangement, and they know it!" How could Hyderabad avoid accession to the Indian Union? Could India accept the disintegration that might result if Hyderabad stayed out? Razvi shot back, "India is a geographic notion. Hyderabad is a political reality. Are we prepared to sacrifice the reality of Hyderabad for the idea of India?" Hyder says Razvi foresaw a time when Muslims would once again become rulers of India and the *Nizam* ruler of Delhi, if only he followed his advice!

Hyder says he was not impressed and recalls how he came back from the meeting frustrated rather than inspired. For him, it seemed "absurd and frightening that this little man could make his position of mastery over Hyderabad." He concedes that the views Razvi shared certainly existed in Hyderabad Muslim society then, though being its lowest common denominator.

In the later chapters, Hyder moves on to his struggle as Collector, his long legal battle with the new government that took over after the merger of Hyderabad, with a series of documentation that makes reading it a bit heavy and taxing.

He concludes by highlighting the fallacy of interpreting Hyderabad's status and its confrontation with India during 1947–48 from the Indian lens of aspirations of the nationalist movement, totally ignoring the concerns of a smaller State being hustled into accession. He goes on to compare the Indian perspective and Hyderabad's dilemma to Thucydides' narrative of the capitulation of the people of the small island of Melos by the mighty Athens. For those craving to know more about Hyderabad's not-so-recent history of the merger, this is the book in which he depicts the history of the *Nizam*. Given this history of the city of Hyderabad, the fall of the *Nizam* directly affected the fortunes and future of the Anglo-Indian society in Hyderabad.

My parents did not live in the city of Hyderabad but moved to the coastal town of Waltair, a natural, beautiful seaside town on the east coast of India. My dad worked in a petrochemical fertilizer company, built by shareholders Chevron Chemicals USA.

My dad had a whole bunch of American friends for whom he worked during the construction of this large petrochemical plant, named Coromandel Fertilizers. Hunting big game was my dad's passion, so regular expeditions with his American colleagues made him a favourite among them.

OUR HOME ON THE GLEN

Beach Road was carved over the rough slopes; it made a sickle shape and hurried downhill from three hundred metres to ocean level towards our home along the shoreline. The constant crashing sound of the waves, influencing coconut palm trees, and the sea breeze blowing the smell of the surf and sea across your face was a daily experience. On these tall coconut palm trees, I honed my wizardry of tree-climbing skills, unmatched by any of my companions. The hot, humid summer days and the sweltering heat, the welcoming freshness of the thirst-quenching water from the coconut fruit, indeed, gave much significance to the boy who was sufficiently gutsy to to climb these tall trees and present them to his companions waiting below.

In my mind is a picture of my mother smiling, at the doorway, expecting the arrival of her youngsters. I could see it if even when she was not at the entryway; as you drew closer, she would undoubtedly show up at some point or another before you entered the walkway from the garden to the entryway. The fourteen tall teak trees that decorated the way towards the house proclaimed the occupants of this house were Anglo-Indians. The pair of wolfhounds that guarded the property, named Beauty and Flash, confirmed that the occupants of this household were different. Local people did not own dangerous guard dogs. We were given a local name that translates as "white men who love dogs." From our terrace roof, we enjoyed the view of the sea. It was a beautiful house that nestled in the valley of hills and more enormous mountains. There was one particular mountain in the far distance that resembled a dolphin in the sea. From a distance, it looked like the rostrum of the dolphin that had just dipped into the ocean, while the melon and the blowhole were the visible parts outside of the water. We Anglo-Indians called the mountain "The Dolphin's Nose," and the beach and caves surrounding this mountain area were called "California Beach." It was a spectacular place for a child to explore sea life—lichens, microscopic plants and cyanobacteria, grazing snails, limpets, and other molluscs. Barnacles, sea squirts, anemones, starfish, corals, crabs and seagulls were also found there.

The colour of the tiny crabs was the same as the sea sand; they were perfectly camouflaged. Now, these crabs would be found running around on the beach; but as a child, the challenge we had was to try to catch some of them—or even *one* of them. It was not an easy task. They were only as big as a two-dollar Aussie coin, a small crab that has evolved with the sharpness of camouflage and matching escape skills from the preying hands of the children of *Homo sapiens*. This tiny crustacean was astute and smart, yet the children of the *Homo sapiens,* with equally swift reflexive skills, emerged victorious from the battle of wits. Statistically, in all cases, the small, penny-sized sand-coloured crab won most of the campaigns, the battles that raged between them and my friends. There was only one trick to the hunt: you had to get the crab far away from the little hole in the sand to have any chance of capturing it.

We little boys surveyed the sand to catch that one elusive little crab that had strayed away too far from his escape hole in the sand. When we found one, we swiftly chased the little crab, pouncing on him on the sand with our hands, catching the little rascal crab before he got away into his tiny escape hole in the sand. We would spend hours running around the beach trying to find this one little crab— pranksters at work.

Once we had a crab in our hands, we walked around the beach; we found other little boys and girls playing on the beach. We would sneak up on them, pull on their swimming trunks, and drop the two-dollar-sized crab into their swimming outfits.

They would be screaming and yelling as the crab wriggled to get away; it was funny. Some kids jumped so high, laughing and crying simultaneously as the crab tickled its way out of their pants. I rarely saw a crab die or get hurt in this struggle. Usually, most kids just ran into the sea, ripped off their swimming trunks, and let the crab get away. It was just pure, naughty, harmless childhood fun. In the evolution of these battles between the kids and the small crabs, the development of the crab outpaced us eventually. Catching a crab became even harder as they developed a sensitivity to the sound of approaching children. They were gone like magic into their underground safety havens. We noticed that there were more holes in the sand; they seemed to have developed a new strategy by digging up more holes to assist them more efficiently in their escape from us horrible pranksters.

This beach was a lot of fun; its shore was the most fabulous place for exploration and swimming in the shallows. Yet, there were also dangerous currents around the bends past the rocks at certain times of the year; it was considered hazardous. As we grew up into teenagers, we moved away from chasing tiny crustaceans to catching big waves, playing with danger, as were the challenges for some of the youth.

Night angling on the shoreline gave you a spectacular night sky that captivated your mind. The early-morning light hit the water line as the sun peered out of the dimness, heralding the break of day. Visions like this touched my heart, and lessons about the glory of creation came alive with thanksgiving and gratitude early in life.

I remember the fishermen singing in cadence as they snared on to parallel ropes leading to a fishing net that had been spread over the water by a watercraft at some point before the early dawn. They sang and dug their feet into the sand, pulling at the rope; I still remember the fervour of the catch and grinning appearances of the fisherman expecting a benevolent haul of fish in anticipation. These events on the shore were exciting and rhythmic.

The hill chapel was a place I often visited as a child; my conversations and prayers to the Lord were held on a mountaintop. Early on, my faith was established and deeply rooted in this mountain. I made an honourable promise to the most beautiful girl, truly loved from the profundity of my heart, at the house of worship on the hill. Joanne Christine was my first true love, the most beautiful girl I would ever know. I would hold her hands on the beach as the waves rushed to greet our feet on the shoreline. She was adorned in a white lace dress, a memory to last a lifetime, a loss to endure forever, the first betrayal of a woman and one that returned to haunt me like a bad dream.

We were surrounded by several hills and mountains along the coastline. As young teenagers, we boys liked hiking them, armed with slingshots made from wood and rubber lines and a leather holder attached to them, where we placed rounded pebblestones, and shot at birds, lizards, and especially snakes. It was a protective device that we mastered with great skill and accuracy. Aspiring mountain climber Steven set out with me on a journey to vanquishing each mountain that encompassed us; we scaled a high number of them. However, the most startling one was on the right side of the map towards the far end, which remained unconquered. While endeavouring to vanquish this precarious mountain, strolling along the shoreline, we suddenly noticed a body, decomposed human remains, lying between the rocks and shore. Terrified, we left—cleared out panicked, never again to attempt an attack on the mountain crest. "Dead Man's Point" was what my friends and I called it. That was our scary place.

The timberland forests held many memories of adventure from childhood to teenage years, enduring severe neck pain straining to see the green bleeding-heart doves camouflaged in the canopy. It was a magnificent bird with a red plumage in the middle of its chest shaped like a heart upside down; it was considered good luck to spot one. The primates were a source of joy, as they defended their territory, challenging our invasion into the forest.

Hopping over a water stream, we transformed into statues, pillars of salt, similar to the scene of the wife of Lot, glancing back at the consuming evil city in a story in the Bible. We encountered a black cobra hissing—our nature to detect danger so significantly inserted in our spirits. Equipped with slingshots and an air rifle, we prepared to strike Satan directly between his eyes. This old expression of hatred between people and the snake had been profoundly implanted inside us, as written in the book of Genesis. The idea was that the snake is used by Satan to assault the spirit of a man. We executed the snake with the air rifle since it was a threat to us. I was the most youthful of my kin, bold and audacious. I regularly heard my mom express her appreciation of my liveliness. I often heard my mother say, "This house wakes up into bedlam with this kid." Even when my parents shipped me off to boarding school, I longed to return to the house on the glen by the seas and to my youthful adventures.

I spent many years of my childhood growing up on this coastline, as my friends and their families started to depart these shores to a new life in Australia. I waited for my turn to leave this country behind. Across the ocean somewhere south, a new adventure awaited me. I never knew then what I know now.

SUNDAY POTLUCK LUNCH AT OUR HOME ON THE GLEN

Sunday was a special day at our home on the glen. My mother was a staunch Catholic, a woman of faith and prayer. She was a beautiful, dark woman, not very tall, about five feet two. She had these pudgy cheeks that stayed the same year after year, notwithstanding when I saw her again following a quarter century after I'd moved away to Australia. She had a beautiful smile and the humblest heart. She was funny, had a witty sense of humour, and always smiled at my childhood antics with a nod of disapproval.

I guess the smile was her blessing; she was a woman who endured so much but walked tall in her shoes with faith and prayer. My mother always reminds me of an angel, a blessed messenger who petitioned to God for me for the more significant part of my life. I felt her presence alongside me regardless of where I was. I always had this picture of her kneeling in her room, praying.

Be that as it may, I was not her most loved child; that was my brother, and she adored him sincerely. I knew he was her indisputable favourite. She didn't show any favour towards my sibling over me, and yet I knew he was her favourite. I didn't give a lot of thought to such things as a youngster since I was involved with climbing trees, playing on the shoreline, vanquishing the slopes and later the higher mountains. Figuring out how to catch waves and bodysurfing was my top pick. If you get it without flaw, it's stunning how far the waves can convey you back to the shore. I felt so thrilled riding the stream, and it was such fun as you rode on top of it, being carried to shore like the ruler of the world. I wished I could educate my wolfhound Flash to surf with me, but he just generally sat on the beach, with pointed ears, watching me. We had such astounding pooches, and they were the best bodyguards you would ever have. I always felt safe with them alongside me.

I don't know how my dad trained them; as a child, I didn't see them as dogs. They were more like bodyguards, incredibly intelligent and understanding. Mother did not like them being inside the house and preferred them out in the big yard. My dad passionately loved them. He called Flash "his son," and Flash was like a son to my dad. One hot summer day, Flash was sleeping inside the house in the hallway when my mother was grumbling at my dad. I heard her say, "Edward, you've allowed this wolf of a dog a bad habit of coming inside and sleeping in the hallway." The next event changed my mother's grumblings forever. Flash woke up; he stood on his four legs, looked at my mother, and walked away outside into the yard. My dad was vexed! He exclaimed, "How can you hurt his feelings like that! It's a hot damn day, and he likes the sea breeze that blows down the hallway. I cannot believe you would be so insensitive to my son in this manner." My mother never offended the dog again and allowed him inside during the hot summer days for the rest of his life.

I hated going to boarding school and being away from this coastline. But kids don't have choices, and we must simply adapt to our circumstances and make the best of every situation—a valuable lesson for me today as an adult. But, as a child, I hated being away from my trusted bodyguards, my beach, my friends, my parents, and my house on the glen.

My mother came from a big family of eleven brothers and sisters. My dad had fourteen brothers and sisters, and fortunately, not all our relatives lived in the same town as we did; some of them lived in the capital city of Hyderabad.

My mother had four of her brothers living in our town about twenty miles away, in the city centre; these were her younger siblings, and every one of them passionately loved her. The Indians changed the name of the town from Waltair (from its British past) to an Indian name that needed every letter in the English language to be utilised to spell the darn thing. Anglo-Indians still called it by its British name: Waltair.

The house on the glen was a magnificent place; we had several fruit trees, vegetable and herbal patches, several chickens, ducks, two parrots, a squirrel called Mickey, two wild-boar piglets called Munna and Munni, and a spotted-deer fawn named Bang (stranded in the forest and found by my dad on one of his hunting trips). It resembled a small mini-zoo.

On the driveway, we had a 1964 Standard Herald car, which was an offshoot of the British variant of the Herald Triumph, proving that we clung to our British ancestry.

Sunday was a special day. My parents would go to church at 6:00 a.m. for the early-morning mass; we had been trained by my mother on Saturday evening to get our clothes ready, polish our shoes, and take our showers and baths and be prepared for the Sunday mass. At 7:30 a.m., along with our Christian friends, we would all be dressed like decent, respectful kids, presentable to visit the house of prayer.

When we returned home, our breakfast would be set on the table, and we would have our Sunday special breakfast of bacon, sausages, and eggs. We got this only once a week because Sunday was a special day.

Around 10:00 a.m., my favourite uncle, Alquin, and his wife, Rhoda MacLeod, along with my three cousins, would show up, followed shortly by my other three uncles with their kids. My friends Steven, William, and Glen, along with Aunty Yvonne, would also show up.

Sunday was potluck day; everyone would bring something for the huge concoction that was arranged by my mum. There was generally much energy and happiness on Sundays; we children got together for fun and games—time to play "Seven Tiles."

You got a heap of seven little clay tiles around two inches in width and put them as a stack amidst a circle and split the teams into two groups. The point of the amusement was to scatter the tiles by tossing a tennis ball with force at them, thus diffusing them over the circle. When the other group hurried to get the ball that had rolled far away, you needed to stack the tiles before the ball was retrieved by the opposite group. If they hit you with the tennis ball while you or your team players were still in the marked circle, endeavouring to stack up he seven tiles, you lost the game, resulting in the teams swapping roles. We played best of seven; the group who first achieved four fruitful endeavours were the victors. The excitement, laughter, and fun at these games were electrifying, and there was a deep sense of community when everyone's kids played like a big family.

We never had any TV in India when we were growing up, so the outdoor activities were extraordinarily innovative and common sense. We played "Monkey on the Tree"; this was another hilarious game. We played it under a banyan tree that had vines that hung from its branches and formed prop roots like pillars to support this vast tree that spread several metres in diameter. The concept of the game involved a stick about half a metre in length, which was placed in the middle of a circle drawn in the dirt. There was always one kid who was the victim, the guardian of the stick. We would throw the stick far away, and when the guardian went to retrieve it quickly and place it in the circle, we had to be the monkeys on the tree; in other words, we had to climb the tree as soon as possible when the guardian of the stick went to fetch it. Then, while he guarded the stick in the circle, one of the monkeys on the tree would try to slide down the vines and prop-root pillars and touch the bat before the guardian touched them. The objective was that everyone wanted to be the monkey and not the guardian of the stick; it was more fun being a monkey than the guardian. I cannot express the joy and laughter we had at these innovative social platform children games; some fell off the tree and broke their arms, and some were brilliant monkeys with amazing tree-climbing skills. We played golden games of great fun. We also played "Box," which was hide-and-seek in the dark; playing marbles, flying kites—this was so much fun. All the youngsters would be shouting with joy and laughter, only occasionally interrupted by somebody crying if they got hurt or wounded falling while running. There were such loud bursts of laughter—they resounded and resonated everywhere throughout the yard. Indeed, even the dogs were energised, and the two parrots would turn out to be additionally chirpy, shaking their heads and shrieking significantly louder in their enclosures. Micky, the chipmunk, would be let free, and he would be up that coconut palm tree with his tail waving and making a squeaky commotion.

A visit to the beach was dependably a part of the Sunday ritual; then, we'd return home for the fantastic lunch made by the women of the house.

Around 2:30 p.m., everyone would be enjoying a Spanish *siesta*; the gamblers of the family would play cards for small sums of money. Around 4:00 p.m., it was teatime; Indian tea is something special. You would never find this taste and method of tea-making anywhere else in the world. It had buffalo milk rich in flavour, a correct measurement of water added, "Three Roses" brand of tea leaves, a dash of fresh ginger, crushed cardamom, and sugar boiled together very slowly. This tea would entice each taste bud on your tongue to a thrilling euphoria that must be experienced—especially if my mum served it to you. Then came the evening music session. There were guitars and singing, and dancing to American country music. Our Sunday potluck days finished around 9:00 p.m. with supper and everybody reluctantly returning home for the week ahead. We had so many happy Sundays to look forward to; these were the most wonderful days of my childhood.

My mum had an extraordinary enchantment in her grasp; as the chief cook, she coordinated everything that happened in the kitchen. I learnt to cook from her—not every one of her recipes but rather the most important ones. My mother is characteristically woven into my soul. I close my eyes and feel these Sundays in my heart. It is astounding how recollections stay so bright and new when you submerge them deeply into your soul.

These recollections convey a kind of sadness inside of me since life changes, time changes, and the world changes. The decisions we make change the present, but the past remains as brilliant recollections. We ache for them once more; I wish I could turn back time. In Sweden, it's like I'm among the living dead, with everyone distant from each other and to themselves—individuals sitting before TV screens like zombies, front yards empty and individuals desolate, kids stuck to their iPhones, and nobody climbing trees in my neighbourhood—except my daughters and me. Today, when I look at what children are playing with and what is considered social platforms, I cannot help but feel a great sense of concern about what we are doing to our society and our children. We have isolated them; they are locked in a lonely cyber-world and in human relationships with very little meaning. We are teaching them antisocial behaviour patterns of loveless relationships and gender confusion. Evil lives in high places of power and greed. We have altered society and elevated more evil than good. Give me those good, old-time childhood days again.

MY FAMILY

There was a saying in my family: "If you had to write a book of my mother's side of the family, you would end up with several volumes about her brothers and sisters. There were many dysfunctional attributes in all of them.

My mother earned the reputation of being a rose among the thornbushes, and our home offered her siblings hope, sanity, and comfort in their troublesome lives. All of this came at the cost of the displeasure of my father. On several occasions, my dad would grumble at my mother regarding her siblings and the financial expenses for the traditional potluck Sunday lunches that were regularly held at home.

Potluck lunches required everyone to bring something for the Sunday cook-up session at our house.

Nevertheless, these Sunday potluck lunches continued. Most of my uncles, aunties, and cousins showed up at our home for the weekly ritual. Despite the occasional quarrel she had with my dad, my mother's sympathy and pleas of compassion overruled my dad's disapproval of her less-fortunate family members.

She had one brother named Kenny, who was a notorious pickpocket, drunkard, and thief. Despised by most of the family not only because he was a thief, more so because seeking every opportunity he got, he stole from members of his own family.

I cannot recall the number of times my mother forgave him for his deeds, pleading with my dad for mercy for the offences he committed; he slowly crawled back within the family because of my mother's love and empathy.

My grandparents on my mother's side of the family were a very successful breeding pair, successfully bringing eleven children into the world in a period of decline for the Anglo-Indian community. Lack of opportunity in education and the financial inability of my grandfather affected the development and the lives of the children they brought into this world.

When I grew older, I questioned my grandmother as to why she had so many children when they could not afford it. She smiled at me and replied, "We did not have a TV in those days, and we had a lot of love in our hearts." Then with a cheeky smile on her face, she added, "Your grandfather was a short cock sparrow of a man." I guess Grandma did not have a choice.

I did not understand what my grandmother was telling me at the time, yet it fascinated me to know how a cock sparrow behaved. It was during one of my bird-watching expeditions that I gained a better understanding of what my grandmother was telling me about Grandpa.

I was watching sparrows one summer in our backyard during the breeding season, witnessing the ongoing courtship of sparrows. The cock sparrow was relentless; the little bugger was chirping, hopping around in a frenzy of love, and never seemed to get enough of loving his mate. I'd see him fly off into the hole in the wall near the shed, carrying grass and twigs and soft organic material, even feathers, in his beak, for building a nest. As soon as he successfully raised his chicks, he was back again courting his mate, making love to her in a relentless desire to satisfy himself. I laughed thinking about what my Grandma told me about Grandpa. Now every time I see a cock sparrow, it reminds me of my grandfather.

When Grandpa died, he did not leave my grandmother a 401(k) pension plan, nor did he leave her any savings, so Grandmother came to live with us. My parents took responsibility for her well-being. Our home offered her the best old-age investment plan, one that could not be rivalled by any wealth-management fiduciary in the country. Grandmother was never lonely, and she was very joyful around us. I developed an emotional bond with her that was profound.

This was my home, a place where you learn such values as giving and sharing—rare virtues you learn as a child, all imparted to me by my mother.

The Anglo-Indian society cannot be described as a wealthy, affluent lot; their financial knowledge about investments and capital growth did not mean a whole lot to most of them. Life was about enjoying the good times, enduring the tough times, sharing what you have with the less-fortunate ones, and mostly sticking together as a family. The richness of this adaptation of life in India secured deep family ties; even with all the misunderstandings that occurred occasionally, families held together, similar to the redneck society I have come to know in Alabama—the big difference being that divorce was not a trait you would find in Anglo-Indian society.

MY DAD

Our wolfhound Flash was probably the only living thing that was not afraid of my dad. Everyone else around him was.

My earliest recollections of him are slightly diminished in my mind, as I stretch out and reach out into the earliest past; I see a picture of myself: a boy in fear of his dad. There were several aspects to my dad in action. He was loved by his friends and the poor people in several villages. He carried out charity campaigns with helping the poor. I remember we had a man from a rural community living with us who was suffering from leprosy. My dad financed his treatment and took great care of this poor man.

In action, his hunting skills and the adventures he exposed us to can only be imagined by most kids today. I cannot fathom, in today's changing world, how children would have the experiences as I had with my dad. His anger was very fearsome and scary, and it's this aspect of my dad that I despised and hated.

Dad was a handsome man. He was of fair complexion, with olive-green eyes, a masculine and manly figure, with well-rounded muscular arms and shoulders. He had a thin-lined moustache neatly arranged across his upper lip in a perfect length and width on either side, always clean-shaven. I never can recall seeing his face with a beard or facial-hair growth; shaving was a regular exercise. It was amusingly funny, but I dare not laugh.

I saw him get his bowl of hot water, a rounded box with a bar of white soap, and his shaving brush. He would vigorously rub the shaving lather and spread it across his cheeks. It looked like white, soft cotton candy all over his face. I always wanted to play with that shaving lather but was afraid to ask out of fear that he would shout at me.

He had an old-fashioned razor, into which he would insert a blade that came out of a box with the name *Topaz* written on it.

I watched him from a close distance as he shaved and the funny faces he made. He would blow air into his face from the inside so that his cheeks would blow up like a rounded air bubble, while he used his razor to remove his facial hair on that cheek. He would switch to the other cheek and blow another balloon from the inside. The funniest one—that made him look like a monkey—was when he blew an air bubble on the upper lip from the inside. I wanted to laugh out loud, but I was afraid to do so.

I don't know why he did that "blowing air bubbles from the inside," but I think it had something to do with the way he shaped his moustache or removed the facial hair on his face. He did spend a lot of time developing his pencil-line moustache.

I did sneak into his room when he was not at home and played with the shaving lather cotton candy on my face. I also knew that I would get a sound walloping if he found out, so I did not do this too often.

I often heard my aunties and uncles say that my dad looked like Clark Gable. I did not know who this Mr. Clark Gable was, but I hoped he was not as angry as my dad. My mother was responsible for all his clothing. The local laundryman was always given strict instructions about his clothing. I was afraid of this handsome man, my dad. I thought my mother was worried, too, by the way she served him.

I never approached my dad directly as a child. I always went to my mother, and she approached him on my behalf. My dad was strict and looked angry, and I shivered when he shouted. Sometimes he would swear and curse at my mother, and I did not like him whenever he did that.

There was a black motorbike with a registration number APK 7244, known as the Royal Enfield Bullet. This was my dad's pride and joy. I saw him spend several hours tuning his bike. It was always in an immaculate condition, polished and shined every day. I did not know that it would become my job cleaning and polishing the bike for a little pocket money, but that's precisely what happened when I grew older. I never got to ride his motorcycle, but cleaning it was my job.

The hunting adventures I had with my dad are genuinely remarkable. Dad got his hunting skills from Grandpa, who was an expert on Indian wildlife, which he explored with a gun barrel and not with a camera. I reckon together they had shot and killed most species of wildlife. Sounds awful today, but it was just like that in those days.

He was a gambler, my dad; I heard that the game is called *cotton figures* in the local town. There was a chart he had in his bedroom where he would sit for hours figuring out these numbers and gamble on the outcome of the next day's draw. I never understood it much; I was too young and did not have a clue. I heard that he hit the jackpot, struck lucky with the number 44, and bought a new motorcycle.

My dad specifically paid for the registration number with the last two digits being *44*. I guess my dad was riding his motorbike in the town like a successful gambler with the name *44* on it.

He had a group of friends who all had the same type of motorcycles. My dad was the master mechanic, so I always saw him working on these bikes, repairing and fine-tuning these great motorcycles for all his close friends.

I heard my mother disapprove of his gambling addiction, the smoking and drinking; nevertheless, she was afraid of him. Hence, she did not bring her complaints to his attention. Like a timid cat, she slipped away into the silent forest of unspoken words. My dad was not a man you could reason with. No one stood in his way. There were times I felt I did not like this man. I always respected him as my dad more out of fear but did not understand why he was the way he was.

He was an angry man, selfish when it came to his addictions, a man of power and strength, unreasonable towards my mother and us; on the other hand, he was a hardworking man who toiled for his family and provided for us. Dad was a generous person to the poor and unfortunate. He was a different person when he was angry.

One day my whole childhood view of my father was destroyed by his raging anger. I don't know what happened between my mom and dad, but screaming and fighting erupted in the room. I was petrified as I saw my mother's hair in his hands and my father fisting my mother in her face. I saw my eldest sister in between them, trying to stop him. Then the madman went into a rage with my sister, and he started beating her as well; as my mother wanted to protect her from his raging anger, he turned once again to attacking my mother. I saw blood on the floor, and I was just shocked and stood in total fear of what was happening.

Pressed against the door in the kitchen and through the gap between the door and its hinge, I was witnessing something terrible; I was watching violence between the people I loved, and it was excruciating. I wanted to protect my mother, but I was scared that my dad would beat me up as well. I found myself crying and shaking in fear.

I slipped through the kitchen door, and slowly through the front door; I ran through the yard and just kept on running through the woods and down a culvert onto the bank. Across was a muddy lake used by local people to wash animals, cows, and water buffaloes, not a very clean lake by any means.

I sat on the bank near the thornbushes and wept for a while. Then I decided to jump into the muddy water and swim with the local kids and the water buffalo. The water was smelly and cloudy, but I did not care. I was sad and did not know what to do. I figured I would get sick and die from the muddy water and all the bacteria in it. So, I jumped into the water.

I did not like my dad that day; I was utterly afraid of him. I did not want to go home but knew I could not stay at the lake forever. I just waited for as long as I could. I felt sad for my mother and my sister. Slowly, in fear, I trudged back and returned to a very silent and sad home that day. My view of my childhood dad changed for a long time. I was unhappy, but, still, I loved him—I just didn't know how much anymore. Soon I would be gone from home, sent to Don Bosco boarding school for boys in Calcutta, West Bengal, India.

My dad was experiencing a changing country. He was passionate about his hunting, friends, drinking, and gambling. He had to work hard to come up in his life, taking every opportunity he could find in a country changing from British colonial rule to an independent nation, unprepared for democracy, and the rule of law to one of chaos and corruption. India was changing, and the British were leaving. This was never going to be easy for the Anglo-Indian community. My father was an angry man in his youth; some things in his life made him this way. These aspects of his behaviour and life were devastating his family, none more than anger and the violence that affected us children; this was painful, especially to my mother.

Although I had a deep emotional bond with both my parents, the one that troubled me the most was the relationship with my father. I admired the hunting adventures in the forest and the beautiful moments of laughter and joy we had during these trips. However, it was always overshadowed by his tendency to suddenly lose his temper. It would turn a happy situation one hundred and eighty degrees the other way around, something like a clock on a bundle of dynamite sticks: you watch the handle tick, and when it got to three o'clock and stopped, phew! No explosion. If it got to six o'clock, it could go either way, back or forth; but when it got to nine o'clock and the blast was set for twelve o'clock, everyone had better get out of the way. I hope you get the idea that I am trying to portray here. It's not easy to live with a person or build a relationship when anger as an emotion is ticking on a clock loaded on a bunch of dynamite sticks. You may say it's a mental ailment, but this was a generational curse because my granddad had the same attitude. We all have anger issues as humans, and if you don't pray these things out and walk a closer walk with God, the demon of anger will get you every time.

My mother was the opposite of my dad; she was a woman who prayed daily and who walked a closer walk with the Lord. It was obvious dad walked in a different direction. There was a demon of anger sitting on his back, willing to destroy everyone around him and blow them to smithereens.

It would be hard for any child to understand domestic violence in a home. This is some kind of a generational curse, a cycle that needs to be broken by a spiritual walk of life with God through Christ. Even if you don't believe in this idea, some intervention of therapy is required to bring a change. Modern people in America call this a mental aliment and put you on medication, but back home, people recognised the demon and unclean spirits that possess the souls of people—addictions, anger, and sexual lust, which are not mental illnesses. People prayed for deliverance from this evil attack on the spirit of a man. He was also unfaithful to my mother and had an affair with another woman who was my schoolteacher. There is an old sin in the world that started at the beginning of time. Many a man—religious men and men of great stature, presidents—have fallen from grace for the lust of their flesh; sexual desire and immorality is an old serpent.

My dad had to deal with his demons and fight spiritual warfare; he was going to need some help. Hence, my mother turned to the church clergy to come and speak to him and pray for him. My father would disparage the Catholic priests and suggest that they needed people to pray for them instead of praying for him. It was a vicious circle of denial and strongholds. Change is as difficult a process for my dad as it was for the idol-worshipping Roman Catholic Church.

The angel who prayed for him was my beautiful mother. We children faced some traumas growing up in a home with my dad, and soon my mother figured it was good for me to go to boarding school. I had to overcome this emotional trauma eventually in my life, but for now, I had to learn to get tougher because boarding school was not going to be any easier. As the years progressed from adolescence, I grew up into a robust young teenager and came to a position where I learned to stand up for myself and against my dad's anger. Although it had gotten better, that demon was always there, sitting on his back. My momma prayed, and resilience kept that evil away from destroying our home and its tranquillity. She was also the peacemaker between my father and me, as I was now at an age that I could defend myself and my mom, and my father knew that all too very well.

I would finally leave home and go away for twenty years, like a Rip van Winkle character. I carried some form of a generational curse of anger, but not to the extent that my dad did. My demon was a smaller version, but it sat on my back as well until I kicked it out of me. That was the spiritual journey in life that gave me heavenly wisdom to understand the spiritual warfare that was raging all around the world. Few people truly recognise it, because you cannot see anything in the darkness if you have no light. Many generational sins and curses rage in the lives of people; humanity uses chemical medicine to treat them, but spiritual cures are more effective in dealing with physical or emotional addictions and unholy alliances of the carnal human being. Anger is a destructive, negative force. What you dwell on is what you will dwell in.

A quarter century later, I would finally address these issues with my dad once again and find amazing healing of his pain, walk with him on a spiritual path that gave him a comforting reconciliation with God. I witnessed the correction of the spirit within a man, an acknowledgement of the mortal death of the flesh, and the reaching out for salvation to a holy thirst within a soul inside a man. I connected to this, and it was my most excellent gift of our healing relationship and bringing repentance of acknowledgement of years lived with foolish anger and pride. Mercy and grace are rich attributes from a Heavenly Father; by this grace, I became the greatest son to both my parents in their lives.

My esteemed reader, I hope you will continue to walk with me on this journey; it is emotional and can tug at the strings of your heart, yet, I know it will be well worth it because no one has a perfect life—in this life on Earth. We are more productive when we share the life we have had and enlighten ourselves with the lessons it teaches us, in order to live a meaningful life while we still can. I am keeping my commitment to you as the story of my life unfolds in the pages ahead.

THE ANGLO-INDIAN CHRISTMAS RIOT

Given this history of the city of Hyderabad, the fall of the *Nizam* directly affected the fortunes and future of the Anglo-Indian society in Hyderabad. As much as our parents may have had closer emotional and historical ties with India, it was surely fading with my generation.

An event that I witnessed as a child made sure that I knew we were a different people in this nation called India. It was the twenty-sixth of December, and I was at the traditional Christmas ballroom-dancing party organised by the Anglo-Indian Association. There was fierce competition in fashion among the women. I would compare it to a scene from the movie *Grease*—girls in short skirts, beautiful dresses, the boys all spiced up with their old-time after-shave cologne called Old Spice, dressed in their trousers, ties, boots, and suits following the dress code. It was like a scene that made you feel you were somewhere else, somewhere Western, somewhere in England or Australia or the USA. For tonight, we could be ourselves. Girls in decent skirts. Western clothing was not worn in public in a country like India in the '60s and '70s, but tonight, my Western culture could be ourselves.

It was customary in those days that the Anglo-Indian Association did not allow Indian people to join our traditional dancing parties. There was ever-growing pressure to allow Indian people to integrate with us, and it was a time of change, a time of dilution, a time to adapt, a time to accept that our British past was slowly fading away, a time for a change, as we were abandoned on these shores by the British even as we were fiercely struggling to keep our identity in India.

We were dancing all night long as the band played on. I can recall that two bands were playing that night. One was called the Black Diamonds and the other was the Psychedelics.

My grandmother, a well-known culinary expert, ran the catering section; all the traditional foods and snacks she made were highly acclaimed by the community. As we youngsters were checking out the girls, feeling shy and afraid of rejection, we mustered the courage to ask the girls for a dance.

There was an ingenious method of getting everyone involved, and it was called the bangle dance. Young men were obligated to buy a bunch of glass bangles and tag another boy who would hand over the girl to the new boy and give her one glass bangle as he left. Every time the girl had to dance with a different boy, she got a glass bangle. When the bangle dance was over, the girl with the greatest number of bangles was declared the most popular lady of the night. Similar to the best-looking cheerleader, proud-peacock-attitude girls who are hard to get a date with. Here on the Anglo-Indian dance floor, if a girl wanted that title, she would have to dance with many boys to earn the title "Most popular lady of the night."

On some occasions, in an attempt to allow for integration, we allowed Indians into our celebrations; many young Indian boys were allowed to join the Christmas ballroom dance. It was during the bangle dance that events took an ugly turn.

One Indian boy, while dancing with an Anglo-Indian girl wearing a short skirt, tried to indecently lift the girl's skirt while holding her, grinning like an ignorant fool; he was utterly disrespectful to the girl, and then world war began. As the boy was escorted out of the hall, it ended in a fistfight between the Anglo-Indians and the Indians.

Now it was a tradition with Anglo-Indian men to go to boxing school, so this event resulted in many Indian boys receiving broken noses and missing teeth. There was screaming and yelling as the fight continued outside and was being brought under control by some of the security staff.

With the departure of the Indians, the Christmas ball continued into the night; it was about an hour after the incident when suddenly a huge mob of Indians returned, armed with sticks and knives to attack the whole Anglo-Indian community. There was screaming as stones were being thrown; the women, all screaming, huddled together while the men were fighting with the rioting mongrel mob. It was the scariest thing I had ever witnessed—the vicious and furious attack by this huge mob of Indians resulted in three stabbing incidents and many broken bones. There were men bleeding, and for every Anglo-Indian injury, the Indians received four in return. But with the overwhelming mob, things were starting to get very ugly. Our women were being attacked, and a few women had their clothes torn off—as I mentioned as a mark of utter disrespect by the Indians towards the Anglo-Indian culture. I heard people saying, "Go back to Britain! Why are you people here?"

Suddenly police jeeps and a riot-control van turned up, and there was chaos as the police force started hitting everyone and anyone with batons. This is the Indian way to stop a crowd from fighting—beat the living daylights of anyone in sight.

I was about eight years old when this event took place, and I was terrified; on a few occasions, the event returned to me in dreams where I saw violence and people attacking one another. It had a profound effect on me as a young boy, and I had a deep dislike for Indians; I knew that this was not my country. We were Anglo-Indians, and we had been abandoned by our European ancestry.

I was Anglo-Indian, so I did not see the need for me to learn the Indian language. Hence, I never did, and for all my school years, I was very proud my Indian teacher gave me a big zero grade for my exceptional knowledge of the Hindi language. I always felt it was an honorary award I received every year for being an Anglo-Indian— true to who I was. I was proud of the grade. This was my identity and culture. I was holding on to it in spite of the social changes.

The Christmas riot changed my perceptions forever; the desire to leave India was propagated in my heart. I would swim an ocean, climb a mountain, grow some wings if I could, and fly away from here. The emotion was penetrating; it infiltrated every cell and tissue of my mortal human body. Travelling upwards, it settled into its homely estate in my brain. I had to wait for adolescence to pass; my mind was in constant disagreement with my father's view of India. I grew up in a culture and a society that was different from the Hindu or Muslim societies that made up the societies of India. We were different because of our British ancestors, who created a mixed-race sub-population of people.

ANGLO-INDIAN PRACTICES

It is significant not to overlook that another explanation behind setting up their own clubs was the distinctive social conduct of the British and Anglo-Indians. Clubs were places where European ladies could straightforwardly associate with men, a practice forbidden for Indian women. European and Anglo-Indian people blended with each other, eating together at clubs, particularly unmarried couples had the freedom to directly interact with each other. This would be considered utter horror to conventional Hindus and Muslims. Women who carried on in such a way with men would have been seen as wanton or even whores.

Islam endorsed that ladies ought to be hidden and observe *purdah*—customary veils worn by Hindus—but enforcement of this custom was not as stringent as with Muslims. However, neither looked favorably on their women associating openly with men outside the family. Although social interaction between these cultures *did* occur—especially during cultural festivals—these were inadequate to change the regulating codes of Hindu and Muslim conduct and practices. English and Anglo-Indian women, in this manner, avoided social interaction with Indian men, more because of reasons of custom and culture, rather than a racist divide between peoples of this era. The apparent lower status of women inside Hinduism and Islam, where veiling was observed—not to mention the arrays of mistresses and concubines that Muslims and some Hindus were allowed to have in their cultures—was another social explanation that deflected Anglo-Indian women from wedding Indian men. These social barriers may have contributed towards racial bias, and this book doesn't deny that types of racial and shading bias existed inside British and Indian society. These societies were apart because India was predominantly a deeply racist nation, with all its castes and creeds and the rules of untouchables. Considerations regarding conventional Hindu and Muslim practices affected the embryonic blended-race network, shaping the roots and trimming Anglo-Indians' separate conduct and dispositions.

The strongholds in the frameworks of this society and its exacting principles of endogamy kept newcomers from integrating. Because of being excluded, newcomers kept up their separate traditions, assembled their places of community, and lived in discrete zones. Along these lines, untouchables contributed to the economic well-being of the higher classes. Simultaneously, this caste separation prevented befouling of highly positioned Hindus by their *mlechchha* views. Indeed, even the British framed their claim to "cantonment zones," and here in Calcutta today, there are discrete locales, *paras* for Hindus, Muslims, and Anglo-Indians.

The philosophy of position and custom immaculateness that is instilled in Hinduism—particularly the contaminating status of *mlechchhas*—kept those of blended race from any decent status in Indian culture. Also, high-standing Indian ladies who entered associations with normal European men lost their position status. Hence, the main alternative accessible to Indian ladies who had lost their status, or to lower-position ladies chasing status, was to assume the character of their male accomplices and enter the Christian crease in the British group. Consequently, Anglo-Indians adjusted themselves to their fatherly social legacy because their blended status was unacceptable as profaning themselves to conventional Hindu society. Anglo-Indians were defensive when it came to their faith in Christianity. A scriptural aspect applied to them. "You shall not plow with an ox and a donkey together." (Deuteronomy 22:9). Anglo-Indians rarely married Indians in the days of old.

These social customs that prohibited blended races and Europeans based on being *dhimmis* or *mlechchhas* challenge the possibility of racial bias by Europeans against Indians. Truth be told, the reverse appears to be progressively precise. Be that as it may, it is obvious that the term "racial bias," with all its harsh ramifications, doesn't accurately mirror the contention between various social practices and convictions that support the reasons various gatherings or races don't mingle together. Rank is an ancient rule; that profoundly various-levelled unfair framework affects every Indian practice and demeanour, which thus significantly influenced the way of life and frames of mind of newcomers to India.

In these conditions, it isn't surprising that Anglo-Indians built up a social personality that was Christian; their first language is English and dress style is Western. These were images that recognised Anglo-Indians from the encompassing Indian societies; what's more, it gave status to Anglo-Indians in British India. Western dress for ladies was an inferred sign that enabled them to stay uncovered regularly, unescorted openly, with no loss of status. A positive result of this Anglo-Indian culture has been that, when most of the populace in India moved to the West after autonomy, they had the option to incorporate effectively into Western culture.

Today, when I look at Bollywood Indian movies, Indians have taken the word *harlot* to an extraordinary level. My mom and sister confronted verbal maltreatment when they wore Western apparel in what was a moderate society. Today, with all its objectifying of love and agnosticism that still exist, Bollywood makes a terrible showing as it has stripped the Indian traditionalist women bare on its screens with the absolutely most revolting articles in the realm of excessive idolatry and avariciousness.

I am not sure, being so definitely Anglo-Indian, that I was an easy child to cope with. I know my mother always understood that one day I would be gone. My attitude at home prompted my dad to send me to a boarding school. I was nine years old when my dad announced that I was going to Don Bosco boarding school in the city of Calcutta in West Bengal. My first journey away from home was set in motion. A few months later, after several recommendations from the parish priest of our church with the school administrators at Don Bosco, my dad secured a place for me at this boarding school.

India was not a country where free education was a privilege for the Anglo-Indian community as it was under the British. These privileges were soon erased once we were left abandoned by our ancestors from the European continent. It was a financial struggle for many Anglo-Indian families; and as a child, I understood this early in life. We could not afford to fail in school or repeat a class due to poor grades. Boarding school was expensive, and the church had to step in to get discounts and concessions for admission to reputed schools and institutions, remnants of the age of colonisation left by the British. Our privileges went with them back to England. We were known as Eurasians, leftovers of the British Empire, abandoned to our fate in India.

As I boarded the train with my dad on my journey away from home, I met the Warring boys on the platform. Mr. John Warring was an Anglo-Indian gentleman who had eight sons and four daughters. Six of his sons were studying at the Don Bosco boarding school, Liluah, Calcutta, West Bengal, India. They would soon become my extended family across this sprawling complex called boarding school.

BOARDING SCHOOL

The journey was exciting. I had new friends, so I did not feel alone, and any trepidations I had about being lonely vanished with the Warring brothers by my side. It was a long journey of twenty-four hours on a steam train that stopped at every station along the way. Excited and tired, we arrived at the extensive complex of the Don Bosco school. My boarding life as a child was now about to begin.

I recall feeling overwhelmed at the size of the building structure in front of me. It was a five-story structure, across sprawling grounds in the shape of the letter *C* in a square form. This was a big school. I also heard that naughty boys would have an appointment with the discipline cane, placed in the hands of the brother Paul, a Salesian priest of the order of Don Bosco, whose job it was to straighten the paths of naughty boys. I was not looking forward to this appointment but had the gut feeling that it was unavoidable.

We walked into the admissions office, where I met an Italian priest, Father Giuseppe; he was kind, and I liked him the very moment he put his hands around my shoulder. "We make young boys good students in this school," he said. "Welcome to Don Bosco Liluah."

He told me the story of Saint John Bosco, an Italian Roman Catholic priest, an educator who was born on August 16, 1815, and died on January 31, 1888. He was the founder of the Salesians of Don Bosco.

Father Giuseppe explained to me the vision of Don Bosco towards the education of boys; then came the rules of the school and the responsibilities of students. I stood there listening to him, realizing this was serious business. Suddenly I felt sad. I was going to miss my home on the glen, my beach and bodysurfing, my dogs, my mother, and family. I did not want to stay in this school. I wanted to go home. The excitement was over, the reality too real.

My dad looked at me with compassion and assured that he was doing the right thing leaving me here in this sprawling complex. He held me by my hand and said, "You will come out of here disciplined and a better child." I stood there with my mouth opened wide. Many years of boarding school—it felt like I would be here till eternity. Oh, my G-d! My little heart was pounding inside. I started beating myself up inside my mind for agreeing to go to boarding school. My imaginary chains were now shackled around my legs—there was no turning back. I suddenly felt a tantrum rising in my head. I wondered if I started crying myself into hysteria, my dad would take me back with him. Yet, as I looked at him, I knew it was not going to work— my little trick.

We shortly met Brother Andrew, who took us on a tour of the complex. Through the labyrinth of classrooms and sports facilities, we arrived at the boys' sleeping dormitory. This was a massive room with rows of beds and wooden cupboards next to each other. Private shared rooms did not exist. Just two massive dormitories—one for the senior boys and one for the juniors.

At the corner of the massive dormitory room, towards the far end, was a square curtained enclosure that housed the priest in charge of the boys at night. There were two enclosures placed at two corners of the biggest dormitory I had ever seen in my life as a child. A total of one hundred and eighty beds and cupboards placed in a row. As I was led to the bed allotted to me, I saw a happy, advantageous boy, my neighbour, smiling at me.

He greeted me with a handshake. "I am Steve Hawkins. What's your name?" he inquired. I shook his hand and told him mine. He was funny; he had freckles on his face, red cheeks, and brown hair. He looked strong and chubby; he had an infectious smile and was friendly. He said he'd been a boarder in the school for the past two years. Looking at me, he reassured me with his words, "You will get accustomed to it." I was starting to feel happy when a tough kid passed by, walking towards the corner of the row of beds.

Steven whispered to me, "That is Wenzel Puxty. He is the tough kid. You don't want to mess with him. He is the toughest fighter here, and you don't want to get in bad books with him. Stay out of his way." My first challenge was presented to me on a silver platter.

A second boy appeared behind me, and, smiling, he shook my hand, introducing himself as Benjamin Patterson. I had found two new friends, and I had the added support of the Warring brothers from my hometown. I felt reassured and confident that I would be all right in this big school. I spent the rest of the day with my dad walking around the school, visiting all the facilities available to me.

Some boys were playing field hockey, and it was my dad's favourite sport; an expert hockey player himself, Dad was encouraging me to take up the sport and to excel in it as he had done when he was a boy. The day had passed by so quickly, and the dreaded goodbye fast approached us. I stood at the huge gate entrance as my father kissed me, and wrapping his arms around me, he gave me a fatherly hug—something he did not do that often. Tears welled up in my eyes as I cried, "Bye, Dad." He walked out of the gate with his bag in his hand.

I was prompted by Steven to climb the wall attached to the gate to get a glimpse of my dad as he walked along the road and disappeared from my view. I felt sad, and that sinking feeling of being away from home gripped me. I thanked my new friends, who put their arms around my shoulder, reassuring me that we had each other.

I stored all my clothes in my cupboard, polished my shoes, and readied my uniform; I prepared for my first day at school. I unpacked all the nice things my mother packed for me—pickles, homemade snacks; tears were rolling down my cheeks. I felt sad. I wanted to sob and cry, but it was not something you ought to do in a boarding school. You would soon be called "a sissy."

I felt this awful pang of separation, and I scrambled down the wall; my boarding life as a child had begun. I thought about Wenzel Puxty, my new challenge ahead. My dad raised us to be tough, and we learned a typical Anglo cultural trait as kids. Boxing was the hallmark of every boy who came from an Anglo-Indian family. So, my adversary Wenzel Puxty was a formidable foe. I just knew in my heart that an altercation with him was certain to happen sooner or later. He was the mafia boss, and a new boy like me was going to get oppressed.

The first weeks of boarding life started to be exciting; it was a drill that I had to get accustomed to. As I lay in my bed in the big dormitory, I was not alone. My trusted friend Steve Hawkins, my neighbour, was funny. I liked him.

It was early morning at 6:30 a.m. when the dormitory lights were turned on and the sound of loud clapping was heard. It was our wake-up call, as one of the Salesian brothers woke us up; it was like being in the army. We jumped out of our beds with toothbrushes and towels, standing in line at the row of washbasins for our early-morning routine.

All dressed in grey trousers, white shirt, and maroon ties, we all walked to the chapel in a line for the morning prayer; after service, we formed rows and marched off to the refectory for the morning breakfast.

It was porridge of some kind, made from broken wheat and milk; certain boys were given eggs and toast. As I looked around, I saw some exchanges of food taking place under the table. Steve told me that those boys with extra privileges were classified as first-class boarders. This means their parents paid more than our parents could afford, and so my first taste of discrimination was the experience of privileges.

I dipped my spoon into my porridge bowl and noticed a small tiny creature that looked like a minuscule worm. I nudged Steve to look;

he smiled at me and said, "Don't look in your bowl; just eat it up." Taking his advice, I gulped it down my throat. It did not kill me, and I did not get sick. The days at school were intensive. I got used to the drill, and by the end of the first month, it became routine. It worked like clockwork—3:30 p.m., we were at the hockey field playing the game. It was fierce and competitive. I loved it.

At times, it got rough when you got whacked with the hockey stick across your ankles; some of the boys were experts, masters of trickery. As you ran dribbling the ball with the hockey stick, the swiftly tripped you with the hook, pulling at your feet with lightning speed. It is hard to catch the foul play, leaving you lying on the grass bruised and defeated. Your only choice was to get up and fight back. As I improved my skills with long hours of practice and ball control, I became a better player with each game, scoring goals and becoming popular with my mates.

As we made our way to the showers after our daily gruelling game, our youthful bodies were taking shape and building muscle. I was getting toughened up for the kill. As I walked into the shower, somebody bumped me from the back—a push, a shove of displeasure. I turned around and saw Wenzel Puxty. He gave me a disapproving look. Provoking me, he pushed me again.

I looked at him and said, "You push me again, and I will smack you."

He laughed, confidently saying, "I will beat you up into pulp," he scornfully told me.

"We shall see about that," I responded.

My challenge was now closer, at my doorstep. I was not going to back down. Even though fear filled my heart, I knew that I had to be strong and fight my way through this one. There was no escape from a bully, and ultimate confrontation was inevitable.

Wenzel Puxty did not know that I came from a family of boxers; my dad had trained us as young boys. We had an uncle named Eugen Adams, who was a powerful man, six feet three, built like a concrete-brick house, a professional heavyweight boxer. As young boys, we went with him and my dad on early morning jogging sessions. Skipping ropes in hands, we had to skip faster to improve our footwork.

He would tie a string between our big toes on both feet and teach us footwork. The idea was not to break the string as we moved around, controlling our feet, throwing punches at the bag. In several sparring lessons and quick handwork, I heard him yell, "Don't waste the punch!

Land it on the bag! Focus, step aside, duck, and dodge! Always make sure you land the punch!" Then there were the one-two shuffles—one punch and then two quick ones in succession, keeping your eye on your opponent, learning a typical Anglo-Indian skill; boxing was intrinsically woven into our culture, and it may have been the Irish ancestry that was also a part of the culture as well.

I went to the gym at school and signed up for a different art of self-defence. It was the first time I'd heard about martial arts called *karate*. I met a Chinese senior student instructor named Fu-Kee Choo. I was impressed with his demonstration. He was swift and smart. He had bulging muscles on his legs, his eyes were small and swollen, his forearms were strong, and the veins running down his arms were dense, filled with blood, flowing like a network of electrical wires, exploding with energy, supplying power to his swift muscles and quick-reflex movement.

I was impressed by our Chinese instructor as he taught us about being committed and gave us a new routine of exercises. It was a new skill and art that was different and intensive. Soon I found myself so involved with the school and sports, my sadness over being away from home disappeared.

The months flew by, and summer holidays were soon approaching; our journey back home was being arranged by the school. Six months had passed me by so quickly. It felt like I'd arrived here just the other day.

After a game of hockey, I rushed into the dormitory, grabbed my towel and shampoo, and headed for the showers. As I made my way through in a hurry, someone tripped me from behind. I went sliding on the wet floor and hit the ground hard. A bump appeared on my forehead almost immediately. I stood up and saw Wenzel Puxty and two of his cronies laughing at me. I charged at him and threw a punch at the boy next to him. I clipped him across the ear; a scuffle broke out, and I was held back by other boys who were there. I yelled at Wenzel, "If you are that tough, let's put it to the test in Field E."

Now, Field E was the farthest playground in the schoolyard. If we were going to fight, we did not want anyone to come and break it up. So, we would have to take it to the remote area of the schoolyard.

Rumours spread like wildfire among the boys; it was exciting for most of them. School fights were a big thing, and like a group of Mafia gangsters, the boys assembled. I wore a hoodie, and my friends camouflaged me. I was going to surprise my opponent with a punch. I figured out that, if I hit him first with a hard punch, he would receive a shock from it and realise I was just as tough as he was; I was going to land the hardest knockout punch and settle it forever.

Wenzel Puxty was standing with some of his buddies as we approached. I sent my friend Steve ahead of us to misinform my opponent that I was coming with the second group. To increase my chances of surprising him in a dimly lit place, as we approached closer and within range, I lunged at Wenzel. I threw my weight with a right-handed punch that landed on his nose; as he went reeling back from the sudden attack, I launched myself with a flurry of punches to his face. I had taken him by surprise, and after three more punches to his abdomen, he fell. I threw myself at him and wrestled him to the ground. I clenched his neck in a viselike grip with my arms, as hard as I could—like a vise-grip stranglehold. I tightened it every time he took a breath. I never gave him a chance. He was strong, but the surprise of the attack was effective. As we both lay on the ground in a deadlock, Wenzel was struggling to break free.

All the months of being subjected to his bullying had built up inside me; my vehemence and anger surprised me. It was scary, but I did not let go. I could hear my friends shouting, "Don't let him go." I tightened my grip around his neck as he struggled to break free; being tossed around, I was covered in mud and grass while his face was bloody. He gave up and was defeated; his days of bullying were over, the image was broken, like a mirror lying on the floor in a thousand pieces—similar to the devil of darkness, just an image. Some senior schoolboys came running, hearing the tumult in the field; they took control and broke up the fight.

Wenzel Puxty was bleeding from his nose; blood dripping, he was taken away. A senior boy grabbed my hand and twisted it at the back and led me away to the dreaded boarding master.

Brother Paul was a ruthless man. His punishment practices were designed to impose pain and scars. We were left to the mercy of the school's punitive methods. I was sent to the dormitory to clean up in the showers and sent to bed without any dinner.

Lights switched off, I waited in the darkness of the big dormitory for Steve to come. As I lay there for an hour and a half, wondering what my fate was going to be, I felt bad for what I'd done to Wenzel Puxty; it was a mean fight—unfair. I took him by surprise, yet, I knew that was the best way to beat him up and teach him a lesson to stop hounding me and my friends.

I heard several footsteps running up the stairs. The boys were coming up to the dorm, and I would soon know my fate. Steve smiled at me as he passed my bed. "Shoosh!" Finger on his lips, he signalled me to be quiet. I closed my eyes and pretended I was asleep.

"All boys in bed," I heard the familiar voice of Brother John. "Lights off, silence in the dorm," he yelled. As I lay in my bed in the dark, I could hear the footsteps of Brother John pacing across the rows of bed. I waited for thirty minutes before I lifted my head slowly to see if I could see Brother John. I suddenly saw him in the far corner in the dark. He was anticipating our tricks, like a game of cat and mouse. I quickly ducked back slowly, throwing my head back into my pillow. If I got caught, this would be an added felony.

My friend Steve was the great pretender; he was fast asleep with his eyes closed, but fully alert and wide awake—an actor of natural talent. I knew he was awake because he wanted to tell me all the rumours, tell me my fate, my destiny, like a fortune-teller; he knew what was going to happen to me the next day. Steve was not asleep; he was blessed with an invisible third eye on his forehead. His instincts were like a periscope lifting from his pillow, scanning the movements and position of Brother John, the shadowy figure pacing the bed rows in the dark.

I waited for a while, closed my eyes, and napped off to sleep. I suddenly felt a tug at my sheet, and I opened my eyes to see Steve sitting on his bed. He whispered, "Wenzel Puxty has been sent to the infirmary. I think they are going to dismiss you from the school. Brother Paul is going to have an inquiry tomorrow." Then like a true friend, he reassured me, "Don't worry—I will tell Brother Paul the truth. Goodnight. Shoosh." Finger on his lips, assuring me of his support, Steve and I went to sleep. The morning came, and the tension returned in my head. I was worried about my fate. Following our daily routine, I went to school.

At 3:30 p.m., as I was getting ready to go for my hockey game, Brother John informed me that I had been suspended from playing any games as a punishment for my attack on Wenzel Puxty. Until further notice.

Later that evening, while I was in the study hall with several of my companions, I was informed to go to the office of the feared Brother Paul, the master of discipline. I walked into his office in total fear of what was going to be my fate. His investigation completed, he told me to stand near a table and bend down. He went to his cupboard and drew out his cane. I stood there waiting for it to happen.

It landed with a swoosh on my butt; it stung badly. Then again, and again—six lashes with the cane, each one worse than the one before, my skin bursting. I felt the swelling rise on my butt. I started to cry. He then held me by the ear and twisted it. As I yelped like a puppy, he switched to the other ear. Then came the slap on the face. "I am sorry," I cried. He then instructed me to go wash my face and to go back to the study hall. "Send Steven down to my office" was the message I carried back to the study hall.

As I walked back limping to the study hall, all my companions knew the punishment I'd endured. I looked at Steve and signalled him with my eyes. I told him, "Brother Paul wants you in his office." I knew his fate. A little while later, Steve came up with tears in his eyes and signalled the call to discipline to Benjamin. A little later, Benjamin appeared with tears in his eyes, and signalled the call to discipline Roy.

As the evening of discipline progressed, it became funny. With the return of each boy from his caning ritual that he'd received from the office of the cruel Brother Paul, everyone started to giggle. Not because someone had been punished, but the anticipation of every boy's hope to escape the caning resulted in disappointment. The look on their faces was so funny.

This was starting to become funnier with the return of every boy in tears. Soon everyone was laughing, and this would only mean more trouble for all of us. So, we suppressed our laughter and kept our heads down and just giggled on the inside. I had never been to a place where you could not laugh out loud. This was corporal punishment. I was responsible for it.

We all walked limping the next day; the broken skin on our rear ends only got worse the following morning. There were no hockey games on Field E for the next two weeks as the wounds on our butts started to heal, while some of us had scars. We were given an ointment to apply on our healing wounds; no one was fighting anymore. No more bullying discipline achieved. There was a definite attitude of "don't spare the rod and don't spoil the child" in this school.

I had to go and meet the Salesian priest Father Giuseppe. He was a kind man who took me to his office and made me read the Bible. I had to read the book of Proverbs. I received instructions from him as he explained how a child should be. I had to go to the chapel and pray and ask Jesus to forgive me for my sins. I did as he instructed, and, kneeling in the chapel of the Lord, I cried and felt sad; my heart was paining as I realised that I was wrong. I wept for a while, and with a contrite heart, I asked my Lord to forgive me.

When I returned to his office the next day, Father Giuseppe told me that I needed to apologise to Wenzel Puxty; even though he was a bully, I had to report his behaviour and not break his nose. "Now you need to humble your heart and amend yourself from the pain."

Wenzel Puxty looked sad and defeated; as I approached him, I felt awful for my attack on him. I was sorry that I had vented so much of my fury. I reached out my hand to him and told him I was sorry. "Please forgive me. I did not mean to hurt you so badly. I am truly sorry," I pleaded. For the first time, our unnecessary enmity was gone, and probity made more sense.

"I am sorry, too," he replied. "It's also my fault." We shook hands. Senior boys facilitated this reunion between foes, and peace returned once again. Wenzel Puxty became one of my best friends in boarding school. We turned around from being fighters to peacemakers and an example to other kids about friendship. Bullying was a different thing back then, but it was not as vindictive or harmful as it has become these days in school. We were even awarded a friendship medal and applied our story to discourage bullying among other kids. Yet, in all this charade, there was something sinister that took place in boarding schools that I feel compelled to tell in this book. It has something to do with the Catholic education system that covered up these terrible events and failed to address them. Boys were silenced, and the victims were those not-so-tough kids.

SEXUAL ABUSE IN BOARDING SCHOOLS

There was a great advantage when you are the tough kid who stands with his fists and bears scars of caning and corporal punishment. Not one of those dressed as brothers in white cloaks in Catholic schools of the Don Bosco system of education would ever consider messing with you. These young priests were called "brothers"; they were on their way to becoming full-fledged Catholic priests. They usually dressed in white or brown long cloaks, rounded necks, with three buttons and long sleeves had supervisory roles in boarding schools under the order of the Don Bosco model of education for boys.

There were some rogue elephants among the herd; solitary in approach and a small gang of three, these preyed on little young boys for their sexual gratification. These events took place in the younger dormitory section of the school where I was located. On the second floor to the right side of the building complex, next to the stairways, were two massive dormitories. You entered through a double door of the first complex, and you would walk into a massive room filled with beds and cupboards in neat rows; there were ninety of them all standing in perfect lines, beds made and neatly tucked, clean marble floors shining like a mirror, ceiling fans, and an array of tube lighting. On the right side of this hall was a set of doors that led to several washbasins and toilets. There were many showers, and it was a place of buzzing activity every morning.

In the massive dormitory, towards the corners, there were large green curtains that hung from steel bars and a cubicle of approximately four metres in height and six metres in breadth; it housed double beds and was set up like a luxurious private room. This is where the solitary rogue elephant in white cloaks slept in the night, among the innocence of youthful boys.

I had no clue about such things; there was an untouched innocence that dwelt within me, so sexual abuse was something I did not understand or comprehend in my mind. I did not know of such things or had any idea; childhood innocence was a beautiful thing.

Steve alerted me about cute boys, who were favourites of the dormitory supervisor, a priestly brother who lived and slept behind the dark-green curtains. Strange things took place in the night, and while the rest of us were asleep, these cute boys who were favourites ended up in the cubicle behind the green curtains. I believe that it was a deeply sinister psychological abuse, in which the confidence of the young boy was his loyalty to the priestly brother. These cute boys were different; they had extra privileges given to them, and they were secretive and aloof, protective of their relationships with the brothers. It was strange and weird. I had not seen any naked people behind those green curtains up until this point of my discovery of what went on behind the green curtains.

As a youngster in a boarding school, it was taboo to talk about anything sexual, so accusing a priest was unthinkable; there were occasions on which some senior boys were dismissed from school on some other disciplinary charges. In a world of hush, rumours also were held in secrecy. It was possible that they may have spoken up about some things that they should have been careful about. We were kids in an educational system, and it was us against them, or it was minding your business, and don't bother if it's not you who is the victim—get your education, and get out. For some kids, this education was the key to their future; their parents could not afford to put them through a better school than this. This institution offered many underprivileged kids a good education. So, losing your education was not an option for many youngsters. In a climate such as this, sexual abuse was rampant, but no one talked about it.

Steve and I made a plan to find out what went on behind the green curtain, to cover for each other, and to alert one another if we saw any boy entering the green cubicle in the middle of the night with the brother. Usually, these things occurred while youngsters slept in the night. The daily evening routine after dinner at 6:30 p.m. was games and play, until 7:30 p.m.; then it was time for the Catholic rosary. We walked in different groups reciting the repetitive Catholic prayers from 7:30 p.m. to 8:00 p.m. I never liked them because I preferred being alone with God in my prayers. I would often be alone in the chapel, praying to God for His protection and a personal conversation. I liked the Lord in my solitude because it was praying from my heart, and I felt His presence near me.

This Catholic routine of walking up and down saying ten Hail Marys and ten Holy Marys and repeating them for fifty times was a denominational prayer made by Romans. It made no sense to me even as a child. Then to think that the brother who was pacing up and down with us youngsters had some lover boys that he would attend to in the nights when his feelings of sexual appetite overwhelmed him made it even more evil. Why don't they get married and have a happy life and leave the celibacy vow instead of preying on little boys and wearing their cloaks of white priestly garments? I had to discover what went on behind those green curtains. Getting the opportunity to discover the wickedness was never easy, because I always fell asleep after gruelling days at school.

Our daily routine of school, games, study, eating, and sleeping now became an integral part of life as a child; eyes were always open, and ears were always wide in a defensive mode, always protecting oneself and friends at boarding school. We had to be tough to survive this place. I had been in the boarding school for two years, visiting my home on the glen for the summer and winter holidays. I did not like returning to boarding school, but my education was important, and I had no choice. I turned twelve years old during my Christmas holidays at home; being a December baby, I got a lot of presents and loved the festive season of Christmas at home. My mom and dad always made it very special. We always ate wild venison, duck roast, wild hare. Hunting for the Christmas dinner was my dad's traditional promise each year. He assured my brother and me that he would take us on big hunting trips if I continued to do well in school. The holidays at home always ended way too soon, and I was back in the boarding school among these brothers in white cloaks. The only thing to look forward to with joy was the reunion with friends at school. Steven, Patterson, Wenzel, and the Warring brothers were the best friends ever.

We had returned to school in the middle of January; the weather was colder, and the winter chills persisted in the state of Bengal. I was having trouble sleeping at night as I wanted to be back home with my parents, my beach, my dogs, and my siblings. I was tired of boarding-school life; it was late, and I did not know what time of the night it was. A shadowy figure walked in the dark towards the green cubicle; the dormitory was silent, and everyone was asleep. My senses were alerted, like a sixth sense; this was the moment I had anticipated—finding what went on behind the green curtain came alive. I slithered out of my bed, covered my pillow with my sheet like I was still in bed, crawled on the floor, and tapped the shoulders of Steven Hawkins. He was slightly startled, but I signalled to him pointing to the green cubicle. He understood, so he did the same; he slithered on to the floor, and we lay there whispering about what we would do next.

I suggested we make our way slithering on the floor like two lizards on our belly and make our way as close as possible to the green cubicle and peep to see what was going on. I was not afraid anymore. I figured out that, in the event of getting caught by any chance, I would be dismissed and return home anyway. After all, I did not want to be in the boarding school anymore.

We crawled on the floor in the darkness towards the green cubicle; this was a daring attempt. No other youngster would have dared to perform a lizard crawl, stop, lift head, swing back and forth, crawl again, and perform the lizard investigation-pose towards the dreaded green-curtained cubicle. We had to be military-trained kids because it's amazing how the body reacts to movement in a survival mode.

We made our way closer and closer; as I could feel my heart pounding against the marble floor, we had reached the south side of the green cubicle. We stopped and froze in silence. We silenced even our breathing by taking slower breaths. A young Indian cute boy was in the bed with the brother; it was obvious he was performing sexual acts on the rogue elephant. He was naked, this boy, and so was the rogue elephant. We had finally seen it. It was shocking as I put my hands over my mouth; we slithered from under the green curtain without being noticed. We backed out silently and made our way the same way we'd come—slithered, lifted our head, looked, head down, slithered a little further, and made our way back to our beds, which were about twenty-five metres away from the green cubicle.

We got into our beds, and it was only then that we whispered to one another, "That dirty fat pig was finally caught." This was the first time we had seen an adult performing sexual acts on a young boy. It was now true; every hushed rumour was no rumour anymore. Our innocence was gone; we saw it, and it was disgusting. It was evil, and it made me and Steven angry. I heard Steven whisper, "We are going to get that fat bastard pig brother." We could not sleep for the rest of the night; we lay in bed, shocked at what we had seen. We knew something was going on, but it was unseen when it unravelled before innocent eyes; it changed forever the eyes that saw sexual child abuse. This sin of sexual immorality is as old as the Earth.

We had an awesome choir in our school; people would come from afar and near just to hear the choirboys of our school. We had a heart for the Lord, and we sang Gospel with voices from our soul. Something was wrong in this Catholic school. It confused me to think that such evil would exist among a few individuals who perpetrated it upon youngsters. I felt angry and wanted to do something about it.

We talked about what we had seen behind the green cubicle, top secret, to only a few friends, Wenzel Puxty, our Chinese martial arts champion, and Benjamin Patterson. We set up a plan to attack this sex paedophile in the field-hockey game.

Quite often these brothers would come and play field hockey with us youngsters, and so it was an opportunity for us to take revenge. It was a perfect place: we were armed and dangerous; we had hockey sticks in our hands, and our footwork and speed skills were unmatched. We lured the paedophile priestly brothers into our games that we turned into rough play, and in the ploy of attacking the ball, we hit them on the ankles with great force and broke bones with hockey sticks. I cannot count the times that we were suspended from hockey games because of rough play, but the paedophile priestly brothers ended up in the hospital. It was a battle of good over evil; it was a setup, a secret gang of boys ready to break the legs of evildoers. But we were eventually going to be busted; they cornered one of the gang members during a suspension, and he confessed the names of the group of boys who had hatched a plan to play rough and attack the brothers to break ankles and legs. Steven and Wenzel were immediately suspended from school. Two days later, seven other students were suspended. It was the end of boarding school for me and my friends. Dismissal letters were sent to our parents, and the end came soon.

I was on a train on my way home. I learnt an early lesson in my life, and it is this: when you fight against evil in this world, you pay a price for it, because it is good to fight against unclean things. I realised I was going to miss the buddies of my boarding-school days, my friends and protectors against sexual abuse. We were the lucky ones who held fists up in the air, the tough boys of Don Bosco Liluah. We made it out unscathed across uncharted waters at a time when such abuse was rarely known or exposed. I hold these memories dear to my heart and always wondered where these friends of mine were these days. Would I even recognise them if I ever saw them again? Yet, I thank God for them because He placed them in my life to protect us from the evils of paedophile criminals. We could not protect the victims, and that was tragic. When I first went to this school, I told my parents that I wanted to become a priest and serve God. But after my experience in a denominational education system among some unclean brothers and priests, I contended with the concept of celibacy. I don't believe it is for all men; it is possible only for some. I thought that I would fail miserably and make a mockery of a Holy God if I ever joined these man-made denominations and systems. Sexual immorality is an old serpent that penetrates the souls of men and makes them filthy and unholy.

These man-made religious institutions cannot be the true light of a Holy God. I was sure of this; I felt this deep in my spirit, even though I was so young. I felt that a sanctified life and a true desire to be obedient to the commandments of God, the ones my mother taught me in prayer and in the Holy Bible, were what made a person godly.

Now, I was back in my home on the glen, safe among my favourite dogs, our mini-zoo, my ocean and beaches, back with my friends Stephen and Richard; the boarding-school experiences behind me made me grow up from innocence to witnessing the corruption and sinful things I had seen in this educational system. Several decades later, when I saw the movie *Spotlight*, I could only imagine what some of those weak kids had suffered. Yet even then, as a youngster, I could not comprehend that such evils existed and that so many vulnerable boys were possible victims.

CHAPTER 3

MOTHER

She was angelic, a beautiful black woman, five feet two, a short woman with rounded cheeks that never had a wrinkle; the elasticity of her delicate skin was so immaculate that it retained the same gleam that complemented her polished character even in her old age. She had curly, bobbed hair, always wore cotton dresses, was conservative, was funny, and wore a captivating smile that radiated with love. She had beautiful, strong legs; her shoulders were broad and reliable, and she had an immensely healthy body and yet a glorious feminine grace that was so powerful. Her spirit was haunting, and her presence was heavenly; and in that beautiful body, she conceived and bore me and gave me life. My mother, the queen of my heart. She was my Madonna; a matriarch like Miriam, she was to be my rescuer, my life-giver, and my spiritual strength, my teacher of great things, my *shalom*, my gift from the Lord who taught me the path to find heavenly realms. She was disguised as a woman, but in her eyes, I saw an angel from heaven. In the twinkle of her eyes, I caught her spirit and soul; we all have mothers, but mine was an angel in real time.

Her hands were not the hands of other women I have seen and known. Her hands were most extraordinarily beautiful, cascading, folding me in their grasp, and feeding me the most delightful culinary food that no one in the world could prepare as she did. She never grew long fingernails; they were not caressed with heavenly creams of exotic oils from distant lands. Her hands toiled on stone, scrubbing, washing clothes, curtains, and bedsheets; she lifted them in the air and dabbed them on the washing stone. She spent hours standing in water in the yard washing clothes. Her feet were so soaked in water that it softened the soles of her feet, and she developed water cracks on them; she applied a turmeric paste to heal them, but soon she would be in the same spot again, doing the same thing. There were no washing machines in those days. When you saw her standing there and caught a glimpse of her marble-black eyes, she gave you the most beautiful smile. She was a Picasso painting of a mother that was never painted.

In my eyes, I was her painter. I painted her in the depths of my soul with brushstrokes of her life with mine; every day I had my brushes ready to add strokes of her beauty to my soul. I kept doing this all my life till she left this world, and the masterpiece of her soul was now the masterpiece in me. I was her Picasso. She was my beauty. She was my mother. I miss her so much, and I missed her all my life. When I look at my legs, I see hers. When I see my hands, I see hers; when I look in the mirror, I see her. Even my cheeks resemble hers. She painted herself when she formed me in her womb. She created me intrinsically in her womb, with brushstrokes of her DNA. She put her spirit of love in me; she imparted also to me her faith in God that she had embedded in her soul so deeply. Some people have mothers, but mine was an angel in disguise. She was a rose among the thornbushes, the rose of Sharon, and a lily of the valley, a delicate flower among the thorns, an almond tree, a giant red tree in a canopy with a shelter under her arms; in the shadows of her love, I grew up from a child to a young man.

She radiated this spirit everywhere she went, was humble and thankful for all things; she endured, suffered, and was afflicted. She was hurt, beaten, and abused; she bled, and she was broken, and she wept. She forgave, she compromised, she committed, she prayed, she hoped, she loved, she never hated, she never spoke a rude word, she never held a grudge, she never had a resentment, she was silent in her travail—and above all these things she did, the best thing that she did was she loved. This black woman, a Madonna of love, is the reason that I know there is a God. Because He lived in her. She reflected Him, and she showed me how to see Him in her. I love her more than any woman I have ever known in this life. I am very confident in this when I write and say this: "They don't make women like my mother in the world anymore."

Besides all the things she taught me, she gave me cooking lessons. Like a warning for the future, she would say, "Women are changing; you men should learn to cook so you will not have to depend on the women you boys will marry in the future." Like a prophetess, she was giving me a prophetic warning about marrying the right girl.

It started when I was a small child. My mother would kiss me on my forehead, sitting on a low stool tending the wood-burning, open fireplaces, preparing family meals, a common feature in a developing country during those early years. Then came the dangerous kerosene pump stoves, and as development progressed, then came LPG.

We lived opposite the Sacred Heart Church of Christ, so the timely, angelic church bells ringing at scheduled times each day was a routine we were accustomed to. For me, they were food calls, sounding the alarm that it was time for food. At noon I heard the bells ring; it was lunchtime for me. I was a growing boy with a healthy appetite, always hungry.

Sometimes this lunch was not ready on time, and, so, as a child, I would roll on the floor, crying for my food. She would draw me near, kiss me on my forehead; I would feel the heat from the open fire and the hot, humid summer days. Then drops of sweat from her forehead fell upon my face, now intermingling with my tears of hunger. She would give me a kiss of comfort and assurance of love, a warm hug, and a voice reassuring me, "Your food is almost done."

My mother smiled and was always patient with my food tantrums; she would pacify me by telling me that I could help her cook and clean so that my food would be available on time. My kitchen lessons started early. She was also my fire-safety officer; she taught me all the dangers of hot steam, fire and smoke hazards, and the risks of sharp knives.

There are some things we never know until people have gone, some things they wanted to tell you but chose not to. I'm not talking about dark secrets or something that is going to hurt you. It's a feeling of love unsaid, a feeling, an emotion, a fact or truth to be discovered only when the person is gone. She had one secret that I discovered when she left the world.

I missed my mother all the days of my life, and my separation from her was painful for me. I would experience sudden emotions of sadness and walk on a lonely beach in Perth, Western Australia, looking at the Indian Ocean. I would scream out her name and hoped the winds would carry my voice to her across the ocean. So I walked into a tattoo shop in Perth and had two lovebirds tattooed across the left-hand side of my chest with the words "Mum and Dad forever." I felt them close to me; they were with me everywhere I went. In my spirit, I carry a beautiful picture of a woman kneeling and praying in her bedroom, an act of daily devotion my mother performed for me her entire life.

THE HUNTING EXPEDITIONS

India was a land of great jungle adventures. I was a youngster growing up with a famous dad who was known as the "Cat Eyes White Hunter" by local people in India, and it was an honourable title. My dad had killed a man-eating tiger that terrorised a forest village several years ago. I believe that he, indeed, was an exceptional hunter with a rifle or 12-gauge shotgun. With such a reputation, he was deeply respected by Indian people in several villages along the way. From the tea vendor on the side of the road to the president of the local town, people respected him. He knew the forest rangers and officers, police commissioners, and politicians. This gave him free passage to the jungles in India, and his hunting skills were unmatched. His favourite weapon was a 12-gauge shotgun Holland & Holland. I believe it was a British-made weapon.

Shooting a man-eating tiger is no small feat; these majestic animals are fearsome predators. They can stalk and sneak up behind you with stealth that would leave you no time to react or a second chance. They are exceedingly dangerous when they become man-eating tigers. Therefore, successfully hunting one down is a crowning glory in a hunter's world.

I asked my dad to write a journal of his amazing hunting stories, which began with Grandpa, but he never got around to it and left me to tell them to the world. I cannot possibly do it justice or tell them as he would have done, but having roamed the forests with him on some hunting expeditions, I will try my very best to share a few important ones. It's only a glimpse into the life and world my father lived in.

THE FURY OF A WILD BOAR

There is nothing more ferocious, dangerous, and mad than a wounded solitary razorback. My grandfather lived in Nagpur, taking care of land and property that he owned in that part of the country. Hence, my dad went to live with his father for a few years. It was there, in the prairie, that his hunting skills were established. This particular story was funny, and I can still see my father's face when he told me the story for the first time.

Dad was twelve years old and often went into the fields with a trusted local tracker guide named Ram Singh, who lived and worked in the farm that belonged to my grandpa. One afternoon as they walked through the fields silently, they heard a sudden thump, and it was a razorback solitary boar. He was big, with six-inch tusks and hair on his back like steel wires protruding upward. Somebody had disturbed him from his afternoon nap, and he was not happy about that at all; he was startled, and that was the sudden thump. This razorback was getting away quickly, and the encounter was swift. My twelve-year-old dad picked up his gun and fired at the retreating razorback; two barrels of lead shot hit the razorback on his back and broke his spinal cord. His back legs fell off, and the loud squealing of a pig sent this twelve-year-old up a tree, as he was mortified with fear. The squealing was unbearable, and for all the braveness he displayed by picking up his gun and letting the pig have it in the back, nothing could have prepared my dad for what came next. They were lucky that the razorback never turned around and charged them, but because its rear legs had given way to a damaged spinal cord, the massive animal was squealing with fury. My dad said he never felt more scared in his life than he did that day.

Ram Singh was imploring the youngster trembling on the tree to come down, but the sound of the squealing razorback kept him up there. There was no way he would come down. With his gun abandoned on the forest floor, a squealing razorback spinning in circles, mad and furious, and a trembling youngster on a tree shaking like a leaf in fear, the tracker guide Ram Singh went running across the fields towards the farmhouse. Raising the alarm, he told Grandpa of the unfolding drama in the prairie. Running across the meadows with a weapon in his hand, Grandpa loaded a ball cartridge and blasted a shot into the razorback and put him out of his misery. The trembling youngster finally came down the tree, and everyone was laughing at him. In my father's words: "That damn pig was demon-possessed. Scared the living daylights out of me. Never heard an animal that could make a squeal like that. I put my fingers in my ears and tried blocking the sound, but it did not help. I have never been so scared in my life." It was a very big razorback; my dad had shot one of the biggest wild boars ever, at the age of twelve.

THE JUMPING BLACKBUCKS

There is no doubt that my dad was the most excellent hunter in the world. He never had a telescope sight mounted on the barrel of his gun; he said, "If you don't have the skills to shoot an animal by the sheer ability of an open sight of your gun, you are not worthy of the animal you are hunting." Therefore, this man had terrific skills, an incredibly steady hand, green eyes with impeccable sight and accuracy. When he squeezed that trigger, he rarely missed.

The jumping blackbucks put his reputation to the test. A blackbuck is a majestic, swift deer with long spiral horns; when the males mature into adults, their brown colour of adolescence changes into a black colour of male maturity with a white chest, as they stand there in the fields among the herd of does. It is a remarkably beautiful animal. There were so many of them in Indian forests in 1940 that hunting them occasionally posed no threat to their existence. These animals were agile and swift, similar to a Thomson's gazelle, and they have an incredible ability at escaping danger by running away at tremendous speed.

My dad had four elder brothers who served in the Railways and British Army; they were visiting my grandpa, and a hunting expedition was naturally inevitable. Grandpa threw them a challenge and declared that Eddy (my dad) was the best among them. They all laughed as the banter raged among the brothers; they were prideful of their British Army training and laughed at Grandpa's suggestion that the youngest, who was still a boy, would outclass them in accuracy and hunting skills. So off they went on a hunting trip in the early hours of the morning. Leaving their jeeps parked in a mountain village, they made their way through the forest by foot into the open fields. Crops and sesame seed production fields were some of the places animals would raid during the season. It was the encroachment of land and habitat that posed a more significant threat to their existence. The three men and the young boy ducked into the fields as they spotted a herd of deer. They silently made their way to get as close as possible, and having reached their advantageous spot, the three men raised their guns, firing at the deer, scattering them everywhere. Shot after shot rang out in the fields, and the blackbucks disappeared into the forest, leaving the areas behind and three British Army-trained soldiers with only one deer lying dead in the fields. Then began a discussion among the brothers as to who had shot the one deer. The youngest stood there, shaking his head. So many shots fired and only one dead deer. This was a big herd of deer, and all they had for all the shots that they fired was one deer that succumbed to their shooting. (I can see my dad's face smiling at me while he related this story of his brothers. I sat there listening to him like I had done many times as a child, always captivated by many of the fantastic stories of his childhood.)

The story continues.

They carried the carcass of the young doe they had shot and discovered two bullet holes in her, so at least two brothers had shot the same deer at the same time. It was funny: in the frenzy of shooting at such a big herd of deer, in their excitement, they fired in all directions, missing with every shot and shooting the same deer twice. It was embarrassing, and they were slightly annoyed with each other. They loaded the dead deer into the jeep and drove off to a different location for some more game.

Sure enough, fifty kilometres away, they came across another herd of blackbucks, spotted deer, and sambar deer, a species of big brown deer found in India. They all agreed to now let the youngest among them do the hunting. They quipped at my dad, "Okay, young fellow, let's see if your reputation is as true as what the old man says."

My dad looked at his elder brothers and told them that he would go alone; he had to go into the fields unnoticed and get as close as possible to the deer to have any chance at shooting them. They were some distance away, and there was enough cover and camouflage available for him to make it to an advantageous point on a small embankment that would give him a fair chance to shoot the deer.

The scene was now playing out: three army soldiers in a jeep, a fifteen-year-old lad with a gun, and a field with a herd of deer. The soldiers were in the perfect position to view the most spectacular natural-born hunter in action, equipped with the most incredible set of skills and accuracy.

As Eddy disappeared into the fields, a silence descended on the jeep, and a sense of tense anticipation fell upon on the three men. As they waited and watched, time stood still for a while; they listened and watched in silence. A head bobbed up near the embankment, the deer grunted, and they were off. *Bang!* A shot fired, and a blackbuck dropped. *Bang!* A second shot fired, and another blackbuck dropped. The rest of the deer disappeared; a fifteen-year-old victorious hunter stood on the embankment, shouting, "I have two blackbucks."

The three soldiers saw it all; it was the most fantastic scene they'd ever seen with their own eyes. Clapping hands, they embraced each other, abandoning the vehicle; they ran into the fields towards their youngest brother and jubilantly hugged him. "What the heck, young man!" they exclaimed. "That was simply terrific."

They were jumping and dancing with their youngest brother in their arms. "Oh, boy—that was awesome." The victory dance lasted for a lifetime among the four brothers. The eldest took off his army cap and saluted his youngest brother. "You are simply awesome."

They carried the two blackbucks, loaded them on the jeep, and drove back to Grandpa's farm. The story remained in the family for generations. My dad, Eddy, was the most excellent hunter in the world.

As I sat there listening to my dad tell me the story, I asked him what his secret skill was. He smiled back at me and taught me a valuable lesson about tenacity. He replied, "Well, if you have missed as much as me trying to shoot running blackbucks, you are going to miss them every time you attempt to shoot them. Oh, boy—did I miss them." He smiled and continued, "I quickly realised that I had to learn the configuration of the way they ran away from me, so I used to go into the fields just to learn that. I would point my gun or a stick and watch them run. I figured out the pattern of their running style—one jump to the right, two to the left, one right, one left, one right, and two left, and so it continued. Now that I had mastered their running pattern, when I lifted my gun at them again, I pointed it at the spot that I *anticipated* where the blackbuck would land on his running stride. I squeezed the trigger, and my bullet met the deer precisely at the spot I had chosen between me and my prey. I never missed a blackbuck again.

"If I ever did miss them, I respected the animal and his life, and I never squeezed my trigger a second time at the same animal. I let him get away because I was not worthy of shooting at him twice. I had enough respect in my heart for an animal that had outwitted me," he finished his story.

I shook my head in utter admiration, listening to my dad tell me how he developed his hunting skills, and I was so proud of him. Eddy was my dad.

THE GREAT DUCK SHOOT-OUT

Hunting wildlife was an Anglo-Indian tradition. Our Christmas dinner table was famous among the community. Our master chef, my mother, was a magician with incredible hands; there was a magic in them I cannot explain. There were secret family recipes, old traditions from my grandmother Adaline De Le Croix; she was the *materfamilias* of the culinary world in our family. She always lived with us, and all directions in the kitchen were given by her hand as she sat on her throne wheelchair; she was such a beautiful grandmother. She was funny, and I had an incredible relationship with her and deeply loved her.

So, going on hunting expeditions was also a part of my education; I had a beautiful childhood even with all its traumas; there were more good times than bad. There was always love and always hope and forever forgiveness.

We had a family friend we knew as Uncle Charlie Bob. He looked like Santa Claus, with a big white beard, and his face looked like it was fashioned from a rock; it had indentations from smallpox that he'd suffered as a child and had survived the terrible disease. He was family to us and a remarkable man. He was a skilful artist who always had white cards with a passport photo, like business cards. He had long fingernails, silver hair and beard; he was white in complexion, came from an unorthodox Brahmin family but became an Anglo-Indian. He married an Anglo-Indian woman, converted to Christianity, and was a dear friend of my father and our family. Those blank-white business cards had a purpose. He would whip them out, make you sit on a chair, and, with his ivory-hardened fingernails, go to work on one of these cards. Skilfully turning the map around with his nails on the opposite side of the cards, he was creating pressed impersonations of your face, a portrait of your face impressed and embossed by the skills of two fingernails, usually the thumb and the ring finger. Indeed, a remarkable picture emerged on that card.

I have never met an artist in the world who displayed such fantastic skill; pure as it was, the prints were impressive and the portrait impeccable. On occasion, he would have fun with little kids. He would make them sit on a chair, and he'd make funny impressions of them on the card with his artistic fingernails, pressing the embossed picture being sketched by them, and wait for their reactions when they saw the funny images he created of them. He was an hilarious man. I recall little girls with wide-open mouths in disbelief at the funny portrait that he intentionally made of them; it was hilarious. He would make Miss Piggy for plump girls, Kermit for skinny boys, and sometimes, he just made their faces funny. We had so much fun with him. Kids loved him dearly. His love for children was contagious because he had none of his own. His wife could not bear him any children, so they loved us as their own.

Now, Charlie Bob lived about 150 kilometres away from us; he owned farming land in a remote village. His wife was a nurse and took care of people in a local hospital. He was my dad's hunting partner. Often a human messenger would be sent, an informant, a human wildlife news bulletin, coming from the household of Charlie Bob. There were no telephone lines in those days and no infrastructure available to support these developments. Human messengers were sent across.

And so we received that messenger one Saturday morning:

Flash News Bulletin—Wild boars causing rampage in the farmlands. Stop. Devastated crops and crying villagers. Stop. The menace of wild boar herds razed a farmer's crop in one night of rampaging. Stop. Alert Eddy! Please come and shoot these damn wild boars. Stop. Charlie Bob.

It was like a distress telegram.

We left the next morning on the Royal Enfield motorcycle; my brother and I were excited as we rode together—a father and his two sons making memories to last a lifetime. I wish I could turn back clocks, turn back time—it just gets away from us.

We arrived in the afternoon, and Charlie Bob was standing there at the doorway of his sprawling country home, with a big smile and open arms; it's incredible, the love that existed between us. There was such a warm feeling of love that always filled the atmosphere every time we were in each other's company. We had Santa Claus all year round, and he even came with us on hunting trips.

An excellent lunch awaited us; we sat down to the array of spicy food and vegan delicacies that were prepared for us. Food in India is an expression of hospitality, of love, of the display of culinary excellency, culture, values, and homely affection. Charlie and Dad started talking about the wild-boar-rampage report, strategy planning, and execution of the herd. Soon, the villagers turned up at the door—simple, humble peasant farmers; they came to pay respect to the hunters who'd arrived to relieve them from the rampaging wild hogs that were devastating their crops. We spent the afternoon with the local village children. Indian village kids were extremely humble and respectful; they had a particular name for British-descent Anglo-Indians. They would call us *dora*; this means *British people* in the local lingo.

The next day, we walked a long distance, passing through the small village of this lake district; due to recent rains, these dirt roads were accessible only on foot. We hiked our way to the cornfields; we saw devastated crops, uprooted vegetation, and hundreds of pigs' footprints. It was quite a sight to see what marauding pigs can do in one night. The local men and my dad made plans to set out camouflage posts at the adjacent crops so they could stake out the place every evening. The plan was to have five hunters placed in strategic locations that surrounded the pigs and to massacre as many as they could; this would scare them away into the forests and make them leave the crops alone. That was the strategy.

While this was going on, my dad allowed my brother and me to take the shotgun and explore the area, so we took two local lads and went off wandering. We hiked for about two kilometres, hunting for green pigeons, quails, or jacksnipes. This was an area that we were not familiar with, but the local youngsters knew their way around these parts.

We came to an embankment, like a dyke, and we stopped in our tracks; there was a massive noise of quacking. We whispered to the local lads; they indicated that there was a lake above the embankment dyke. They were wild ducks, cotton teals, my mother's favourite duck for roasting. It was so delicious, the way she prepared them.

My brother and I crept on our belly on the muddy slope and peeked silently at the lake. I did not see any water, but the shore was covered with wild ducks, of all kinds of species; the recent rains had brought them earlier than usual. I levelled the double-barrelled gun on the embankment, I pointed my barrel at the largest congregation of ducks that I had ever seen in my life, and I pulled the trigger. *Bang!* A cloud of ducks lifted into the sky in front of me. I pulled the trigger a second time at the darkness; number-one bird shot filled the air, and ducks fell from the sky.

Then water appeared on the lake, and the sky was filled with a massive cloud of birds flying off in the distance; there were ducks lying on the water. The local lads jumped into the lake, retrieving ducks, and we collected twenty-two ducks that late afternoon. We started to walk back with all the ducks tied to a string, carrying them on our backs, like little warriors following in the footsteps of a great hunter, our dad.

He met us halfway as he heard the gunshots and knew we boys had shot something but was surprised to see four youngsters carrying wild ducks on their backs. My dad congratulated me, "Twenty-two ducks with two shots—even I have never done that in my entire career." He was proud of us. The wild-boar-hunting expedition was postponed till the next week; we had cotton teals to bring back home to mother.

Growing up in India was an adventure of a lifetime. There are so many amazing real-life hunting stories; when my father started to tell them, the audience would be riveted to the extraordinary details of the hunt and the dangers that he overcame. Hunting was not a hobby, but it was his way of life and an addiction in some way. The excitement and adrenaline rush was all a part of the story, and you could feel it just listening to him relate the stories to you because they were so authentic and real.

There were two miracle stories that he told us, near-death experiences. One was when he had shot a wild boar and strapped it on his Royal Enfield motorbike. He was riding in the darkness among lonely forest roads on a stormy night and pouring rain, when he had a problem with the headlamp on his bike and had to ride in the dark, with the assistance of only his two tiny parking lights. Riding in the darkness coming back home, he felt a tap on his shoulder; he described it as a strange feeling, like a voice in his ear. Soaking wet to his skin, he stopped his bike in the darkness, parked his motorcycle, and rummaged for his tiny little torch; he heard the sound of gushing water, a powerful force ahead of him. With the assistance of his tiny flashlight, he discovered that the small bridge had been washed away by a mighty flood that had cascaded from the mountains with impressive force and had swept the bridge away. He stood there shivering, cold, wet, and shocked at the sight in front of him. If he hadn't stopped in time, he could have ridden it straight into the cascading flood and been swept away and surely would have died, along with his motorcycle and the dead wild boar. It was the first time I ever heard my dad say that God saved him that night with the voice he heard in his ear. He waited all night in the pouring rain till the morning light revealed the miracle he'd experienced. He was shocked, realising how close he had come to death on the night of the storm.

Our home was a hunter's trophy museum; we had deer skulls and big antlers mounted on wooden shields hanging on the walls of the living room. One particular antler had a round bullet hole right in the middle of it. Dad would proudly display it with a prideful story of accuracy and gun skills. I heard that story so many times that it was almost like a daily morning prayer of hunting stories. Nevertheless, the truth is admired and told. He was in a very dense forest and had a head-mounted flashlight, scouring through the maze of dense undergrowth, when suddenly all he could see in the blackness of the night were just two eyes shining in the darkness.

That was it, just two eyes and nothing else; it was an extremely dense forest, illuminated by two eyes looking at the flashlight. Dad picked up the rifle, took aim, and fired a shot between the two eyes. This man never used a telescope his entire hunting career. He loathed the invention of the telescope. The result of that event was a ten-pointer deer antler sitting up on a wall with a hole in the middle of its skull.

Of all the ghastly memorabilia of beautiful animals, sadly dead, there was a beautiful and painful one. I think it was the man-eating tiger that he shot, but he never said it was; he was silent about that tiger. I guess it almost killed him, and there was a fear within him when he talked about it, and he didn't talk about it much. Some regrets existed between man and beast.

We had a huge tiger skin in our house; it was displayed on the huge wall in the living room. Its head was mounted, and its mouth opened with a big snarl; marble eyes were inserted, like real tiger eyes. It was like the tiger was pouncing at you from the wall. I am sure that was the cat that had almost killed him. That is another story. The man was a legendary hunter.

I hold back tears writing these events. I see faces of people. I close my eyes and see images of my dad and his smiling face, my mother roasting cotton teal ducks, Uncle Charlie Bob smiling at the doorway. I can't help it; tears fill my eyes. I just wish I could turn back time and hug them all again. I pray I will see them all again. I miss them so dearly. These events marked an epoch in their history as they flash into the memories of my heart. Life always ends in death, and the ones we love leave us behind; our fragile lives are an episode of meaning. We leave memories everlasting only in the hearts of the people we have touched the most. Nobody else will remember you.

CHAPTER 5

JOANNE

Let me introduce you to the most beautiful girl I ever met. I was seventeen years old when I first met her. It was a late afternoon, and a gentle sea breeze was blowing through our kitchen window; my favourite place at home was Momma's kitchen. The scenery from my kitchen window was a breathtaking view of the ocean; the house was nestled in a mountain valley, adorned with beautiful greenery and a variety of tropical exotic plants. On hot summer days on the coastal plains of the Indian east coast with unbearable humidity, the smell of the cool ocean breeze was always a breath of relief from the relentless humidity and stickiness of it.

There was a knock at the door, followed by the doorbell ringing; my sister went to open the door. Standing outside was a beautiful lady named Sherly Whittle. She was dressed elegantly. Her smile and voice were so joyful.

She was a British/Portuguese Anglo-Indian lady, a well-known childhood family friend of my mother and father; standing behind her was a beautiful girl with green eyes, a gorgeous face, a shy smile, holding on to her mother's dress.

Oh, my good lord! What a wonderful surprise! My dad affectionately hugged her. Sherly turned around and gave my mother a big bear hug. "Oh, Valarie!" she exclaimed. "I am so overjoyed to see you. I know where to find great love in this city, so I just thought I'd give you all a big surprise."

While all of this was going on, Valarie looked at me from across the room, to the entrance of the kitchen door, where I was standing; her green eyes met my brown eyes from across the room and kissed each other. I was motionless. I stood in awe looking at the most beautiful girl my eyes had ever seen. She was sixteen years old. We'd already met before any introduction. She gave me *that* smile—the one that said a thousand words at the speed of light. This all happened in thirty seconds as she walked in.

Here is an example of a typical rich Anglo-Indian culture of hospitality. You don't need to make appointments to meet people; you are always welcome to show up, anytime you like, and you can stay as long as you want. You will be greeted with tremendous love and laughter; everyone will be talking at the same time and forget to sit down; the excitement is contagious, and the noise is usually loud. The love is real, the laughter is loud, the dogs start barking with excitement, the parrots are whistling, and someone making tea in the kitchen makes the announcement that tea is being served, and then, finally, everyone gets to sit down. Perhaps it is the Indian tea that does it.

"This here is my daughter Joanne." She was now introduced. *Oh, my god!* My mother exclaimed, "She is a picture of you, Sherly. What a beautiful girl. Don't feel shy, my girl." My mother gently held her hand reassuringly. My three sisters gathered around her, and she was blushing at the compliments and all the attention she was receiving. I offered her tea and biscuits, and she smiled at me as she took one; she smiled at me again, and my heart just stopped beating for every smile she gave me. I did not have a clue what the heck was going on in my head, but I was in some kind of crazy stupor of being mesmerised by some emotions that I had never experienced before. As much as they made me feel so great inside, I did not like it, because I did not know what was going on, and they made me look stupid in front of her, like I wanted to be by her side and keep admiring her and never leave her. In a few minutes, it was getting worse because it was showing on my face, and I was starting to look stupid and nervous. It was so weird, so alien, so overpowering, so controlling, so crazy, and I could do nothing about it. I just wanted to be by her side. I have never experienced this feeling ever again in my life. The only woman I ever loved deeply was my mother. Now, a girl with green eyes, red cheeks, brunette hair, and an angelic face; her lips produced a smile that did something to my heart, and I had no control of myself.

My three sisters gathered around her, and I shook in a daze when my eldest sister said to me, "Give her a break! You have not stopped looking at her." I was so embarrassed! I disliked my sister almost immediately and disappeared into the kitchen. I heard Joanne say to my eldest sister, "It's okay! He did not do anything wrong." She was ready to defend me.

Under my breath, as I walked into the kitchen, I was mumbling words of disapprovement towards my sister who had embarrassed me. I just loved the way Joanne came to my defence. It made me feel special. I was in my momma's kitchen looking out the window towards the sea and feeling the strangest feeling in my stomach. I just wanted to go out and be with her. I did not know what became of me in those twenty minutes of my life. I fell in love with the most beautiful girl I had ever seen. I did not realise that this day of my life would not come back again to me, ever again; I would never experience this emotion again in my life. This innocence is lived only once in life, and it never comes back.. You fall truly in love only once in your life.

This was my moment. I smiled at the sea, shook my head, left the kitchen, and went out to be with her again. I walked into our garden, where she was sitting among the trees and flowers, chatting with my sisters; she smiled at me when she saw me. I took it as a reassurance that she was also wanting to be with me. It was so beautiful that we both were feeling the same in different ways but still had the same outcome. Falling in love—awesome, so beautiful, pure.

Our parents were having a long conversation in the living room, and then I overheard Joanne's mother's request for my parents. "Can I leave Joanne with you for a week? I am conducting the state nursing examinations in this city. As you are aware, I am the senior nursing board examiner, so I have a hectic week ahead." My parents were delighted that she was going to be with us. I could not believe it. She was going to be with us for a whole week! I was excited and could not contain my joy. I could not shut up.

I quickly joined in the conversation to reassure her mother that I would take very good care of Joanne. I offered her my qualifications of honour and skills. "I am an excellent swimmer and would protect her from crashing waves when we take her to the beach, and I will be happy to cook some good food for her in Momma's kitchen." It was all so instinctively done, and I did not realise that our parents kind of figured out what was going on.

Sherly looked at me and said, "I am confident you will do an excellent job protecting my angel, young man. I trust you will." I just told them I was in love with Joanne. My dad was about to say something to embarrass me, but my mother gave him a look with her eyes that silenced him. I left the room feeling embarrassed.

The following seven days were the most beautiful days of my life. I was in the company of the most beautiful girl in the world. I told my youngest sister about all the crazy feelings that were going on in my heart and how shy I was to ask her if she felt the same about me. For the next few days, I was always in her company, doing everything to make her stay as comfortable as possible. I had to contend with some stiff competition from my elder brother, who also showed a keen interest in this beauty. As the battle of the brothers raged for the first two days, she put an end to the competition when she bravely told my mother that she liked her younger son more. My elder brother was kind, met me privately in the garden, and said, "You are a lucky bugger—she is in love with you."

We went to the beach one afternoon when the weather was calm and the waves were smaller. She was wearing a beautiful white petticoat; she looked radiant and stunning in it. This girl was as pretty as an angel. We stood waist-deep in the sea jumping at the waves and having a great time. My youngest sister was in the middle, between us, holding hands, anticipating the next crashing wave as we played in the surf. Slowly my sister slipped away and put my hand in Joanne's hand and left us both while she went back to the shore to sit in the shade of the coconut palm trees.

My youngest sister was so cool; she knew we'd both fallen in love with each other and never had a chance to even hold hands. Now for the first time in four days, from the moment I first saw her when she walked in the door, I was holding her hand. I felt so happy; every time she jumped, laughing at the waves crashing, she shouted in excitement.

The city where she lived was landlocked. Hence, the ocean was a very exciting place, but also frightening when you are not accustomed to waves and sea currents. I was holding her hand tight and protecting this angel next to me. She looked magnificent in a white dress that showed the beauty of her body as the wet clothes gently caressed her youthful innocence. We both were pure in heart, and this love was so innocently beautiful. I held her around the waist as we jumped at another crashing wave. The saltwater splashed on our faces; the fierce sun was shining through her brunette hair, and her lips were irresistible as she smiled at me. I pulled her close and kissed her on her lips. We were now totally in love and sealed it with our first kiss. We walked back home together, the three of us holding hands and walking back home. That was the most beautiful day of my life. I had the most beautiful girlfriend in the world. I squeezed my sister's hand and said, "Thank you." She smiled and replied, "Don't be shy—you both love each other. I already knew that two days ago."

We laughed, running on the sand chasing each other and hugging one another; it was so cool, so wonderfully innocent and pure. These are those happiest days in life. The whole week was romantic and blissful. I dreaded the thought of her leaving; it was going to be unbearable. Her mother spent the last two days with my family, playing cards, drinking tea; laughter and fun filled the house. I was in my momma's kitchen with my sisters making her breakfast, cooking some great lunches with the family, and lavishing all my affection for her in the food we prepared. I wanted to kiss her every time I saw her smiling. She was just so beautiful. I was now totally in love with her. Later that afternoon, I approached her mom, sat beside her, and popped the question. "Can I visit Kitty Girl [Joanne was fondly called *Kitty* by everyone]?" I asked. She looked at me and smiled and said, "From what I have seen in these past few days, young man, I think Kitty Girl would be happy if you came to see her. Of course, you are welcome to come and see her whenever you both like."

I was so delighted with her approval; in my mind, I was already making plans to go and visit her as soon as possible. The days passed, and I found myself in a magical world of ultimate joy in my heart. I wanted to do something special and seal this with a blessing.

There was a beautiful church—Ross Hill Chapel—on top of a mountain overlooking the sea and the natural harbour. It was a place where I had learnt my faith; it was a popular place of worship among the Christians. I would often go there and be alone in the presence of the Lord and pray for my family and many blessings for my life. It was a sanctuary for me, a place I went whenever I felt sad and needed to have the assurance of the hand of God in my life. I asked that He would take care of me. I even climbed the mountain on my knees, all 482 steps of it. My knees were bleeding, a sacrificial act that expressed the love I felt for Jesus Christ. He would always remember my heart, a child's heart that loved Him.

India was a mixed spiritual country, and an act of sacrifice was an common expression of faith and love. But climbing the hill on one's knees—that was taking faith and sacrifice to a completely different level. There was a saying in the culture, "A family praying together stays together." Anglo-Indian culture was Catholic. Sunday church service, potluck lunches, get-togethers, picnics, and parties were a common feature of this unique culture.

I climbed Ross Hill with the most beautiful girl and walked into the holy sanctuary, holding her hand in this holy place. I made a promise that I would love her truly and forever always, a promise before God. Then I kissed her. That is truly how I deeply felt in my heart, and I have never loved anyone like this again. Her mother saw this from a distance, and I believe she thought it was a beautiful thing that happened to us.

The Anglo-Indian culture was a Western culture but with some stricter values; falling in love was accepted, but a girl's honour and rules of engagement were strictly protected. Holding hands was allowed, but nothing more than holding hands. You kept your hands to yourself and waited till the relationship blossomed. Your intentions had to be honourable, which led to you getting married to the girl. You were allowed to date each other; parents would trust you and give you your space, but the rules of engagement had strict limitations. If you took the girl out, you would have to bring her back on time—no late nights. Sometimes her brothers accompanied you to keep an eye on your behaviour. The honour of a girl was respected and protected.

This was a rich culture; fornication or having sexual relationships before marriage was not accepted or allowed. Hence, the decency and family reputation of the boy was important. You don't throw pearls to pigs. It was a culture of profound values; the longing to be with each other made loving each other so beautiful that you would wait a lifetime for the one you loved.

These were the rules of engagement. It was not always perfect, and breakups did take place; pregnant girls got married, and family feuds resulted. Broken hearts happened, just as in any other place in the world. With some rednecks I know in Alabama, cowboys with broken hearts crawl into a bottle of whiskey and stay there forever. Some even died with a bottle in their hand. Country music about broken hearts belted out of a broken home. We had towns that were called Little England, Funky Town, California Beach—a people and culture holding on to its Western roots. Anglo-Indians strictly married their kind, and getting married to Indians was a big *no.* We were trying to preserve what was left of us.

In the background of this rich culture of mine and with all the written rules of engagement, I had found the most beautiful girl in the world; she came from a wonderful family. And now the days had come to an end; the dreaded goodbye came. My heart was breaking, I could not stand it; this was already becoming unbearable. I did not want her to go. I wanted a life with her.

I walked her to the coach on the train; she was sitting near the window, smiling as I stood there on the platform. I saw the guard signal the green flag to the driver. The train started to move. I held on to her hand. My mom and dad were waving. I ran for a little while, holding her hand; and then I had to let her go. The train moved away. I stood there, watching her leave. I wanted to burst into tears. I was empty. My brother came and put his arm on my shoulder. I had tears in my eyes. I was totally in love with her.

I had to wait for six agonizing months to see her again. She was going to study nursing, and I was going to go to technical school. I wrote letters to her, and I learned to love the postman. I gave him a tip when he brought me a letter from her. I even showed him her handwriting on the envelope so that he knew my letters were precious. My relationship with the postman was so cool; even he was warmed with the love in the air that followed me everywhere I went. It was infectious, and the sheer joy of my love for her poured out of my heart and filled the whole world around me, and the world never looked more beautiful than it did with her in it. I was just warmed each day with thoughts about her. I walked to the beach, and I could imagine her right there in front of me, laughing and jumping in the waves, holding her around her waist, her wet clothes on her beautiful body, the sunlight in her hair, the smile on her face, and the most innocent, beautiful kiss. It was like a beautiful movie scene that stayed with me my whole life. I have never loved like this ever again. She was my first love.

I got off the bus at the central bus station, and I saw the postman on his bicycle. He smiled at me. "Good news!" he said, "I just dropped a letter from your sweetheart." I hugged him and went running home as fast as I could, with a big smile on my face. I was so happy—just a letter, and my joy was everlasting. My joy spread like a canopy of stars falling all over my siblings. I could see they were happy for me; my sisters would tease me and call me "lover boy."

I am so glad I fell in love in a place and time when falling in love was simple and true. It was innocent and pure, and it was just holding hands and a beautiful little kiss.

Six long months came to an end; the agony was excruciating, but the joy was like a catastrophic event. The postman was given time off. He was overjoyed to know I was going to see her; he hugged me and said, "Sir, you give my best wishes and blessings to her as well—tell her that it's from the postman." I hugged him and replied, "I will do just that; don't you worry about that now."

My mother helped me pack my suitcase and gave me instructions. "Be wise and carry yourself with respect and dignity. Don't go beyond your limitations with the girl; she is precious to her parents. Be respectful, and carry yourself with respect and dignity. Don't lose your temper; control yourself, and help around the house." My mother had one commandment, one word; when she said it, you had to lift your head and look at her—the word was *listening*. I looked at her, and she smiled at me. "Behave yourself with that beautiful girl, and just hold hands." I closed my eyes and felt embarrassed. "I love her, Mom. I will do all you have said." I hugged my mother. "Thanks. Love you, too."

It was 4:00 p.m.; the same train that took her away from me from the same platform started to move. I was on it this time. I could not wait to reach my destination. This train could not get there fast enough. It was an overnight's journey; it would have been easy for me to just go to sleep and awake the next morning, but sleep just would not come. My journey took forever, and in between falling asleep and staying awake, I was mostly awake, only to look out the window at the next station to see how close I was getting to her once again.

I finally fell asleep and awoke with a startle. I looked out the window and felt overwhelmingly excited; the train was making good time, and we were on the outskirts of the city of Secunderabad. *Another thirty minutes.* I brushed my teeth, washed my face, combed my hair, put on some cologne, grabbed my suitcase, and waited at the door. The train pulled into platform number 1.

I could hear the brakes being applied as the wheels came to a stop. I was the first passenger to get off the train.

I just wanted to see her face again. Now I could not wait anymore. I'd waited long enough. I took happiness to another level. I grabbed a three-wheeler taxi called a *tuk-tuk* and told the man to drive fast and get me to the address. Off we went, whizzing through the maze of early-morning traffic; after twenty minutes of crazy veering from left to right, scurrying through some narrow streets, and taking shortcuts, we pulled up to her mother's house. I paid the taximan and walked through the metal gate. She was standing at her doorway. I wanted to kiss her and just hug her. But, after all those months of missing her, all I could do was say, "Hi."

Her parents were at home, and it was the first time I met her dad. I was timid and afraid, but he quickly put me at ease; Monty was his name, and he was a wonderful man. He was funny and had a joyful smile on his face. He greeted me and asked me about my journey. I hugged her mother and met her younger brother, David; she had an elder sister and an elder brother.

I guess they all knew that I was the boyfriend. It did not take long for me to feel at home. She took me around and showed me her house. There in the kitchen was an older Indian woman dressed in a traditional *sari*; she greeted me with a smile. I was introduced to her. "Well, this is Kashamma [*Amma* means *mother* in the Indian language]. This lady is the eldest member in this house. She runs the kitchen and cooks for the family. She lives with us, and she is our family." I shook her hand. "Nice to meet you, Kashamma." She smiled at me and said, "Baba [*Baba* means *son* in the Indian Language], I am so happy for my Kitty Girl; she has found a nice boy. May God bless you both." I hugged her. "I am very happy as well to find her," I replied. She smiled approvingly.

We walked outside into the backyard, and it was like a mini-zoo, with parrots, dogs, and cats. It had a guava tree and a wall about four feet high that surrounded the entire house and grounds. I held her hand and smiled at her. She was so beautiful. "I missed you," I whispered. She blushed. "I missed you, too." I could have kissed her. *Shoosh, behave, young man!* My mother's words were ringing in my ears.

I spent the rest of the afternoon with the family, meeting all her siblings and becoming a part of this wonderful family. Her parents were simply wonderful people, and the house was filled with love and laughter. They were a proper Irish-British-Portuguese Anglo-Indian family. I did not feel out of place, and after only a few hours of being here, I was a part of this family.

The kitchen was buzzing with activity; music was playing, and it was like being back home. Anglo-Indian homes were always joyful, happy places; music, eating, dancing, and being happy were cultural traits.

It was quite normal for Anglo-Indian families to have a servant who lived with them; it was traditionally English. When the British ruled India, they would employ the service of servants and maids to do their household chores. India was "the jewel in the British crown," and India served the best interests of Britain and not the best interests of India.

However, the Anglo-Indian community polished this "servant and maid" business to a far better level. Servants became family members; they learnt English, their families were also taken care of, and their children were given free English lessons as well as education and medical attention. Corporate social responsibility started a long time ago with the Anglo-Indian community.

Hence, the servant of this house, Kashamma, was deeply loved and regarded. She was an adorable faithful family member who provided impeccable service in the best interest of the family she served so diligently. She was even consulted on some family issues, and all decisions in the kitchen were under her supervision. Instinctively, I went to the kitchen to give her a helping hand; she sure appreciated that. She held my hand and said, "Baba, I am so happy for my Kitty Girl. Your mother has raised you well, and you are perfect for this beautiful girl."

Then she walked right in, my sweetheart. "What are you doing here chatting with her? You ought to be with me." She grabbed my hand, and we went into the living room, where the music was at full blast and everyone was dancing. "Foxtrot, my dear?" We danced in our happiness of finding love with each other. I was home with her, and it was perfect.

Having the most beautiful girlfriend in the neighbourhood was not going to be easy. I was to soon find out what I would be up against. I was walking down the road from her house when a bunch of Anglo-Indian boys on the street corner were giving me the evil eye. As I passed them, I heard them comment, "We should give him a good walloping, *macha* [*macha* is the Anglo-Indian term for the Aussie word *mate*]." I realised these were my contenders for the hand of my bride; there was a whole bunch of them in line, all crazy about the most beautiful girl in the neighbourhood, every one of them claiming that she was in love with one of them. Hence, they were allied with each other to impress her and win her love. I was public enemy number one. Oh, the audacity of me, a young man from another part of the country who just walked into town and took the most beautiful girl by her hand, kissed her on the beach, wrapped his arms around her, and claimed his bride. My rivals had spent their teenage years contending with each other and assuming she had fallen in love with one of them. They stood there in their arrogant demeanour, burning up in jealousy across the street, threatening to give me a walloping. Now, I was ready to fight the whole world for her, but I did not need to—she was already mine.

I looked at my opponents and said, "I am not afraid of any of you. I will take you all on anytime. You stand here and watch while she walks with me hand in hand going to church on Sunday. That should be enough to shut you guys up forever. Now back down, or I will break somebody's nose for interfering in my business." I walked back up the street to her house as they watched me go. My sweetheart came home from nursing school in the afternoon, dressed in white, pretty as she could be, joyful and in love; she looked radiantly happy.

"Well, Miss Beautiful," I said, "you did not tell me about the many contenders down the street who claim that you are in love with them." I laughed. "Did you see them on your way home?" I asked.

"Oh, those silly buggers," she replied and laughed. "They are crazy. They have been after me for a while. Did they bother you?" she asked. "I will go out and give them a piece of my mind."

"Don't do that," I said. "Just walk with me hand in hand to church on Sunday. That will settle this 'contender' issue once and for all." I told her about the incident, and we both laughed.

Sunday came, and we walked hand in hand to church. It was a small town; people were inquisitive and nosey, part of the culture. Eyes watched us as we walked down the street. The contenders all disappeared the following week. Animosity took its place.

The next two years of my life with the most beautiful girl were the happiest times, and love is such a beautiful thing. At this age, it was not complicated; it allowed you to dream of endless things. The periods of separation in between, as painful as they were for us, the longing and the eventual reunification was like a huge seismic event in my heart. I will forever cherish those moments I spent sitting, reading a book on a chair, watching her sleeping, feeling the endless burning of my heart, the admiration I felt for her presence, and the joyful spirit that she had in her. I have never loved like this ever again. We deeply loved each other; we were young and innocent; we fell in love at a time when innocence was real; we were two beautiful young people whose desire for each other was pure and beautiful. It was hard to keep hearts away from each other, and the desire in us was like a raging fire, impossible to be calmed until we met and held each other in an embrace of its beautiful expression between two lovers. We had to wait till we were married, and we were too young to be married. The rules of engagement—respectful honour and family values—applied, and we had a deep respect for our parents. Love like this cannot be contained, cannot survive forever in this sphere of influence; it has to break forth. This love was larger than the world we both lived in.

I was back home with my parents, finishing my studies at the technical college, and my separation from the one I loved was now unbearable. I wanted to get married, but I was too young and did not have the economic status to do this. We would both still have to wait. Yet, I was worried that our love had gone to the point that our parents may not have a choice and get us married.

Then something terrible happened; my whole world came crashing down on me. I could not contain it. I was shot in my heart. I was killed and murdered. Someone, some terrible evil, a hidden demon, a terrible creature, had risen from the depths of animosity, betrayal, destruction, and blackmail. She stopped writing to me.

I was completely distraught. I waited for the postman every day, and no letter came, and I could take it no longer. I got on a train and went to see her. I went to her house and waited for her to return from her nursing college.

Her wonderful mother was very sympathetic to my concern. She said, "I don't know what is going on with this girl; she has not been herself lately. She will not talk about it, and she seems to be very upset and has been crying; she will not tell me anything."

Then she appeared, in white. I looked at her. I had tears in my eyes. She was upset the very moment she saw me. I had never seen her angry.

She looked at me and said to her mother, "Mum, please tell him to go. He betrayed me, and I don't want to see him." She went into her room and was crying. I was shocked, totally confused.

"What are you talking about?" I protested. Standing outside her door, I begged, "Please tell me what I did wrong."

"Please go away" was the response.

I was traumatically trembling, shaking at her reaction, totally confused at her behaviour; she was young and immature, and so was I. We were just older kids; love happened between us that was so magical and beautiful, and like all great love stories, we were experiencing the worst trauma of the heart. Mine had just suffered an earthquake, and it resulted in a string of aftershocks; eventually, it would be shattered into a million pieces, and I would lose the one I loved the most. Gone forever. I did not understand or know why. That was the worst—not knowing why.

I pleaded with her mother, and even she wept with me as I cried over her shoulder; she was distressed with my broken heart.

She could not understand the behaviour of her daughter. She reassured my brokenness that she would talk with her; she told me that I should have patience and give her time. The more time I gave her, the more I was losing her, and she was moving even further away.

I would go to a restaurant near the hospital where she worked and wait there for hours, hoping to catch a glimpse of her. I felt I should just walk up to her and firmly take hold of her and ask her what the hell was going on. I was too young to understand, too confused about what action I needed to take; her mother's advice to give her time seemed a better option, and time flew past. I never got a chance to talk to her again, and I lost the one I loved the most. My first love was my first broken heart forever. She was gone. It's a cruel world, and my contenders were back on the street jeering at me as I walked past her house, hoping she would come out and just run into my arms once again.

Amid this beautiful love, invisible animosity and jealousy were raging; it was like a hidden evil waiting for an opportunity to destroy what was beautiful. It is inconceivable to think that anyone would attempt to destroy such a beautiful thing.

You don't need to fight for your bride when the bride is in love with the groom. The only thing that keeps the beautiful bride from the groom is the evil that surrounds her. And the groom will always love his bride. He will die for his bride. He will wait and be reunited to her, because, no matter what she goes through, the love he has for his bride will never change, and time is endless for the bridegroom. Similarly, his love for his bride is an endless love.

"For indeed man was not created for the woman's sake but woman for the man's sake" (1 Corinthians 11:9). The bride can only return when she has shed all defilement and is washed clean and made holy once again.

CHAPTER 6

THE ROAD TO AUSTRALIA

Amid all the beauty of a home, the closeness of family, and the greatest adventures of an amazing childhood—even with all its pains and traumas—Anglo-Indians were leaving India for the Commonwealth nations, of which Australia was the most favourite of them all. I firmly held the view that, as a people without any nation of our own, free passage for all Anglo-Indian people should be given. I was only a young teenager, and no one was going to listen to my views. I had to make my way across. I believed that I had a greater future in Australia. I'd been a cowboy from early childhood. I never watched Indian Bollywood movies; I watched only Western movies; and when I first kissed a girl, I left her breathless. I recall her face all blushing and turning red and her asking me, "Where did you learn to kiss this way?" I smiled back, kissed her again, and whispered to her, "Those cowboys in the movies kiss this way." Now I had a broken heart and only memories of her. I was always grateful that I'd experienced that kind of love with that kind of special girl that she was to me.

The immigration procedures to Australia were a daunting task for me to do on my own. My father had no interest in immigrating to Australia, even though all his brothers and family were moving away. My father reckoned that India was a much better country. He would often say things in a philosophical tone, "When you look at the banks of a river and look across the other side, it may appear very lush and green. It's only when you get across to the other side that you realise that the place you left was also green, but you have to get to the other side to realise that."

Another one was, "When you get old, they dump you in a home for the aged, and you will die lonely in these countries. Here in India, you may not be richer, but you sure won't die old and lonely. My son, they don't have the same family unity and values we have here in this country."

I could never agree with his views and told him that there was no future for Anglo-Indians in India. Therefore, we were always at loggerheads, and I could not get the support I needed to make my way to the land that I'd dreamt about as a child. I was also running away from a broken heart, and I think my dad understood.

Every time my cousins came from Australia, I wanted to go back with them to the "land down under." No one wanted to help me, and my need to get away was growing every day; this *land down under* was a childhood dream. My desperation to get away from India and leave my broken heart behind was intense. I turned to prayer and my faith to the one I loved the most, Jesus Christ. I would go to Ross Hill Chapel and pray; I would just break down sobbing in tears at the foot of the cross. My heartache followed me even there. I could see her standing there at the altar, her smiling face, the love we felt for each other, my promise to her, and my honourable intentions to make her my bride. It was unbearable. Now, I could lay it all at the foot of the cross. I wept and wept and moved heaven with my tears. "God, please make a way for me. I just want to go to Australia. I just want to get away from here."

It was 1987; it had been almost a year that I had been living with a broken heart. I had no choice but to find some happiness in my life; even when there is an emptiness because the one you love is not there, you have to move on. Well, at least, that is what they tell you: you've got to move on. And yet no one seems to know how to successfully do it.

I got a breakthrough from the most unexpected source: if you want to believe in miracles, you should, because they were happening to me. I was introduced to a very rich Muslim man in India. I told him about my predicament. He liked me a lot; he was kind and a very benevolent, good-hearted man. I visited him on several occasions, and he told me that he would help me go to Australia.

What he did surprised me. He legally transferred the title deed of one of his mansions to my name and made me a real estate agent in his company. He made me a rich young man and applied for a status on me that said, "Young, rich, and successful." I then prepared all my papers for a visa to Australia. I took a train to New Delhi and applied for a visa to go to the land of my childhood dreams. I was nervous but confident that grace and favour were following me.

Dressed in a suit and looking very smart, I went to the Australian embassy and applied for a one-year visa. I handed over all my documents. I was rich and had the legal title deed to a very expensive mansion. Still, there was no guarantee that a visa would be granted.

I waited for three working days, and on the appointed day, I knelt, said a prayer, and went to the embassy. I handed over my token receipt, and I received my passport. I was so nervous I did not ask the lady anything but just said, "Thank you." I walked out of the embassy and onto the street. I opened my passport to look through the pages, and there it was. The image of a kangaroo and an emu with a shield. I looked at them; it looked like they were smiling at me, saying, "Gidday, mate! We have been waiting for you for years. Welcome home to Australia." I closed the book and leapt in the air; my face was covered with tears as I thanked the one who'd heard my prayers and answered me in the most unexpected of ways.

It's amazing, the vanity of the world I live in. "Young, rich, and successful" astounds people and governments more than words that say "honest, hardworking, spiritual, good character" means less chance of getting a visa. I was nineteen years old, and I was leaving India forever. This was a one-way ticket for me because I was broken-hearted. I'd lost the girl I loved, and I never felt I belonged to India. My childhood dream had come true; I wanted to preserve my Anglo-Indian culture and all the years I'd lived in a country that was not ours anymore; I wanted to leave behind the discrimination I felt in India as a child. It was the love of my family that kept me here, but now I could make a way for my siblings, and soon they would be in Australia with me. I longed for the eventual reunification of my family in Australia.

It would have been ethically moral if those pompous British colonisers would have had enough respect and decency to respect the plight of the Anglo-Indian community. All these Commonwealth nations would have just repatriated Anglo-Indian families. We had British, Dutch, Portuguese, and French ancestry but were left abandoned by these kingdoms of colonisers who operated around the world in an endless spiral of greed and piracy—slave trade, control of mineral wealth, and serving only their own interests. Here we were holding on to our culture on the edge of a sword hanging on a thin silk thread, waiting for it to fall on us repeatedly until all the Anglo in us was cut to shreds and the only thing left was the Indian, with the Anglo-Indian soon to disappear into the history books like a story that said, "Once upon a time there was a group of people in India no one wanted to recognise. These were an amazing people, and they were fun-loving, hardworking, good people. They were called 'Anglo-Indians..'" Would anyone be willing to even write a story about them? It was not the Indian part that made us unique; it was the Anglo part that did it, and we wanted to go home—to have a place and island or a nation that was our own. We were like the Jewish people. Like the American Jew of today, his home will always be Israel; in spite of all the evil the world has perpetrated on the Jewish nation, it has existed; it cannot be destroyed by nations. Kingdoms have come and gone, and Israel still exists. As a child, I had a deep affection for the Jewish nation because I connected to its struggle in the stories I read from the Bible with my mother.

For the Anglo-Indians, the nation that would always become their home more than any other place in this world was that "red land down under." I was going home alone, and I wished I could have taken all my family with me.

It was December 15, 1988. I was scheduled to leave everyone I loved behind.

The goodbye was heart-wrenching; there were many tears. My beloved grandmother was sitting there crying. I had always brought joy to her life and taken care of her; we'd laughed so much, because we had an amazing relationship. Now, the sobs of her crying as she held me, saying words of final goodbye: "I will be dead and gone by the time you come back." Oh, those words of hers tore me apart. My beautiful mother was crying; my siblings were crying. I was so deeply saddened by this goodbye that, momentarily, I entertained the thought of changing my mind. It was suddenly clear that it would be many years before I came back. I was going to an uncertain future in an alien land; even though I had so much family in Australia, I was going to depend on me, and me alone was all I had. I had faith in the holy one in my heart and spirit. I saw what He had done for me.

My family took me to the altar of the Lord at home, and they prayed and were blessing me with their hands placed over my head; final hugs and painful tears of goodbye overwhelmed the home. I realised how much I was loved. Goodbye is so overwhelming and crushingly painful.

The taxi came to the door. I stepped in. I broke down in tears; it killed me. I was so broken inside. I could have had a heart attack: how does a heart take so much pain and still beat? I was in a pool of tears, and then I was gone. I held on to my dad and hugged him; he was sitting next to me in the cab. My father was silent; all his emotions hidden inside, he was sitting there being strong for me, and all his own sadness and fears were bottled inside of him. He never said a word; he just hugged me and put his arms around me. I think it was the first time in my life I'd hugged my dad this way. It was going to be a very long goodbye, and he knew it.

My dad accompanied me on the train journey to the city of Madras. I had one more goodbye left, the one with my father. I felt like just turning back and saying, "Let's stop this madness. It's too much—I've changed my mind." If I could have just said that.

I checked into my flight and dropped my baggage. I did not want to prolong the agony of goodbye any longer. I hugged my father. We held each other for a while; I felt him holding me like he really did not want me to go, but he did not want to keep me away from my dreams.

I saw tears in his green eyes, and he grieved. "God bless you, my son. Love you, my son." It was the only time I had seen my father cry. I was truly shaken. I stumbled in my walk towards the gate. I truly was feeling nauseated; this emotional goodbye was just too hard to take any more. I felt dizzy walking a few steps but held on. I turned back one last time and looked at him. I waved him goodbye, and I went into the departure lounge. I was done. I had to look forward to my new life down under and make a way for my family to join me someday soon.

Singapore Airlines was delightful even back then. I was tired and exhausted, and soon fell asleep thirty-five thousand feet up in the air, sore and broken from a deep emotional goodbye.

It was 10:00 a.m. when I arrived at Changi Airport in Singapore. The airport was impressive, and, now, for the first time in my life, I was in a different world. I explored the airport for the next two hours.

I went window-shopping. My connecting flight by Qantas to Sydney was still five hours away. I ended up at a bar/café and got myself a drink.

I was of athletic build—broad shoulders, a stocky lad, five feet six, long hair. My legs had been genetically programmed by my beautiful mother, so they were short like hers; they refused to grow the extra four inches that I would have liked them to, so I always wore boots with 2.5-inch heels. I bought myself a hat, slapped it on my head, and now was having a drink at the café/bar.

A dude sitting across from me was eating a steak, a bowl of salad, and a big glass of beer; he was looking at me and smiled at me. "Gidday—where are you headed off to?" he asked.

I replied, "Oh, me, I am off to Sydney."

"Well, that's great, I am headed home to Sydney, too," he replied. He was very friendly and offered to buy me a drink; soon we were sitting at the bar and drinking a few Tiger beers. We were heading in the same direction but on different flights. An hour into our beer-drinking conversation, I learned his name was Geoffrey Healy; he lived in North Sydney and was a businessman. He was very friendly, very generous; he did not allow me to pay for any of the beers and was willing to help me out in Sydney. I was thankful to find that such good-hearted people lived in the country I was going to embrace as home. I felt confident. He gave me his business card and insisted that I call him in Sydney.

SYDNEY, AUSTRALIA

I arrived in Sydney, Australia, on December 17, 1988; it was slightly overcast, with bright sunny spells. It seemed like the heaviness of my emotional departure from home had followed me. This was peak summer in Australia, and a heavy cloud was hanging around the city, presaging the arrival of a sad new kid on the block. I had a friend pick me up at the airport and drive me to Rossmore Avenue, Punchbowl. I felt happy that I'd finally made it.

I was slightly apprehensive as I walked into this four-bedroom house; it was filled with seven Pakistani occupants. I was introduced to all of them. They were friendly, and all of them were dressed in their traditional clothing. I felt awkward but knew in my mind that this was only a temporary arrangement. I had to share a single bed in a room with my friend and two other Pakistani fellas. I soon settled in with them as my friend gave me the rundown on how to get certain things for me organised. Accordingly, all the paperwork was prepared for me. I was able to apply for a tax-file number and a learner's driver's licence. I went to the local Commonwealth Employment Office and started to pursue a suitable job opportunity for myself.

I had an excellent technical background and a three-year apprenticeship as a mechanical technician working at Coromandel Fertilizers. I was confident and knew I could do any job in the technical field. I registered myself at the CES, had a resume made, and was a local lad looking for a job. I had a tax-file number, I'd passed my driving examination, and, pending my practical test, I would soon have my driver's licence. I was able to achieve a lot in the first four weeks of my new life in Australia. Then came the breakthrough.

I was praying for a job, and it came. A company in Revesby, BHP Steel, would be glad to have me come over for an interview; the lady at the CES called me on the phone to tell me this. I went to the office the next day, collected the relevant papers, and went for the interview.

It was great; these blokes were impressed with my technical knowledge. The supervisor was pleased. "I reckon you are pretty sound mate," he said. "I am looking forward to having you in the maintenance department. When can you start?" I was slightly baffled at my job offer. I told the bloke I could start the next week. That settled it, and I had my first job.

I left the office and walked down the road. I said a prayer of thanks, jumped up, and punched the sky—happy with my new job. The next week I got up early and went jogging to work; the blokes at work were a bunch of good lads. They made me feel at home. I worked earnestly and was always happy to please my boss with every task he gave me. I was ready to do more. I would hear my mates tell me, "Oh, mate, you better slow down. You will not be able to keep up this pace," but every week, I did. You see, I was thankful to have this job.

I remained in the Pakistani house; my money-related commitments were critical to support those fellas who did not have an occupation. I discovered these folks had exceeded the conditions of their visa and were wrongfully remaining in Australia; they had poor English aptitude, and they were attempting to secure positions. This house was a setup for "overstayers." I was legal for a year, so no one could hurt me. I could not live here for too long, sooner or later I needed to get away. Yet, I had to do it carefully.

The house had home standards concocting and cleaning days for the inhabitants of this house. I would sing along with tunes on the FM radio station. I got into an incredible Aussie band, Cold Chisel. I adored their music, and as I was cooking supper in the kitchen one day, singing ceaselessly, a guy I saw strolling over the tight road stopped and said to me, "I've heard you singing, mate, and I figure you should keep your everyday employment since you ain't going to make it as a vocalist." *Cheeky bugger*, I thought and snickered. I grinned and answered, "I am apprehensive; this is all I have, mate—you should endure me." He snickered. "Here, mate, get yourself down to the bar and come join the band. They may give you a possibility with that singing. It would be ideal if you whack a couple of lagers down ya." That sounded so Anglo-Indian. I had connected; I felt comfortable. Here was my first mate in Australia, a great guy, definitely a social heavy drinker. In this way, I went down to the nearby bar and met the local blokes, the regulars at the pub, the daily, devoted pub-goers. I was not into drinking. Before long, I discovered that would be somewhat hard in a nation where lager is significant. I began to drink only a little brew sometimes, as I needed to fit in with my mates. I had never been a drinking individual, so I would clutch a lager till it went flat on me sometimes. I would never drink lager the way these blokes in the bar did. With that much Toohey's draft on tap in my gut, I would be sick as a parrot on a roost.

I was invited to go to the Punchbowl Country Tavern to meet a few new people; sure enough, I was soon line dancing. Every week I was in my country pub, becoming a familiar face in the crowd.

I remembered Geoffrey Healy, the bloke who gave me his business card in Singapore. I produced it from my wallet and called him up. He answered the phone, and we talked.

Geoff said, "I was wondering what happened to you, mate. Hope you like Sydney, and if you are keen to come out on the weekend, I can pick you up."

"Sure," I replied, and we agreed to meet on a Saturday.

True to his word, on Saturday, a Porsche 911 pulled up on Rossmore Avenue at around 10:00 a.m., and we were off. We went on a cruise around Sydney.

The following two Saturdays, I spent with my new mate Geoffrey; he was a decent bloke, very friendly. He gave me his time, and I was very pleased to have met him. I got to know Sydney much better because of him.

This was a beach Saturday, so we hit Bondi Beach, swam in the ocean, and had a couple of beers; then he suggested we go to a La Perouse beach later in the afternoon and have dinner.

"Sounds great, mate," I replied as I ran into the surf to dive into it. I swam out among the surfers; it was buzzing with activity. It was a fun place to hang around.

Later in the afternoon, we drove up to the La Perouse beach—and it was a nude beach. I honestly had never been to a nude beach in my life. I was certainly not going to run around the beach naked. I was surprised to see a whole bunch of naked men playing some silly games with a ball and bat, running around naked.

Further up the beach, there was a mixed nude beach where everyone was naked. For me, this was something new. Around the corner from us was a nude beach with only naked women; two of them were kissing each other. I turned around and looked at the beach I was sitting at; two men were holding hands on the beach, walking and kissing each other.

I was naïve. I'd never seen anything like this in my life. I did not know what to make of it. I assumed it was a strange culture, but it was weird, and seeing something like this was alien and new.

Then there were some men dressed as women on the beach. I did not know the Aussie term, but this was not alien to me. I'd encountered this in India, but it was different. It was more visible in India and had been accepted very well in Indian society.

We had a particular type of people in India called *hijras* (eunuchs). *Hijras* possess a unique spot in Hinduism. Be that as it may, their relationship to current Mumbai, where transgender individuals are lawfully perceived, remains tenuous. In India, these looked like men, but they dressed like women and would always be found in a group, dancing on the streets with drums and tambourines; they would go from shop to shop performing a dance and get paid money. It was said that misfortune would befall you if you never gave them anything.

The La Perouse beach was secluded, and it was clear to me that a certain kind of people came to this beach, and my mate Geoff was showing me all the differences in this diverse city. We spent the evening at one of the bistros/cafés near the Sydney Harbour Bridge. I asked Geoff where he lived.

"We are going back to my place, mate, if you want to see it," he suggested.

"Sure," I replied, and so we went, driving in a northerly direction, crossed over Sydney Harbour Bridge, and came to a big building. The door opened to an underground car park; we drove in, parked the car, took the elevator to the fourteenth floor, got out, walked left in the direction towards the ocean, opened a door, and walked into a penthouse.

Awesome place! Wow! It was a beautiful place; there some cool paintings on the wall of naked men. The furniture looked expensive, the carpets were Persian, and the art décor was stylish. I walked to the balcony, and it was the most beautiful view I could have ever imagined of Sydney. Sprawled out in front of me was the view of the Sydney Harbour Bridge, Opera House, the boats sailing, the whole harbour—it was just astonishingly beautiful.

Geoff got me a gin and tonic and met me at the balcony with a drink in his hand, smiling at me, and said, "Pretty awesome, ain't it?"

I shook my head and replied, "I was not expecting to see such beauty. It's exceptionally stunning. And you live alone in this awesome penthouse by yourself? Are you not married, or do you have a girlfriend?"

He smiled at me and replied, "I had a boyfriend, but we broke up a while ago."

His response shocked me. I was so naïve, almost stupid. I had no clue until then that my friend Geoff was one of those nude guys on the beach who was kissing another man. I freaked out. "Okay," I replied. "I understand," I stuttered slightly. A weird thought came into my mind. It was saying, *Don't go inside the house. If he tries to rape you, jump from the building; then at least you'll have had a beautiful view on your final day.* I felt so weird.

I gathered myself and put on a cool attitude, like "I am pretty good here." Then came the bombshell. Geoff looked at me with a seductive smile. I almost died when he did that. *Oh boy, I've got myself into some bother here.* He said, "Well, Lyndon, I like you a lot. From the moment I saw you at the airport in Singapore, I figured you understood."

A voice in my mind was saying, *Creepy! Get away, get away from me! Don't you come any closer. I will jump!* I smiled at him and said, "Geoff, you are a good man, and I like your friendship a lot, but I am not inclined to like men in the way you may have thought. I am a friendly person, and I like women so much more." I smiled and continued, "I know women may be more complicated than men in relationships, but I am a man for a woman." The voice in my head was saying, *Shut up! You have said more than you should. He may try to convince you to try a man instead of a woman.*

Instinct is a pretty powerful thing when you are in a bother like that was; you have to listen to that inner voice all your life—it's your soul.

Geoff looked at me and said, "Yeah, mate, you are right." My mind was going, *Oh, crap!* Geoff continued, "Yeah, I cannot have a relationship with women. I prefer blokes like you."

I had to stop this conversation. I looked at him firmly but in a good way. "I am sorry to disappoint you; I appreciate this wonderful day I had with you. I am going to consider your suggestions about me having a relationship with a man like you, but I need time to think about it. Are you okay with my suggestion?"

"Oh yeah, it's cool. You should think about it; we can have a great time together in Sydney. You can live in this penthouse if you like."

I was speechless.

I needed to get out, and I did. He dropped me at the train station. I did not want him to drop me by car to my place; it all felt all so strange. I just needed to get away from this man. He was a nice person, but it was uncanny; my soul and inner spirit told me it just wasn't natural.

There was a term I came to know the week I was in the pub telling my mates about how I was hit on by a bloke. "Yeah, bloody pooftahs, mate," they yelled at the bar. "We will give him bloody hiding if he comes around to Punchbowl chasing after you." Everyone was laughing. "Bloody hell, bloody pooftahs, mate, they are starting to appear all over Sydney. We need to bash their heads, ey, mate."

In 1988, there was a lot of hostility in Australia to this gay movement; it was out of the closet, and I survived almost being raped by a man. He was a big fellow and could have overpowered me. What if he was dangerous? It was a time in history when acceptance of the gay lifestyle was in its early stages in Western societies. I questioned this kind of alien, distorted nature of human beings that I had never known. It was something I was encountering for the first time in my life. I was surprised that I was able to deal with it in the way I did and escape unharmed. Yet, I was somewhat perplexed at the dangers of my new society. I never saw Mr. Geoff Healy again and never answered his phone calls. I changed my land-line phone number to a private number.

I was nineteen years old, naïve, innocent, and encountering something alien and new in my life. My mother's prayer for my safety always accompanied me like a ring of fire and protection.

In my initial half year in Australia, I changed over into a local bloke; my evolution into this land of my dreams fit like a hand in a glove. I tossed my Indian passport in a trash bin in the city. I was finished with that. It made no sense. I was rarely returning. It was likely not the shrewdest action, but, rather, I did it simply out of impulse. I had all the Aussie identification I required. I sealed myself off from this nation, India. As an Anglo-Indian, I was home and had a particular resentment when I saw real Indians settle in Australia.

As much as we Anglo-Indians were so Western in our upbringing in India, we struggled to keep to our Western identity; we endured discrimination and abuse to remain who we were. If there was anyone more deserving to immigrate to the West, I believed that all Anglo-Indian individuals ought to be given that human right to come back to their Western roots. I couldn't comprehend why the Indians, who thought their Indian qualities to be so significant and especially hallowed and clean, would need to come and live in the West. It befuddled me. I therefore shed everything that was Indian in me, and everything that was Aussie became a part of who I was. I was true-blue and fair dinkum because I felt I was finally home.

MELBOURNE

One day, I got a phone call from my cousins in Melbourne, re-establishing communication with lost family relatives. He convinced me to leave Sydney, suggesting there was more family in Victoria than any place else in the nation, recommending I would be in an ideal situation if I came and lived with family. As I pondered my choices, I understood that living in a house in Punchbowl with illegal immigrants was not in my best interest. I decided to leave Sydney and head down to Melbourne.

I soon unobtrusively left Sydney and took a trip to Melbourne; it was a decent choice. I was home, with a ton of family. The city had had the biggest Anglo-Indian settlement here since the 1950s. Australia is a 100 percent outsider country. Everybody originated from elsewhere, and it was the most varied country on the planet. The Anglo-Indian people group were very much settled and set up in this country.

Before long, I found a new line of work with Holden Car Company in Dandenong, and life was how I would have preferred it to be. I felt natively constructed. I had achieved my fantasy of being in a nation that I could call home. Life, for me, was immaculate. I could now build up myself, and demonstrate that my augmentation and immigration justified each legitimate explanation behind me to be free as the red kangaroo—even an animal was destined to be free. I had no criminal record. I had never hurt anybody. I buckled down and made good on my regulatory expenses, safely settled myself as a supporter of the income of the government and monetary prosperity of the country, and I was not one of those numerous dole bludgers.

William Taylor turned into a decent mate of mine; we met each Thursday night for a round of squash, do some fitness training in the exercise centre, and end up with ten laps in the enormous pool. On the weekends, we went out downtown to some favourite BYO's cafés. William was married to Charmaine from the UK; she was a delightful, appealing lady; she had a genuine Pommy accent. I would regularly go with Crystal, a companion of William's; she was a young lady with an extremely charming comical inclination—what she didn't have in magnificence, she made up in character. In all actuality, she was most likely a passionate woman; however, our regular weekends did not spark any romantic fire between us that would prompt some sort of dating between us. The chemistry was just not there. She was a big girl for a little person like me. In any case, she was consistently there on the weekends, arranging the eateries or the dance-club scene. It was customary that, as companions, we would consistently hang out together. William was an awesome mate, and we had some extraordinary occasions together. I truly enjoyed him from my heart; he generally made great efforts as a friend.

I moved into another condo and made it my little home, committed myself at work, and had an incredible life. Melbourne City is probably the best place on the planet for international cuisine and nightlife. Melbourne was a blend of societies in its brunch eateries, bistros, and bars. Whether you're after present-day, customary, colourful, or hand-crafted flavours, Melbourne's diverse eating scene offers a surprising exhibit of the world's incredible cooking styles, from prominent top picks to the genuinely noteworthy. This was now my city, and I loved it.

It was a Friday afternoon. I was on my balcony, just relaxing. I had a day off from work and was looking forward to our regular weekend bash. I saw Charmaine step out of her parked car and wave at me. I was surprised that she had come to visit me; as she made her way up to my apartment, I went to open the door.

"What a surprise!" I said. "How did you know I would be home?"

She smiled. "Well, William told me last week you were having a long weekend. You did not invite me to your condo, so as I was passing by, I thought I'd drop in."

"Sure, well, of course," I replied. I tried to hide my surprise. "Can I get you a drink?" I asked.

"Sure, passion fruit, sweetie!" she replied.

Although I knew her very well and we met almost every weekend, it is still very surprising when your friend's wife suddenly shows up at your apartment.

I sat across from her on a chair near my writing table as she sat on my bed, chatting with me.

She wore a red high-collar top, a denim skirt; her fingernails were painted red. She had a matte-red lipstick, long hair and heels; she always liked her heels. She was a beautiful woman, but she was the wife of my best friend. She was sitting on my bed in my room and smiling at me with a seductive smile. Then she dropped a bombshell.

She told me, "Crystal used to be my husband's girlfriend many years ago. William and I have an open relationship, you know."

"What does that mean?" I asked.

"Well, we don't own each other. We are married, but we are both entitled to be happy. Lyndon, you are wally, you know that?" She laughed. "Did you not notice how I pulled you close the last time you danced with me?"

I was shocked because I did not have a clue. I had no such thoughts in my mind.

I was nervous. I stumbled in my speech. "Uhhh, oh, I did not notice," I replied. "Sorry." My mind was trying to correct me. Damn, what was I saying! I felt very uncomfortable, but there was an evil voice in my head telling me, *She is sexy.*

She was a beautiful, seductive woman who had had her eye on me in a way I was not aware of, and she had made a big move on me; she knew that she could easily seduce me, and I was baffled and in a terrible quandary within myself. I told her that I liked her but that I was confused because of my close friendship with her husband. I needed time to think about it.

I stood up to go to the kitchen and get a drink of water. I was in a nervous sweat. She was a very attractive woman. This was morally and physically difficult.

She followed me to the kitchen; she stood in front of me, put my glass of water down, put her hand around me, and kissed me. I was trembling. Taking my hands, she put them around her waist. I was helpless and liked her kiss; it was very sensual, but I got ahold of myself. I gently moved her away. "Please give me some time, please."

We four continued to meet on weekends. I was very tempted to end up having an affair with my best friend's wife, and I struggled through an awful moral battle within myself. I made excuses so that Charmaine would not come to my house. There were moments I wanted to have a heart-to-heart talk with my mate William. Then, as I went through those desperate thoughts, I realised that, if I did go ahead with it, then it might end his marriage to her. I would be the cause of it.

There was an evil inside of me urging me to just have an affair with her. She was surely worth it; she was a very attractive, sensual woman. Nobody would need to know; it could be a secret.

I would fight those evil thoughts in my mind and started praying. I felt desperate and weak; every time I saw her, I pictured a sexual relationship. It was sinful, and I hated it. I had sinned already in my heart, so committing the evil makes no difference. Such evil conclusions plagued my mind. I knew if I did not get out, I would be immersed in total adultery.

I was desperate. I was lying on my bed in my apartment looking at the ceiling, thinking. Then I made up my mind to do a Houdini act, an unobtrusive vanishing. I thought Outback—Perth, Western Australia. I knew for sure that, if I did not leave Melbourne, Charmaine would end up in my bedroom eventually and be lying next to me naked, and I would be living in the sin of adultery, wearing a mask every weekend and sleeping with a good friend's wife. We all have choices. I chose to leave Melbourne forever.

ACROSS TO THE GOLDEN WEST

I quit my job, gave up my apartment, and, one cold winter morning in June 1990, I boarded a Greyhound bus and went across the great Nullarbor Plain across South Australia, a weeklong journey right into the city of Perth, Australia, and a life in the Outback. I was truly amazed at the distances between places; the meaning of the words *massive, infinite, immeasurable, enormous, gigantic, colossal, cosmic, great, space, dry, beautiful, desolate* all came together, forming a union of words that displayed their true meaning as I was crossing this huge mass of land in front of me.

I had contact with an Anglo-Burmese family in Perth who were happy to have me to board with them. So, I found myself in a secure home with Christian people and started a new life yet again. My job hunting was a relentless process. I focused on getting a job as a heavy-equipment diesel mechanic, but I had to study some courses at a TAFE college.

I found a day job in the neighbourhood, at the assembly line of a sheet metal factory. I did extra jobs, the evening paper run, and supported myself, paying for my education and living expenses.

The family I lived with had two sons around my age and an adopted blond kid, Willy, who had an alcoholic mother and an unknown father, speciously in prison somewhere. Hence, he'd been adopted by this family as a kid, and he'd been raised here in this home. He was about sixteen years old.

With my newfound family, things were great once again; this family were relatives on my father's side who had settled in Burma many decades earlier, during the days of British rule. Many Anglo-Burmese families had also moved to Australia and made it home.

Colin and Judy were a couple who had four sons and one daughter; the older kids had already left the house and moved away. The two younger sons, John and Benny, along with the adopted Willy, lived in a big five-bedroom house with a big yard. There was an awesome blue heeler, a cattle dog, whose name was "Bud." He was a sturdy type of Aussie cattle dog, and his eyes had two black rings that made him look like a bandit; sometimes when I looked at him sitting and thinking his dog thoughts, he looked like a dog psychologist's professor of some sort that wore a pair of black spectacles. Then when he acted silly in the backyard, he would look like a comic character from a comic book. The blue heeler is an outstanding dog and friend. I was emotionally involved with this dog Bud.

There was a great atmosphere in this home. I was soon to become very connected to this family, as it became like my own.

Colin was a devout Christian who had Bibles placed in many strategic places in the house; you would always find him reading the scriptures. He was a member of a Christian outreach centre, devoted to church activities, and involved in evangelism with members of his church. Colin had a brown skin tone. He looked younger each year; this man never seemed to age. He was short, about five feet five, medium built, had five grown-up kids; he was about fifty-two years old, but he looked like he was in his early forties. It amazed me how certain people look younger than their age. He was a very vocal man when it came to preaching.

Judy, on the other hand, was less vocal; she was a dedicated woman of the house, a mother who raised boys. You would hear her comment on how she preferred her four sons to the one daughter she had. This was not said in a negative manner, but she was rather suggesting that the daughter was difficult to manage and was spoilt by the father, since she was the only girl in the family. Judy was a typical woman of the house; she was an awesome cook and managed her household impeccably well. She always had a smile on her face, adorably loving and kind. She had fair skin tone, black long hair, a round face, well-dressed, and took care of herself. She loved knitting and sitting at the front of a fireplace in the winter months watching TV.

John was a stocky lad who did not pursue any studies or higher education; he had no interest in such things. He believed in being tough and doing a man's job, and so he worked as a bricklayer in the construction boom market of the northern suburbs of the city of Perth. He'd always loved building houses.

Benny was the youngest of the family; he was the funny one, a comical lad who was always up to some silly antics around the house. He nevertheless possessed a musical talent and played the piano remarkably well; while Judy admiringly watched him play, she dreamed that he would become an awesome pianist, performing in famous places.

We would have some music sessions together; I played the acoustic guitar, and we would perform songs together, especially those classics from The Beatles, songs like "Hey Jude," "Can't Buy Me Love," "Imagine." Judy always insisted we sing some of her favourite, Cliff Richard, a very popular artist with the Anglo-Indian/Anglo-Burmese folk.

My coming to this family brought some kind of tranquillity. I was a regular churchgoer with Colin, while his two sons resisted the churchgoing business; on a few occasions, I was able to convince the sons to join me, which they reluctantly did. However, it did not last long.

This pleased Colin, as he began to see me as a good influence among the three lads at home. There was a communication issue between him and his children; he was always preaching to his sons, and they rejected him in subtle ways. He was not able to connect to them, and my presence now began to fill in a gap, creating a connection within the family.

Judy did not come to this particular church and insisted on attending the Catholic church. Therefore, we had a family that were all united at home but not united together in church. Sunday morning, everyone went their ways and came back together in the afternoon for the traditional lunch. I always returned from church and helped Judy cook the great Sunday lunches. We always had guests or friends over on Sunday for lunch. It reminded me so much of my home in the glen. It made me emotional as my thoughts of my mother and father would come flooding through my mind. Nevertheless, I was grateful that I had a similar atmosphere here.

I was a positive influence around the house, especially with the lads at home. Judy would always hug me and tell me how happy she was that I had come to be with them. Colin always talked to me about preaching to his sons. While I advised him that he should be more lenient with his views because his children had been born and bred in Australia. I suggested that he accept that children were raised with more obedience in Burma in comparison to Australia.

On the other hand, the lads were happy that I was around because their dad was finally off their backs. Judy was also pleased because she was also tired of Colin's preaching at home. In the complexity of the different entreatments and opinions that existed in this home, I was the peacemaker, the sedative guru, the comforting counsellor.

I lived amid this family and this home for almost a year. I was thankful to be there. I could not have asked for a better blessing than the one I had. Some issues existed, of which I was unaware; nevertheless, my presence and energy around the home made a difference.

Then, one day, it changed. Colin came home upset and asked me to accompany him to his brother Harold's house. I never knew he even had a brother named Harold. As we entered the house, I saw Judy slumped on the couch, completely intoxicated. Colin and Harold got into a heated argument.

Colin grabbed hold of his brother and shouted, "Damn you, Harold! You have been giving her drink and turning her into an alcoholic like yourself."

Harold shook off Colin, pushed him back, and, with wobbly feet, slumped in the chair and yelled at his younger brother, "Your wife comes here on occasions to drink. I don't force her to drink. She is neglected and unhappy because you don't give her any attention, you moron." Harold continued, "Stop your preaching and take care of your wife, dipstick! Don't come here accusing me of giving her drink. She is welcome at my house anytime she wants."

I heard profanity being hurled between the brothers, and I was no stranger to this kind of domestic drama. I stood there thinking to myself, *No one has a perfect life in this world. We all keep up appearances.* I stood between the two brothers and introduced myself to Harold during the chaos. I went to the couch, picked up Judy, walked to the car, and put her into the back seat. I sat with her and put her head on my lap while Colin drove home.

The next day, the home was gloomy. John and Benny disappeared to their friend's house; Willy was gone, too. I had my trusted spectacled bandit blue heeler Bud with me, so I was not alone. Evil is never far away; destruction and accusations are never far away. Human life is fragile. I would bring peace to this home. I prayed with Colin. This was not something new; this was an old demon; there were issues in the family. There was a calm before the storm rose up again. Colin had neglected Judy for a while, and she protested by going to Harold's house and binge-drinking on sherry. The elder kids had left the house and had their own lives and did not want anything to do with an old problem between Colin and Judy, their parents. A day of drunkenness can narrate history.

The next day, I stayed at home while Colin went to work. I had to take care of Judy, who was very sick. She kept apologising to me every time I entered her bedroom to assist her. She had consumed so much alcohol that she'd passed out. A few days later, she had recovered and was back to her normal self; she kept apologising to me, feeling genuinely embarrassed, and started to express her frustrations about her husband, Colin. I was the peacemaker once again, and the home came back to its normalcy once again. The lads were back home; things would continue.

I had the experience from back home when my dad would drink and destroy the peace and tranquillity of the home. Based on the experience of my childhood, I knew that this pattern would surely crop up again.

A few weeks later, Judy came home after her grocery shopping; she was happy, always wearing a smile. I was the regular cook with her in the kitchen, and often we would share our culinary expertise; she knew some awesome Burmese recipes. While I was preparing the meal, I noticed that she would keep disappearing and reappearing from her bedroom. I sensed it. I looked at her and asked, "Judy, what are you drinking?"

She smiled at me and said, "I am having some rather nice sherry. I don't give a damn about what Colin thinks. I like a little bit of sherry. I am tired of his preaching. I don't give a damn anymore."

I smiled at her; she looked so funny with that little glass of sherry in her hand.

I told her I understood, but I begged her not to get drunk. I suggested, "Colin is going to be home in the evening, and we could talk about you having a little sherry once in a while."

John walked in the door while this was going on, came to the kitchen, and said to me, "Is Mom having a drink?"

I looked at him and said, "She likes to have a little sherry once in a while. I don't see how it can harm her. What do you think?"

"Yeah, mate," he replied, "Mum is good; she is a happy person and likes to be happy, but Dad is the one who makes her sad and does not allow her any drink. Hence, she goes off to Harold's place and gets wasted. If he allowed her to have a little sherry once in a while, Mum would be fine." He continued, "I drink beer in the pub, mate. My dad does not know that I do. I am eighteen years old. I don't give a damn what he thinks anymore, and I don't want his preaching."

Colin turned up in the evening, and there was trouble in the house. I could hear him being upset, protesting, "I don't want any alcohol in this house."

I heard Judy shouting back at him, "No one gives a damn about what you like or don't like in this house."

John disappeared and left the house. Benny, who was sixteen years old, did not show up; he was hanging around with his friends, and Willy was with him.

I was the psychoanalyst once again. I tried to make peace. I reasoned with Colin that his total intolerance of a little sherry in the house and the application of such stringent house rules caused more harm than good.

I was not a very good mediator when it came to Colin. In the midst of this discussion, I did my best to calm him down. He was still upset; he took a shower, got dressed, and said he was going to a church meeting. I patted him gently on his shoulder, reassuringly, in peace, and I said to him, "Be calm."

He acknowledged me, looked at me, and said, "Take care of things around here."

I looked at him and replied, "You must consider some flexibility—please."

Colin got into his car and drove away. "I will be late getting back home," he added. I walked back into the kitchen and got myself dinner. Judy walked back in with another glass of sherry and was happy that she had stood up for herself.

I could see she was starting to drink more than the agreed-upon amount, so I suggested she have dinner. She walked to the living room and turned on the music, came back, grabbed hold of my hand, and said, "Come and dance with me. Life has been so dead with that man. I can have a drink, I can have a dance. I am tired of his preaching, and I don't give a damn anymore." She swung her arms, pulled me to the living room, and danced the foxtrot.

I was sympathetic to her as much as I was to Colin. I understood that they needed to compromise and that a fair balance needed to be struck with home rules.

Judy continued to dance with me. Then she left and came back with another glass of sherry in her hand, turned on another of her favourite songs, and I didn't seem to have any choice but to dance with her. With every song and every dance, I believe she finished about four glasses of sherry, in addition to the several other shots she had been having earlier.

"Do you want a glass of sherry?" she asked me.

I looked at her and replied, "Judy, I don't drink sherry. I sometimes have a beer, but I have never been into drinking, and I don't get drunk."

"Come and dance with me again." Now she was getting tipsy as she swung me around and danced with me. I continued to be accommodating and tried my best to persuade her to have dinner. My thoughts were that, if she ate some food, she would stop drinking, and I could talk her into controlling her happy mood and her drinking at the same time. Then she grabbed my hand, pulled me, and said, "Come follow me—I want to show you something."

I was walking with her and saying, "Judy, please, you have had enough, and you promised you would not get drunk."

She smiled and said, "I am not drunk, just a little tipsy and happy. Come," and she pulled me into her bedroom. I had been in her bedroom before when she was very sick, and I cleaned up the vomit, so it was not something alien for me to stand in her bedroom.

She took my one hand, wrapped it around her behind, and took my other hand; she put it on her breast and started to kiss me. She started undressing and said, "Come make love to me like crazy. Oh, please just ravish me."

I stood there dumbfounded. "No," I replied, "please, I cannot do this." She was half naked. I didn't want to see. I pulled away from her.

"Oh, no, Judy—please, I cannot do such a thing. Please, please." I hurriedly left the room. I walked out into the yard and on to the street.

The evil one in my head was telling me otherwise. I was holding my head. "Get away, you filthy, evil devil." I was shocked and upset; I did not expect that she would want me to have sex with her. I looked up to her like she was an aunt. I was perplexed. I followed the road straight ahead then took a left. I kept walking, into the big park, and found a park bench, sat down in the dark, and started crying. It was terrible. I returned home very late that night because I walked back home. I walked past the living room and saw Colin sitting in the living room. I said goodnight, and I silently went into my bedroom and lay in my bed. I had to get out of there and go away once again.

I dreaded the next morning. I woke up and wore my happy mask, just like Judy did every day of her life. I went into the kitchen and made breakfast for the family. Judy was in the shower; she got dressed and came out and hugged me. Judy, in reality, was a lovely person; she was a woman who was neglected, and she was desperately trying to be happy. Colin was a good man but completely in another world, and I found myself with all my good intentions bang right in the middle of the gravest sin, being caught up in an abysmal form of adultery, with a woman who was as old as my mother. Colin was silent, sitting on the couch, reading his books. Benny and Willy came out of their rooms for breakfast, and I wore my mask as if nothing had ever happened to me.

Judy was going to win this battle. I knew the opportunities were many for her. I was often alone at home with her, and I knew she would try to seduce me again. I would avoid being alone with her anymore and try to escape from this horrible temptation. I had to get away. My studies at TAFE college were almost at an end, and I had to hang in there for another two months. Hence, I found excuses to be away from the house more often and stayed focused on the completion of my studies.

My hard work paid dividends; I was awarded an excellent grade in my national tradesman diploma. I was twenty-one years old; I was now ready to go and find a job in the mining sector in the vast deserts of Western Australia.

I went on a job-hunting spree, knocking on doors, and circulating my CV at every contracting company I could find. Skilled Engineering was a well-known contracting company for the mining sector. I would make regular phone calls, chasing a job in the mines. I was begging for a job, as I just wanted to go away. I did not want to end up in bed with Judy.

Then came my breakthrough; one morning I got a call from Taipan Resources. I went for the interview and got the job as an underground mechanic/contractor for Western Mining Corporation in a place called Kambalda. My safety training and certification would be conducted at the site, and I was asked to join as soon as possible.

I came home and announced my leaving; it came as a surprise to everyone, and for me, it was the best that could have happened. I started to gather all my gear, booked a ticket on the Greyhound bus to Kalgoorlie, and left three days later. I felt really sad for Judy; she was a caring woman who was unhappy. Colin needed to fix this problem. I was deeply grieved because I loved this home and everyone in it, but there was darkness and an evil lurking; adultery and sexual immorality would surely get ahold of me sooner or later. I left with a heavy heart and took my sadness with me. I was baffled by thoughts in my mind about the constant attack on my life by women—women who wanted sexual gratification, drawing me into the act of sexual immorality. I was so tempted by my flesh; my mind fought against it, but I had come so close to yielding to this evil.

I got on that Greyhound bus and journeyed into the distance, to a new life in the goldfields of Kalgoorlie. I could see a pipeline along the way; it would disappear into the sands of the desert and then reappear along the highway, and then disappear and reappear once again. I missed home and my family. I looked over the desert badlands like a meandering soul with an insane dream that currently had turned into my world. Australia was presently home for me.

The pipeline is the story of an Irishman, Charles Yelverton O'Connor, who engineered the pipeline construction project; O'Connor is best known for his work on the goldfields pipeline. Ostensibly the world's longest central pipes, it conveys water 530 km from Perth to Kalgoorlie—provoked by the Gold Rush and the population boom that resulted.

In 1896, Premier John Forrest acquainted a bill with a raise of £2.5 million (more than a billion dollars in terms of today's money) to build the pipeline from a dam on the Helena River, close to Mundaring, to the Mount Charlotte reservoir in Kalgoorlie; the water at that point reticulated to different mining focuses in the goldfields. O'Connor was exposed to a delayed analysis by the press and government officials over the plan.

One journo composed a proceeding with battles against O'Connor that is thought to have added to his demise. It blamed O'Connor for debasement and corruption. One urban fantasy is that O'Connor ended his own life since, when the pumping began, the water didn't stream. Truth be told, it was overwork, extraordinary weight, and analysis of his plan that drove him to discouragement, and allegations that he was degenerate drove him to suicide.

According to the driver describing the story to the passengers on the bus I was travelling in, the next day, the water showed up. Then the driver added something of his humour to the story. "Silly Irish bugger," and he chuckled. "Takes time for water to travel nine hundred kilometres. He miscalculated flow rates in proportion to time and distance. Therefore, the pipeline was a reminder of this poor soul who shot himself."

It was a hot day as I got off the bus, walking along the main street of Kalgoorlie town; the place was beset with bars. This was, no doubt, a hard-drinking town. I walked past the post office, and right there in front of me was the name "Excelsior Hotel Pub." She was a classic building, very European, colonial Victorian, Edwardian style. There was a huge bar, always filled with people, since drinking was a human necessity; the warm weather and cold beer formed a coalition that became an embraced creed and ethos in Kalgoorlie.

For a youngster like me, who was definitely not a major consumer of alcohol, to plunge myself into a rough environment of hardworking, hard-punching, hard-drinking, fair dinkum, true-blue "get stuffed, you wanker, or get a cue stick broken across your skull," the Greyhound bus may have dropped off a wrong passenger in this town.

Walking into Kalgoorlie, I imagined all these fingers pointing the word *misfit* tattooed on my head. I got myself a Coke on ice and sat at the bar.

I was to meet two blokes from the mining company, Mike and Wolfgang. Pubs were the most important places; they were the communication hubs and the nerve centre of the town. It connected people, businesses; it was the employment centre. It was the word of mouth that moved opportunities along the line. Australian mining towns were predominantly white. Gold has always had that kind of attraction.

I made enquiries about the two blokes I had to meet at this bar. Tim, the barman, laughed at me when I told him the names. He eyeballed me and said, "You are in trouble with the Wolfgang fellow, crazy German Aussie. Oh, mate, you are in deep trouble—you will not be drinking any damn Coke on ice when he gets here." It wasn't long before the two blokes showed up.

Tim yelled out, "Hey, Mike, Wolfie—one of your blokes from Taipan Resources here at the bar."

Mike walked up to me and said, "Gidday, young fella. Welcome to Kalgoorlie."

I shook his hand and replied, "How ya going? It was a long trip down here from Perth. I am glad I am here."

"Yeah, no worries, mate," Mike replied. "We have you booked in here for a night at the Excelsior, and we leave to Kambalda tomorrow lunchtime to the mining town. It's about eighty kilometres from here."

Wolfie rocked up, shook my hand. I looked behind me, and Tim had served three large beers, smiling at me. Wolfie just shouted, "You bloke's beer."

"So, what are you? Diesel hydraulic mechanic, mate?" asked Wolfie.

"Caterpillar heavy earth-moving equipment," I replied.

Wolfie said, "Shall be all right, mate, but you know you're going to be down a long shaft—it's more a *wrong* shaft, if you ask me. It's a long way down the hole. You'll get accustomed to it; don't worry."

I looked at Mike and asked, "What's life like at Kambalda?"

"Well," he replied, "you are out in the sticks, mate. All-day work in the hole in the ground and then get holed up in a pub and drink till you are ready to go to bed, and do it all over again each day, every day for almost the rest of your life. Don't mess with another man's woman, or you will get your head bashed in. There are not many women in these parts." He laughed at me. "It's rough as guts, mate, but you have good blokes to help you. Welcome to Kambalda." And Mike laughed.

"I prefer to call the place *Cambodia*," said Wolfie. "You can go to Hay Street in Kalgoorlie if you want a woman for the night, mate." The two men laughed. "That's if you like ugly women," they added and laughed some more.

I honestly was baffled and naïve to these conversations. I did not get it at first. I was lost in some of them. I later found out that Hay Street was the red-light district of this town, Kalgoorlie. I had to keep up appearances and drink a few more beers with these men. I was not sure I would survive the night; the beers kept appearing, and my mind kept thinking, *You are going to be sick.* I left the crowded bar, collected my keys, and told the men I was tired and going to rest.

Wolfie protested, "You can't go, mate, the party is just starting. With the bands all ready to fire up, you will not get any sleep in your room until closing time."

I replied, "I've got to go, mate, and take some rest, get a shower, and I'll probably come back down later. See you blokes later." I escaped my first night of heavy drinking.

The next day in the afternoon, I drove the Toyota Hilux to Kambalda Western Mining Corporation SPQ (single-person quarters). Mike and Wolfie were wrecked; they were still drunk from the night's party. It was a hot day, and the desert heat was intense in the afternoon; as we made tracks, I heard the popping of cans. The men had a twelve-pack of Victoria Bitter in an Esky cooler box.

Wolfie smiled at me and said, "To avoid a hangover, you stay drunk, mate."

"I am not drunk, you see," I replied.

"She'll be all right, mate."

I refused the beer. Up until now, I had not seen individuals drink so much and ventured into an authentic universe of alcohol abuse to a different level, as I had witnessed in the frontier mining towns of Kalgoorlie.

CHAPTER 7

LONGSHAFT

LONGSHAFT NICKLE MINE—KAMBALDA, WESTERN AUSTRALIA

I checked in with the camp boss at the western mining site and took my keys to my *donga*. (The *Donga* or the *dog box*, as they called them, were live-in accommodations for single men.)

These were portable house structures, like cubicles, that consisted of a bedroom, a table and two chairs, a small refrigerator, a cupboard, a bedroom lamp, one fire extinguisher, and a large window. These structures, arranged in rows across this camp, housed hardcore men, who worked, drank a ton of liquor, played eight-ball pool, fist-fought each other, and then became friends again a week later.

The public toilets and showers were outside among the gum trees. On the right-hand side was a large pub, a courtyard with benches and chairs. In the middle stood four barbecue fireplaces; several gum trees made it a perfect garden for the men. A graffiti sign on the *dunny* wall said "Bro's Beer Garden." *(A water closet is called a "dunny" in Australia).* And in the middle of the beer garden stood a tall white gum tree.

I went for a wander around my new surroundings, meeting some of my new neighbours. Harley Davidsons owners, men with goatee beards and covered in tattoos, polishing their prized possessions. They were big men with long beards like the fellas from ZZ Top, smoking and drinking beer, in a Sunday-afternoon session—recovery mode after

108

a weekend of hard drinking. Hangovers are a rare thing for regular beer-drinking men. This was home for now.

I was now in the Outback, frontier towns—the new young kid on the block. I kept a low profile, stayed in my *donga*, unpacked my clothes, hung my guitar on the peg near the cupboard, lay down in my bed and continued reading my book—*The Fatal Shore*, by Robert Hughes. I fell asleep.

Early the next morning, I walked across to the mess hall, had my breakfast with Wolfie and Mike. Everyone looked sober and ready for the hard, dangerous work underground. Here was the second-deepest nickel mine in the world. Longshaft—1900 meters down—two shafts—one for the men and the other were the skips that carried the ore out of the ground.

I met my boss, Terry Groombridge, the man in charge at the mining site. He was of Irish descent, with fiery red hair, freckles, and sunburnt skin, a veteran in the mining business and a well-seasoned, dedicated company man of WMC. He was a man who had made a lot of money and a name for himself out here. He was a tough guy, a short man, like some Napoleon of Kambalda. I was in the hands of a tough fella, known to be ruthless. On his table was a wooden logo that read, "Cows may come, and Cows may go, but the Bull in this place goes on forever."

I spent the next week training on the safety-induction program. I learned survival and rescue, firefighting, alarm systems, and sequences of the ringing codes for the cage man. I was taught about emergency alarm systems and when and how to trigger them on. Some added practical-training programs led me down one of the older mine shafts. As the cage descended into the darkness of the hole in the earth, I held my breath and then relaxed. Here was one eerie, dark world.

After a successful week of safety training, I found myself in the workshop, working under the watchful eye of the Napoleon of Kambalda. Mr. Terry Groombridge gave me a brush, a shovel, and a bucket. Then he announced his orders: "Every day, you will keep this whole workshop clean. I want to see the floor clean and everything in its place. That's your job."

I spent the next four months cleaning everyone's mess. I shovelled, mopped, polished, and swept that damn workshop floor in an endless sequence. I had had enough by the end of three months; I was here to develop my technical skills. I wanted to work on the big machines underground and master them, an opportunity for which I had been waiting a long time.

Soon I found myself disillusioned, a great disappointment as far as I was concerned. I was reduced to a young chap holding a mop, a bucket, a shovel, and a brush. For those four months, I cleaned every other person's mess. I was the cleaner about whom no one gave a damn. It was my initiation into the mining world, a test to see if I had the will to do the shit jobs first. Everyone was on the ball game—everyone except me, like they were breaking in a wild horse. Four months of abuse was more than I could take.

One morning, I stood outside the office of Terry Groombridge. I twisted my face to guarantee my displeasure of being the cleaner for the past four months, and I wanted to quit and tell him to shove the job.

I vented my displeasure about the lack of progress in my career under his leadership. Terry Groombridge listened to my complaint, lifted his head, and gave me an imposing look. I stopped talking.

He replied, "Young man, if you are distraught carrying out your responsibility, I will sign your papers, and you'll be down the road around lunchtime. I can assure you no one will miss you around here.

"I suggest to you that I am not kidding. So, quit messing around with that sad face of dismay you came here to demonstrate to me. I recommend you return to that open workshop and sweep it clean, or I may need to fire you and ensure you are off by tomorrow."

I was all shaken up.

I scrubbed and mopped the workshop floor for the next two weeks, silently, with a smile, minus the whimper. I even had to clean the men's toilets. Now, working even harder, I kept everything spotlessly clean.

Three weeks later, Terry Groombridge came and patted me on the shoulder. "Young man," he said, "a good mechanic is a man who learns how to keep his workshop and tools clean and in good condition."

I smiled at him and replied, "Fair enough. I sure learnt that lesson, Sir."

Mr. Groombridge handed me my new responsibilities. "You will be working with Wolfgang for the next three months underground at level fifteen. Your workshop duties include working on Elphinstone boggers, Jumbo Drill Rigs, winches, rock breakers, and several other pneumatic types of equipment. I will be watching you, so don't screw up when you are down the hole. It does not take much for you to be down the road if you screw up while you work underground. We don't keep hazardous workers around here."

I had passed my test of humiliation.

The next morning, I was down the square shaft, descending into the darkness with twenty other men. We were all packed inside a huge metal cage, suspended by a steel wire, dangling above a chasm that led into the blackness of the earth 1900 metres below the surface of humanity. I was now a miner.

Mike, the cage man, made his regular stops, dropping off men with all their assortment of equipment. There were nineteen levels in this mine, but it all stopped at level eighteen. Nobody went down to level nineteen, and it was probably too dangerous. Wolfgang and I got off at level eight.

As we closed the safety gate behind us, I stopped and watched the cage disappear into the darkness of the shaft. It was all so chilling. There were small rail tracks that led to a tunnel that brought us to the charging station for the electric train and Grambie.

Diggers unearthed adits and cross-adits into the metal body and removed the mineral, utilizing the mining strategy known as "sub-level stoping," including the unearthing of the stone in a progression of vertical shafts, or "stopes." The stone impacted from the top of the stope, utilizing gravity to drop it into shafts for extraction. The metal ore was carried by Grambie vehicles, a mini-electric train pulling a tipping container on wheels and dumping earthly treasures at loading pockets to be hoisted up by the skips and transported to the process plant nearby. Longshaft was a twin shaft; one carried the miners, and the other the precious ore.

The diggers would enter the underground condition from a different level, going down the incline by walking, four-wheel-drive vehicles, and a railroad framework. At that point, arriving at working levels, they would begin their day. Groups armed with pneumatic drills impacted the rock, drilling holes with incredible noise; others would tidy up and utilize hydraulic rock-breakers to break up large rocks to smaller sizes. They would utilize Jumbo diesel/electric-driven machines to bore two-inch holes into the rock face, eight to ten metres deep from top to bottom at specially marked areas made by the geologists.

When finished, they would pack these openings with explosives and detonators with various timings, framing an arrangement of planned impacts and blasts that exploded the stone and shook the entire establishments of the earth. I was terrified when I first experienced this kind of explosion.

It resembled a little city underground, a system of passages and safety signs, modified Toyota four-wheel drives. There was a mini-rail network; Grambie trains were hauling rocks, a place where threat, danger, and death were consistently present. Even though you don't consider it that way, you don't think along these lines, but mining is this way. If you did not overcome fear, you couldn't last more than a day underground. It was a well-established reality. A few people came to labour for a week and soon left. They just got claustrophobic and feared the danger. It could be overwhelmingly claustrophobic, more demanding than a man can take. Mining was not an occupation for a faint-hearted man.

I boarded the small electrical train on level eight, with a nutter, a crazy German Aussie. As we moved into the darkness, the German lunatic turned on the lights and put the train into its maximum speed, flying into the darkness on a roller-coaster ride. Wolfgang was singing in a loud voice. He had a small leather strap on his hand, and he slashed it to the side of the train. We headed off into the darkness, singing this song.

Rawhide

Rollin' rollin' rollin' keep them loco's rolling
Rollin' rollin' rollin'
Rollin' rollin' rollin'
Rollin' rollin' rollin'
Rollin' rollin' rollin'
Rawhide
Keep rollin', rollin', rollin'
Though the streams are swollen
Keep them locos rollin', rawhide
Through rain and wind and weather
Hellbent for leather
Can't feel my balls by my side

All the things I'm missin'
Good vittles, love and kissin'
Are waiting at the end of my ride
Move 'em on, head 'em up
Head 'em up, move 'em on
Move 'em on, head 'em up, rawhide
Cut 'em out, ride 'em in
Ride 'em in, cut 'em out
Cut 'em out, ride 'em in, rawhide

I was not laughing; I was petrified, scared to death. The train finally slowed down about two kilometres into the ride. We drove along, with collapsed areas of the mines at level eight. Excessive rock bolting and several metal supportive structures appeared in the darkness visible only to the miner's light on our foreheads. I understood it was unstable ground; it was the creepiest part of the mine. Wolfgang was laughing like a lunatic, *Hoodoo, Hoodoo;* He made some scary noises, like there were ghosts of fallen dead men surrounding us. My skin turned from brown to a whiter shade of pale.

We reached stope 28, and the train stopped. I walked alongside Wolfgang onto the tracks, my headlamp lights blazing in the obscurity of the mine. This was a tour of duty, a survey of the area, and inspecting equipment we were responsible for as the maintenance team.

We got back on the train; Wolfgang started singing the same songs again. Occasionally, we'd slow down and wave at the rock bolters and miners making their way by foot to their locations of work.

We took the cage down to level fifteen, where a large workshop was located. There were greasy maintenance pits, where heavy mining equipment was serviced. It was a polluted place, with the smell of oils, diesel fuels, hoses, tools, spare parts, fittings, connectors, and grease monkeys.

I was one of the new grease monkeys. Soon I would be concealed in these same pits, covered in sweat, oil, and grease, as black as the darkness of this nocturnal world underground.

I had just survived the roller-coaster ride by the skin of my teeth, riding through the eerie tunnels of level eight on a train with an absolutely crazy German/Aussie bloke, a man who had a moustache that extended across the breadth of his face. His eyes were bloodshot, he was loud and obnoxious, and I figured out that he had been in the mines so long that it had driven him to a certain level of craziness.

I met the other blokes who worked at level fifteen and complained to them about the scary experience at level eight with Wolfgang. To add more detail to the scary mine, the miners told me the story of the men who died due to rock falls at level eight, and some reckoned that it was a haunted place. It was my first day at Longshaft nickel mine in Kambalda.

Three months later, I was completely integrated into the mining culture, and I was one of the boys. I'd built a reputation of being a hard worker, and I always learned all the competitive innovations and aptitudes from the more-experienced blokes. My enthusiasm for work and knowledge rattled the office doors of Terry Groombridge, and he appreciated my work ethic.

The weekends always were a binge-drinking party, with regular barbecues and get-togethers at the "Bro's Beer Open Garden" behind the pub.

As I walked over to join the group, I heard an uproar progressing as men attempted to scale up the white gum tree that stood in the center of the beer garden. With the agitation of giggling that followed, it was the most humorous sight. Drunk men were attempting to climb up a white gum tree that had a bark that was as smooth as glass. They battled to climb towards the top, where the tree trunk split into a fork of two branches, around ten metres above the ground. They descended its glass surface quicker than they could climb it, and no one had ever made it to the top.

This entertainment on weekends carried prize money of one hundred dollars and two cartons of beer from the pub if you made it to the top. No one ever did succeed. It remained an unconquered quest. Hence, every weekend, a few men tried to climb the slippery tree, accompanied by the laughter and encouragement of the blokes.

The characters of the men in this place were funny and bizarre—a certain kind of craziness. Like hikers on a trail receiving a trail name, miners did the same. A person would end up with a name that described their character. So, Billy the Fish turned up with wet trousers returning from the *dunny*, staggering towards the table to get himself another beer. He was so drunk that he'd peed himself in the process. Unaware of his mishap, he stood holding the tree, boasting to everyone that he was going to make it this time.

The place filled with laughter; it was undeniably comical.

The crowd shouted out, "Hey, Billy! Did you just pee yourself?" Another bunch of fellows yelled words of encouragement, "Go get it—good on ya, mate." "Billy the Fish—way to go, digger," while others hurled insults at him calling him a "silly old git."

Billy was a notorious challenger; he made many false claims of his ability to perform incredible tasks when he was drunk. He was about 58 years old, five foot three, a slim fella who drank more than he ate; he was good-hearted and an hilarious man, a well-loved character among the miners.

As he held on to the tree with his wet trousers, wrapping his legs around the tree, he launched his one-hundredth attempt to scale the tree and broke the record for the fastest slide down the tree as he fell. As blokes went to pick him up, the laughter that followed was contagious.

I walked up to the tree, looked at it, and held it with both my hands; I had climbed coconut trees as a youngster most of my life. Some were about twenty-five metres tall, but this gum tree was different. Its bark was smooth as glass, and it would be a tougher climb. I was confident I would make it. I held the tree and started to scale it, I made five metres, holding on to it with a tight vise-like grip. I was up seven metres, with everyone yelling encouragement below: "Go, mate, go, mate, go, mate." I started to slide, and I tightened my grip as the skin on my thighs was rubbing against the smooth bark. I felt a burning sensation. I tightened my grip and scaled, and I slid down a little, with another tighter grip as my skin burned from the friction. I kept going for the last three metres. I was almost there. With one serious attempt as I grabbed the forked branch, I scaled the gum tree—the only one who'd ever climbed the "Bro's Beer Garden— Ghost Gum Tree Challenge. I sat there, victorious, on the top of the forked branch of the tree, with everyone clapping their hands below; they threw me a Swiss army knife and asked me to engrave my name on the bark of the tree.

The bloke who ran the pub came outside to witness the "Great Conquering." Then he rushed back inside to bring back the prize money and the two slabs of beer. The crowd all cheered.

I sat there for the next ten minutes revelling in my victory and knew the hardest part was not getting up there; the slide back down was going to burn my skin. You cannot climb this tree with long trousers. It was always going to be chafed skin climbing up this tree with satin barks. I slid down the tree in pain as my skin burned and bruised as I reached the ground. My thighs were red, and my skin was chafed and burnt. It was painful, but my victory was resounding. Nobody succeeded in climbing the tree ever again. Some drunks even attempted to burn it down a few years later.

The Bro's Beer Garden was a place of entertainment, a circus, bonfires. Occasionally when thing got outrageous, crazy Steve turned up with his motorbike and jumped over the big bonfires. He sometimes rode his bike into the fire and came out the other side. On one occasion, his hair was on fire and was put out by three blokes pouring three cans of beer over his head.

And this is the way I got my nickname: I strolled over to the "Bro's Beer Garden" with my guitar. In the company of the greatest banjo player in the world, a notorious plonk drinker, Mr. Shaky Dave. We joined forces and sang a blues tune that we composed and performed, a song called the "The Kambalda Blues." The crowds cheered as we sang along, drinking beer and singing the blues. I did a few solo Elvis Presley tunes, followed by an Irish lad who sang the classic Irish Song "The Sick Note." It was a memorable night, one that went down in history as the most fabulous night of entertainment, booze, and song. Out in the whop-whops of the frontier mining town and camp at Kambalda, stars were born.

The following Monday morning, as I strolled into the workshop, there on the black notice board, written across with white chalk in big letters, was a caption of dedication.

"Elvis is back, but this time he is black." I had just received my official nickname—"Black Elvis."

Although I was a light-brown man, the colour is not well known in Australia; everything that was dark was "black." It was with great affection that one could get a nickname down under. It truly means you are a fair dinkum bloke and everyone likes you dearly. I had never experienced such caring friendships, such crazy people. Many were dysfunctional, and almost all had an alcohol addiction or mental problems; some were teetering on the tipping point of insanity.

Mining in Australia was a way of life, and the Western Australian government was not well prepared to manage the mining industry or the goldfields during the 1890s. Water was one noteworthy issue; security was another. As profound underground mining built up, the related threats, including the dry and dusty conditions, turned out to be more than a challenge. In 1894, four miners had died in mines. By 1899 this number had expanded to 45, of whom 38 were working underground. A Royal Commission on Mining prompted new laws identifying many issues, such as ventilation, assurance of deserted shafts, long stretches of working hours, and assessment of alcoholism and mental health.

Progressively, mine well-being—including ventilation, endorsements of competency, just as defensive gadgets, for example, boots and safety helmets presented in 1939—expected high need.

By 1900, working in the mining industry was a very hazardous business that resulted in several deaths. In those early years, miners were notoriously unsafe and ill-equipped. Mining wound up to be known as the "widow creator." A significant number of the diggers who worked them carked it, either from pulmonary sicknesses attributed to exposure of breathing in the fine dust or from alcohol-related liver diseases.

By 1910, "miners phthisis," a general term for silicosis, tuberculosis, or a blend of both was commonly found. Fine dust silica particles inhaled into men's lungs caused scar tissue and fibrosis. All this made the digger progressively vulnerable to chest ailments, for example, tuberculosis. The use of explosive chemicals likewise added to more health-related issues affecting miners.

In isolated Outback locations, extended working hours, mental health, excessive drinking, and drug addictions were common among miners. They were contributing to social issues that affected the mining cultures.

Do men feel an enormous brotherhood peer pressure? To belong, to become one of the blokes, and to go to the bar and drink, whether they're huge consumers or not, irrespective of whether they love or loathe it. You become a part of this drinking culture.

After three years in this town, I had become a miner. I began to realize that I was drinking like the rest of the crowd. I would swear profanity like it was my normal, everyday vocabulary. As much as I liked this way of life, there were days when I hated it and wanted to leave. There were days when I hid in my *donga* and switched off the lights, pretending that I was not in my room, hiding in the corner in the darkness, to avoid the drinking parties. Suddenly a fire extinguisher came crashing through my window, and my drunk mates invaded my *donga*. Men grabbed me around my collar and whisked me off to another beer party with the blokes. They were forcing me to go down the path of alcoholism with them.

FISHING WITH TERROR

Terry the Terror, Filthy Phil, Crazy Steve, Billy the Fish, Wombat, Stretch, and a bunch of other blokes drove through the bush in the Ford Falcons, Holden Toranas, and HQ's, four-wheel drives, heading on a fishing trip, a few miles into the wilderness. They would camp near a billabong, loaded with cartons of beer, steel barbecue hot plates tossed on top of a wood fire, not to mention snags—spuds rolled up in silver foil and thrown into the fire—and sizzling steaks on the hot plates. Terry "The Terror" went fishing. He ran a wire cable to the battery of the car, along the bank of the billabong. He attached a detonator to a few dynamite sticks and wrapped it in plastic. He threw it into the lake, where there were signs of fish. With madness and crazy laughter, like a scene from *Mad Max*, they returned to the car and connected the two wires to the 12-volt battery and set off the charge. There was an explosion in the lake as the sticks of dynamite blew up, A little while later, fish were afloat and were collected by these men.

The nights were filled with drinking and singing; men were throwing nets into the lake and fishing for "yabbies"—a sweetwater crawdaddy-crawfish jumbo. The drinking party continued until the early hours of the morning, till the return to the camp.

I woke up one morning in my *donga*, and a picture of my mother flashed across my mind. I was not sure if she would be proud of me if she saw me that day. I saw a picture in my heart of her praying on bended knee for me. I realized that I had changed, that I had forgotten my core values, that I had become an Aussie miner. The drinking was not my thing, and I needed to get away from here. I had forgotten prayer and church. I had squandered everything I had received through prayer in my life; I had squandered my blessing. I felt lonely, sad, and depressed. Suddenly this place lost its relevance, and my soul felt guilty.

I was down at level fifteen, working on a list of jobs for the afternoon shift that stretched from 3:00 pm to 11:00 pm. There was a mutual understanding between us: the moral obligation to always give the night-shift men a comfortable night. Hence, we tried to complete most of the planned tasks during the day and afternoon shifts. In this way, we helped make it a little easier for those who worked the night shift. Teamwork is a powerful camaraderie found among miners.

There was one pending job in stope thirty-two at level eight; a pneumatic bogger had a control valve that was not working.

I asked Neil, "Are you coming with me, mate?"

Neil replied, "Sorry, digger. I am feeling a bit crook—not really up to it today."

"Alright, then," I replied. "I will go by myself and knock off this small job. It's just a control valve."

I left Neil in the workshop on level fifteen and took the cage up to level eight. I hopped on the battery-fueled train, turned on the lights on my headlamp, and drove straight ahead into the dark passages. I had lost all dread of the murkiness. I had no fear of the darkness, ever since Wolfgang scared the living daylights out of me the first time I'd descended this hole in the ground three years before.

Stope thirty-two was a long way off, and as I moved in the darkness, through the tunnel, flashing my lights at the reflective numbers, I realized that the rail network did not go all the way down to stope thirty-two. I stopped the train on the track at stope thirty. I walked approximately fifty metres towards the reflective sign of stope thirty-two.

It was a small tunnel, away from the main track. There was a large opening at the end of this tunnel, where a large ore body had been discovered, and it resembled a small hill at the end of a passage.

There was a small pneumatic bogger parked there; I saw a winch and a scraper with cables that miners used to drag the ore into two big holes in the ground. The ore scraped down these chutes carved out of the rock; they were about one metre wide and approximately one hundred fifty metres deep, leading to the loading level eleven. There were two of these big holes in the ground. I carefully walked a safe distance from them and approached the bogger. I had my tool bag and grabbed hold of a ½" socket set and took the control lever and assembly apart. I discovered that the circlip lock was broken, causing the control valve to malfunction and incapacitating the bogger from being operational. I replaced the broken circlip and put back the control valve and lever assembly.

I walked over to the bull hose and turned on the air pressure that connected to the pneumatic bogger. I climbed on to the operator's platform and worked the control levers, and the bogger darted forward. My helmet fell forward, and my light went with it. Everything went dark.

I had the cable still connected to my battery, so, I slowly pulled on the cord and retrieved my helmet and headlamp light. In the darkness, I turned the switch on my headlamp into emergency mode. It did not work. I kept turning the switch; the light flickered, and then it went dark.

My headlight was damaged. I kept trying to get it to work, but it had failed. I realized that I had been complacent and never really inspected my headlamp properly at the start of my shift.

There is a policy in the mining industry of daily checks and repairs of headlamps that were routinely carried out by a particular department at the surface. Nevertheless, it was also the responsibility of every person to double-check their lamps before descending into a mine.

My lamp had been damaged and was malfunctioning, and I was in total darkness. I could not see my hands in front of my face; I had never experienced the blackness of darkness like this before.

I was in serious trouble; my only option was to stay put near the bogger. The consequence of my actions would cost me my job. And I had broken a critical, fundamental mining rule: "Never work alone underground. Have a second person with you at all times."

Such an offence led to the termination of an employment contract. I had breached this rule. I had become fearless and complacent and, in this tunnel, I held my hand to my face and pondered my plight in the utter blackness of darkness at stope thirty-two.

If I walked in the darkness, not knowing my exact location, then I might be moving in the wrong direction. My gravest danger would be to walk into one of those holes in the ground. And such an error would send me down a chute one hundred and fifty metres to a particular rocky grave. I stood petrified at the thought of lying dead on a heap of rocks.

My second option was to stick my back to the wall and keep moving along it, making my way out of the tunnel. I knew that, once I'd made it out of the tunnel onto the mainline, I would be safe. Then if I felt the rail line and kept walking along with it in the darkness, I would find the loco train that I had parked fifty metres away. In reality, it was a mammoth task with incredible danger.

I stood there cursing myself for my clumsiness, blaming myself for my arrogance and complacency. I decided to move along the wall, and I moved forward with my back against the wall at all times. I moved my hands in the dark, feeling for anything in front of me. As I slowly progressed with small steps forward, I repeated the same sequence of check, feel, and move. It was not easy by any means. I moved carefully forward and stopped. I was trying to move forward in total darkness. I kept trying to stay calm, but fear was ever present all around me. My mind was racing, and I decided to focus. I felt sweat all over my face, and it dropped like raindrops on my hand. My heart was beating faster, and so I stopped and stayed with my back against the wall. I believe I had moved only about half a metre in the darkness, and it felt like forever.

I kept moving forward again, and, with each step, my calmness slipped away, and fear started to replace it. I was shaking in the dark, and then the thoughts of ghosts came into my head. I froze in total fear and started shaking. My mind remembered the story of the four men who'd died in this part of the mine. I was shaking, and fear had now overtaken me. I stood there in the darkness and started crying. I could not stop crying. Then I remembered God.

I began to cry and pray; I cried and prayed some more. I wept and now was in total fear; crying loudly in a tunnel does not make it any better. It was even scarier as my crying bounced off the walls, and

I imagined the ghosts were there, making fun of me crying in the darkness. I shook myself; I slapped my face with my hands, telling myself, "Get a hold of yourself."

I moved forward slowly with my back against the wall at all times. I lost track of time, but it may have taken me an hour to get out of the tunnel. I knew I was moving forward, but, in the darkness, it's challenging to know where you are going. I sat down in the dark and wept. I prayed to God and asked Him to forgive me.

I had lost all direction in my life and pleaded to Him to get me out of this mess. I cried from the depths of my heart.

I even said this: "Lord, if I don't make it out of here alive, please forgive me. I have let you down and have forgotten you." I had back-slid in my life and was living an awful experience as an Aussie miner. I cried intensely. I started to feel better again. "Forgive me," Lord, I said and stood up. With my back against the wall, I crept agonisingly slowly. I was feeling every inch of ground with my hands on my way, moving precariously forward until I found myself out of the tunnel of stope thirty-two.

I had finally made it out of the most dangerous part. I was still crying and saying, "Thank you, Lord." Sauntering forward in the dark, yearning not to trip and fall, I moved forward, step by step, bending down and feeling for the rail line. I kept up this sequence of two-steps ahead and bend down and feel for that rail line. I did this several times, and then I felt the steel rail. A portion of my mind was still praying relentlessly, for all the months I had forgotten God. This night, my prayers and tears flooded these tunnels of darkness.

I did not have any idea of time; in darkness, time felt like forever, and the very thought of being in it for much longer made me feel dead inside. I kept moving along the track now and was sure that, sooner or later, I would walk into the loco train. We were destined to meet again.

I never stopped praying. Every prayer of my mother came to my heart; I could feel her prayers shroud me like a mantel. I stopped, bent down, and moved my hand forward; I touched a metal block—it was the loco train. I'd found it. I forgot to say, "Thank you, Lord." I held onto the loco train in the dark, made my way to the driver's platform, found the switch in the dark, and turned on the lights. They did not work.

I realized that I had used my headlights on my helmet coming down the track, and, in doing so, I didn't even think about checking if the lights on the loco train worked. I put it in reverse gear and moved in the darkness, back towards the main shaft. I moved backwards at a slow speed, and it took ages to get back. It was the most terrifying experience of my entire life. I felt my trousers were wet and realized that I had also urinated in fear and did not even know it.

I kept moving forward; in the distance, I could see the lights of the main shaft. I burst into tears once again—I had made it out alive! I got to the main shaft and parked the train in its parking bay. I connected the charging system and left a notice—"Do not use"—on the loco train. I approached the bell-ringing codes and rang the emergency bells to the cage man. I felt wet and cold, and I was shaking in fear. I was breathing heavily and feeling claustrophobic.

The yellow cage stopped, and Mike stepped out—blond hair and beard, big fella he was, too.

"Hey, Elvis," he shouted. "Are you alright, mate?"

I was in tears, and, in shock, I whimpered, "Please get me out of here!"

He held me, took a bottle of water from his bag, and gave it to me to drink. "Calm down, mate! She'll be alright. What happened?" he asked.

"I want to go out, mate!" I cried. "Just get me out of this stinking hole, mate!"

He assisted me into the cage, closed the gates, and we shot up in an emergency speed—straight to the surface. I stepped out into the open, fresh air and took a deep breath. I just wanted to see the sky once again. Mike walked me over to the workshop. I went into the showers, dumped all my clothes, walking naked into the showers, turned it on, and cried while the water fell over me. I had never experienced so much fear in my entire life. Darkness is a dreadful certainty. That night, my soul caught a glimpse of something I needed to learn about this life.

I was creeping and crawling through the aphotic tunnels of Longshaft, trying to make it fifty metres ahead, with a certain threat to a horrific end to my life. This gruesome death would surround me if I stumbled or crawled my way, in the darkness, into one of those holes. I would have surely been lying on the rubble of rocks with a nickel grave as my decoration.

I took the company utility vehicle and drove to the Kambalda camp, opened the door to my *donga*, slumped into bed, and went to sleep.

The next day, I went to see Terry Groombridge. I'd been summoned to the office to report about the terrifying incident. I honestly did not care anymore if I was fired or down the road. I knew how I'd gotten out of that hellhole alive. I knew who held me in the darkness and brought me to that loco train, and I saw the picture of my mother praying for me when I closed my eyes. I could not care less about the job anymore. I would be happy to leave anyway.

My boss issued a severe warning about the safety rules I had broken and the gravity of the incident and complacency of my actions. The reality was that I had never put the mine or anybody's life in danger except my own. Terry Groombridge did not fire me; secretly, he was glad I'd made it out without any injury. I knew that he knew it was a gutsy performance of getting out of stope thirty-two. He was a very seasoned individual and knew better than me; he knew that it was a miracle I did not get killed.

Two months after the experience of stope number thirty-two, I was working with Wolfgang at the same level eight. The deadly harrows, the place where men had died a long time ago, a place where rumors existed that the spirit of dead men moved in the darkness, was an eerie place. We were in a tunnel looking up a shaft, as the men at level five were lowering an electrical motor, with ropes and slings, down this rocky hole. The motor of the scraper was damaged and needed replacement. We kept looking at the chute upwards as the motor was lowered down. We were shouting messages back to the men at level five. It was a dangerous operation—a primary method using pulleys and an "A" frame with ropes.

Wolfgang and I stood directly under the hole as the motor was lowered, shining our lights up the dark shaft. Suddenly this feeling came over me—like a rush of blood to my head. A voice, an instinct, was telling me to get out of there, a message I understood in my spirit.

It was like an unknown power of protection. I grabbed Wolfgang's hand and pulled him hard; He was surprised, I think. I must have yanked hard, as it was an instinctive reaction, a feeling of danger, death, and destruction.

"What's wrong?" he asked.

"I don't trust it, mate," I replied. I had barely said it when we heard men shouting from the level five above us, "Get out! Get out!"

We were already out; then we heard a big rumbling noise down the shaft. The electrical motor came hurtling down the shaft. It crashed at the bottom at level eight, where we were standing about a minute earlier.

We would have been killed or seriously injured. It was all just too much for me. In three months, I came close to being killed twice. I needed to get out of the Longshaft.

I had made up my mind that I was going to quit my job and leave. I did not want to see an underground tunnel again. I was not afraid of underground mining, but I wanted out. I returned to my room and lay there, wondering if I was ever going to miss this place and all the mates I had met here. It was tough to decide to leave them. I had come to this place as a youngster, and in three years, I had become a real man.

As I contemplated my thoughts, I realized I had to get out to save myself from this life of dangerous work and alcohol abuse.

The following week, I resigned my job and gave notice of my departure. It was not well received by some of my mates. They figured that I should reconsider my decision, but I knew the time had come for me to take a break and revaluate my life once more.

I worked at level fifteen underground for the next three weeks; I did not attempt to return to level eight or stope thirty-two again. I never wanted to see that hellhole anymore. I was thankful that I did not end up dead in this place.

After working the day shift, I walked back to my *donga* and found a package left near my doorstep. It was a bag of liquorice candy, shaped in the form of small brown people, with a handmade card written in black ink. I opened the packet, popped a few candies into my mouth, and began to read the handwritten card. It happened to be my birthday this day.

The card read as follows.

An Ode to Lyndon
Happy Birthday to the Happiest Black Fella
we have ever known.

Miles and Miles, he travelled, he did come from afar
A dusty pack in one hand and the other he held a guitar.
He entered Kambalda SPQ to have a hard-earned beer
When his mates cried out from the back, hey black Elvis is here.
He played all balmy night, and he played all sweaty day.
They told the little bugger to stop, but he said no bloody way
He's got a cheery smile to match his happy mood
Nobody knows his real name they just call him the dude
But when he leaves Kambalda as smoothly as he came
They all know deep in their hearts; it will never be the same.

I wrapped up the sonnet, while my eyes welled up with tears. I was leaving my mates. I felt profoundly dismal. They were like siblings to me, and I was the wanderer of OZ.

The following week, there was a big "Barbecue Grog" party arranged by my mates, in the town of Kambalda at Janes Place. It was a huge party; everyone turned up with a slab of beer. There was a 205-litre drum filled with ice and beer, two barbecue fireplaces arranged, heaps of food, and music blasting. It was a rage.

Then came all the jokes and the banter, followed by the "shoey"—drinking beer from someone's shoe, some kind of Aussie beer-cult tradition. The others were getting drunk and resorting to having cans of beer turn into a shotgun competition. Famous Aussie Beer Games.

Then someone fell into the swimming pool or got pushed; that triggered laughter and fun while another ten people got into the pool. Billy the Fish almost got drowned as he lay in the bottom. As they fished him out, I heard other blokes say, "Silly old git." It was not a serious incident. Billy the Fish was never going to change. The more beer-filled his gut, the more he took on incredible challenges. These were wild parties that ended only in the early hours of the morning. The following day, there were a bunch of blokes laid up in the garden and people crashed all over the place. I managed to survive this night.

I somehow escaped the heavy drinking; I collected twenty-two big garbage bags of empty beer cans. My Goodbye Party was a classic Outback farewell.

I left Kambalda the following week; it was now a part of my history. I loved the whole experience, and I did meet some good people there. I formed some fantastic friendships, and I learned the deep, rich culture of Aussie mate-ship and teamwork while I worked underground. The drinking was not my thing, and I struggled with something that I knew would ruin me and my life. I had descended into the world's second-deepest mine and survived to tell the tale. I looked back for one last time as we drove out of the SPQ site. I waved at the blokes, as we turned left and headed off to Perth—I knew I would never see Kambalda ever again.

I drove the old Volvo 240 Deluxe that I had picked up at Kambalda for $1800 and made the journey to Perth with two mates, Tony and Big Dave. We had all quit our jobs simultaneously. Working underground does get to a man psychologically. It felt great to be on the road again. We made a few pub stops along the way, feeling relieved that we had no more underground days to endure anymore at Kambalda.

We drove past Southern Cross as the music played and Dave was sleeping in the back seat. Big Dave was from New Zealand. Six feet six, 240 pounds of a big man, who always landed with a big thud when he parachuted on Sundays at the Kambalda flying club. I recall one incident when his parachute got caught on some gum trees on his descent, while he was trying to steer away from landing on them. He ripped the parachute and still managed to land with a big thud. When you heard it, everyone would joke and say, "I reckon Big Dave has just landed."

We drove past a lonely service station about 250 kilometres from Southern Cross, when the Volvo 240 started coughing and jerking; then, she just died. It was 42°C outside. We moved to the side of the road and attempted to start up this old Swedish beauty. She cranked, but she would not fire up. I looked at the fuel gauge, and it indicated half tank. We tried again, but she would not come to life. We checked the cables and the spark plugs, and they were all excellent, but she would not fire up.

We looked into the tank with a flashlight. I ducked underneath the car and tapped the fuel tank with a spanner; it sounded empty. We had run out of fuel. The fuel gauge was faulty and had malfunctioned. We were fortunate that we did not end up stranded in the middle of nowhere. We pushed the car about 2 kilometres to the service station we had just passed. We were lucky.

It was a hot day, and the sun was beating on us. We got into the station and parked the car at the pump. When an older lady approached us, she smiled and said, "Sorry, Love—I reckon we are both in the same bother here. We have run out of fuel this morning and are awaiting the supply truck to turn up today or by tomorrow." I stood there dumbfounded.

"Are you serious?" I replied.

"Sorry, Love," she apologised. "Hope you fellas have a couple of jerry cans. I can give you some if you need some."

I shook my head in disbelief.

Tony and Dave smiled at me and said, "At least we don't have a pub that has no beer."

The old lady disappeared back into the roadhouse, while we men discussed the hitchhiking trip that I was going to have to make to Southern Cross to bring back some fuel.

As I prepared to move the car to park it and remove the two jerry cans from the boot of the car, the old lady returned, smiling, just as I was about to move.

I had this strange feeling that she was enjoying the misery we were in, because of the smile she was wearing on her face. She never stopped smiling. She stood there and said, "Do you want me to fill it up?" She took hold of the hose and the filling nozzle. I was surprised and confused. I protested.

"You told me just a little while ago you had no fuel."

"I know what I told you, Love," she responded, laughing jokingly. Pointing to the window, she said, "Can you see the old bloke at the window?"

I looked up, and the old fella was smiling and waving at me. I said, "Yep, I see him."

"Well," she said, "he has had a damn good laugh at your expense." Then she laughed hysterically.

I laughed with her because it was funny. I knew that I was the joke of the day, and, when the laughing died down, she spoke again.

"Well, he saw you blokes pushing the car in the hot sun. He told me to come out here and tell you fellas that we had run out of fuel—said he'd love to see the look on your faces.

"He is a mean old sod, you see," she said and then laughed again. "He was having a go at you fellas, but he has a few free beers for your blokes. So go and get them while I fill up the fuel for you."

We all cracked up laughing.

As we walked in, the old bloke was still having a laugh at at us.

I looked at him and said, "Cheeky fellas—you had us cobber."

"Oh, mate, that was a pearler," he replied. "The look on your faces!" Then he laughed out loud again. He handed us three pints of beer as we all laughed together.

The old fella smiled and said, "Well, the old girl and I live out here in the whop-whops, and every once in a while, we have people like yourselves who run out of fuel. We don't miss out on the opportunity to have a good laugh, mate. Then he added, "It does get lonely out here sometimes, but we love it."

We appreciated this fantastic couple, and it was a classic Outback sense of humour. We had some meat pies, a few more beers, and some good laughs at the pub. We learned a golden rule that day: "Never drive around the Outback without some extra fuel in jerry cans in the boot of vehicle."

We arrived in Perth the next day and drove straight to the Holden Car Yard at Quality Motors at Inglewood. I traded the Volvo Deluxe for a Holden Statesman V8 five-litre engine, a car painted in metallic blue. It included an edge and semi-monocoque (unibody) development. It was the primary full-size Holden to have curl spring-back suspension. As a cost-sparing measure, it was built for right-hand, so it was a unique Australian car. We took it for a test drive and struck a deal with the car salesman. I told the man to get all the papers ready and that we would come back in an hour and pick up the car.

I thanked Tony and Big Dave for all the assistance I had received and for the great friendship we had shared along the way. We parted that day, and I hoped we would meet up again someday, yonder. Sometimes you never see some people ever again.

CHAPTER 8

THE OUTBACK FOREVER

After spending a few weeks in Perth meeting old friends, I packed all my tools and gear into my Holden Statesman HQ and drove into the Outback of Australia forever. I was an endless nomad. My skin was now innately merging into the red dust as I disappeared into a painting of a culture and a people waiting to embrace my destiny with theirs, something that would change my love for this red land forever.

I drove back to Kalgoorlie and stopped along my favourite places where I had become acquainted with the people who chose to live the Outback way of life. I stopped at the roadhouse of the old couple who'd made a laughing stock out of me the last time I ran out of fuel. It was like meeting old friends. They had an awesome Outback sense of humour. I was so much the wiser from the experience. I always carried forty litres of fuel and essential spare parts at all times. A few blokes at the pub in Kalgoorlie told me about some work at an open-cut mine in Leonora. So, I picked up the phone and called the man about it, giving him details of my experiences and credentials and references for the reputation I had established in the goldfields. I soon received a call back that I could come to Leonora and start up with a new job offer. It was just that simple in Australia—your reputation and character were worth more than the qualifications you possessed on some silly academic paper.

I drove the following morning through the wilderness towards Leonora; it was January 14, 1991. I entered into an ancient historical place that the Aboriginal people called *Wongatha*. My first real contact with an ancient people was about to originate at this Outback town. Before the appearance of gold miners, the region had been scantily populated by individuals from the nearby Wangkathaa Aboriginal community.

In April 1869, the pilgrim John Forrest went through the territory, searching for the lost pioneer Ludwig Leichhardt. He named Mount Leonora on June 20, 1869.

In 1895, a miner named Booden found alluvial gold in a crevasse around thirty-seven kilometres northwest of the present site of Leonora.

In 1896, Edward "Doodah" Sullivan discovered gold six kilometres from Leonora, and in March of that year, he pegged the Johannesburg rent. In May 1896, the Sons of Gwalia Reef was founded by miners named Carlson, White, and Glendinning. By September 1896, the Sons of Gwalia Mine had pulled in £300,000 from the capital venture.

On May 1, 1898, Herbert Hoover, later to move toward becoming president of the United States, was elected general manager of the Sons of Gwalia. In 1904, the assistant government geologist C. F. V. Jackson completed a topographical review of the territory.

The Leonora townsite was announced on April 15, 1898; the town was officially gazetted on August 21, 1900. In 1903, a steam tramway connected Leonora and Gwalia. After two years, the tramway was connected to Menzies and the primary railroad line to Perth. By 1925, various pastoralists had moved into the region, proposing to raise sheep for their fleece. In 1949, managing a deficiency of work, the Sons of Gwalia dispatched sixty-seven excavators from Italy. Just thirty-one were still working at the mine a year later. On December 13, 1963, it was declared that the Sons of Gwalia Mine would close. When it shut on December 27, 1963, the Sons of Gwalia had created more than 2 million ounces of gold. The expanding cost of gold in 1980 saw the mine's revival. The celebrated Tower Hill mine was revived in 1983, and the Harbour Lights mine appeared in 1985.

In the late spring of 2012 or 2013, named the "Angry Summer" by the Climate Commission, the temperature in Leonora arrived at another recorded high of 49°C. I don't believe this record to be accurate. I remember a blistering day in Leonora when the mercury measured 51°C.

The Wongi people, extremely dynamic in their customary nation, were the first to show European and British travellers their nation, prominently water and valuable minerals in their nation. The Wongi demonstrated to Irish wayfarer and pioneer Paddy Hannan his first gold chunk. Being an important stone, the Wongi revered it due to their conventional *tjukurrpa* (lore) under their customary practices and administration frameworks. Still today, the *tjukurrpa* is regarded and exceptionally respected. During the mid-1900s, the Wongatha/Wangkatha were considered the "most savage wild-people" out of all the Aboriginal tribes in Western Australia. The Australian government didn't have a clue on how to manage these individuals. They did not care about these individuals or consider the impact of a beer binge-drinking culture that mining was.

The Wongi, as an indigenous Australian social order, showed impressive social variety yet stayed discernible from other Indigenous Australian tribes. I would, before long, observe the annihilation of an antiquated people segregated and called *boongs*. I heard a significant verbal presentation of numbness among white alcoholic individuals who said the most unfeeling words to depict native individuals. *Boong* was alluded to the sound you would make if the bull bar on your four-wheel drive hit one of these native individuals; the sound would seem like *boong*, like running over a kangaroo in the Outback.

In the words of author and researcher Stephen J. Bedells, from Cowan University, "Nearly 90 percent of the detainees at the Eastern Goldfields Regional Prison in Boulder were indigenous, although they accounted for just 10 percent of the populace in the district. While investigating the veracity of these claims from a few government workers inside the criminal equity framework in Kalgoorlie and found that the fact of the matter was considerably, additionally surprising? Since the nearby gaol was packed, countless Wongi detainees were moved 600 kilometres to serve their sentences in penitentiaries in Perth. As a police officer, I was playing an accidental piece of a framework where Wongi individuals were, in effect, over-represented in the equity framework. Stunned by this disclosure, I talked about conceivable research extends with Dr. Milnes that would give me a progressively more-precise point of view about the impacts that such a high imprisonment rate was having on the Wongi individuals. We chose that the Wongi network pioneers, some of whom I had fashioned associations with over the past seven years, could talk with power and knowledge about the impacts of Wongi imprisonment in their locale." The author further started to "take a look at the over-portrayal of indigenous individuals at each phase of the criminal equity framework crosswise over both Western Australia and Australia." He discovered that "Western Australia detains about twofold the national normal of indigenous individuals proportionate to their populace than any other State in Australia, furthermore, above multiple times the pace of the standard populace." I had lived in Leonora in 1991, twenty years before several research reports and studies regarding the incarceration of indigenous people of the Wongatha lands in the eastern goldfields of Western Australia.

I was deeply moved to see the plight of these ancient people. There was a beaten-up old pub in the town that was filled with miners; it was predominantly Caucasians who filled the pubs with the daily drinking ritual. Out on the dusty streets, native Aboriginal men would beg for a smoke or a beer. The adjoining red, dusty corner streets that connected to the main streets occasionally were inhabited by Aboriginal women who would solicit for cash or beer. Some would cheekily supplicate offers of sexual favours.

As I walked towards my camp with a bag of soft drinks, a native woman walked up to me and offered me sexual favours in exchange for the beer she imagined was inside my bag. I reached into my bag and give her a soft drink.

She took the soft drink and then asked me for money so that she could buy beer. I was not going to play any part in the destruction of the native people; I walked away with a heavy heart. I wanted to give her some money, but the thought of seeing her lying in a drunken stupor would be heartbreaking. I felt deeply sad for the Aboriginal people, and my encounters with them in Lenora gave birth to a desire in my heart to know them better.

I wanted to understand, learn, and help them. I saw the hopelessness in their eyes as the descending of the white man's demons of alcohol abuse had infiltrated an ancient culture, while the wealth of the land was being separated from the profundities of the earth. Similar to the dull shadows in the red dust, their reality overwhelmed me, such as being burned by the flares of sadness. Aboriginal men, women, and their children were being destroyed.

The sweltering balminess at the open-cut mine was savage, and by the end of the day, the exhaustion was overwhelming. The mining camps were filled with men, imprecation, sweat, and beer; it was the way of life. Jerry, the lord of the Esky ice boxes, maintained the status quo as the keeper of the jokes and the beloved cold, golden-yellow-blond-coloured beverage—beer.

He would toss a can at you with a familiar phrase: "There you go, bloke. The first beer is better than your mother's milk." Another one was "Get that down you, mate—it's like an angel has just pissed on your tonsils fair dinkum." Beer was a beverage and not considered alcohol in this part of the world. Alcoholism was a potentially dangerous addiction—you had to keep your wits about you. I was not going to let this portion of the Outback culture get the better of me. I refused to drink like my workmates. I had to find a balance and not become a social outcast.

I started to reach out to the native people and make contact with them. I felt a deep attraction to their history and culture; my first encounters were with the ones who had been infected by the white man's disease of alcohol. From as far back as when white men set foot in Australia more than two hundred years prior, they have abused, bugged, tormented, and tyrannised the individuals they found there. The more inhumane decised that the best method for managing a world of people groups who might always be unable to adjust to the "white fella" system was to dispense with them as fast as could be expected under the circumstances, so they shot and harmed them. Others accepted that they owed it to their God to protect the misguided savage, strip him of his agnostic culture, dress his bareness, and show him the estimation of work. Disregarding the first occupants was never a choice; gaining from them was past any idea of what was correct and legitimate. To the extent that the pink individuals were concerned, dark Australians were crude people groups, survivors from the Stone Age in a land that time had overlooked.

Out here in the Outback, drunken white men who worked in lonely Outback mining towns took sexual favours from native women who sold them for the same alcohol that destroyed their spirit and souls. White men called these women *black gins*. In the desperation of their lustful spirits and flesh, they took advantage of the young Aboriginal women and had sexual relationships. A few children were conceived, and they were called "half-caste." These things never happened openly, yet it was cryptic. There was a term for white men caught having sexual relationships with native women. They were known as *gin jockeys*. No white man wanted to be called a "gin jockey," but half-caste children were being conceived.

I developed friendships with Aboriginal people and played footy games with these half-caste children. I could feel an association with them, since I was an Anglo-Indian, and they were Anglo-Aboriginal. I additionally saw that their ancestral language bore a few similitudes to the language of individuals from the profound south of India.

I was naturally teased by my working colleagues and being accused of being a "gin jockey," but there was enough respect in my heart that did not exist in theirs for the native people. It astounded me how individuals can erroneously pass judgment on you because they see the world from a wicked soul and chuck misleading indictments against you by believing your soul to be equivalent to their lost paths.

I spent my weekends with the native people and tried to talk them into controlling their dependence on the white man's poison alcohol. I wanted to make a difference, but it was a terrible reality, a continuing heartbreak, to see Aboriginal people lying drunk under a tree; it was like some demon had possessed them. They had lost themselves and had descended into an abyss of self-destruction. Nobody cared for what was happening to these people and how this mining industry had no respect or any form of corporate social responsibility. Such terms were not known in the early 1990s, and even if they were known, they amounted to only a policy written on a piece of paper but never carried out in reality.

I struggled in my heart seeing the plight and dependency on alcohol among Aboriginal people. I was caught between the devil and the deep blue sea, for the first time since I had lived in Australia, a country where I had never known of racism or discrimination. It simply did not exist until I left the cities and came to live in the loneliness of the Outback. Out there, the reality and plight of the Aboriginal people was a stark reminder that kept me awake at nights thinking about the terrible injustice being done to these people. I was no better than the other white fellas and felt compelled to do something about it. I first had to make friends and gain the trust of these native people.

One night, as I lay asleep on my bed in my *donga*, I kept my doors open to allow for some natural breeze to blow through from across the open desert plains that lay before me. I was suddenly awoken, attentively, to see a dark, shadowy figure of a large Aboriginal woman. I recognised her from the town of Leonora. She had entered my bedroom, opened the icebox, took two sixpacks, and walked away with them into the darkness. I watched her go and failed to say a word. I lay there, still feigning sleep. I noticed she was not interested in the several dollar bills that were available on the table; she did not touch the money, just the beer. Aboriginal folks are hunters and gatherers; they don't steal and aren't thieves. She was just gathering what she wanted. I felt sad for their plight, realizing how they were self-destructing themselves, and the white man could not care less.

This attitude was not uncommon among Australian people; maybe it was the agenda of the white man from the day Captain Cook landed on these fatal shores. They never considered the native people as human beings. These policies, bent on the destruction of the native Aboriginal people, have had a long, dark history in this country. I did not know the history then; I was not educated about them. Nevertheless, I was in the Outback; the reality was before my very eyes, working with the white fellas, watching them destroy the black fellows, and caught in between were the half-castes—the brown fellas like myself.

I was now experiencing the truth among the people, perceiving their destruction. It was a clash of two worlds: one was white, and it was filled with endless greed for mineral resources and privileges of pride and sense of superiority; the other was an ancient world of peace within their spirits and belonging to the land of their ancestors, a way of living life in total harmony with nature. It did not make sense to me that evil would overcome good; the darkness of the night gives life to the rising of the sun.

However, the reality on the ground with the clash of these two worlds was the total lack of respect of the white illegal immigrants towards the native people. White illegal immigrants had come to settle on this land without any permission from the original inhabitants. I imagined if the Aboriginal people had a proper government set up 219 years ago, the native government would have set up a point system for the intruders, discouraged criminal-record holders, and denied alcoholics entry into this land, considered a threat to the national security of the native people. It's an imaginative thought.

Meet the warrior of Australia, the Sitting Bull of Botany Bay. Two years after the appearance of the First Fleet, Aboriginal warrior Pemulwuy started to oppose the invasion of white pioneers onto his kin's customary grounds. In spite of being injured in 1797, he escaped being apprehended according to the white man's desires to steal his freedom.

He was born a free man and lived until 1802, when he was shot dead. Pemulwuy's head was sliced off and sent to Sir Joseph Banks for his accumulation. Ever since that day, Australians have been cutting off the heads of their native people one way or the other. I learned about Aboriginal communities where alcohol was banned, and I desired to go up north and find a way to live with them. Australian politicians were never deeply interested in the welfare of its native people; it has a dark and dreadful history, which every Australian should come to recognise and accept.

The destruction and killing of the Aboriginal people's culture and way of life was the greatest annihilation in human history, perpetrated by men who had the evil notion that they were superior as a human race. As the saying goes, "Actions speak louder than words." The record shows: Cain killed Abel, the commandment says, "Thou shall not kill," but you have killed—men, women, and children.

I spent six months in this dusty town called Leonora. I was tired of the life out there and of the constant pressure and culture of alcohol consumption. The destruction of my spirit within me was taking its toll, and the plight of the native people made it even sadder. I quit my job and left Leonora. I drove the Holden Statesman into the dusty road that took me to a remote place called Wiluna. There was a period, back around the 1930s, when Wiluna was a flourishing mining town with a populace of around nine thousand individuals. In 1991, it was a solitary, lonely town. Wiluna is situated at the southern end of the Canning Stock Route and the western finish of the Gunbarrel Highway. These are the absolute most risky and testing drives on the planet. The Canning Stock Route is 1,500 km from Wiluna, north to Halls Creek (or the other way around) through the Great Sandy Desert and the Gibson Desert, past immense salt lakes. The Gunbarrel Highway makes a trip east from Wiluna to Uluru and Yulara and is rough enough to test the determination of any vehicle and its occupants. It is a fundamental place; you can get yourself killed if you are stranded. I did not know of the real risks, but I went there anyway. Preceding the appearance of Europeans, the Ngangganawili Aboriginal people lived and travelled through the region, and I was now one of them.

I drove in the night to avoid the blistering heat of the day. It was dark as my headlights scanned the dusty road ahead. I maintained the engine speed slightly above idle and cautiously rolled into the darkness. I realised that I was in a remote part of this immensity and did not want to find myself lost out here. I did not even know why I chose to drive out to Wiluna. I had no idea. I just wanted to get away from Leonora, I suppose.

I slowed almost to a crawl as a wombat crossed my path. I saw bandicoots and other types of marsupials scurrying across the dirt road. As I moved into the lonely darkness on the dusty road, I saw him sitting with his back facing towards me. *Bang!* Right in the middle of the dusty road, tall and robust, the most magnificent red kangaroo I had ever seen. I honked at him; he stood up, looking in the opposite direction. I eased back my vehicle to a slither, loosened up my window, prodded my head, and called out to him, "Hello, *Macropus rufus*. Here, mate, you silly bugger." He stood up on his incredible rear legs; he was a big red male kangaroo, more than six feet tall. He turned and took a look at me. I affectionately called him out, "Ain't you a handsome-looking roo-mate. Get off the road, you silly bugger." He remained there, looking at me as I ground to a halt, a chance to appreciate him. I killed the high-beam light, as I did not want to hurt his eyes with the glare. He stood his ground for more than thirty seconds.

The message translated into his calcaneal tendon that probably stretched all the way back his hind legs; like an elastic band that was released from its point of tension, he released himself from the surface of the dirt road. His big, red, muscular body and tail lifted into the air in one enormous graceful leap, and, with a second bounce, he disappeared into the darkness. I sat in my car and embraced the moments I had with him; this was an Outback country.

I drove slowly for several hours until I felt tired. I parked the Statesman across the dirt road under some gum trees. I grabbed my blanket, dived into the back seat of my car, and slept like a child in the cradle of the Outback.

Wiluna was a classical, lonely Aussie town with only a few people around. The mining town is a classic example of human greed. When the mines and gold have shut down and the people who are all materialistic have all gone, the native people and the kangaroos remain true to the land. I drove to the only service station I could find and filled up my car and jerry cans with fuel. I spent the day talking to the local Indigenous people.

If I worked for *National Geographic*, perhaps I'd find this one of the most interesting places to make a documentary film and stay here for a while. I waited for the early-rising sun the next day and drove on to Meekatharra. I had slightly missed the peak season of spring, and, judging from the flora and unique plants around me, the territory around this area is one of the most astounding in the Murchison district, with emotional presentations extending over the scene. It is prominent, especially for the Sturt's desert pea.

> Captain Charles Sturt (1795–1869) noticed the event of *Swainsona Formosa* in 1844 while investigating among Adelaide and central Australia, and the regular name, Sturt's Desert Pea, remembers a striking pilgrim of inland Australia, just as showing the plant's environment and family. Sturt's diary, *Narrative of an Expedition into Central Australia*, alludes a few times to the magnificence of the desert pea in bloom and the cruel idea of its natural surroundings, and notes that past the Darling River: "As he portrayed it, we saw that excellent blossom, the *Clianthus Formosa*, in astonishing bloom on the fields. It was developing amid futility and decomposition, yet its long sprinters were secured with blooms that gave a blood-red tint to the ground."

> —(Australian National Herbarium "Floral Emblems— Australian Plant Information." South Australia—Floral Emblems—Australian Plant Information. February 15, 2020.)

As I caught the remnant of the spectacular spring flora exposition of the beautiful Australian desert blooms, I stepped into the mind of the early explorers and caught a glimpse of how their minds must have operated, seeing the beauty and the ancient people who lived here. In the beauty of the vastness, they neglected to notice the remarkable beauty of the ancient people who lived here, considering them the flora and fauna of this nation, writing it into their psyches and constitution.

I came across wild emus and many kangaroos along the way; suddenly, sitting on a rock, was the most outstanding sight of the wedge-tailed eagle (Kurrawurra). I stopped dead on my tracks; my heart suddenly felt deeply drawn to his majesty on the rock. A deep sense of admiration and love burst forth inside my heart as I watched him sitting there. I instinctively killed the engine of my car. I had come face-to-face with something spiritually, iconically beautiful, and in this moment of mutual admiration, my spirit and the eagle embraced each other like two wanderers under this desert sky. We were so close to each other, I could see his talons and sharp beak; his plumage was shining in the sun, and he was aware of my presence. I could sense his wisdom; nothing could escape the gaze of his eyes. I wanted to hug him—step out the car and just hug him. For a brief moment in time, the amazing connection was established. I felt deep spiritual pangs in my heart. I remembered the childhood hunting times with my father, the wanderings in the Indian forests, the duck-hunting shoot-out. I suddenly remembered my loved ones. I looked at the eagle and wondered if he'd share his hunting stories for mine around a campfire while we dined on some prey. Could he tell me about his wanderings and listen while I tell him of mine? Maybe his wisdom could point me in the right direction, show me the way to go. I was completely wrapped in his gaze and beauty. I looked on as he spread his wings and lifted with utmost grace into the blue sky; then, like a blessing or a goodbye, he screamed into the wilderness and flew away. I watched him as he soared into the sky. I felt more connected to the spirit of the eagle than all the other creatures in the world. For that brief moment in time, I closed my eyes and wished I could soar alongside him. This encounter was a lifelong association, and its lessons were only beginning.

Author Penny Oslen in her book *Wedge-Tailed Eagle*, describes in great detail the beauty of the Australian Wedge-Tailed Eagle:

> First showing up in Aboriginal rock painting artworks over 5000 years back, the Wedge-Tailed Eagle was minimally more than an anomaly to the early European pilgrims. The author Penny Olsen in her book *Wedge-Tail Eagle*, follows the ensuing changes in discernment—from the white man's given reputation as an awful sheep executioner to a notable species deserving of preservation.

—(*Wedge-Tailed Eagle*, Penny Olsen, 2005)

It has long, genuinely expansive wings, completely feathered legs, and an indisputable wedge-moulded tail. In light of the two—its tail and its size—it is perhaps the biggest winged creature of prey on the planet. It very well may be recognised initially as a "wedgie."

The promptest human records of the wedge-tail hawks are found in the stone-art compositions that were a piece of the religion and practical existence of Australian Aboriginal clans. In Western Australia, the natives of the Kimberley painted some especially wonderful and simple, conspicuous art onto a rock-cave sanctuary, in any event, 5000 years back.

Wedge-Tail Eagles are so recognizable, incredible, and inescapable that it is amazing that they have had firm eminence in Aboriginal custom and folklore. A few south-eastern moieties, a division of society that governs customs and relationships, are named after the eagle and the crow. The ancient story of the Eagle and the Crow is at the centre of Aboriginal culture. Albeit based for the most part around the Murray Darling River framework, variants of their antiquated legend have been transmitted, similar to the upper-east regions of Western Australia.

The Eagle-Crow legend recounts Wildu the Eagle, who was vexed because his nephews the crows had not welcomed him to their dance celebration; the crows were all white back then. Eagle watched them from a slope, and, following the ending of the late-night party of the crows, they went into a cavern to rest. At that point, Wildu the Eagle came and consumed them with fire, and that is how the crows came to be dark. The legendary otherworldly and mental importance among ancestral individuals informs them regarding social exercises that are even scriptural.

Likewise, with increasingly nitty-gritty renditions, the straightforward story communicates the essential human wants and their outcomes. Without social controls. Normally the Eagle-Crow fantasy is worked around the polarity of solidarity—tricky, father-child, and contention over their moms and spouses. In this way, it is frequently sexual, strengthening taboos over inbreeding and other socially endorsable sexual associations. Fire speaks of sexuality or life itself, and, when the crow behaves recklessly, as a discipline, the more-dominant Eagle guarantees that the Crow gets burnt.

—(*Wedge-Tailed Eagle*, Penny Olsen, 2005)

Because the white man considered them to be savages, it was clear that the eye of the spectator was defective and regrettable; it was drained of all learning and comprehension. It was the obliviousness of the white man that was predominant. The average Australian neglected to understand the profundity of these accounts and how these ancient stories protected a social order that existed among these astounding individuals. There was no requirement for some white-man laws to be authorised here. These people were true environmentalists; a profound culture existed here in the Outback.

The laws that were enforced by the settlers and conquerors were certainly not in the interest of these ancient people; they were draconian and made to oppress, depress, and drive them into a terrible drudgery of all manner of poison, including the alcohol the British convict colonisation inflicted on these people.

According to researchers Raymond Evans and Robert Ørsted-Jensen, "Provincial states additionally made native police forces, that watched and 'scattered' Aboriginal individuals. Convicts were enrolled in these and other twisted gatherings. Investigation of volunteers uncovers that many had earlier military experience recommending that the provincial government utilised convicts with fitting abilities as a feature of its endeavour to 'assuage' the Outback." According to the researchers (Raymond Evans and Robert Ørsted-Jensen 2014), "there was evidence that, between state police and native police, the state-supported Outback killings in Queensland alone counted more than 65,000 individuals, between 22 and 26 percent of the pre-colonial population of Aboriginal natives." According to authors Hamish Maxwell-Stewart and Deborah Oxley, from the Digital Panopticon project team:

> Convict Australia is an account of sharp differentiation. The provincial concoction blended intimidation with opportunity, hardship with circumstance, an expression that was both solid and feeble, a financial supernatural occurrence with disaster, black with white.

> Colonisers demolished property rights and all the while commended them. A so-called cultivated country legitimised massacre. This came about because of a correctional approach, yet that strategy was likewise at the administration of British majestic aspirations, particularly against the French. The British government had handled exactly 160,000 offenders in Australia's

convict states and initiated a procedure that confiscated maybe one million Indigenous individuals. Persevering results over the hundreds of years make Australia's frontier history a live political subject.

—(Stewart and Oxley, 2004)

Today, one of the oldest known tribal cultures in the world are these Aboriginal people. I was now in the Outback, and my genuine love for these people opened doors that would take me into the world of Dreamtime. That wedge-tailed eagle sitting on the rock was an ancient spiritual call. I did not completely understand the journey ahead or the significance of his close appearance. I know most people would not think much of it. After all, it was just an eagle. Yet, I knew in my spirit that it was far more than this. I was in Dreamtime Outback land.

I'd heard about this ancient Dreamtime, but experiencing it was something else, so to best describe this, I employed the words of native people to cite the following research by Reconciliation Australia (2006):

"Imagining" or "Dreamtime" are English words that depict a rich Aboriginal and Torres Strait Islander idea. As a general rule, it is difficult to discover words that sufficiently catch this central component of what their identity is. Nevertheless, it's something you feel when you sit with them like family and hear the accounts with an acquiescent attitude and heart.

Dreaming is additional of a legendary past; it endorses the Aboriginal individuals with the profound embodiment of everything around them and beyond. Visualising stories are not just from the past; they are outside of time—constantly present and offering significance to all parts of their life.

The Dreaming is passed from age to age through stories, melody, the corroboree dance and expressing dreams in art. The deep connection between man and beast, like Adam taking care of the animals under his dominion in the Garden of Eden, all of this information gives them an extraordinary obligation and is viewed as a significant privilege.

For instance, they are encouraged to tell a story or dance about the movements of antiquated creation spirits and predecessors from water-hole to water-hole; they become the holder of this deep spiritual connection from the past to the present.

The idea of Aboriginal Dreaming has been portrayed as the mantel isolating physical life from presence outside of genuine life is far less unmistakable and undeniably more penetrable than that accomplished by non-indigenous people groups. The collective information and insight of the grandparents and extraordinary ancestors in their living and the spiritually connected state are stored into the aggregate "asset bank" when they pass on into death.

With the dreadful history of the convict colonisation of this nation as a backdrop, I was venturing into a land and a culture that were far more spiritually richer than I was prepared to receive. My recent associations with Aboriginal people and my genuine affection for them were opening windows of greater understanding of them. Of all things that a human can possess, the feeling of genuine love would have to be the most gratifying emotion of human life, a fundamental spiritual sensation necessary for building relationships. Without love, a man is as empty as a hollow, wood-carved creation of himself. I pondered as I drove on to Meekatharra. I remembered my mother teaching me to pray as a child, and the lessons she taught me from the Bible. "Do unto others as you would want them to do unto you."

I started to measure the scale and the enormity of Western Australia, similar to the endless highways that can lead you into extinction. Every town we passed through had a similar country framework: a mail depot, a few taverns, a provision store, a church, and a police station. Every township had proof of history but bore signs of human struggle. The number of inhabitants in every town we passed through was low—a nearly phantom-town feel. When I left Kalgoorlie and headed across to Wiluna, the principal indications of the immense salt pans started to show up. The tone of the sky and the earth started to appear into gold, to shades of blue and ochre. Notwithstanding the superficially dry surface, hidden underneath the sun-heated surface, thick pockets of dampness were concealed. Similarly, the concealment of the treatment of Aboriginal people by the convict settlers was all far too apparent to my eyes. It pained me as I watched the wretchedness that had descended on an amazing people.

CHAPTER 9

THE ELIMINATION HISTORY

PRIDE: THE UNCLEAN ACT

In the 1890s, the life expectancy in Australia was 47.2 years for males and 50.8 years for females. According to Cumpston (1928) and Lewis (1989), life expectancy had risen to 59.1 years for males and 63.2 years for females. Nevertheless, these statistical records did not count the Indigenous Australians; they could not care less for them. The myth that Europeans portrayed of Indigenous ancient people as savages and primitive people was an excuse; they used to eliminate them rather than truly understand the people they were conquering. The author Greg Blyton writes in a research journal titled *Healthier Times: Revisiting Indigenous Australian Health History*, "The perception that indigenous Australians were primitive hunters and gatherers who lived in a nomadic 'Stone Age' culture resonates through most narratives found on indigenous people in pre-colonial times. This narrative is better placed in the realm of myth; I contest claims that the life expectancy of indigenous Australians was only 40 years in pre-colonial times, by providing suggestive evidence that there is a strong probability that longevity favoured indigenous Australians in comparison to many poorer sectors of the European population living in slum habitats. As well, I will challenge notions that indigenous Australians were more violent than supposedly 'civilised' nations. Finally, I express the

146

hope that future researchers will revisit archival sources to develop a more-nuanced perspective on the past" (Blyton 2009).

On my journey across this Australian red land, I was on the path of discovering the truth. What is that truth? The search for truth has been the journey of many men for centuries.

> This image of white Australian historians and physicians who describe the indigenous Aboriginals of the pre-colonial era as people of a primitive hunter-gatherer society portrayed a non-caring and capricious people with a low life expectancy. This truth has been so pervasive for a long time, because, for a long time, the white Australian has been telling the story according to his perception, through preconceptions of their early colonists who generally held a rather hostile attitude towards indigenous Aboriginal Australians.

> —(*Health and History*, Greg Blyton, 2009)

Mainstream ethnographic presentations of indigenous Australians in precolonial society tend to portray simple hunter-gatherer primitive images of Aborigines. These conceptualisations were accepted willingly as the perceived vision but fall short of a deeper understanding that required to be carefully analysed by these researchers. Australian historians may have operated with a sense of pride that they were a superior race studying some form of primitive man from the Outback. This attitude of pride or sense of superiority may have distorted their views. It is similar to the story of the six blind men examining an elephant with their hands and characterizing what the elephant is by how they perceive it to be. In other words, such preconceived notions and perceptions most likely led to misconceptions and led us far away from the truth.

Manning Clark, an Australian, initially perceived the Aborigines as a primitive culture but realised later on in his career that he was one of those six blind men examining an elephant and concluded that this blindness came about because of the inherent pride that came from a superior culture that he belonged to. Hence, he wrote, "For despite all the egalitarian ideas and inclinations, it never occurred to me that if Aborigines were allowed to decide for themselves which way of life they would prefer, they might have chosen their traditional way of life. All I knew then was that, in the presence of what I had accepted without question as a 'vastly superior power,' they decayed; they went to pieces. What I did not know was that, when an Aborigine is uprooted from the land of his Ancestors, without the land, life lost its meaning for him. He became a vagabond on the face of the Earth."

Indigenous Australians have been represented in literature as violent, club-wielding assassins, lurking savages, waiting to ambush, ever ready to kill each other or invaders—a primitive man, a hunter-gatherer with a random, capricious, instinctive nature packing a low-life expectancy and a high level of social immorality. Now, most of these historians were more likely to be Caucasians; they had never lived with Aborigines or among them. How would they have truly known? George Finkle was another one of those blind men examining an elephant. Similar to many other historians, he held the view that Indigenous Aborigines were hunters and gatherers and a Stone Age man, constantly roaming as nomads in the country in search of food and relying on the simplest of tools. His assumption is that these people came from a static culture who waged war with their neighbouring tribes.

Such judgmental, weary motives with Caucasian historians such as Pat Price claimed that Aborigines lived for a thousand years, living as a hunter-gatherer in the Outback of Australia. Now throwing some archaeologists into the fray, we get into a more mixed view that completes the poem of the six blind men and the elephant. Josephine Flood wrote that another significant factor of Aboriginal depopulation was black-on-black violence: punishment duels, pitched battles, and payback murders were witnessed in Sydney and elsewhere during the first contact between white European Caucasians and native Aborigines. Yet, after scrutiny of Flood's views and claims, there is very little or almost no evidence to substantiate her theory. Likewise, Flood admits the impact of colonisation may be a momentous cause of this supposed indigenous uprising and conflict.

On the contrary to these views by white historians of the colonial era, the story of Pemulwuy comes to mind—the native story of Australia's Aboriginal resistance hero, Pemulwuy, who kept British settlement around Sydney restricted for twelve years, 1790–1802.

Hence, it can be counterclaimed that labelling Aboriginal people as violent and club-wielding savages was propaganda, fake news of the colonial era. This was a European invention; the expression "propaganda" obviously first came into regular use in Europe because of the missionary activities of the Catholic church. In 1622, Pope Gregory XV made in Rome the Congregation for the Propagation of the Faith.

The provision of propaganda as a tool was widely used to distort the truth; it was a tool that gave the European settlers the false impression that they were a superior race to the native people. Propaganda portrayed them as savages who needed to be subdued, overpowered by brutal force, if need be, and encouraged overtaking the land and colonising them. The estimated lifespan of the Aboriginal people was now reduced to forty years since the arrival of the colonisers, who brought along with them their European diseases. As the historians and archaeologists agreed and disagreed with one another, Daisy Bates, an anthropologist, claimed that Aborigines lived till their eighties and had a much higher life expectancy than Europeans. The archaeologist Flood, along with historian Geoffrey Blainey, vehemently suggested that Aborigines could not live longer than forty years; they were unable to care adequately for the sick or a proportion of their newborn and elderly. In any case, neither of these two academics presented any evidence, statistics, or solid evidence to corroborate their claims. The dilemma among these academics was summed up by Richard Broome, who said, "What we know about traditional society is somewhat speculative." Unfortunately, there is very little evidence available about the nature of the precolonial society of Indigenous Australians. Yet there are indications that the image provided by these authors needs to be revised.

Propaganda has been termed as fake news. In the wake of this type of propaganda that was mastered by the European colonisers, such ethnographic projections rarely provided any platform or opportunity for Indigenous Australians to tell their story; they were not considered human beings by their European counterparts. Hence, they could not portray themselves favourably in comparison to those whose derogatory, prideful attitudes remained from the past, the present, and the future of Indigenous Australians.

Much of the credit score for European colonisation success in the New World can be handed to the superiority of their weapons, their literary heritage, even the reality that they had special load-bearing mammals, like horses. For example, these factors combined gave the conquistadors a big benefit over the state-of-the-art civilisations of the Aztec and Inca empires. But weapons alone cannot account for the breathtaking pace with which the Indigenous populace of the New

World had been completely wiped out. Within just a few generations, the continents of the Americas had been, without a doubt, emptied of their Native inhabitants; some studies estimate that approximately 20 million humans may have died in the years following the European invasion—up to 95 percent of the population of the Americas.

No medieval force, no matter how evil or bloodthirsty, ought to have completed such huge stages of genocide. Instead, Europeans were aided via a deadly secret weapon they weren't even aware they were carrying: smallpox and the spiritual disease of pride.

THE SIN OF PRIDE

One must not confound pride and self-esteem, two interests altogether different in their inclination and their belongings. Self-esteem is a characteristic assumption that prompts each creature to look out for its very own preservation. Pride is just a relative, counterfeit feeling conceived in society, a supposition that prompts every person to connect more significance to himself than to anybody else (Rousseau 1984, p. 167).

As a reluctant frame of mind, pride regularly has been viewed as having a place with a dangerous arrangement of sentiments, separate from the evident basic sentiments of confidence that are accepted to be normally based and far-reaching. Recent research shows that pride has a particular distinctively observed nonverbal verbalization that is unequivocally seen by children and grownups (Tracy and Robins 2004b, 2006). Tracy, Robins, and Lagattuta (2005) propose that pride may meet the fundamental criteria to be viewed as an essential tendency. Truth be told, pride may serve basic adaptable points of confinement. The flood of pride may pass on a person's prosperity (which propels the tendency) to different people, along these lines refreshing the person's social position; the energetic experience of pride may strengthen the practices that produce fulfilling feelings, reinforce sureness, and provide for the person that she or he merits a decent status. All things considered, after a socially respected achievement, pride may enable to keep up and advance a person's cultural position and set up attestation (Leary, Tambor, Terdal, and Downs 1995). This affirmation about the importance of pride in open public raises the question: What, unequivocally, *is* pride? In what limit may we depict its mental structure? What is its otherworldly peril?

I might want to initially address the profound threat of pride. Pride is superfluous certainty, known as vanity or pretentiousness. Pride is bad behaviour in the demeanour of the central core of the heart and soul of a person. Included are the musings of egomania, negative wantonness toward the prerequisites of others, and suspicion. Pride is both an airframe of the brain and the soul, a kind of terrible profound conduct.

Pride, in this manner, forces the individual, in the end, to move to trust in self rather than humbly trust in God. While there is a positive inclination of being satisfied in achieving what is extraordinary and sound, by a wide margin, the majority of the references to pride in Scripture are negative. Heavenly scriptures light up to us that this offence of pride has a consequence. As pride is irrefutably in the order of offence, people who are proud in heart will suffer discipline. The Proverbs reflect this perception of conditions and wise outcomes.

A lot of our present thought in Western nations can be accepted as being prideful as described in scriptural terms. Everything considered, current humankind has, in any supposed historical event, outflanked the prerequisite for a "divine being." The academic elites of our day disdain, on any occasion, drawing in the credibility of the remarkable. They love the naturalistic heavenly power of science and self-effort.

> The Lord tears down the house of the proud, but he sets the widow's boundary stones in place.
>
> —(Proverbs 15:25)

The Holy Bible depicts many stories of the danger of pride; for example, the story of King Nebuchadnezzar of Babylon and the stature of his pride. God brought him down and transformed him into a wild wandering beast for seven years.

> The highway of the upright is to depart from evil: he that keepeth his way preserveth his soul. Pride goeth before destruction, and a haughty spirit before a fall. Better it is to be of a humble spirit with the lowly than to divide the spoil with the proud.
>
> —(Proverbs 16:17–19)

The danger of pride from a spiritual aspect is that it is associated with the darkness of Lucifer, the fallen angel; it is also associated with the story of Narcissus, a hunter in Greek folklore, son of the river god Cephissus and the fairy Liriope. He was a handsome youngster, and many experienced passionate feelings for him. Nonetheless, he just ventilated prideful scorn and disdain towards them. Foe, the goddess of reprisal and vengeance, realised what had occurred and chose to rebuff Narcissus for his conduct. She drove him to a pool; there, the young Narcissus saw his appearance in the water and became hopelessly enamoured with it. Even though he didn't understand first and foremost that it was only a reflection, when he got it, he fell into the hopelessness of falling in love with himself and could not leave the image of himself; eventually, it drove him to destroy himself unto death by suicide. Pride is associated with narcissism, describing an excessive interest in or admiration of oneself and one's physical appearance.

Ezekiel 28 and Isaiah 14 depict the spiritual sinful nature of the pride of Satan.

> Your pomp has been brought down to Sheol, with the music of your harps. Maggots spread out beneath you, and worms cover you. How you have fallen from heaven, O Morning Star, son of the dawn! You have been cut down to the ground, O destroyer of nations. You said in your heart: "I will ascend to the heavens; I will raise my throne above the stars of God. I will sit on the mount of assembly, in the far reaches of the north. I will ascend above the tops of the clouds; I will make myself like the Highest.

> —(Isaiah 14:11–14)

The Bible teaches us that the two greatest virtues we must possess as a creation of God are to love God with all our heart, mind, and soul and love our neighbour as ourselves.

> Jesus declared, "Love the Lord your God with all your heart and with all your soul and with all your mind." This is the first and greatest commandment.

And the second is like this: "Love your neighbour as yourself." All the Law and the Prophets hang on these two commandments.

—(Matthew 22:37–40)

From a spiritual perspective, it's conceivable to state that the early colonisers didn't see the Aboriginal people as equal to themselves; the demolition, segregation, social decimation, and the historical backdrop of Australia has demonstrated the obscurity of a prideful race annihilating overwhelmingly straightforward, humble people who were the inverse of the promulgation among the colonisers about the Indigenous Australians. On the off chance that the European colonisers were professing to be Christian, they didn't show any of these Christian qualities. Despite what might be expected, they were narcissistic by nature, for they saw the Aboriginal as crude and savages; they thought of them as terrible and called them *boongs* or *coons*, and instigated institutionalised discrimination against them.

In spite of its centrality to social conduct, pride has gotten pretty much no consideration in the social-character writing, even compared with other unsure feelings, for example, disgrace and blame. As a hesitant feeling, pride customarily has been seen as having a place with an optional class of feelings, separate from the supposed fundamental feelings that are believed to be naturally based and general. Nonetheless, late research demonstrating that pride has a particular diversely perceived nonverbal articulation that is precisely recognised by kids and grown-ups (Tracy and Robins, 2004b, 2006; Tracy, Robins, and Lagattuta, 2005) recommends that pride may meet the imperative criteria to be viewed as an essential feeling. Truth be told, pride may serve significant versatile capacities.

The outflow of pride may convey a person's prosperity (which evokes the feeling) to other people, in this manner improving the person's societal position; the abstract involvement of pride may fortify the practices that create pleasing emotions, help confidence, and impart to the person that she or he has status. Along these lines, following a socially esteemed achievement, pride might have the capacity to keep up and advance a person's social status and public acknowledgement (Leary, Tambor, Terdal, and Downs, 1995), subsequently forestalling gathering dismissal. This proof for the significance of pride in public activity brings up issues about what, precisely, pride is. How might we describe its mental structure?

In my endeavour to comprehend why Australians treated me well even though I was a brown-coloured person, there were types of the profound misconception that existed with my white companions towards local individuals. I needed to comprehend the psychological aspects of the conceivable outcomes of pride that framed obstructions in the minds of individuals to see old, local individuals so rudely as some of them did.

Pride is a significant emotion that assumes a basic job in numerous spaces of mind functions concerning the attitudes we adopt. Specifically, sentiments of pride fortify prosocial practices, for example, altruism and adaptive practices, as well as accomplishment (Hart and Matsuba, in press; Weiner 1985). The loss of pride is a contributing factor that incites hostility and other solitary practices in light of self-image loss or abuse (Bushman and Baumeister 1998). The guideline of pride is inherently connected to confidence regulation and moral self-esteem; numerous demonstrations of self-upgrade are likely endeavouring to expand one's sentiments of pride. Truth be told, pride is the essential emotion (for example, similar to its opposite emotion of disgrace in intensity) that gives self-esteem its full potential of this prideful emotion (J. D. Darker and Marshall 2001) and confidence. Thus, this impacts a wide scope of intrapsychic and relational procedures. Regardless of its centrality to social conduct, pride has gotten little consideration in the social-character literature, even comparative with other hesitant feelings, for example, disgrace and blame. As an unsure feeling, pride customarily has been seen as having a place with an optional class of feelings, separate from the supposed fundamental feelings that are believed to be naturally based and widespread. In any case, ongoing research demonstrating that pride has a particular diversely perceived non-verbal articulation that is precisely recognised by youngsters and grown-ups (Tracy and Robins, 2004b, 2006; Tracy, Robins, and Lagattuta, 2005) proposes that pride may meet the imperative criteria to be viewed as an essential feeling. Pride may serve significant versatile capacity. The outflow of pride may convey a person's prosperity (which evokes the feeling) to other people, along these lines improving the person's economic wellbeing; and the emotional experience of pride may strengthen the practices that create glad sentiments, support confidence, and impart to the person that she or he merits expanded status. Therefore, following a socially esteemed achievement, pride may function to keep up and advance a person's societal position and gathering acknowledgement (Leary, Tambor, Terdal, and Downs, 1995).

WHAT IS PRIDE?

A few scientists have contended that pride is too expansive an idea to be viewed as a solitary emotion; combined with other emotions, a better perspective may be achieved (Ekman 2003; M. Lewis 2000). Consistent with this point of view, pride has been experimentally and hypothetically connected to exceptionally different results. From one viewpoint, pride in one's victories may advance positive practices in the attitude and behaviour in one's achievements (Herrald and Tomaka 2002) and add to the improvement of a veritable and profound established feeling of confidence. Then again, hubristic pride hypothetically is also connected with narcissism (M. Lewis 2000), which has been named the deadliest of the seven deadly sins (Dante 1308–1321/1937). This kind of pride might add to animosity and an antagonistic vibe, relational issues, relationship strife, and a large group of maladaptive practices (Bushman and Baumeister 1998; Campbell 1999; Kernberg 1975; Kohut 1976; Morf and Rhodewalt 2001; Paulhus Robins, Trzesniewski, and Tracy 2004). By what means can a similar feeling serve such differed opposite emotion, from various perspectives, agonistic roles? This oddity can be settled if we examine apart from the prosocial achievement-oriented form of the emotion from the self-aggrandizing, hubristic form and postulate two distinct facets of pride (M. Lewis 2000). An enormous group of research demonstrates that disgrace and blame are unmistakable, negative, unsure feelings with dissimilar elicitors and results (see Tangney and Dearing 2002), and it may bode well to conceptualise pride along these lines (M. Lewis 2000; Tangney, Wagner, and Gramzow 1989). In particular, the pride that proceeds from a particular accomplishment or prosocial conduct may be unmistakable from pride in one's worldwide self. This distinction parallels the conceptualization of blame as derived from an attention on negative aspects of one's conduct—what was done or not done—and disgrace as derived from an emphasis on negative parts of oneself—the self who did or didn't do it (H. B. Lewis 1971; M. Lewis 2000; Tangney and Dearing 2002).

In various investigations, specialists Tangney and her partners (Tangney and Dearing 2002) have shown that this differentiation portrays the key contrast among disgrace and coercion and may be the wellspring of the wide scope of dissimilar results related with the two emotions (e.g., blame and disgrace have divergent affective factors, extending from confidence and good faith to discouragement, tension, and recidivism). Expanding on these thoughts and discoveries, these researchers built up a hypothetical model of self-conscious feelings in which they speculated the presence of two unmistakable variations of pride, inspired by particular psychological procedures (Tracy and Robins 2004a). As per the model these scientists created, self-esteem feelings (pride, disgrace, blame, and shame) are inspired when people direct attentional concentration to oneself, actuating self-portrayals, and emulate a feeling applicable to these portrayals.

Quite a while ago, therapists noticed that pride happens because of inward attributions—that is, the point at which one-self is credited as the reason for the occasion (Ellsworth and Smith 1988; M. Lewis 2000; Roseman 1991; C. A. Smith and Lazarus 1993; Weiner 1985). Notwithstanding, expanding on past hypothetical work, it can be contended that two features of pride can be recognised by ensuing attributions. In particular, credible, or beta, pride (*I'm pleased with what I did*) might result from attributions to inward, insecure, controllable causes (*I won since I rehearsed*), though pride in the worldwide self (*I'm glad for who I am*), alluded to as hubristic, or alpha, pride (M. Lewis 2000; Tangney et al. 1989), might result from attributions to inner, steady, uncontrollable causes (*I won since I'm constantly extraordinary*).

These analysts have marked the principal feature legitimate to underline that it is regularly founded on explicit achievements and is likely joined by real sentiments of self-esteem. This idea of *hubristic pride* likewise means the full scope of scholarly, social, moral, and relational achievements that may be significant elicitors. In any case, these scientists don't wish to suggest that hubristic pride isn't a true emotional encounter. Or maybe, from a hypothetical point of view, in any event, the elicitors of hubristic pride may be all the more freely attached to real achievements and might include a self-evaluative procedure that mirrors a less-real feeling of self (e.g., mis-shapen and self-glorifying self-views). In like manner, this hypothetical model determines that there are two features of pride, yet it doesn't show whether these two aspects establish particular feelings in the manner that disgrace and blame are, for the most part, conceptualised.

These present discoveries provide knowledge into this issue; notwithstanding explaining the idea of complex feeling, the distinctions and difference between the two features of pride may help settle dubious inquiries regarding the manners by which people manage confidence. Analysts have noted similarities *and* contrasts between high confidence and narcissism, two-character attributes that include significant levels of pride yet that are related with unique subjective and conduct structures (Bushman and Baumeister 1998; Paulhus, Robins, Trzesniewski, and Tracy 2004; Twenge and Campbell 2003). One approach to conceptualise the contrast between the two-character measurements is to propose that each is driven by an alternate full-of-feeling centre—an alternate aspect of pride. In particular, real pride may fuel high confidence, while hubristic pride may be the premise of narcissists' abstract-inclination state of mind (M. Lewis 2000; Tracy and Robins 2003). Indeed, hubristic pride may be a piece of a unique administrative example through which narcissists smother sentiments of disgrace, to some degree, by communicating and encountering misrepresented sentiments of (hubristic) pride (Tracy and Robins 2003). As indicated by this view, narcissists have profoundly separated positive and negative self-portrayals, to such an extent that the understood self is increasingly negative and the unequivocal self progressively positive and romanticised. This separation appears to be related with inner, steady, wild attributions for progress at the express self-level (*I am an ideal individual; I'm constantly impeccable*), which, as per our model, would inspire hubristic pride.

Proof of precoloniser Aboriginal life is incredibly rare in that you're searching for it in the libraries of the Caucasians. Maybe this proof exists only in the libraries of the lives and Dreamtime accounts of the Aboriginal individuals themselves. Native people were profoundly human social orders; similar to every other human culture, they likewise confronted well-being challenges. They lived in adoration of their elders, and care was given by the youthful to the older; even the handicapped got backing and traditional medicine. History and truth can be judged according to who is narrating this history and facts; in other words, we have been given so much fake news these days that it's completely baffling to distinguish what is true and what isn't.

The native people had no control in the media propaganda that was established in colonial Australia. If they were portrayed as wild, uncivilised savages by an arrogant, prideful people, then they couldn't change that false perception. The savages could have been the ones who were making major decisions and executing these phoney updates. "Fake news of their times."

PUBLIC HEALTH IN AUSTRALIA

In Britain, Sir Edwin Chadwick, who was a legal advisor and social reformer, pushed for the state to make a move on sanitation. He spearheaded strategies to address unsanitary conditions, understanding that significant dangers to human well-being begin from such situations. Working with financial specialists, structural designers, and lawmakers, he was the engineer of the primary British Public Health Act of 1848, showing that the state can act "in an empowering limit" (Scram and Ashton 2007, p. 8) and, in fact, that the state has a duty to ensure the well-being of its natives. The German doctor Dr. Rudolf Virchow was additionally calling for government Kunt activity on social issues, for example, neediness and the absence of training, which he saw as components behind the plague of typhus. Urban areas in Britain, Europe, and Australia were dangerous spots to live because of fast urbanization and an absence of arranging, which offered ascent to urgently packed lodging of poor people, debased water supplies, and an absence of sanitation. In London, John Snow's activities to close down the water being siphoned from the Broad Street Pump, which was tainted with cholera, has stood out forever. In early Sydney and Melbourne, steers were permitted to wander through the lanes, and trash was dumped unpredictably, giving reproducing grounds to flies and vermin. It wasn't until local governments passed sanitation laws that the avenues turned out to be less dirty. Australian specialists attempted to gain from the issues of Britain and Europe, gradually presenting Public Health Acts and urban arranging controls. Regardless, in 1890s Australia, future during childbirth was 47.2 years for males and 50.8 years for females. After thirty years, the future had ascended to 59.1 years for males and 63.2 years for females (Cumpston 1928 and Lewis 1989).

In Sydney during the mid-1880s, paces of baby and youngster mortality were higher than rates in London simultaneously. Newborn-child mortality in Sydney crested at 194 for every 1,000 live births in 1875 (Fitzgerald 1987); however, the pace of baby mortality among the poor were triple those of progressively special classes. By 1900, baby death rates were falling because of a scope of general well-being activities. In Australia, the main Public Health Act was passed in the state of Victoria in 1854, and different provinces pursued with comparable enactment (Cumpston 1928 and Lewis 1989). Instances of early enactment that upheld the Public Health Act incorporated the Noxious Trades and Cattle Slaughtering Acts, Nuisance Prevention Acts (to limit the entry of material conveying smells and scents), Dairies Acts, Water Pollution Prevention Acts, and Factories and Shop Acts (Keleher 2000). While the primary Public Health Acts were generally feeble, they flagged the aim of governments to make more grounded moves to secure the strength of the individuals. Reinforcing of enactment for general well-being changes was given catalyst by rushes of destructive illnesses, including typhus, typhoid fever, cholera, looseness of the bowels, tuberculosis, and flu, which compromised the little populaces of the settlements. Crosswise over Europe, the USA, the UK, and Australia, the bacteriological revelations of the second 50 percent of the nineteenth century slowly gave general well-being and prescription a more-grounded reason for making a move, particularly on irresistible (transmittable) illnesses, which were regularly of epidemic proportions (Keleher H. 2001).

Just as maternal mortality, tuberculosis (TB) was an essential driver of grown-up death in Australia. In 1885, the demise rate from TB was 197 for every 100,000 individuals; be that as it may, it tumbled to 61 for every 100,000 individuals by 1919. This decrease, in no small part, was because of interest in sanitation, clean water, upgrades to lodging and sustenance, fundamental training, and in working conditions (for instance, employing plant changes), particularly of the urban poor (Graham 2007; Keleher 2000). As Health Acts were continuously created in the provinces, different irresistible maladies were broadcasted, requiring local governments to make explicit arrangement for assets to oversee them—and, especially, reveal their occurrence to well-being offices. Smallpox, cholera, plague, and yellow fever were declared by 1885; however, it took a few additional prior years when phthisis, tuberculosis, diphtheria, typhus, and measles were announced (Schultz 1991, referred to by Keleher 2000), even though they were infections liable for high demise rates. This lag in taking action is a marker of the feeble limit of governments to create measures for a purposeful general well-being reaction to dangers to the strength of the populace.

Australia developed into a country through the alliance of the colonies in 1901. The White Australia Policy was alive and solid, with citizenship denied to Aboriginal individuals and to the Chinese, a large number of whom had landed during the earlier decades to join the (Caucasian) race to the goldfields of the different Australian settlements. Moreover, frames of mind to race were underscored by genetic counselling, which backers particular reproducing of the population. At the end of the day, the health of the population was considered regarding reproducing and race recovery (or what was called racial cleanliness). Developing hypotheses declared thoughts not just about the number of individuals expected to continue and build the Australian population, but also about the nature of that population. These ideas influenced debates about how much to invest in improving the lives of the working classes, and whether they should be given assistance to improve their environments, which, in turn, would improve infant- and child-mortality rates. Practical eugenics was promulgated, aiming to "rear a strong and healthy race by constructive, not restrictive, means. The object was not primarily to eliminate the unfit, but to prevent their production by aiding in the full development of the healthy" (Barrett 1918, p. 307, cited in Keleher 2000). Eugenic theories were held more strongly in Europe than in Australia, where, Bacchi (1980a) argues, the movement was relatively weak. Nonetheless, it existed.

Regardless, white Australians were viewed as fundamental to the improvement of a sound national character, and white youngsters were viewed as the future of the country (Keleher 2000). Some contended that children of poor families ought to be permitted to bite the dust, since that was nature's method for permitting "characteristic determination." Be that as it may, social reformers in Australia kept confidence in an ecological change to encourage social change, taking a humanist position by participating in what has turned out to be known as the nature-develop banter (Bacchi 1980b). Social reformers, medical officers of health, attendants, and network pioneers contended that improved endurance relied upon sustaining, requiring ecological change, and frameworks to help moms, particularly in poor territories.

By the mid-1990s, the baby-welfare development had started to give a general arrangement of exhortation and instruction for new moms to attempt to control the high newborn-child death rate. The social-change development of the late nineteenth and mid-twentieth century was additionally worried about joblessness, production-line changes, mature-age annuities, and town arranging, with a desire to build the populace, to make it more advantageous (Hyslop 1980, p. v), and the objectives of the social-change development started to associate with beliefs of the early general well-being development. The period 1900–1930 was one of extreme patriotism. This period is frequently viewed as a time of "social designing," described by tremendous enthusiasm for cleanliness and sanitation to deliver a superior-educated and fitter populace who might better serve the British Empire at war and in industrial facilities. Extensive exertion was placed into well-being "puposeful publicity" (Keleher 2000), which nowadays would fall into the classification of well-being "efforts"!

General public health was accordingly poor for the native individuals, in a nation where ethnic purifying and narcissistic social orders loaded up where a hubristic, unclean pride existed. Native individuals suffered enormously at the hands of the colonisers' hubristic pride. These frames of mind continued to flourish under the initial 150 years since the convicts arrived on these fatal shores. As much as this country may have advanced, it showed itself to be deadly in its decimation of the native individuals. While the colonisers developed in the certainty of overcoming the huge Outback terrains, finding tremendous mineral assets, the contrary impact of pride was being practiced against the Aboriginal people.

The Aboriginal individuals confronted fast change and lost their local terrains; the discrimination, melancholy, the loss of personality, the reliance forced on a people, like a meanderer who had lost his motivation, lowering Aboriginals' status to that of a forager lying out and about, mooching for a cigarette or attempting to suffocate himself in the trouble of his reality by the alcohol that was presented by these narcissistic new leaders of the land.

While the white man worked with bona fide pride, which was determinedly related to narcissism, the opposite effect occurred for hubristic pride; it ended up being even more positively associated with narcissism. Two things were occurring at the same time: the land was being vanquished by narcissistic colonisers, and, tragically, an ancient culture was confronting a social decimation to their lifestyle.

In addition to all the changes this nation inflicted on these ancient people, the mining industry was not run by God-fearing Christian people; on the contrary, it bordered on a paganism of drunkenness and debauchery that was the scourge of the land and the humanity it affected. I often looked at the plight of the native people in these Outback towns where I worked. It tormented my heart that, although overt scorn didn't exist in Australia, rather unpretentious, politically sanctioned racial segregation existed. Christian estimations of adoration and seeing the astonishing picture of God in these inconceivably ancient people were not the sort of considerations that were processed by the descendants of the colonisers.

POLICE BRUTALITY

My long stretches of working in the goldfields in Western Australia allowed me the chance to come into contact with Wongi individuals. Increasingly, the disingenuousness of the early colonisers, with their phoney news about these individuals, never persuaded me that these individuals were capable of any genuine criminal conduct. Engaging with the community, I saw them in the genuine light of what these individuals were, regardless of all that they had lost and of the considerable number of changes that they may have endured. When the Wongi were inebriated, it changed them into a different people, like being possessed by a demonic force capable of lashing out and becoming disorderly and in conflict with the laws that criminalised this kind of behaviour. The true culprit in the criminality was not the people but the alcohol that was brought into an ancient culture by a new set of people who had settled the nation and brought this poison into this new land.

In this way, any reasonable person would agree the Australian law requirement was pointing at the injured individuals and victims as the *cause* of the problem. Rather than manage the reason for the *ailment*, the government treated the exploited *people* as the reason for the problem. It was only a short step from there to treating the natives harshly because they were viewed as less human. The wickedness of pride deliberately or instinctively instilled in the psyche of the governing authority enforced a systematised type of inconspicuous, subtle separation driven by prideful individuals.

The only difference between Australia and South Africa is that one was open with the way it treated its Indigenous people and separated themselves from them by favourable laws that protected their interests. The other was pretending to be a fair, democratic society but proceeded to perpetuate apartheid in subtle ways; take, for example, the condition of the local lockup cells in "...Goldfields Regional Prison Boulder-Kalgoorlie, where most of the people incarcerated were Indigenous people, even though they accounted for only 10 percent of the population in the region."

Living in the Outback, I was a visual eyewitness to the views expressed in this book. It's a known truth and researched fact that Aboriginal people were discriminated against and put into prisons. Various research articles added to the credibility of what I saw in the reality of the Outback.

Out here in the Outback, it was no secret coincidence that the criminal justice system in Kalgoorlie systematically incarcerated Aboriginal people; these claims came from government employees within the criminal-justice system in Kalgoorlie. The truth was even more startling. Because the local gaol was overcrowded, a large number of Wongi prisoners were transferred six hundred kilometres to serve their sentences in prisons in Perth.

I was always seeing the police pick up Aboriginal people and throw them in the dog box. In the name of law and order and regulations passed by man, I believed that there was an over-representation of Indigenous people at every stage of the criminal-justice system across both Western Australia and Australia. Truth speaks for itself; it needs no support or evidence. On the other hand, lies and deceit are not the same; they cannot stand unless it has support and hidden aspects that help it camouflage itself as the truth.

So, the truth is that Western Australia imprisons nearly double the national average of Indigenous people proportionate to their population than any other state in Australia and more than thirteen times the rate of the mainstream population. The fact that 8 percent of all adult males in Western Australia currently incarcerated are Indigenous people is alarming, but the incarceration rate within the Wongi community is even higher.

POLITICAL DISCUSSIONS

The number of inmates at the local prison in Boulder had grown dramatically. In a Parliament Question Time in 2009, the Attorney General, Hon. Christian Porter (2009), claimed that during the period 2001–2008 there was a 58.6% increase in the prison population of the Goldfields Region, and because of that increase, 180 Goldfields prisoners now have to be incarcerated in Perth (Porter, 2009). This dramatic rise in the number of Wongi prisoners means that nearly 16 percent of Wongi adult males are currently incarcerated (Australian Bureau of Statistics, 2007a; Porter, 2009). I suspected that imprisonment was having a substantial impact on the life chances of a great proportion of Wongi people, a phenomenon worthy of urgent research.

The truth is that the Western Australia criminal-justice system was incarcerating people faster than almost every other criminal justice jurisdiction. Chief Justice Wayne Martin claimed, "The judges of Western Australia send more people to prison, and for longer terms in prison than almost any other jurisdiction in the world … (in fact) … we're the sixth highest in the world" (Fan, 2009). Furthermore, a reduction in parole applications being granted in the last two years (Department of Corrective Services, 2009a) has resulted in Wongi people being incarcerated for longer, contributing to a further greater prison population. Increased incarceration rates in Western Australia cost the taxpayers of Western Australia dearly. The average daily cost of incarcerating an adult prisoner is $273.17 and $610.79 for a juvenile (Department of Corrective Services,

2009a). Imprisoning the Wongi people was becoming increasingly common and increasingly expensive.

Many academic articles are debating why indigenous people are over-represented in prisons, and why indigenous people apparently commit so many criminal offences, but I am still questioning what is going on and what effects this is having on indigenous communities. If we can better understand the "what" questions, we may be in a better position to answer the "why" questions at issue. From my previous Indigenous studies, I knew that Indigenous problems required Indigenous solutions or at least the involvement of Indigenous leaders in any resolution process.

In all the technical literature research I have presented to you in my book, there was no Aboriginal literature I could find in white people's library books, despite the British, European, and American appetite for trying to study, research, and explain the whole world by proof according to how they see it. Nor did I did find any reference to encouraging the participation of Indigenous community leaders to describe what they see happening to their communities. This was my journey of discovery. I was on the road to Meekatharra, driving around like a nomadic person, alone and searching for the truth that lay hidden in the red sands of this vast nation. What I discovered instead was the lack of human ethics and morality that exists in this country.

THE LOSS OF MORAL AUTHORITY

Ever since a permanent European colony was established in Western Australia, the diverse Indigenous people groups have been subjected to a system of justice that is foreign to their traditional culture (Brooks & Shaw, 2003; Gale, Bailey-Harris, & Wundersitz, 1990; Thomas & Stewart, 1978). Indigenous Western Australians are now vastly overrepresented in all stages of the criminal-justice system hand are currently being incarcerated at a rate 13 times greater than the mainstream population (Australian Bureau of Statistics, 2008b; Graham, 2009; McGinty, 2006).

The purpose of this literature review was for me to write the truth, to paint the picture of what I saw in the Outback, and to expose the sadness that I saw in the eyes of Indigenous Aboriginal people.

If the coloniser population came from a Christian nation like England, then there was not much Christianity that came with them. To treat the original people in this way was nothing else but exercising white supremacy over an ancient culture, overpowering them, and shutting them up into submission.

The history of Indigenous Australian interaction with colonial Anglo-European authorities has been replaced by unreasonable detainment and over-representation in the criminal-justice system. Indigenous Australians understand their own history and continue the traditions of storytelling to maintain sacred and important knowledge within their family groups (Edwards, 1988; Schmidt, 1990). Similarly, the *Bringing Them Home* report into the "stolen generations" (the generations of Indigenous children who were often forcibly removed from their parents and institutionalised from colonial times until the practice was finally abandoned in the 1970s. On 13 February 2008, Prime Minister Kevin Rudd formally apologised to the surviving members of the stolen generations.) of Indigenous children found that the past has profound power in determining current and future events (Human Rights and Equal Opportunity Commission, 1997). To demonstrate the effect incarceration has on the Wongi people, the principles of Indigenous social order before colonisation will be outlined, and the historical literature describing incarceration of Indigenous Western Australians over successive government administrations will be reviewed. From each period of government administration, the intended outcomes of incarceration will be contrasted with the actual, unintended, and profoundly adverse outcomes.

THE PHILOSOPHY OF INCARCERATION

Condemning a guilty party indicted for offences considered illegal is a troublesome and complex issue. In Western Australia, a sentence of detainment should be a last-resort tactic. A definitive judgment permissible under the Sentencing Act ("Sentencing Act," 1995) states in Section 6 (4), that court must not force a sentence of detainment on a wrongdoer except if it chooses that—

(a) the earnestness of the offence is such that no other resolution except detainment can be advocated, or (b) the protection of society requires it.

There are two basic premises on which sentencing a prisoner is based: retribution for offences committed and prevention of offences in the future (Gur-Arye, 1991; Hatzistergos, 2010; Spohn, 2002). In the moral dimension, retribution "… aims to express our condemnation for wrongdoing to confront the wrongdoer with the evil of his ways" (Gur-Arye, 1991, p. 452). Whereas in a practical dimension, as Spohn (2002) explains, retribution is the public expectation that whatever advantage the offender has gained by breaking the law should accordingly be taken from them. The prevention of further offences involves a combination of many approaches: specific and general deterrence, incapacitation, rehabilitation, and, possibly, restoration (Gur-Arye, 1991; Hatzistergos, 2010; Spohn, 2002). Sentencing should result in improved public safety, but as Hatzistergos (2010) correctly points out, almost all intended outcomes of sentencing require strong punishments more akin to retribution. For both retribution and prevention, there is a natural tendency for society to demand stronger and stronger punishments, to which governments tend to acquiesce (Hatzistergos, 2010). Given the marked and recent increase in prison population across Australia and especially in Western Australia (Australian Bureau of Statistics, 2008b, 2010a; Department of Corrective Services, 2009a), it would appear that the moral disapproval of society is being expressed, but that the preventative value of prison is less certain.

The author Lyn Stewart examines in her book *Blood Revenge* the first time that white men were held to account in a criminal court of New South Wales for killing Aboriginal people. It happened in 1799, just eleven years after the New South Wales colony began. This book answers the disturbing question: Why were five men found guilty of killing two Aboriginal people—yet were never punished?

The story lays bare the nature of black-white relations at the colony's Hawkesbury River frontier settlement. Governor John Hunter tried to carry out his orders and stop the wanton killing of Aboriginal peoples.

There is a pattern the world has come to know and see; these deeply held white-supremacy attitudes have existed for centuries. As a Christian, my Bible teaches me something completely different from this man-made, unclean ideology. White hegemony certainly goes entirely against every word of God and His holy creation.

Odinism is the first, original faith of the English people. Odinism is the name we provide for the first, Indigenous type of pagan religion practiced by the Anglos, Saxons, Jutes, and by the related Teutonic people groups of Mainland Europe. It is, in like manner, the familial, local religion of the English individuals and, in that capacity, our one-of-a-kind profound legacy. Odinism is an old religion whose inceptions are lost in the fog of time; however, it has been re-established in modern times by individuals who trust that it offers an answer for modern people's spiritual emergency.

This is similar to the time of Nazi Germany and Hitler's belief that white people—especially Germanic whites—were from some superior Aryan race.

Many "folkish" Ásatrúar, Odinists, and Wotanists confine the religion to those with Northern European families, much as local Americans rehearse strict Indigenous convictions. The contrast between the clash of two ancient cultures, obviously, is one of intensity. Native Americans endeavour to keep up their social and strict religious practices despite the repercussions of hundreds of years of colonisation and destruction. White Odinists, conversely, took advantage of racial oppression and precluded others' participation in securing concerns about white "immaculateness" rather than social survival, in the midst of mass slaughter, constrained sterilization, and the abduction, misuse, and social "re-education" found at Native American boarding schools. Australian missionaries stole Aboriginal children and attempted to eliminate the native people by breeding them out, similar to the "re-educating" of the Chinese Uighurs.

Given that white individuals were the culprits in this colonisation and annihilation—and don't have a unique claim to the land—proclaiming an association with Vinland empowers racially oppressive Odinists to "assert a verifiable case over North America," as indicated by David Perry, associate professor of history at Dominican College in

Illinois. As such, by making a case for Vinland, Odinists tap into the possibility of Indigenous people having a place while advantageously disregarding their status as pioneers on stolen land.

NORTHERN WESTERN AUSTRALIA

I did not stay long in Meekatharra. I advanced toward Port Hedland and found a quaint little inn at which to leave my vehicle and lay my head to rest. The journey was a long one, and I took a couple of days to rest, totally sitting idle. I decided to visit the local pub one evening to get myself a meal across the bar. An Aboriginal woman hanging around the bar asked me if I could buy her a drink. I always felt guilty if I gave a native person a beer. I told her I could give her money for anything else she wanted but that a beer was not good for her.

She offered to take me home to her place. I declined her invitation and said that I was a Christian and not at all interested in with becoming involved with her in any such way as she was soliciting at the bar. I loathed doing this, yet I bought her a brew and left the place. I went to a bar over the road to escape from being bothered. I would have honestly loved to sit and talk to her, but I knew from my experience that alcohol was ruining them, and I wanted to be a part of some kind of solution out here, not a contributor to the apostasy. I did not realise that, by rejecting her the way I did, I was no better than any other white supremacist in the attitude that I had. It was not easy, for the dynamics of attitudes were already established in this country before I got there. I did not see myself different from Aboriginal people; in fact, I had a deep desire to get to know them without the influence of alcohol.

I'd had a few drinks at the bar when a woman came up to me, put her hand on my shoulder, and tapped me. I spun around and looked: it was pretty Linda, the gold sampler test-lab technician who worked with me in Kalgoorlie. I was surprised to see her. It's a small world in the mining sector; it was not uncommon to meet your workmates as they moved from one project to another. We had a few drinks, and as the band played, we danced, sang, and drank a few more beers. It was a great night until I decided to leave.

As I walked in the dimly lit street, I saw three Aboriginal women. They yelled at me, started to use profanity, approaching me with anger. I noticed that it was the woman at the bar whom I had rejected earlier in the evening. I heard her say, "Give this bloke a flogging. Son of a bitch, he like them white girls, and he don't likes to talk to us black girls! Give him a good hiding," as they approached menacingly towards me. I figured reasoning with them would be impossible, so I ran as fast as I could. I bolted like lightning across the road and took a left turn, spun myself at the next right into a lane, making a zigzag pathway of my escape. I knew I would confuse them and that they would never figure out where I lived.

The following day I went into town searching for this native woman; as insane as it appeared, I needed to find her and clarify that I didn't intend to dismiss her. I needed to be companions with local individuals, and I wanted to apologise on the off chance that I had made her feel dismissed or treated harshly. I was attempting to stand in her shoes and understand her point of view. I looked but didn't find her, so I returned the following day to look for her. She was at the local Aboriginal bar, a place where most of the Aboriginal people hung out at. I was walking into a lion's den. I bought her a beer and went across to her table. She recognised me. I smiled at her. "Look here, sister, I apologise if you felt hurt that I rejected you. I am here now among you people. I was dancing with those white girls because they were my mates at work, but today I will dance with you people." I spent the rest of the evening in the company of native Aboriginal people; everyone expected me to buy them a beer, and so I had no choice but to drain the $150 I had in my pocket that night. As much as I hated to encourage the alcohol, I wanted to get a better understanding of the issues that affected them, and so I had to embrace them as well in some way to get a better comprehension. I did not want to be hated by them; I did not want to inflict a discriminatory attitude towards them.

These were a friendly bunch of people. It was an uproarious gathering, a vivacious one; from multiple points of view, it was progressively fun at the local bar. I hit the dance floor with them and befriended an entire bunch of local individuals. I was not surprised that they were such a carefree people, wandering this endless land for centuries of nomadic DNA. However, I realised they'd been demolished by the liquor that was gradually slaughtering and changing the mob.

I found a job as a mechanic in Port Hedland and stayed in the area of North Western Australia for six months. I had developed some close friendships with Aboriginal people, but I was not satisfied. I already had a deep understanding of their problems with alcohol;

they were lost among the pubs, like wandering souls lost in time and in space through the era of colonisation. Their self-esteem had almost vanished as a people.

But I wanted to meet them at a different time, a different era, a precolonial time. I realised I would not find it in Port Hedland. I would have to go to even-more-remote places, where I would be cut off from any white man's influence.

I got a phone call from a workmate named Peter Stone, who said he wanted to go to Melbourne to see his fragile grandad. He told me that he had never met him in his entire life and wanted to see him before he passed away. He was wondering if I was interested in going along with him on an adventure to Melbourne. Two weeks later, I called him back and told him that I would drive to Kalgoorlie and that we could make this trip together. I left Port Hedland and headed down to Kalgoorlie. I picked up Peter Stone, and we drove to Norseman, heading south into the vastness on a long road that lay like a black line of rubber drawn across the red desert sand. Peter looked like Wez, from the movie *Mad Max*; like night riders, we headed off into *Mad Max* territory.

ACROSS THE NULLARBOR PLAIN

Next to me sleeping on the desert sand, an image of a shooting star out of orbit in the night sky, burning up forever into the vastness of oblivion—drunk, drugged, stoned, lying like he was almost dead on the desert floor, was Peter Stone. I went through hours alone in absolute wonder gazing at millions of stars and galaxies that showed up in the extraordinary southern night sky. Somewhere close to paradise and earth, I nodded off into a blissful slumber in the utter joy and the impossible magnificence of creation.

The morning sun rose early on the desert plains, and as the warmth hit the earth, the coldness of the desert night soon dissipated like pouring boiling water on cubes of ice. It gets warm pretty fast when the Australian sun shows up. I got my act together and grabbed my gear; I packed my sleeping bag and loaded my car. Peter Stone was still lying on the desert sand, being roasted in the sharp morning sun. I grabbed a bottle of water and went across to wake him up. I figured out he would wake up with the dry horrors of alcohol abuse and dehydration—a deadly combination out here in the desert plains.

We drove for hours across the plains. Peter was suffering with a bad hangover, so he reached out into his Esky and grabbed a beer. He had this alcoholic philosophy: "To avoid a hangover, stay drunk." We arrived at Cocklebiddy roadhouse, and it's one of these places in Australia that if you blinked while you were driving past, you would miss it. Back in the 1980s, there was not much going on out here in Cocklebiddy. It was a blessing for the weary traveller and a haven for anyone crazy enough to make the crossing across the great emptiness of the Nullarbor Plain. Cocklebiddy is the third stop from Norseman in Western Australia on the Eyre Highway. It started out as an Aboriginal mission located on the Eyre Highway in Western Australia. We spent about two hours checking the car and servicing it for the long journey ahead of us. Peter restacked his Esky with ice and beer; we ate some food and chatted with the locals.

The old bloke from the Wedgetail Inn roadhouse told us about some underground caves farther down the road that were worth a visit. Peter and I figured we would go there and camp out there for the night. When we arrived at the underwater cave system, it really blew my mind; out here in the desert sands was a marvel of nature. It was an underwater cave system filled with clear lake waters. It was not long before I found myself taking a swim in the waters of the lake. It was hard to imagine that, above these cave systems, lay a dry desert that could kill you for the same water that she held secret inside her belly. Its places like this in Australia that take your breath away. The old bloke at the Wedgetail Inn roadhouse told us that the first underwater cave dive took place somewhere in 1961. Ten years later in 1971, some other divers were able to penetrate farther, and a few hundred metres of underwater-cave explorations had taken place. Fourteen years later, Peter Stone and I spent a night out here alone in the empty desert sands, lighting up a small fire. We chucked a hot barbecue plate on it, cooked up some snags and steak, downed a few beers, and watched the sun go down. We found some solid dry logs of wood and had a fire that would last all night long as we camped out in the wilderness under the awesome night skies of the great southern hemisphere.

We drove for the next seven days across the open plains into South Australia, stopping at places along the way, sleeping out in the bush under the stars; I was truly amazed at the peculiar differences that existed in this country. We had some fishing gear and stopped over at

Ceduna. While fishing at the shoreline, we saw a school of herring; since they are a great source for live-bait-fishing techniques, we put our throw nets into action to bag a few herring to be used as live bait.

The local chaps corrected our words of describing the species of fish and the terms used to describe fish out here in South Australia. The old fisherman commented, "You blokes must be from West Australia. We don't call them herring around here, mate!" He exclaimed, "Out here, you'd have to call them Tommy Roughs."

"Similar to the expression we have in West Australia, you are too bloody right, mate. Fair dinkum, Tommy Roughs they are," we replied. It was a great day fishing with the old chaps at Ceduna.

We decided to take a tour of Iron Knob and checked out the area of the Great Australian Bight. As we drove into this ghost town, there was not much to see except the final days of the iron-mining industry that, like the population, was fading away. We drove on to Port Lincoln and finally made our way to Cape Carnot. The sheer isolation of these places out in the wilderness was emphatically an awesome experience. The coastline and the views of the mighty Southern Ocean, the reminiscence of the breakaway from Antarctica, the remnants of ancient Gondwanaland—these were ancient tracts.

We camped out there on Cape Carnot, and the view was awesome. Although dangerous at times on the slippery rocks, it did not take too long before the reel went screaming into overdrive as the attack on the lure went wild. Our dinner was blissfully awesome: fresh fish for tucker; you just cannot come close to eating a fish any better than from the ocean into a pan. I made no attempts to swim in this ocean, knowing that this sea harboured numerous white sharks. There were a few occasions on which I had this terrible feeling that my alcoholic mate Peter Stone would not make it across to Melbourne. As he dived into the dangerous shark-infested waters of South Australia, I thought it might be the last I time I would see him. I sat on the shore imagining the worst scenario: an image of a white shark appearing from behind a wave, and a sight of big jaws gobbling up Peter Stone. How ghastly were my fears and thoughts!

We had spent eighteen days on the road crossing the Nullarbor, and it was truly the most memorable journey I'd ever made. We were now heading into Melbourne, and Peter started to sober up. He was excited to meet his grandad and wanted to present himself a little more decently.

Grandad was an Anzac veteran. He was truly an optimistic war hero. He opened the door with a great sense of joy as he greeted his grandson for the first time in his life. He was glad to have us stay with him for a couple of days, so Peter and I decided to spend a week with him. I witnessed an emotional reunion as they went through an old photo album. Peter got a different perspective on his mother's version of the story of her fallout with her relationship with her father. He kind of teared up a bit as he hugged his grandad.

Peter said, "I did not want to come to see you at your funeral, Grandad. I wanted to make sure that I got to see you before that ever happened. Thanks to my mate Lyndon here, he decided to join me on the journey across to come and visit you."

Grandad replied, "Good on ya, blokes. I appreciate you fellows coming all the way across. Now that's some kind of a trip, hey! Your mother was a stubborn girl who gave me endless grief, mate, but I am truly stoked, happy that you came, Peter." There was a tear in the old man's eye. Peter gave the old chap a hug. It was a Wednesday afternoon. Grandad was getting dressed to go downtown to get his pension money, and then he was heading down to the pub to meet this old sheila; he said he was dating her regularly on Wednesday-afternoon pub sessions.

We spent a week with a true Anzac solider who was the most optimistic and cheerful old man I'd ever met. Grandad was truly happy that he'd met his grandson, and now that these relationships were renewed between them, it healed old wounds.

CHAPTER 10

THE NORTHEAST COAST

My journeys with Peter Stone took me to Sydney, a city that did not appeal to us. We arrived in the morning; by the end of the evening, we were driving into the blue mountains of New South Wales. Our adventurous journey was surely not going to last forever. As the funding started to dry up, we knew that we'd have to find a job soon, make some money for a while, and then make our way up to Queensland to visit Peter's uncle Leslie.

We were now in the land of the Snowy River. Orbost is a pleasant rural town on the river flats of the Snowy River. The town is principally a service-supply centre in the production of meat and dairy products; several farms produce vegetables, beans, and maize, including timber products. Orbost is basically a one-street town with the majority of the town's lodgings and other noteworthy structures situated on Nicholson Street. A history of early European settlers' farmlands offer the tranquillity of a good harvest of crops on this rich and fertile valley.

We got jobs there picking bell peppers for the harvest season. We found a place to stay at a local pub. The next day we rocked up to the farm and were handed rubber kneepads and gloves. Bell peppers grow on low-lying plants, which means we boys would be crawling on our knees all day picking them and loading them into baskets.

It is truly a remarkable experience when you realise that crawling on the ground all day plucking bell peppers and loading them is a labour-intensive, back-breaking job. There were a couple of local sheilas who worked with us, pleasant, friendly local girls, the kind that would make you want to stay and make Orbost home. We had heaps of fun with the daily work and the humour we shared each day. Even though the work was labour intensive, the group of people were truly pleasant. We spent eight weeks through the harvest season and saved as much money as we could for the journey ahead, up the east coast to Queensland. Peter Stone did not save as much money as I did, because he could not resist going to the pub to chat up the sheilas and keep up the vices and weaknesses that dominated his life.

I was always concerned about getting into trouble with the law. Peter had a small bag full of marijuana among his belongings. I believed he had grown it in some plantation somewhere out in the bush, back in Kalgoorlie. I did not want to get stopped by a police trooper. For all the distance we had travelled together, I was never stopped or pulled over by any law enforcement/traffic police/cops all through this entire journey. We made our money at Orbost, in the town of Victoria, and the farmer was so pleased with the hard work that we had put in that he gave us a $150 bonus and a full tank of fuel for our journey up northeast. We bid farewell to the country girls we'd worked with. I even considered asking one of them out on a date, but that would have only complicated our journey, and we were nomads.

We hit the road once again and made our way into the state of New South Wales and drove up to Newcastle. We stayed for cheap at the Salvation Army for two days. There was not much to keep us nomads shacked up in this town. It was a bright, sunny day; we drove out of Newcastle and headed on the highway towards the Gold Coast. There were two female hitchhikers up ahead.

Peter said, "I reckon we should pick them up for some female companionship. Who knows—I might even get lucky? What do you reckon, cobber?"

"It all depends, Peter. Where are they heading? I am not so keen, but let's stop and ask them."

We pulled up near the hitchhikers. "Gidday, sheilas," he greeted them. "Where are you headed to?" he asked.

"The Gold Coast," they responded.

Peter exclaimed, "Well, hop in because you are in luck—we are heading to Brisbane." I was at the wheel, so he got out to help them load their backpacks in the boot of the car. We drove on, and now there were four of us.

The girls were from the UK, Pommy sheilas travelling around Australia on a one-year working-visa experience. The girls started to relate their story of woes, having spent six months in Sydney working as barmaids and doing all kind of odd jobs on the way. They cried of poverty and moaned about their endless struggles to earn enough money to keep travelling. Now they were heading up to the Gold Coast, hoping to find some work and enjoy the coast in Queensland. Now, I truly understood the expression we have in Australia—bloody whining Pommies.

We drove the 380-kilometre trip from Newcastle to Coffs Harbour; this mid-north coastal town was a beautiful place. Peter and the Pommy sheilas got stoned on a few joints and drank a few beers along the way. I understood his devious plans, but the girls were on the same playing field and were enjoying all the attention they were getting from him.

My mother raised me up with different values; girls getting stoned and drunk were not my cup of tea. I was the least interested to have any hanky-panky ideas that had filled up inside the head of Peter Stone. He was looking to get laid. He suggested that I should take the ugly one and that he was going for the prettier one. I laughed at his proposal. "How about you have them both, mate?" I eagerly quipped back. "Not my type, mate—you should know that by now." Peter suggested we treat the girls to some Aussie hospitality; the only problem with the suggestion was that the hospitality was on my expenses. My alcoholic mate was running out of cash. Hence, I paid for the camping and the tents; we went down to Target supermarket, bought a whole load of food, and spent the evening in the camping grounds near the ocean having a barbecue. The British girls got drunk and stoned that night. They laughed and joked late into the night with Peter Stone.

I was tired from all the driving and left this mob right after dinner. I retired into my tent and turned myself in for a good night's sleep. I awoke up early the next morning, grabbed my fishing pole, and headed onto the beach to do some surf casting. My idea of eating good fish was to catch it and cook it on the beach.

It was a great day; the water temperature, the tide, and waves were perfect on this immaculate coastline. I landed three good-sized silver bream. I rigged up some size-6 long-shank hooks with a 1-metre monofilament leader, with a running ball sinker and a swivel, dug up some beach worms and hooked them up, and cast the rig out onto the sand flats, where I was sure there would be a whole bunch of whiting fish. I was back in business. I did not have to wait long before the whiting started to bite, and within the next half an hour, I had caught six more fish. I put my live fish into my netted nylon bag tied to a nylon rope and threw them back into the sea to kept them alive for a fresh meal in the afternoon. With the rope fastened to a wooden pole, I secured my fishing bag.

Peter Stone and the Pommy sheilas turned up on the beach, hung over from the night's party; they looked wrecked. Yet, there was lust in the air. Peter Stone had had his way. Now, she was all over him like a cheap suit. I did not disrespect people for their beliefs or behaviours. Nevertheless, it's the spirit of alcohol, drugs, and fornication that was very persistent in societies.

The beach in Coffs Harbour was truly remarkable; the body surfing was superb. When I caught the perfect wave, I sailed with my body all the way back. We spent three days in Coffs Harbour. My generosity was gracious. I found myself paying for the food and the fuel as these backpackers were very reluctant to spend any money. With sweet words, they were enjoying all the hospitality they were getting. Peter was having all his lustful desires being fulfilled by the Pommy sheilas, so he kept complimenting me for my generosity. The only time Peter spent any money was when he bought alcohol.

We left Coffs Harbour and headed up towards the Gold Coast; it was a beautiful day, and the drive up north was pleasant. We decided to stop at a roadhouse to fill up on fuel and get some food. Peter went with the girls into the restaurant while I took care of my car. I serviced the car and filled the tires with air, checked the oil levels, and went with it through the car wash.

We drove to the Gold Coast and arrived at the backpackers' location, where the girls had planned to stay. Peter's lustful romance had come to an end. As they unloaded all their gear, the girls started to panic. The panic started to get desperate as they frantically searched for something they were missing. I stood there baffled at what had gone amiss.

Then they were getting upset with each other. I did not have a clue as to what was going on, and then one of them started crying. Finally, I asked them, "What is going on?"

Julia said, "It is our little black handbag—it's missing."

I replied, "What do you mean, 'it's missing'?"

"Are you thick, mate?" she replied angrily. "It's not here!" I did not like her arrogant tone. So, I let Peter deal with his lusty lover. They searched the whole car, and there was no sign of the little handbag. Then one of them declared that they had five thousand dollars in cash in the bag, and now they had lost it.

Looking at me, they said, "Hey, mate, if you have taken it, please return it back to us."

I was dumbstruck. "Excuse me," I replied, "I have been the kindest person you have ever met in your entire life. I did not even want to pick you up, but thanks to my friend Peter Stone, I obliged. I have showered you with hospitality, fed you, protected you, even accepted your lies that you didn't have much money. May I ask, what are you insinuating, young lady? You have protected your stuff all through your journey, and now you don't remember a bag that you have lost, and I have not even the faintest idea what it looks like. I am not a thief or an alcoholic and a drug addict. Please be careful with your accusations."

The other girl apologised. "Sorry, mate. She did not mean that, but if you found it, please return it to us."

I could not believe it. I found it rather distressing. Peter was getting upset with me because I was not compassionate to their loss. I walked away from this drunken mob and went to the local telephone booth. I remembered the name of the roadhouse where we last stopped.

I opened the Yellow Pages and tracked down the number. I called the bloke up who told me his name was Dan.

"Hey there, Dan!" I said, "A few hours ago we passed by your roadhouse and filled up some fuel and serviced my car. A couple of my mates got some food at your restaurant, and we left. We are currently in the Gold Coast, and it seems these Pommy sheilas may have lost a black handbag. Did you happen to find a small black handbag? I don't even know what it looks like. I'd have to get these distressed girls to call you for a better description."

Dan's response was a sound of regret. "Oh, no—are you kidding me? We found a small black handbag left near one of the tables. It had actually fallen on the floor. We asked people if anyone was missing a small black handbag. A woman said it was hers, so we gave it to her. You know many people pass through this place, so we don't track them all, mate. We announce if we find anything. I am so sorry, but we don't have any handbag here. We gave it to what we honestly believed was the owner."

I thanked him and said, "I reckon one of these distressed girls would surely call you back. Let me pass the message on to them." I thanked the man and hurried across the road.

I felt very distressed by being called a thief by these biased white people; I was thinking, *Why are they holding me responsible for their loss? Why did they not accuse drunken Peter Stone? He was the one with them all the time. He was drinking and drugging himself, having sex with the girls in their tents. I was the one who kept a distance from them.*

Oh, I got it! How could I be so naïve? I was the brown fella, with the fancy car. I looked more Aboriginal than Peter Stone. He was a white fella, and so it was more unlikely he would be a thief. It is more likely I was the one who would do something as low as rob people.

I walked across the road toward them. I felt hurt and upset. I wanted to call them "white trash" but restrained myself.

Peter walked towards me and said, "If you have their bag, give it to them, mate! They are getting ready to call the cops."

I looked at him with disgust and walked over to the girls. "Well," I said, "if you want to know where your bag is and how it disappeared, you better call Dan at the roadhouse because he just told me that he found a black handbag that you girls forgot at the last place we stopped. The number is available in the Yellow Pages at that telephone booth over there, and if you don't have a coin, I suggest you ask my alcoholic friend Peter Stone to help you out." I emptied Peter's backpack and all his gear on the sidewalk. I looked at them standing there on the sidewalk. "I don't deserve being called a thief when I have been so good to the three of you. The only ones who are thieves are those who say they don't have money while they do. What you sow is what you reap! Have a nice day." I left them standing there. Peter Stone threw his beer can at my car as I drove away. He was always stoned and drunk, and I'd just about had enough of it. That was the last time I ever saw Peter Stone.

I drove up to Brisbane and found myself a place to stay in Fortitude Valley. I needed to find a job and get myself together. Clyde Babcock was hiring at the Tarong Power Station for a major shutdown project. I went for the interview and had a new job. It was a twelve-week project. Food and accommodations were provided for working twelve-hour shifts; it was the perfect thing to get me back on my feet again. I had a week's time on my hands before I started my new job.

I walked past the local pub, so I popped in to get some lunch. I was happy that I had a new job. I would soon have enough money to continue my travels around Australia. A door led to the TAB, where many TV screens were displaying horse racing. I found it interesting. As much as I love horses and cowboys, I had no clue about horse racing. Curiosity got the better of me, so after my lunch, I went through the door that said TAB.

It was exciting; there were a whole bunch of fellas cheering on their favourite horses as they sped across the big TV screens. No sooner did one race end than another began somewhere else. The whole rhythm of cheering began once again; some faces were smiling, while others tore up their tickets and threw them into the bins. Hurriedly, they scanned the boards with slips of paper coupons in their hands, marked with squares, with letters and numbers; they were fanatically searching for a winner as they scribbled their hopes on pieces of paper.

A big bloke with a huge beer gut, a fair dinkum true-blue punter with a loud voice, was asking questions like, "What is the weather like? What is the ground like? Yeah, she is a good bet, mate." I was impressed by this man. Hence, I approached him with a pen and a paper coupon.

I said, "Excuse me, sir." He looked at me with a friendly smile on his face. "How do you fill out one of these coupons?" He gave me a crash course in gambling on horses so efficiently perfect that it went straight into my head without any need for further instruction.

He held my ticket coupon and took me to the board. "Well, the next race is in half an hour in Rosehill NSW. It's a class C race, so you pick a horse, and I will tell you if it's good enough to win the race. What do you think of that?" he remarked.

"Yeah, mate, sweet as. I'll do just that," I said. "I like this one, number eleven, 'Majestic Mission,'" I responded.

He laughed at me. "Well, mate, young fella, I hate to tell you this, bloke, that is not a horse, it is a donkey." He laughed at my face; it was quite funny. I laughed with him. "Bloody New Zealand galloper, mate; never ran in Australia; bloody thing has been running with sheep." And he laughed some more. "On those odds, it's a rank outsider; you'd be wasting your money on that donkey."

"I liked the name," I said assertively. "Can you write out a bet for me?" I politely asked.

"Fair enough!" he replied. "It's your money."

"How about twenty dollars to win and ten dollars for a place?" I placed my bet.

He smiled at me. "It's a donkey," he said.

I smiled back. "Thanks, mate—it's a funny bet," I said.

I went back into the pub and sat down at the bar; a few minutes later, the race started. I was not inclined to look, as I had picked the donkey among the horses. It seemed like an endless race as the horses ran around the circuit on what turned out to be a 3,000-metre race.

It took so long to finish that I finally stood up and saw the last part of the race; the commentator was getting excited, and I heard him say, "Now as they are taking the bend for the home run, Amber is ahead by two lengths, Carlie's Smile is behind in second place, Misty is in third place, and Majestic Mission is in fourth place and moving strongly at—"

I stood up as the excitement started to take ahold of me as I watched the TV screen. I heard the commentator, "Autumn Rain is tiring, and Carlie's Smile has nudged ahead, but here comes Majestic Mission from the outside with two hundred metres to go. He is moving strongly, this unknown galloper from New Zealand. Looks like he is going to win it here. Carlie's Smile is tiring, with another fifty metres to go, and Majestic Mission moves his head forward. Carlie's Smile is fighting back, but it's all Majestic Mission to the winning post, and she has it." Majestic Mission, the rank outsider, had surprised the punters at Rosehill. "Fair dinkum," said the commentator, "these are big odds, and some lucky punters may have money on this horse."

I held my ticket in my hand and pinched myself. I wondered if he'd written the right number on my ticket. It was there—Number 11. I had the winner; the odds were 189 to 1.

The big bloke with the big beer belly came rushing into the pub from the door of the TAB, shouting with joy; pointing to me, he exclaimed, "This young fella has thirty bucks on that donkey that became a horse." The whole bar cheered; it was a joyous celebration. I went and rang the brass bell at the bar, and the whole pub erupted in a joyful uproar.

The lady at the TAB office said to me, "In all the years I have been here, I cannot recall anyone winning 4,100 dollars on a single bet. Good on ya, mate."

I spent three hundred dollars at the bar and shouted everyone a drink. Majestic Mission had made me famous one afternoon in a pub in Fortitude Valley. The big bloke with the big beer gut came and hugged me. He looked at me and said, "Listen up here, young chap, it's a mug's game, this horse racing; you just had beginner's luck; more people get addicted to this, but you lose more than you win." That was a golden piece of advice, and I grabbed his hand and slipped him a $100 bill. I left the bar with many happy cheers, met the lady at the counter of the Commonwealth bank, and stashed all my winnings into my bank account.

A week later, I was at Tarong Power Station and, for the next three months, grafting at the shutdown job with a bunch of great blokes. I stayed in Queensland for the next six months working at Charters Town and Townsville. I met a pretty girl named Vera Tichbourne at Charters Towers in Queensland. I really thought it would turn out to be something good. We dated for a few weeks, but her instability and drinking assured me that blue eyes don't always make an angel. I did not want to get entangled in the love triangle she was having, and in reality, I'd have to play the spare guy who always buys her stuff and takes her places. If it starts off bad, it is most likely going to get worse. You know the gut-wrenching feeling. I listened to the instinct within me.

A group of backpackers were looking to head up to Alice Springs by car, and my constant urge to travel towards the Northern Territory and get into real Aboriginal country was now a reality before me. I just had to make a decision.

The next day I picked up the German girl and two British lads, and we headed out across from Townsville to Alice Springs in the Northern Territory. It was a journey of 2,097 kilometres in a country of humongous, vast, empty spaces; long distances were the norm in the sheer vastness there. Lonely highways sprawled across the changing landscapes.

The Holden Statesman was proving to be an excellent car. She was clocking up the miles, and her lovely V8 engine was perfect. I kept her in good nick, put on a set of new tires, and regularly serviced her. I started to get attached to her reliability and the way she moved with me across this vast expanse. I fell in love with this machine. She was always there to cradle me in her bosom, as I slept in the back seat often during these long journeys and tiredness.

The agreement between the four of us was a simple arrangement: I would pay for all the fuel, and at the end of the journey at Alice Springs, we would split the bill four ways. We stopped in several places, camping along the way, making this a four-day trip.

I put up my tent out in the desert sands as we watched the sun go down. I grabbed some blankets for the night's sleep. The British lad laughed at me.

"What are you doing with blankets out here in this heat, mate?"

"I have a spare blanket if you need one later on," I replied.

We chatted around the campfire cooking some food, talking about each other's travel adventures. The red desert land cooled down rapidly, and the British backpacker started to see the wisdom of a woollen blanket wrapped around me. I was not going to let him freeze out there in the cold; I gave him a blanket to keep him warm. It's just something you do for people—be kind and show some care. The cold winter night was challenged around a warm campfire out in the middle of the "whop-whops." It was the kind of experience that resonated with backpackers: the need to be free, to escape the drudgery of city life. The bond between the earth and human is an ancient relationship that echoes the delicate actuality in the vastness of the Australian continent. The Outback can be a dangerous place if you are caught between a devil and a deep blue sea, similar to the sight outside the windscreen of our car as we approached Devils Marbles (*Karlu-Karlu* in Aboriginal language). Large and small red, well-rounded boulder rocks perilously lying one on top of the other, fragile and mercilessly baked in the blistering sun of the Northern Territory. It was a reminder of life's fragility and the merciless world that surrounds us. I was becoming deeply attached to this country as I wandered like a nomad with strangers across this red land.

Devils Marbles—the myth of the native people; rounded rocks and boulders are considered the fossilised eggs of the mythical rainbow serpent.

We finally arrived in Alice Springs and checked into a backpackers hostel. I tallied up the bill and presented my fellow travellers the fuel costs that each of us had to pay. A British backpacker suggested that he'd pay me later in the evening and requested that he would like to keep my quality blanket for one more night. Benevolence is a usual character of travellers in this country when you are on lonely roads across great distances. I did knock on his door later on in the night, but he did not answer. I figured he may have gone to the pub, so I decided to collect my money the next morning. I was duped once again when I was surprised to learn that my British pirate had checked out early in the morning and had disappeared with the money; he owed me and decided he'd keep the blanket as well. My experience of the British was a negative one, developing into a view that I did not want to have. After the experience of the two British girls and Peter Stone, I was deceived again by another British backpacker. Once bitten, twice shy. I was now twice bitten, never try. Benevolence towards the British started to change in my heart. I understood the character of colonisation.

While travelling from Townsville to Alice Springs, we passed by a place called the Threeways Roadhouse. We had stopped to stock up on fuel and other supplies. I had seen something that stirred me in my spirit. I saw an eagle sitting on a tree; when I approached to observe him closer, he screamed and lifted into the atmosphere. I watched him fly northwards, towards Darwin.

I stood outside the backpackers hostel in Alice Springs contemplating the next direction of my vagabond nomadic life; the eagle's scream drew me to head back the same way I came. Back to the Threeways Roadhouse. I returned the same way I had come. I contemplated going back to Queensland and trying to work out a relationship with Vera, although I had this sinking feeling that it would be a mistake to go back. Something about eagles held more sway in the inclination of my emotions and sense of direction.

I stayed overnight at the Threeways Roadhouse, a place that inspired me, a location in the heart of Australia that splits into three ways. One road took you to South Australia, another that drew me to Darwin, and a third that would take me back to Queensland and to a girl with whom I did not have any hope of building a steady relationship. Threeways was my pivotal point of reference.

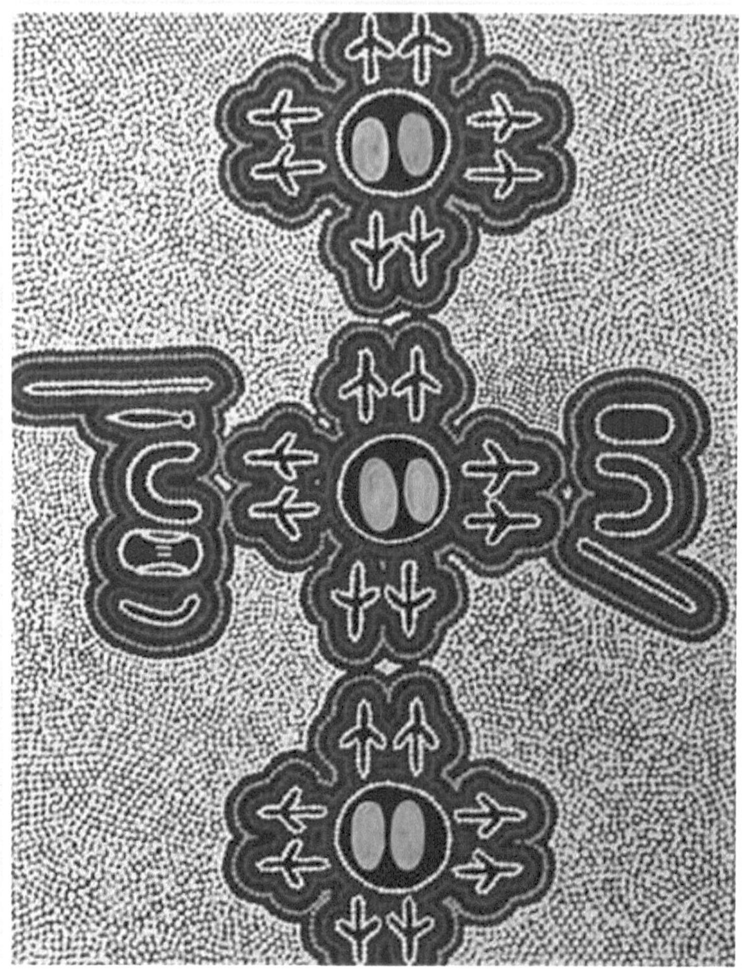

Wedgetail Eagle, *a native Australian painting by Linda Walker Napurrula.*

Like the eagle, I was a wandering soul. I had no place to call home and no family to visit. I was an illegal immigrant. I'd abandoned my family for a new life in Australia. Having discarded my Indian passport to the rubbish bin in Sydney, I was now a wanderer in this red land, a prisoner of my own dreams.

This painting, when examined closely in the centre, looks like two hands with fingers pointing in different directions. This was the eagle's scream directed at me, recommending me to head up north. Just like the wedge-tailed eagle, I had choices to fly wherever I wanted; the spirit of Australia was embedded in my soul as I sang the song from the movie *Paint Your Wagon*, "I was born under a wandering star." I stood on the crossroads between civilisation and freedom.

Completely interwoven with the spirit of the native people, I chose not to take the road to western civilization. I swung my car right and headed off to the Outback. I had an appointment to meet "Story Man" in the Outback, a man I did not know yet. There were still more lessons to learn about art and the people who paint it. Like a finger pointing my wandering soul, I followed the screaming wedge-tailed eagle.

> A wandering dream to meet me there,
> A place and time—a memory to hold.
> Go forward on, mate, don't think too much about where?
> An old man waiting, a story to be told
> A smile and Mirriwa to meet and greet
> (Mirriwa is a frilled lizard)
> A grey-haired man to help you walk with your feet.
> Can you now find water in a hole, out in the desert sand
> I am told?
> Look for footprints of birds and beast converging close
> or be lost wandering and die of thirst.

—(Lyndon Berchy)

CHAPTER 11

VICTORIA RIVER DOWNS

I drove for the next ten days slowly across the Northern Territory, stopping at small towns along the way, sleeping in my car parked at Outback service stations. I moved to Darwin, relying on signs I had seen and followed—on the wings of an eagle.

I found a city that was very laid-back. This was not like any other city I had seen in Australia. There was a beautiful coastline, beautiful beaches, and a fantastic ocean that lay in front of me. The top end was top-notch.

This city was twenty years behind in time in comparison to any other city in Australia; the atmosphere was unlike anything that I'd ever experienced in this country. It started with my noticing that most people were in short pants and rubber thongs. The weather was humid, sweaty, and almost unbearable. I was now in a tropo country. More alcohol was consumed here than in any other place in Australia. The two-litre beer bottle, a Darwin Stubby, was the legacy of this city.

I locked my car and wandered to the beach. I came across a couple of young blokes living in tents on the beach—beach bums equipped with fishing poles; they were able to haul a good catch of fish; they were living off the sea and just being free. These were the days that Darwin would never see. For the first time, I was to come across a new word in the English language that I had never encountered or quite understood: *long-grassers*, social untouchables, people who reject society and live in the long-grass, where they are not unmistakably visible to the general population. There is, in any case, "solidarity in vagrancy and dismissal." White, dark, and darker are altogether joined in the long-grass living space.

As opposed to the impression of different vagrants sleeping harsh, these "long-grassers" were applying a long social custom to manage the circumstance wherein they get themselves. For a few, living in the long-grass is a social decision. Numerous camps are intended for transient living. They have proof of eating and resting, yet not cooking. Aboriginal people group in remote territories; individuals at times cook on open-air fires. Outdoors in the shrub is an exceptionally esteemed social action. From this viewpoint, living in the long-grass expands parts of their ordinary lives. The number of individuals in Australia who are destitute was growing. They live existences frequently concealed—either an escaping view or avoiding acknowledgement. Their numbers were only growing, as more people came to Darwin for various reasons, more for the desire to free themselves as they got away from an old life searching for a new one.

I went down to the local Commonwealth Employment Service (CES) office and registered "looking for a job." I'd had a solid experience in the mining industry, so finding a job here was not going to be a difficult task for me. I surveyed the vacancies that were pasted on the employment boards and discovered a job that caught my eye: Wanted Station Mechanic for Victoria River Downs Cattle Ranch. I approached the lady at the counter, made an inquiry, and expressed my interest in applying for the job.

I handed her a copy of my resume, and she assured me that the CES would get hold of the station manager and notify me in a week's time. Furthermore, she suggested that I visit the office once every day to see what progress they could make to set up a joint interview.

I walked into the CES office one morning and was greeted with a friendly smile.

"Well, good morning. I am Julia," she said. "I am not sure if you know where Victoria River Downs cattle station is, but I can assure you it is one of the remotest places on the earth."

"I'd go even to the moon if I could," I replied.

Julia smiled and said, "Well, here is the good news: the manager is very keen to have you on board. Let me call him on the phone, and you can chat with him. Once you have finished, we can discuss your travel plans and what assistance we can offer you."

Brian Williams said, "You have been around, mate."

I smiled to myself and replied, "I sure have been around. Tell me about the stuff you have there that needs maintenance."

Brian Williams laughed. "I have ancient stuff here, mate! Single-cylinder BDC engines built in 1942, Toyota Land Cruisers and pumps and windmills. You reckon you'd be able to fix them?"

"Sure thing," I said.

Brian said, "We will meet you at the airport when you get here. You will have to fly down here because you could not possibly drive out here and not kill yourself trying."

I found a safe, secure place to store my car while the CES arranged my bus ticket to a town called Katherine. In addition, I was given a flight ticket on a seven-seater Cessna aircraft and a cheque for $140 as supportive money to get me back on my feet again with employment.

A week later, I took the bus from Darwin right down to Katherine. I lodged at the Kookaburra Backpacking Hostel. I made my way the next morning to a small airfield, where there was a little Cessna aircraft waiting for me. Suddenly I felt insecure; if you cannot drive to a place in Australia and you have to fly to get there, then you know that it is an incredibly remote location. When I saw it on the map at the airport, it was like a tiny dot among the red landscape.

Soon we took off from the airport and lifted up into a clear blue sky. I was right in the heart of the Northern Territory. I was wondering if this is what the wedge-tailed eagle most likely was telling me to do when I encountered the majestic bird at the Threeways Roadhouse. Now, I was actually in an aircraft soaring like an eagle, flying to the most-distant, least-likely manageable place on earth.

Victoria River Downs was a very iconic and the largest cattle station in the world. Now as I flew on the little Cessna aircraft for hours, I knew that I was going to the most isolated distant place in the world. From the sky, the empty spaces of red land below me were just incredibly mind-blowing.

According to its history, Victoria River Downs started some way back, in 1880; it was 41,000 square kilometres, no kidding. Honestly, you would look at it, and you would think, *Why would anyone in a sane frame of mind decide to start a cattle station out in the middle of absolutely nowhere?*

The little Cessna aircraft touched down, and as it threw up red dust behind its landing wheels on the dusty red runway, I was happy to get out and put my feet on the ground, after a gruelling long journey. I have never seen a country so vast and so enormous.

Station manager Brian Williams was happy to meet me, and I was so excited that I had finally made it there; he shook my hand and said he'd been waiting for a mechanic for a long time. He smiled and said, "I think I just found one." I thanked him for the opportunity, loaded my gear in the Land Cruiser, and drove for another two hours before I got a glimpse of the cattle station.

Brian Williams gave me a tour of the cattle station; it was a little green oasis in the middle of nowhere. It was a beautiful place—green grass, two long asbestos corrugated sheet-roofed houses that consisted of several rooms, enough to house twelve people comfortably; in addition, a few self-contained houses—one big dinner/lunch house with a big kitchen, a small, circular waterfall facing a big house towards the east side, which housed the cattle station manager, his wife, and children. There was also a large workshop shed, with a few chain blocks hanging from the overhead steel bars, six diesel Toyota Land Cruisers, and two massive trucks built to transport cattle. On the southern side of the station in the distance was a building and fencing where the Brumbies were broken and all the horses were kept. As you walked east from the main building about five hundred metres away, there was a man-made lake.

The first thing you learn about Victoria River Downs is that it's always going to be hot—consistently hot. I reckon it was the hottest place in Australia. Ever wonder why they never called the Northern Territory "the Sunshine State"? To escape the destructive heat, cattle station workers usually start early in the morning. I was so tired from the journey that when I got into my room, I just unloaded all gear and had a power nap, forty winks. I woke up later on in the evening, around about 4:00 p.m., to the smell of meat roasting on the barbecue, a welcome party for the new station mechanic. I met a whole bunch of remote people that day. There was Bob the Englishman, the multi-tasker who fixed fences and everything else except diesel engines and water pumps; Duncan, the bore pump mechanic; Heather, the cook from England; six ringers, two Jillaroos who amazed me with their knowledge and passion for horses. Then there was Steve, the horse whisperer, a legend with a formidable reputation as a man who could break in any wild horse. Then there were two weird-looking fellows they introduced me to: the gardener, who everyone reckoned was a tramp, Dero. Finally, there was a big, overweight fellow they called Cook (Captain James Cook). He was the field cook for the cowboys when they camped out in remote places working with the cattle. These were the two most awkward-looking fellows I had ever encountered. I believed they had lived out in this remote location for so many years that they were incapable of living with society ever again.

I started my first weeks with a deep commitment to repair all the BDC single-cylinder diesel engines. I salvaged parts from redundant engines and restored four engines into good working condition. I serviced the power generators and the standby emergency units, and by the time I was finished with all my endeavours, Brian Williams was the most pleased man in the station. The annoying gardener, Dero, would stop by the workshop and give me suggestions about my work. I wanted to tell him to bugger off and go mow his lawns. Nevertheless, I was polite and did not want to have any strife with people; we were already living in utter isolation, and I did not like to have any kind of animosity.

I continued to work hard and keep myself busy each day, fixing all the equipment that required service and repairs. At the end of three months, I became well respected by the station manager and by most of the blokes at the station.

Every other cowboy was trying to hit on the English cook, Heather, and behind her back, Dero, the gardener, would be bad-mouthing her with his chauvinistic remarks about her wide hips and large buttocks. When these blokes gathered for lunch at the camp, they would talk about horses and cows as if they were people. Their lives were intrinsically woven into the landscape, but horses, bulls, and cows dominated every other conversation at the breakfast table.

Steve, the horseman, gave me riding lessons on Mr. Popgun, my favourite horse. I was truly impressed by this man's skills with horses. The two Jillaroos, Jane and Lucy, were his companions, looking after the horses in the stables. These were highly talented horse people. I was always amazed at the amount of work they put in to break in wild Brumbies. I learned a fair bit about horses from these folks.

One day outside my window, I caught a glimpse of a Willy-Wagtail courting his mate near the lemon tree. I spent many days watching these birds raise several young ones. The Willy-Wagtail is a black-and-white small bird that has the most amusing attitude as he wags his tail from side to side, busily searching for food on the ground. The male had a peculiar white eyebrow, like a design of his proclamation of beauty to attract a sweetheart for himself. The other male birds who were his competitors raised their eyebrows with animosity during their struggles to win the battles over the female during the regional war of the territory of the lemon tree, which raged for a few days and was finally settled by the female when she picked him from the batch of feuding bachelors. In an act of total defiance, she allowed him to mate with her in full view of all the bachelors. The war was almost immediately over. The bachelors all disappeared and took their squabbles elsewhere. Mr. Willy-Wagtail was now presented with a new task. He had to build a nest.

I would throw some bread crumbs under the lemon tree, offering him some added nourishment, and I was astonished at the agreeability of the bird to my presence around him. A recycler by nature, I watched him collect grass, horsehair and hide, along with some wet mud, returning a hundred times a day, building the nest. Then as a bonus for all his dutiful endeavours, his mate would allow him to mate with her. I often laughed at him whenever I saw them mating under the lemon tree. I found it particularly amusing because it was usually in the afternoon or in the evening; he mated with her like he was receiving a bonus each day for the great nest he was building. He was a fair dinkum Aussie bird. It was similar to the Australian male who would come home from work, kiss the missus, and say, "Grab me a beer, love." "What's for tea, love?" "Do you fancy a root, babe?" Mr. Willy-Wagtail was Aussie to the core.

I spent my weekends lying on my bed near my window watching the amazing love story of the Willy-Wagtail. I often thought of home and missed my family. There I was, lost now in the middle of nowhere. I tried to put my sad emotions away so that I would not feel homesick, but the images of my mom and dad haunted me. I had not been in touch with them for more than a year. I wondered how worried they must have been. Nobody even realised that I was from India; most of the blokes figured I was a half-caste mixed-Aboriginal bloke. I was very Aussie by now, and my heart and soul now enveloped into the land of my dreams. Then one afternoon when I returned for my lunch break, I heard a lot of chirping under the lemon tree; his tail was wagging from side to side, and I went close to peek into his nest, and there were three tiny eggs. They both took turns incubating the eggs; the birds trusted me wholly, and I developed the most invigorating bond with the two tiny birds.

The days passed, and I went out with the ringers for a few days, camping at some water holes and mud dams that held a reservoir of water, supplied by a windmill-driven piston plunger pump. These are iconic symbols of Aussie cattle ranch equipment. I returned back to the station after spending three days camping in the wilderness.

I was lying in my bed feeling tired, and I looked outside my window. Willy was on a branch, twitching his tail from side to side with a worm in his mouth. I turned to look at the nest, and a tiny little head appeared from the rim of the nest. The chicks had hatched. I was excited. He hopped next to his young chicks and started to feed them. Soon his mate appeared, and he flew away; when he returned, she left. This flurry of activity was intense, exciting, and plenty of hard work for the birds. They raised two sets of fledglings that summer. My heart rejoiced greatly with the friendship I developed with the birds. I even had the opportunity to pet his kids under the lemon tree. He was like family to me; he reminded me of my mom and dad.

> I saw you under the lemon tree
> When the wars raged on in your battle for love.
> You stood your ground, eyebrows flashing, tail wagging, your opponents you set free.
> She looked at your robust power and lifted you above.
> With a daring move, she submitted in broad daylight to you with a bow
> "Go take your prize," I heard myself say, "for she is all yours now."
> You were confident, gentle with your graceful approach
> If there were a church for birds, I'd marry you both.
> You gave me such feathery joy, drawing me to memories when I was a boy
> Your spirit of freedom, you exemplify to me each day
> Oh, Willy Wagtail, this memory of you in my heart forever will stay.

The hot summer days were hectic, as the cowboys worked on the cattle, setting out in the early dawn and camping in remote places.

Quite often they rounded up cattle by utilizing two light helicopters (Heli-Muster) and driving them into large pens made from steel piping. It was a lot of hard work. I watched them brand them, line them up in holding pens, and move them along in a line in the channel that trapped the animal's neck in a clamp while they dehorned them; cauterization is generally accomplished with a dehorning hot iron after the region is desensitised with local anaesthesia. A bent blade can be utilised to cut the horn off when the calf is a few months old. It is a straightforward methodology, in which the horn and the development ring are sliced off to remove the horn. It is not an easy business when you try to do this with an adult animal. And as the majestic Brahman bulls stood with large horns, the attempt of dehorning big bulls was futile. These were wild cattle, powerfully dangerous.

Some Sundays, rodeo mornings, these macho, driven, testosterone-raging, cowboy competitive fellas would round up the mean-looking bulls with a couple of dogs trained to be aggressive towards the bulls; they would drive these massive Brahman bulls into a holding pen, shoving them against the steel fences, while dogs drove them into their rodeo boxes. It was intensive, noisy business. Suddenly a 2,400-pound bull would aggressively charge as the dogs' barks agitated them; the dust kicked up in the air, like a leaf blower of considerable pressure, the breath of expelling air released from the nostrils of the bull, as dust filled the air into a crazy atmosphere. Rodeo—where men's testosterone clashes with bulls'.

The ringers threw ropes across the beast a few times, wrapping him in three bands of rope around the ribs. "Let us ride," I heard them shout, whistling, swearing, and laughing as they mounted the bull. With the gates swung open and madness ignited into the brain cells of the bull, they went crazy, vaulting into the air, trying to throw the rider off his back. I must admit it was exciting but insane to see a 2,250-pound animal jumping up towards the sky—that's a lot of strength, that's a lot of power, and you wouldn't want to fall down on the ground and be gored by those horns.

I witnessed these crazy rodeo shows out there regularly among the competitions of ringers who competed to be the best bull rider in Victoria River Downs. They even got me to ride a bull, and I almost died as I was thrown and slammed against the fence; I heard a crack in my shoulder. I had no time to even contemplate the shooting pain I felt. I saw the bull turn around and come straight towards me. I don't know how I got out of that. I mustered my strength instinctively and threw myself in a backflip somersault over the steel fence. Then the head of the bull came crashing, and the fence rattled. I considered death approaching. I did not like it anymore. These men were cruel, and those bulls really like to be left alone. I never approved of riding bulls, and that was my last rodeo.

Brian Williams assembled a three-man conference; Bob, Duncan, and myself were gathered to discuss the issues the farm was confronting. Brian disclosed to us that there was no water at a specific place called Four Corners for the steers; dry season had set in, and this location was around six and a half hours driving on dirt road. He proposed that we blokes would need to camp for a couple of days and fix the bore pump.

It was early, about 4:30 a.m. We loaded the Land Cruiser with all the tools, clamps, three-pole tripod stand, and a two-ton chain block, a .303 Lee-Enfield rifle, gas cutting tools, oxygen and acetylene cylinder. We loaded our swag bags and tents and sixty litres of extra diesel.

We set out on this journey with all the provisions we needed. Our vehicle was heavily loaded, so we drove slowly. The Englishman, Bob, was an excellent driver. Duncan was a hillbilly; he was not the brightest spark. Yet, he was not a fruit-loop, just a simpleton with a good heart; six feet tall, he had this dopey look about him—fair dinkum Aussie bushy. "Duncan, you don't need to be smart and talented to have a good heart, mate." I generally complimented and shielded him from those harasser cattle jackeroos.

What I loved about him was the magic of his simple ways. There was no corruption in him; he was a genuine mate, and he had more truth than most people in that cattle station. If this is what it took to be a simpleton with a genuine spirit, then I would always want to be like Duncan.

As for Bob, he still retained every British accent, but he had been long enough in Australia to start losing it; he didn't talk much about himself. It was like he wanted to keep his business to himself. He was the handyman; he could do everything and work with everybody—from fixing fences and windmills, from bore pumps to diesel engine. His favourite equipment was an old Fiat Tractor that he drove, ploughing the land, growing crops for the settlement, like a shadow that had found some form of solace out in the middle of nowhere.

We had driven for two hours, and the sun came out; it was bright, and it warmed up pretty good; the Australian Outback is an unforgiving place. And as we moved along the dirt track, Bob looked out of his window, popped his head out, and noticed that we had a flat rear tire. We stopped and jacked up the Toyota Land Cruiser and changed the flat tire. Now we had two spare tires left. There were all kinds of stuff on this dirt track; it was not unusual to have flat tires. This place was quite rough—some sharp stones, spinifex thorns and grass, a lot of drywood of dead trees. It was not a forested area but mostly prairie plains with ghost gum trees scattered around the landscape. The dirt road would sometimes lead down into a culvert that was an old flash-flood riverbank that may have been carved in ancient times.

This was also bird country. The flocks of budgies were amazing; they would fill the sky like a swarm of bees, darting around in the sky, sketching images that left your imagination to explore the fantastic array of images they created in the sky. They moved in thousands across the atmosphere like some Dutch artist's painting images, leaving you to guess the mystery of them as they changed the patterns in flashes of time, changing with every movement of the flock adorning the sky.

Australia is bird nation; the flocks of budgies left me gasping in excitement as the flocks of birds were adorning the heavens and their creator. We stopped to watch this show of artistic skills of these birds. Bob was like me, or maybe I was like him. We loved the Outback and its magic.

This landscape sheltered winged, feathery beauties: Spinifex doves perfectly camouflaged; several different parrots, cockatoos, pigeons, and lorikeets, singing bramble songbirds, button quail, and flocks of bronzewing. This was also reptile country, with some of the most lethal, scaly, slithery snakes that could kill you instantaneously. We continued our journey as the show was now over and the birds had sheltered on some ghost gum trees; the sun was now rising higher in the sky, and playtime was over for the birds. We drove on, trying to reach our destination before it got scorching hot. It started to turn ugly when we stopped to fix the second flat tire on the right-front wheel. Bob was not so happy about this. Duncan jacked up the car and changed the tire along with me; looking at me with his silly smile, he commented, "Crikey, mate—looks like we boys are on a bad journey. Can you bloody imagine getting two flat tires in four hours of driving?"

Bob responded, "Now, we've got one spare tire left. If we have another flat tire, that's it—we will be up shit creek."

I smiled at both men and suggested, "Let's change drivers for good luck. Bob, you take the back seat while I do some driving here." We continued to drive slowly across the dirt track, passing through the open country; this region was like a wasteland, so humongous and vast. There was nothing you could see for miles and miles, and, yet, it had a richness of bird and animal life that was stupendous. This is not a state I am talking about here, but a cattle station, 41,000 square kilometres.

Finally, around 3:30 p.m., we reached Four Corners Station. We parked the vehicle, unloading all the gear; we set up camp for the night. Duncan and I raised the three-pole tripod stand and hung up the two-ton chain block over the bore pump; we neatly placed the clamps, tools, and flaw-check spray cans used in detecting cracks on metal. We walked over to the water reservoir and found the water level to be low, and the troughs for the cattle to drink water were dry. We got into the reservoir and cleared the blockages on the outlet piping. We dug around it with a shovel and channelled the water into the inlet as a little water flowed into the trough for the cattle. We locked the windmill and shut down the operations of the piston plunger pump.

Bob set up the kitchen tent for our cooking and grabbed all the gear in the boxes, stacking them up for extended trip out in the middle of nowhere.

We set up our sleeping tents, laid out our sleeping bags, and decided to call it a day. We cracked a few cans of beer and prepared for an evening meal. It was a memorable evening as the sun set. Duncan said, "And the Lord said to the shepherd, 'Piss off, mate, this is now cattle country.'" He kept us entertained with his funny ways—a talented one-man show he was, good old Duncan.

We drank a few beers around the campfire, thoroughly enjoying the excellent meal we men cooked together. As the light faded and darkness covered us like a blanket being pulled over, the great southern sky lit up once again, and I lay there once more baffled at the enormity of this creation.

There are a few encounters for which I have no words to express them, something that I have never found in my life and presumably will never observe anything like this, anyplace, until the end of time.

I was about to witness something spectacular out here in the middle of nowhere.

The morning sun rose, heralding a beautiful day filled with song and rhythm; the natural world awoke with its adoration of the beauty of creation. It has always fascinated me how all the living creatures around me appreciated the birth of a new day, whistling tunes of joy or announcing the marking of territories. Birds are such a crucial beauty of our world.

Finishing a good breakfast, Duncan and I went about our task repairing the bore pump. As we disassembled all the piping and the plunger pump, we set up the clamps and started to lift the tubing out of the ground. We clamped the first tube and secured the connecting metal pipe with a clamp, securing it as we unscrewed the tubing for inspection for cracks. Bob came and gave us a helping hand in this labour-intense activity.

We had removed six pipe tubings from the ground and discovered a crack that had developed. We were now satisfied that our intense efforts had paid an early dividend. We took a break for lunch, and I sat under the shade of a gum tree with Duncan.

I saw that the winged creatures were energised. There was a breeze blowing dust; it was abrupt, such as proclaiming something wonderful was to occur. The sky out there was beginning to seem shadowy; some sort of murkiness was dropping upon the earth. It heightened in the far separation to the extent the eye could see. The breeze went past us again, and it was somewhat more grounded. Duncan said in his bushy astuteness, "It doesn't rain around here that regularly. However, when it does, it's generally quite evil." He had scarcely said this, and another whirlwind blew past us, yet now it had an unmistakable smell. It was lovely to the point that getting its breath was energizing. It occurred to me that the birds had just made sense of what was coming. An immediate thought entered my psyche: *Sure thing these winged animals and their progenitors have been here longer than me. Sure they comprehend what's coming.* I respected their intuitive structure. We raced to our camp, unloaded our tents and swag sacks, and stacked them into the Land Cruiser. The tempest was rapidly drawing closer, and the entire scene was presently quickly evolving. We men understood this was something humongous drawing closer; this was not something small. Every winged animal vanished into spots of asylum, while others just took off. We hurried around stacking stuff into the Land Cruiser; the splendid sky was presently transforming into obscurity.

We rushed to get into the Land Cruiser, our place of refuge, when a blinding dust storm hit us; darkness had descended on us like an apocalyptic nightmare. The dust was formed not just by the wind but by the rain that was like the size of golf balls hitting the ground. As the dust rose, the wind pushed it forward. The dust hit us like a freight train as we scrambled into the Land Cruiser and got out of the way; the biggest raindrops fell, and darkness covered us. The day had turned into night. We huddled together as the sound of a freight train passing through raged around us for the next two hours. It felt like the world had come to an end, biblical in portion to the days of Noah.

Our Land Cruiser could become our death trap if we were swept up in any flood. The rain was so heavy, and the darkness so dismal, we could barely see anything outside our windscreen. We had no choice and remained in the Land Cruiser. The vehicle shook in the stormy rain, and the sound of golf balls kept falling on the roof. It was relentless for several hours, and then the intensity started to decrease. An hour later, it began to die down and clear up; the storm had passed through, and we were still alive. I believe ten years' rain fell in one day.

We started to get a view outside the windscreen, and there was only water around us. We were in a deluge but lucky at the same time. We were on higher ground by chance. We did not even consider it when the apocalyptic storm hit us. We could have been washed away had we found ourselves on lower ground.

The rain was now over, and the darkness lifted; we got out of the Land Cruiser and stood in utter shock at the transformation of the dry land. There were flash floods everywhere. Water was gushing, creating new ducts and transforming the area before our very eyes. The tripod stands and the chain block had fallen. Mud covered our tools, our project decommissioned.

I had never observed anything like this in my life; what I saw was, to be sure, an exceptional otherworldly change. With the twinkling of an eye, the land changed. I understood a man could live in the Outback for his entire life and never experience anything like this, ever. These are rare events that happen when you are at the right place at the right time.

Bob smiled and said, "Goodness gracious, I have never seen anything like this in my entire life. There is enough water for the cattle for a long time. I reckon we should abandon Four Corners and head back to Victoria River Downs."

We tried to hook up the radio and set up the aerial, but the radio had conked out, and in this storm, our communications with the station was cut off; it was not working. So, we left the tripod stand and heavy tools back at the bore pump, loaded only the light gear, and started the journey back to Victoria River Downs Station. The land was so incredibly saturated; it didn't help that the Four Corners area was well-known for a darker black soil, rather a clay type of soil. The dirt road had now transformed into a potter's haven; the ground had become a clay pit as we struggled along with the driving. We slowed down at a culvert when the worst thing we were hoping not to occur happened.

The rear wheels of the Land Cruiser just started to sink into the ground; it was like a mini-quicksand of clay gobbling up the rear wheels. As Bob attempted the forward and backward movement of shifting gears and moving back and forth, it started to prove futile, and we only got bogged deeper into the mud. We were now in a hopeless situation. There was no tree anywhere close or a winch wire long enough to drag ourselves out of the grave of clay.

The Toyota Land Cruiser was now buried at the rear end into the clay, in an embrace of death. Reminded me of a dead crocodile that got trapped in a clay mud pool as the grip of the drought got tighter, and death was inevitable as the beast lay there to become fossilised into the history books.

Our Land Cruiser was an old six-cylinder diesel vehicle that had served the station well, but now she was trapped and desperate to come out. We needed help, but that is a desperate thought around these parts. Nowhere starts here, in the Outback of Australia.

Bob looked worried and disappointed. "Well, we cannot sleep in the Toyota, and I am ready to start walking back to Victoria River Downs. What do you fellas reckon about that?"

I enthusiastically agreed that I would join Bob on the journey on foot and hike the way back with him.

Duncan looked at us in astonishment, laughing with a dopey smile. He said, "I reckon you blokes are nuts to think I'd walk back with you all the way to Victoria River Downs, mate. That's friggin' eighty kilometres from here. I am staying in the Toyota."

Bob and I were hoping that we could put some sense into his head, but this dopey bloke would have nothing to do with our hiking plans. Reluctantly, we left him behind with his obstinate ways, not something you do easily. No matter how much we coaxed him to join us, he refused to walk all the way back to the station. Two is company, and three is a crowd; I decided to go hiking with Bob, walking all the way back, and we split up with Dopey Duncan, who decided to sleep in the Toyota Land Cruiser.

It was late afternoon, so Bob and I started our hiking journey; we carried our swag bags and a few provisions and some tucker. Bob had a little billy hanging around from the side of his bag, holding a promise of a nice brew around a campfire. Traveling light with a few provisions, we both set out, leaving Duncan behind.

This land was now transformed. The smell of rain and a freshness of life hung in an ecstasy of joy: sweet-smelling rain, awesome in its transfiguration, was the language of life spoken over the land. It just overwhelmed everything living to sing now in a joy of this great event—everything this land had anticipated and waited for a long time for it to come. And now, because they had received rain, it was like a joyful celebration. As I walked across the land, it felt like the land was singing with you, a rejoicing sound that you could feel all around you: the spell of the dry spirits that had gripped the land vanquished by the power of life-giving water.

Now I felt like we were walking through a land filled with happiness; you could actually, literally feel the earth beneath your feet singing for joy, because this rain had come after…how many years? I don't know. I had never lived here long enough to know if such a storm like this one ever came to these parts. Yet, when it did come, it was truly a remarkable thing; it's hard to even imagine. How do you explain this? How do you express this? You literally feel the earth rejoicing with the rain, and the smell of the rain remained embraced to the ground. In this love embrace between the sky and the earth, it is water that gives life to the dry ground. I walked silently behind Bob while my spirit was intrinsically entwined with the romance and love embraces of nature that surrounded me that day.

Bob and I started a conversation as we broke the silence after a two-hour steady walk; the sun had disappeared on the horizon, and the moon rose up like a beacon of light guiding us through this vast land.

"Hey, Bob," I asked, "what brings you out here to these parts?"

"Oh, well," he replied, "if you really want to know, I like it out here, mate. It's peaceful, and no one bothers you, right!"

"Yeah, for sure," I replied, "I am a wandering star, Bob, maybe just like you, mate."

Bob smiled. "I left England twenty years ago with my wonderful wife. She was a kind woman, and then I lost her," he said.

"How did you lose her?" I asked.

"She died of cancer, and she was like an angel," he replied.

We walked in silence for a little while as Bob was with her in the silence of his happy memories.

A woman he had loved and lost was still alive in his heart with her memories behind.

Then Bob broke the silence and said, "Several years later, I got married to an Australian sheila who was a rough woman and the opposite in comparison to my first wife. Oh, this one put me through hell," he said. He stopped, turned around, looked at me, and said, "Put it this way—my first wife dying was a tragedy, and my second one staying alive was another tragedy." Then he laughed at the misery of it all. "Now, I am here in the middle of nowhere, and I have peace from all the turmoil," he added.

We laughed together as we walked for the next four hours. It was almost 10:40 p.m., and we were getting close to a place the cowboys called Black Gin.

Black Gin was a campsite, a regular Heli-Muster spot, a place for a cattle roundup. The cowboys would come out here and camp regularly during the mustering season to work the cattle.

The full moon was splendid up in the sky and lit up our way well; we didn't have to utilise any flashlights; we continued hiking even though our legs hurt. We propped up till we arrived at Black Gin.

We dropped our swag bags with a sigh of relief; we set up camp and started a fire and secured the billy and hung it over the flames. We brewed some coffee; relishing this warm mug of coffee in my hand, I stretched out my legs to relax them. We had come a long way down the dusty road. I was concerned for Duncan and wished he were with us, but that stubbornness in him was pointless; this is no place to be alone. Bob and I decided to take a break and sleep for a few hours.

I rolled out my swag bag and quickly secured my body into a comfortable position and went to sleep almost immediately. I was tired and exhausted. I fell into a sort of coma and disappeared into a deep sleep for a few hours. Then something stirred in my spirit; something unsettled me. At that point, something mixed into my soul; something disrupted me. My eyes opened, and the twilight was inconceivably splendid and magnificent. I took a gander at the moon in the sky. I felt something move, and I lifted my head off the ground and looked towards my feet that I had securely tucked inside my swag sack. I was solidified to death; I felt a lump up in my throat, and I was not able to move. I was transfixed as the slithery snake crept over my swag pack close to my feet. I needed to run and bounce up, and as much as I needed to do it, I solidified to death; some unexplained power stuck me to the ground and shielded me from going into a craze. The slithery reptile crept over and moved away from me. I lifted my head and watched it crawl away. I connected for my spotlight, turned it on, and sparkled it to check whether there were more snakes around. I changed from a profound rest into a total condition of readiness. I escaped my swag sack and went nuts as I envisioned snakes surrounding me and the possibility of one inside my resting pack. The musings sent shudders down my spine, and I needed to flee from here. I got out of my swag bag and went over to wake up Bob.

I didn't have the foggiest idea that Bob suffered from ophidiophobia. He was vexed and responded in an absolute frenzy at the reference of a snake. This man was out of his swag bag like a blaze of lightning. As he began to pack his rigging, Bob was reviling the snakes: "I abhor reptiles, can't stand the idea of them," he continued protesting. We gathered up all our stuff, and we left the campground of Black Gin.

We kept on strolling for some time, and Bob was currently over the abrupt interruption to his blissful sleep. We walked for a few minutes, and Bob thanked me for cautioning him to the presence of slithering snakes.

Bob said, "You made the best choice, mate, and if we ever get bitten around here, we are dead. These damn Aussie snakes are the deadliest on the planet."

We walked for an hour in the moonlit darkness on the winding dirt track, with ghost gum trees like silvery white shadows reflecting the moonlight across the landscape. We kept walking in silence, and I looked at the time; it was 4:00 a.m. Then we heard cattle in the darkness.

Over here in Victoria River Downs, cattle have insignificant contact with people and live a wild presence, so the sound of cows in the haziness was somewhat concerning. I strolled in front of Bob and stated, "I will shoo them away." I cusped the palm of my hand together, put it towards my mouth, and shouted a *whooooaaaa* sound that vibrated and went out into the haziness. I needed to shoo the creatures from us, so I followed up with a similar activity and three quick *whooooaaaa* hints of caution.

We stopped on the track and heard a sound of hooves; a herd of wild cattle were moving toward us. They were frightened, and they were going out of control.

Bob shouted at me, "Get up the tree, damn it." He hollered, "They are coming in our direction."

I tossed my swag pack across the track into a ditch and clambered up the tree as quick as I could. Bob was on the contrary side, climbed up a tree. As the approaching sound got stronger, a herd of raging bulls and cows came charging down the track. They were running mad.

I was chuckling at the sight; despite the fact that it was dangerous, it was funny. As the distraught cows and bulls drew nearer, I realised we could easily be trampled to death. They ran past us in a furore of franticness and vanished into the obscurity. I was convinced that there were at least three hundred head of cattle in that stampede.

Bob and I got down the tree and were laughing. "I didn't expect them to come our way," I apologised.

Bob chuckled and said, "We would have been trampled to death." It was funny and dangerous at the same time, but we were lucky to escape unharmed. We took a break, lit a fire, and brewed some coffee. We laughed at the experiences of the night, and Bob and I had become good friends through this journey together. We continued our journey back home and walked for a couple of hours.

It was around 10:00 a.m., and we were about five kilometres away from the station when we saw a Toyota Land Cruiser approaching. It was Williams, the station manager. He drove up to us, and there was a look of disbelief written on his face.

Williams said, "Don't tell me you blokes have walked back. What the heck happened?"

Bob replied, "I have never seen a storm like this in my life," as we related the adventure we had survived.

"Why did you leave Dopey out there?" Williams inquired. "Well, Dopey did not want to listen," Bob replied. "He is still out there, and we need to rescue him."

Williams called in the Heli-Muster guys and requested them to fly out there and bring Duncan back.

We got into the Land Cruiser and drove back to the station; we were exhausted and sore from the gruelling journey. The cook made us a great lunch; we had a few cold beers, and I went to sleep on a camp bed under the lemon tree. I didn't wake up even once over the next twenty hours.

The following week, the boys made a poster about the "crazy two who walked from Four Corners." We had become legends with our story in the station.

The seclusion of the prairie fields of the northern region at Victoria River Downs had a few disadvantages. Individuals who live in confinement for quite a long while become exceptional and contorted. Rustic psychological wellness was going to uncover some terrible substances, and I saw a few people who frantically required some assistance here.

The gardener was a weirdo. I regularly observed him with a .22 Remington rifle shooting birds. Six excellent cockatoos were lying dead. I was bothered at the sight and asked the purpose behind the severity of the killing of the birds.

He strolled past me and stated, "Noisy damn things, mate, a grisly disturbance." The way he looked and carried on, I realised something wasn't right. He was a wiped-out individual and required assistance; he worked with mental hindrances. He preferred slaughtering things over getting joy from them.

It was not long before certain events showed his psychological well-being issues. These were the occasions that made me extremely upset.

There was a dog we had in the camp; she was a robust dog. For a bitch, she was very muscular and well-built. This dog liked everyone except Dero, the camp gardener; she never trusted him.

One day the ducks in the pond were found dead, and Dero the gardener told the camp manager that he knew that it was the female dog that was the culprit. He hated the dog for some reason that none of us could understand. Apparently, the manager was sick and tired of his constant complaining about the dog and gave him the orders to get rid of the dog.

Accordingly, he loaded the dog in the back of the Toyota Ute, drove her down to the valley of dead horses, and shot the dog. He apparently hit the dog with some blow to her head after he shot her. When this violent killing occurred, no one was around, as we had gone into the field, finishing out errands for the afternoon.

The next morning, while we were having breakfast, Steve, the horseman, drove up to the camp, and he looked outraged—like he was ready to kill someone. He walked up to the gardener and grabbed him by his neck and stuck him up against the wall and yelled, "Did you finally get your way and shoot the dog? You son of a bitch—you couldn't even kill the dog properly! She is still alive out there!" He shouted again, "Son of a bitch, did you use a hammer to bash her head in? You're a sick man! Go and put a bullet into that dog and put her out of her misery right now."

The gardener, looking all weird and mentally disturbed, panicked and rushed out to go and complete his evil deed.

There was a ruckus that morning at the breakfast table; it was inconceivably upsetting and a horrendous occasion. "I never addressed that dog executioner until kingdom come in my life." I went to my workshop and sobbed for that canine. It just tore me up to realise that its death was a horrible demise. I thought that it was challenging to conquer this sort of cold-bloodedness. The horseman disclosed to us that when he went to get the ponies toward the beginning of the day, he saw the canine sitting on its fours with her belly on the ground moaning and snarling, and he thought that it was yet alive.

A few weeks later, I was at the water reservoir checking a water pump when I heard a young dog yelping; it was a wild dingo pup, about five months old, trapped by the youthful cowpoke, Marty. He had the canine lassoed around his neck, and with his boot, he stuck it to the ground and was attempting to hold it down while his mate hurried off to get the firearm.

I snapped. I raced to free the pooch. I grabbed the rope in Marty's hand and solidly said to him, "Nobody is killing anything today."

He dissented. "It's a bloody dingo, mate—they kill sheep and young calves. We have orders to slaughter dingoes at the site."

I released the young dingo pup, and it ran off, yelping in fear; the little wild dog was running across the field—petrified, yelping, turning back repeatedly—looking at me, mortified with fear. When the pup reached a safe distance, it stood there—howling, protesting—against white farmers and cattle ranchers for their cruelty toward his natural-born talents of survival in the outback.

The pup had been born near the waterhole and had four other siblings. I watched him rejoin his family, and I stayed on until the cowboys had left the site. I had seen Aboriginal cattle men shoot wild hare and feed the dingoes; as for the dingoes, they never trusted the white man out here.

I had spent almost a year out in the deep wilderness. I found it challenging to hang around weird people, especially those cowboys, who had so little respect for the wildlife and animals around them. There was an isolation in the outback that made some people with mental-health issues behave strangely. I felt so sad that I had to decide to leave. It got a little too weird to my liking after the incidents of animal cruelty.

A month later, I left Victoria River Downs forever.

CHAPTER 12

MY ABORIGINAL PEOPLE

I was back in Darwin amid civilisation, and it felt strange, another world. I was happily reunited with my Holden Statesman. Yet, I started to struggle to live in the city. I felt disconnected to the world around me and missed the wilderness.

I went down to the Commonwealth Employment Service and zeroed my eyes in on a job that I found on the board, an opportunity working for an Aboriginal community. I applied for the position and received a favourable response. My long-awaited dream had finally come true. I was to find myself among a people I admired, and yet it was precisely this very desire that moved me across this red land. I had spent some years wandering like a native nomad in a car across this country. I had no place to call *home*. There were times that I felt deeply distressed, thinking about my beloved parents and siblings; my silence towards them was excruciatingly painful on both sides. I knew I would have to call my mum and dad soon.

I did not want any of my relatives in Australia to know about my whereabouts, so I kept silent and disappeared into the wilderness far away from everyone I knew. It was painful for me as well as for my parents, whom I missed deeply.

I gathered all my belongings, loaded them in my car, and drove to a place called Belyuen, near the Cox Peninsula. I travelled along the dirt road that led me along with tropical forests and mangroves.

I was excited and looking forward to being among people that I'd felt deeply connected to over the years. I was now leaving the civilised world behind. I did not need any influence from it anymore; not that it was terrible, but there was an emptiness that I felt in the madness of it, and the connection I felt in the wilderness was more satisfying. As I drove across to Belyuen, when I looked out the window, the scenery was just breathtaking.

During the wet season, I figured out that it would be challenging to drive out here. My job with this community required me to be the technical expert, a position of responsibility, to look after all the equipment, which included Caterpillar graders and shovels, water treatment, and pumping systems. I was also required to train and develop Aboriginal youngsters so they would learn how to look after the equipment. I was now the workshop supervisor/mechanic trainer. The road that led to this community was a dirt road, and during the wet season, it would get damaged due to the weather. Maintaining the way and performing regular grading and road maintenance were required. I was needed to share my technical skills and teach these ancient people new things. I had no idea that it would be, ultimately, the other way around. They were going to show *me* life. This was about to become the most significant impact on my life.

I drove the last few kilometres in anticipation towards the Aboriginal communities of Belyuen. I passed by a few houses scattered across the sprawling grounds. They did not look well maintained, and I saw some broken windows and frames missing; there was a thick forest on both sides of the road. I saw a white house on the right side of the dirt road, and it looked newly built. Next to it were a few trees around spreading branches, a shady spot, and open gardens. I drove two hundred metres, turned right, and drove to the community office of Belyuen. I was greeted with smiles along with the way as everybody curiously looked at this new car driving into the community. My window down, I waved at all the people greeting me with friendly enthusiasm.

This was wonderful. I felt embraced upon my arrival as if I were one of them; my first impression was heartwarming, comfortable, and reassured. I reported to the community leaders in the office and discussed my roles and the priorities that I needed to take care of. I was reminded that I was now in Aboriginal land and did not need to stress out like I did in the city. The priority was to meet all the people in the community and spend time with them so that everyone would know me; becoming a part of them was important.

There was a newly built apartment ready for me, a two-bedroom house, fully furnished, under the shady trees. I checked into my new place and spent the morning setting up my new home. I went down to the workshop and met all the young fellas who were there. We talked about fishing; these were fertile fishing grounds, and the mangroves held some of Australia's most excellent green mud crabs. I couldn't wait to go fishing with them.

I was introduced to one of the elders, whose name was Claud; he gave me a tour around the entire neighbourhood, so that I could meet all the people. I felt so comfortable and warmly accepted. Kenny was a well-built Aboriginal man around thirty years old—not to say he actually cared about his age. I began to realise that date of birth was not an essential thing around these parts. You are born on a particular day, and you go back to the spirits of your ancestors on a specific day. Kenny just told me he was born during the wet season and that it may have been thirty years ago. We laughed, and I just loved that concept of looking at life from his perspective. I invited Kenny back to my place and offered to cook him dinner. A strong emotion of happiness filled my heart and spirit, and I started to feel a great sense of belonging like I'd never felt before.

While we unpacked all the provisions and filled the cabinets in the kitchen, Kenny was helping me to sort my stuff out, while I started to cook some food. Then I heard it—from my kitchen window through the mosquito-proof screen—a voice, singing, under the trees. The lyrics were echoing in the darkness of the night.

> I found my thrill on blueberry hill, on blueberry hill when
> I found you,
> The moon stood still on blueberry hill and lingered until
> my dream came true.
> I found my thrill on blueberry hill.
>
> —(Fats Domino)

This was the song's first verse, and it was repeated over and over again. As the shadowy figure moved farther away, the song followed him and faded into darkness. Kenny smiled and said, "That is Henry, the Story Man, a respected elder of the community."

*****

Six months of living with Aboriginal people had transformed me into a new person. I was now weaving myself into the tapestry of native life. I became a part of this community and felt a great responsibility to fix and repair everything. I took care of the equipment and shared my knowledge, graded the road, fixed the sewage, did the plumbing, and fixed the taps.

I had never realised how exceptionally advanced and environmentally friendly their lives are; their knowledge of the land and everything connected to it made for a union of harmonious living unmatched in my entire existence. I became deeply aware that I was living among the most advanced people in the world, and my gratitude for and appreciation of this oozed out of my spirit daily.

The people now saw me as one of their own; there were no barriers between us. I took out my shoes and walked barefoot with them. I grew my hair longer, and the tropical sun burnt my skin from brown skin to a darker brown. I was adopted into the fold like a native son.

The most profound bond I developed was with King Henry, the Story Man. I never told him that I called him "King Henry" in my mind. I did not think that British royalty could compare to this man. Story Man had a more significant ancestry than British royalty.

I sat with him on many of his happy nights around the campfire. He told stories of the past to the kids—great stories, with his facial expressions and funny, quirky moves and sounds he made mimicking animals, causing the spellbound kids to synchronise their every motion to every action of his storytelling. I sat there totally feeling like a child and then laughing like one along with the kids when he characterized the funny parts. There was no greater storyteller I have ever met.

One day, Story Man and I walked together in the bush, looking for signs of long-necked turtles buried in the mud, when we came across a frilled lizard. The reptile went up the tree, opened his frill, and, like a dragon, hissed at us. Story Man spoke to the lizard in his own language, and I did not know what he was saying to it. The lizard put his frill down, and they exchanged some pleasantries, on another level that was not physical. Henry smiled and told the lizard something in his native words. I just watched this interaction in silence.

We walked on, and I asked Henry, "What did you tell him?"

"Old man," he said and smiled.

Then came the story. "This fella is Mirriwa, his name, 'old man.' Long time ago, he walked with us, but, at that time, he was just a grumpy man. His people told him to stop being grumpy because his neck had become shrivelled, causing him to become even more grumpy. This old man became Mirriwa the Lizard, grumpy old man." As the story vibrated through me, I asked him what he said to the old-man lizard.

Story Man said, "I told him to take care."

I was astonished when I caught the magic of the moment; it was so deeply profound and has remained embedded in my spirit ever since.

I had seen a frilled lizard dragon. Story Man saw an old Aboriginal man.

I saw a reptile on a tree. Story Man saw an ancestor of the past.

I was not connected to the realm of the land. Story Man walked in a different dimension.

These Aboriginal stories are different among different tribal people, but they all have a deep connection to the humanity of Aboriginal people. My days of living with them was a daily joy of learning the intrinsically woven tapestry of life as I had never known it before. The harmony—between birds and insects, reptiles and ants, animals and man—was the dance of a balanced life together.

I was transformed daily as I learned to sing and dance and perform the "Carobree." I went on hunting expeditions with the men. We would hunt fruit bats (flying fox). As we shot them among the trees, some of them remained hanging on the branches in the final grip of death. I would climb the tree and shake the branches till they fell to the ground. They were roasted on the open fire. Kenny was dancing and doing the fruit-bat dance; he said it was his Dreamtime, and so he would not eat it. He suggested that I try it because it was medicated meat. I tasted a piece for the first time; it had a peculiar taste that I was not accustomed to.

I went out with the women one day looking for long-necked turtles, a species of turtles that buried themselves in areas where there was moisture in the ground. They would immerse themselves and keep their bodies moist. Their long necks would allow them to sink themselves into the deeper ground while they continued to breathe air through their tiny nostrils above the ground. The women were equipped with thin, long wooden and metal probes, which they would dig into the field ground, looking for the turtles. They would also dig deep into the ground and find yams.

Even though we had a food store in the community, a bush tucker was a necessity in this culture. It was a natural instinct to remain connected to the land and to hold everything in reverence, to remember survival, an ability that was built into the DNA of a people who have walked across this continent far longer than we can imagine.

We followed the small river that led us through the creeks where the river met the sea and the tides of the ocean flowed back into the river and mangroves, in a back-and-forth water dance of the ocean and the river. I began to see the earth as I never had before. I was aware of the relationships between man and his world. If this was the Garden of Eden, then I understood what it would feel like be to be Adam. I felt a responsibility of having dominion of all the nature around me in a balance of life in the profoundness of relationships. That is what I was learning—the bonds of every living creature with every other, and man with dominion over them all. He could trap them, hunt them, plant them, do everything to sustain himself, and live with them; most importantly, man should take only what he needs and protect all creatures. That responsibility was almost sacred.

As we dug in the sea sand with the women and kids on the beach, we collected turtle eggs, some of them freshly laid the night before. Then a few eggs from different nest sites were collected, and the remainder were buried in their nests.

I had a fishing line out when I felt a tug. As I retrieved the hand-line, I noticed that it was not acting like a fish. I found a big, green mud crab at the end of my line.

Kenny smiled at me, pointing to the big crab; he said, "That fella is good tucker, mate."

We finally subdued the crab to give up his life and washed him in the seawater. We rolled up his parts in silver foil, dug a small pit in the sand, buried the silver foil with the crab in it, and lit a fire on top.

The women and children all gathered around the fire as we barbecued fish and other seafood we caught during the afternoon session of foraging, hunter-gathering. If such living is considered primitive, then I am having more of it for the rest of my life.

Story Man was always never far away from me. I would sing "Blueberry Hill" with him, and he sure loved that. I managed to get him to learn the second verse of "Blueberry Hill," and he loved me for that. And so, we sang "Blueberry Hill" around the fire as we laughed, sang, and ate together. Kenny moved the fire and dug out the silver foils that we had buried earlier.

The mud crab was the tastiest food I had ever eaten; this was a culinary Michelin three-star dish that you would never get anywhere else but on that sandy beach.

This was Aboriginal land, and there was no white man allowed here. This was their land and their home. As I lay on the beach with all the people, looking at the stars once again, I was humbled and felt a great sense of love for my people.

I had eaten the most wonderful seafood, sung the most excellent tune, and felt the greatest love of family. Most of all, I felt deeply loved. We all slept on the beach around a campfire under the stars that night.

The next morning, there was an excitement in the camp. I did not have a clue as to what the excitement was about. The kids were also excited.

Kenny told me that they were going to find a delicacy called *milka*. I didn't know what it was; the excitement among the people was so joyful that I was excited as well but did not know what to be excited about. It was such an excellent feeling, a new emotion I was encountering in my life, a surprise of a different kind—a hunter-gatherer surprise, I would call it now. We all gathered together in the mangroves; the tide was moving, and the mangroves started appearing as the sea receded. Everyone spread across the mangroves searching for something among the prop roots of this shrubbery plant that was so iconic along this coastline. The excitement was contagious; someone shouted, laughingly excited. With axes and machetes, they chopped the wood and pulled out these white worms. Some they ate raw, and others they collected to take back home to boil them up in hot water. We hopped around the corals and oyster beds for a few hours, and then the worm harvest was over. I learnt about this worm much later.

Teredo navalis, the maritime shipworm, is a type of saltwater mollusc, a marine bivalve mollusc in the family *Teredinidae*, "the shipworms." This species was of the variety *Teredo*. Like different species in this family, this bivalve is known as a shipworm since it looks like a worm in appearance, while at the front end it has a little shell with two valves specifically for drilling through the wood.

This species may have started in the upper east Atlantic Ocean, however, it has spread far and wide. It burrows into submerged docks and pilings and is a significant reason for harm and pulverisation to submarine timber structures and the frames of wooden vessels.

—(Wikipedia contributors, *Teredo navalis*, Wikipedia, The Free Encyclopedia, accessed February 17, 2020)

I did not feel brave enough to eat the worm raw the first time I saw it and opted for the cooked version. When I realized it was good tucker and tasted like an oyster, it became a delicacy on many shoreline expeditions.

I had lived among amazing people here for almost two years, and yet it felt like I'd been born among these people; they had become my family. I had wandered this red land and found myself a family among the ancient people of this land. My spirit, for now, was not restless anymore; it had found some peace in a vast territory—a people, home, and a family that I hadn't had since I had abandoned them on a distant shore in exchange for a dream.

I would still go through emotions of crying alone when I thought of my mom, dad, and my siblings. It felt like my dad was with me on these hunting trips, and I saw Story Man as a fatherly figure in my life. I had become primitive, according to society, but if being primitive is what this is called, I realised the first ones were those who lived across the Cox Peninsula in the city of Darwin.

In 1991, I knew the world was a mess; the environment was going to turn ugly on this white man. I was in the bosom of the ancient native man, in complete equilibrium with nature, and I understood that the world across, where advanced men lived, was setting out on a course of self-destruction. The partition between man and the world was a divisive destiny that was drifting on the slope of a streaming waterway, cascading to a possible tipping point, ending the mess of humankind forever. I likewise acknowledged they would never, at any point, have the option to return; they had lost the association with the earth. My contemplations from back then have been affirmed today as I compose this book. The world and environmental change are the headways of men who have labelled themselves as "advanced." My heart races, and I can close my eyes and stroll back among the mangroves with Kenny, Claud, and Story Man even till this day. I feel tears and realize the world is headed toward end times. Who is crude? They just couldn't let the Aboriginal people live the way they had lived for thousands of years. They had to come and conquer and decimate this antiquated land. Even a friendly sentiment can't fix what is broken until the end of time. Individuals think Australians are Caucasians; however, Australians are Europeans. Aboriginal people are the real Australians, people of the Never-Neverland.

Australians have transformed the land into a consuming inferno, similar to the seeming end-time prescience of the seething bush fires in the year 2020. It seems to be some kind of punishment on the nations that have turned away from God and have for decades refused to learn from the ancient people of Australia.

There was a hidden sadness in this place, and I never knew until it confronted me one day. During the days of the missionaries, native people were separated around these parts of Australia. While the Japanese bombed Australia's top end for a long time during the Second World War, the Catholic church had destroyed the Aboriginal people earlier, being responsible for taking away children from their parents. There was this distorted belief among the missionaries that these ancient people had no clue as to how to live as human beings and that their children were living in an uncouth manner. The reality was far from the truth.

This tragedy came home one day to Belyuen when the elders told an older woman that her son was coming back from New South Wales. They had managed to find him through the agencies. The small community office had been established by an Aboriginal couple who worked hard to make the reconciliation of the lost generation happen. I did not know the details of all the history, but I witnessed the unfolding reality of pain and separation.

They were attempting to make the older woman understand that her stolen child was coming; she was old and delicate, and it was an emotional scene that influenced everybody in the camp this day. There was an expectation of mixed feelings filling the air; it was something I found myself caught up in. I was bewildered, like every other person, and the older lady was the centre of the unfurling occasion.

I didn't have a clue as to how to respond. I didn't have a full grasp or comprehension of the conditions and history of this country. All I could feel was that someone had done something unnatural, evil, and inhumane to this poor woman; they stole her infant away from her, and life had stopped for her since that day. Like a phantom, she walked among her people, dying to her emotions each day. Now, frail and old, the community was advancing an event to relieve her agony forever.

She would find closure to her enduring suffering with the delight of this reunion, an embracing of something so valuable that had been lost. The older lady was confounded and sincerely unconscious of what was in store. She did not know how to respond, so every other person felt a similar way; her life touched the pain of everything these ancient people endured when their world changed forever.

The cars approached on the dusty track towards the community, and the elders gathered around it; an Aboriginal man stepped out. The people all gazed upon him; they were frozen for a moment in grief *and* happiness. Everyone felt the truth of the moment, and it seemed like everyone wanted to hug him. But the elders walked him over to his old mother, the one the white man had taken him away from. The sun stood still, and the trees did not move. The birds stopped and gazed; the lizard lifted his front leg, acknowledging the new visitor. I was capturing this most painful scene of my people. He bent down to give her a hug, and a son saw his mother for the first time. She did not hug him back but said something to the women in her language. She asked them who he was, and they told her, "This is your son." She said she wanted a baby and not a man.

I ran away. I could not bear it. I held onto a gum tree, and I was overcome with terrible grief. They'd stolen the children away. I cried for an hour and could not stop. I felt anger and hatred for a brief moment. How could they have done such things in this country?

People cried as they explained to her that her baby had become a man. I had come to realise that time had stood still for her the day they took her baby away.

In the following week, happiness returned once again as the son and mother were reunited, and lost time remained lost time. I could never understand how primitive men like the Europeans could come over here and perpetrate the most inhumane crimes against the most advanced people on the planet Earth, the Aboriginal people.

I went for a walkabout with Story Man; Kenny and Claud came along. We spent three days out in the bush, hunting and living off the land; we found a tree filled with small white berries they called bush apples, so I ate them.

"This was men's land," Story Man told me. "Here, boys become men." Pointing to a different location, he said, "That side there was women's land, where girls become women." Clad explained that, when a girl had her first menstrual cycle, she would be brought to the women's land, and the women would gather her favourite food and initiate her into womanhood.

I was now one of them. I had become a family with them; this was my family in Australia. My days were beautiful; I found a life among good people, abundant in joyful living, in spite of all the tragedies they had suffered.

It was late afternoon in men's land; there were a creek and a small stream of water that flowed around this rock. So, I lay there on the rock as the wind blew through the gum trees; it was a shady place, good for dreaming. In the midst of this tranquillity, I fell asleep.

I saw an eagle again, and this was the most majestic bird I'd ever seen. I stood in front of it in utter amazement. Our eyes met, and I asked the bird, "Can you teach me to fly?" "Come," said the bird, "spread your arms like me," so I did. And as the bird lifted, so did I. We were in the sky together, and there was a wind blowing under me that raised me. I soared and flew, and in this dreamtime, I could have stayed forever. Suddenly, the sound of kookaburra birds, sounding a loud, noisy chatter, alarmed me out of my dream and deep sleep on that blissful rock that I lay on. My eagle dream was over. I did not want it to end, but it did; I wanted to go with that eagle wherever he was taking me.

On our way back later that day, I told Story Man my dream and how I first encountered this eagle in Western Australia, driving up in Wiluna. Story Man said, "Kurrawurra—you are a Kurrawurra; this is your Dreamtime. That eagle has followed you every way."

My days in this community were profoundly moving. I had found a place to live and a unique family to behold. Yet it did not change the fact that I was not supposed to be in this country illegally. I knew that the original people of this country would never tell me that I was "illegal." I was going to be united with these people forever. They had become my people.

One morning, two Toyota Utes pulled up in front of my workshop. I was servicing the Caterpillar grader when the boys came to pick me up for a hunting expedition. We were off to shoot some wild pigs. I closed the workshop facilities and grabbed some of my gear and went with them. I was excited because it reminded me of home and connected me in my heart to the memories of my dad. We drove through the bush for a few hours and stopped at a large swampy area. Claud had shot two wild turkeys on the way. We camped and lit a fire, spiced up the turkey, cooked it over the fire, and ate lunch.

They split up into three groups, armed with shotguns, and moved to different parts of the swamp. I stayed at the edge of the swamp with a young teenager named Daku, while the other group moved into the bush to flush out the wild pigs. I had a .22 Remington rifle with long-range hollow-point bullets. I had learned something about wild pigs from my dad. I recalled his advice as a professional hunter on the correct way to shoot wild pigs with a high-powered rifle. His words were ringing in my head: "Always be patient; wait till he presents you with a good shot. The best place to aim your bullet at is just behind the pig's ear. That, my son, is the vital spot." For a moment, I could feel my dad's presence right there next to me.

I stood there at the water's edge with Daku waiting for any wild pigs coming our way. I handed him the gun and lit a cigarette. I was looking one way and Daku the other way.

Suddenly some dark shadows appeared, and the young fella moved quickly with the gun and ran into the swamp. I was distracted because I was smoking a cigarette, and before I could react, Daku had run after the pigs into the swamp. I felt a little upset because my dad's advice on how to shoot a wild pig couldn't be realised.

I moved about thirty metres along the water's edge of the swamp when I heard them snort. I hid behind the tree, and I could see six wild pigs walking along the marsh. I could not do anything. I had bullets, but no gun; my young brother Daku had run off with the gun.

I felt frustrated and let down. I waited, and Daku returned, sweating, smiling, and empty-handed.

"Did you get any?" I asked.

Daku replied, "No, mate. Them pigs can run fast."

I looked upset, and I told him what had happened after he had run off. "Six pigs were walking in style in front of me, and I had no gun to shoot them.

"You don't run after them, young fellow. You wait for them to get closer and aim well. Then you pull that trigger and lodge that bullet just behind the ear of that pig. My dad taught me that," I added. "You will always kill a wild pig this way."

"I am sorry, mate; I got excited," he replied.

I took the gun from him and knew the opportunity had slipped away. Then I heard magpie geese landing close by. I left Daku near the campsite and walked into the swamp with the .22 in my hand and about twenty hollow points in my shirt pocket.

I circled around the swamp and trees and found an opening where a whole bunch of magpie geese were hanging around; they were swimming around as I slowly sneaked up knee-deep in water. I levelled my gun on the branch of the tree, took aim, and squeezed the trigger.

Feathers ruffled in the air, and birds took to the sky with loud trumpet sounds of panic; one magpie goose stayed behind. I waded my way through the water and picked up the dead goose. I was surprised at how big and bulky the bird was. I was sure my family would be happy that I had contributed to the hunt—although I still would have liked to have shot a wild pig. I turned back with the gun in one hand and the goose in the other, wading my way through knee-deep water. I stopped, looked, and was confused. When I walked into the marsh, my view was different, but when I turned back, it all looked the same. I was sure that the direction was straight ahead, but I found myself getting into deeper water. I turned around and realized that the water level should be decreasing and not increasing. I was surely going the wrong way. I walked the other way and kept going. I tripped on a dead tree trunk and fell into the water with my gun and the goose. All the .22 hollow-point bullets fell out of my pocket, and I was a soaking mess.

I put my hands in the water and started searching for the gun. I felt logs of wood, and then, luckily, I felt the thin barrel of the .22 Remington rifle and pulled it out of the water. I felt relieved at recovering my firearm. I removed my boots and tied the laces to the neck of the goose. My shoes were hanging in front of my chest, and the magpie goose was hanging on my back; I was holding the gun firmly in my hand. I was wading in the water, completely lost and disoriented.

The swamp was a dangerous place. It would be almost impossible for a helicopter to locate me if a rescue were to be attempted; such thoughts went through my head. I kept walking, but the more I moved, the more lost I got. I found a tree with a small piece of land around it. I put the gun against the tree and climbed up the tree. I figured that maybe I would be able to see people from a distance. Yet, when I reached the treetops, I was in a canopy and realised that I would not be able to see anyone on the ground. I did the next best thing: I started the howling-monkey trick. I was calling out for people, but no one could hear me.

I realised that my situation was getting desperate; the sun would go down in two hours, and I would be lost. I got down the tree and started to cry. I felt a great sense of desperation descend on me, and I began to pray. I was complaining to the Lord in utter agony. I knew I could not stay under this tree and needed to keep moving, yet, I did not know where to run or which direction to take.

Then I heard a gunshot. *Pow! Bang!* It came from an opposite direction. I heard it, and suddenly I felt relieved; hope returned to my heart. I walked in the direction of the sound. As I kept walking, I noticed that the water level was falling and suddenly knew that it felt right. I walked even faster in the water because I just wanted to get out of this deadly marsh. The water reached my ankles. I was on dry land, and I called out. Story Man, Claud, and Kenny quickly approached me. Story Man was very upset. He walked towards me, gave me a firm slap across my back. He shouted at me with love and anger, "Where did you go?"

As I explained to him my ordeal, Claud and Kenny came and hugged me. They looked at me and said, "We did not think we would see you again today. There are saltwater crocodiles in this marsh. They come from the sea and use this place during the nesting season."

Story Man was relieved that I was alive. He reprimanded me, "You will never do this again in any swamp in this country. Young fellow, you are a lucky boy to live to tell the story. Good spirit protected you. The season of the crocodiles is approaching. Eagle spirit Kurrawurra may have protected you, but you are a lucky boy not to be dead. Few people come out of this swamp alive, where crocodiles are known to live."

There was a dead wild pig in the rear of the Toyota Hilux; we bounced on the vehicles on the dirt road as the men drove around the marsh for around thirty minutes to an alternate area, and we halted for a bush-reality lesson. Story Man instructed me to bring that magpie goose I had shot; we jumped on the embankment of the marsh and looked at the still water. "Now, watch and learn," he said. Claud and Kenny joined us with sticks in their hands. Story Man started to bang his hands on the banks of the swamp. "Look," he said. I saw a clear surface like a dark mirror. "Look," he said again; as the banging on the bank continued, a crocodile's eyes started to appear on the surface, then another and yet another. I saw five crocodiles appear. Stealthily, as they moved towards us, Story Man threw the magpie goose in the water, and they attacked it. "Let's go," he said. I think it was a spiritual gesture, like thanking the crocodile for not having me for dinner this day. I looked and learned a lesson. Aboriginal people had respect and reverence even for the dangerous creatures around them. These people are intrinsically woven into the land and creation, unlike any other people I had ever known.

It was the early start of the nesting season. I was lucky to be alive; there were no crocodiles in the area where I'd gotten lost wandering in the marsh. It was a miracle that I cannot explain. How a crocodile did not get ahold of me remained a mystery: either it was not my time, not my destiny, or there was a Holy God protecting me. I have never attempted to find an answer to this question. Yet, Story Man believed that the power of spiritual blessing of good spirits rested over me, and I was blessed to be alive.

I almost died at the Western Mining Longshaft Kambalda mine, and now, this was the second time I had escaped death. Australian saltwater crocodiles are no ordinary reptiles; this is death that grabs you at 3,700 pounds of bite force, and when the teeth on the upper and lower jaw trap your body between them, you can expect to feel the power of 350,000 pounds of force. This beast would spin its body like a turbine and rip off your body parts, while another one of his friends grabbed you from another side and did the same. It's an awful death; Seeing the magpie goose we threw at the crocs ripped into shreds before my very eyes was wrenching and sent shivers down my spine.

We returned to the community, and families gathered as we divided the carcase of the wild boar that we'd brought back from our hunting trip. In the evening, the people lit a campfire while the meat was being barbecued. Then they danced the native *corroboree*—with young men playing the *didgeridoo* and others clasping rounded wooden sticks, making a rhythmic sound. Another expert musician played a tune from a leaf that he placed in his mouth that sounded like a small flute, another man was swinging the bullroarer at a safe distance. A fire was burning in the middle, with meat roasting on the fire. Young men decorated themselves with white chalk markings over their bodies, framing lines and specks all over. In an emblematic rhythm, they moved around the fire, singing and dancing like the wild boar, moving around the fire, while the hints of wild hog reverberated from the *didgeridoo*. Snorts and screeching sounds blended in a musicality of thanksgiving to the spirits for the nourishment of all the tribal individuals. This was a sort of thanksgiving ritual before a meal. I was impressed.

I propped up through the musings of the day. I realized that I was fortunate, blessed, and grateful to be alive.

My days with my people were like a magical fairy tale. I had never known a people more advanced in wisdom, knowledge, and environmental skills; their responsibility for the balance of nature was amazing, wandering as true environmentalists, leaving almost no carbon footprint wherever they went. I see them as ancient scientists who walked daily in the university of life, with profound reverence for their life and for every other form of life that surrounded them. Even the perils and dangers that could tip these balances were respected and revered.

They have excellent sense of family, community, and togetherness, and their own healthcare cures astonished me. For example, Kenny took a piece of cloth and planted it at the nest of bull ants, disturbing the nest in his attempt to bring out the aggressive marauding ants. They can pack a stinging bite, and yet, they oozed out an antiseptic enzyme around their bodies that medicated the piece of cloth Kenny had thrown on the ground. Kenny then returned to pick it up once the ants had settled down, returning to rebuild their damaged nest.

Kenny wrapped the cloth around the wound on his leg, preventing it from any further infection and becoming healed in the process. I stood there baffled and astonished at the many medicinal solutions that existed in the mind of Aboriginal people. Who taught them these things? How did they learn such things? Was it by accident or just a simple, deep connection between man and the Earth? I believe this is called *function*. When man was created on the Earth, he was given power to subdue all things, and the lord God gave man the ability to *function*.

Here was a family and a community that touched the core of my human heart, and I learned to dance, paint, and weave their culture into the very fabric of my own life. I was walking with the most advanced people in the world. When I close my eyes, I can still see their faces, feel their spirits dancing around the campfire nights, the evenings of our thanksgiving and celebrations of life in the Outback.

As I write this book, I look at the current condition of the world—the disasters and the climate change that have jeopardised humanity.

We have moved from petrol cars to electrical cars, from plastic cups to plastic spoons, from fast-food chains to figures of obesity, from food production to drug prevention, from the state of human need to the state of human greed. We have destroyed ourselves as a species and call ourselves "advanced."

There has never been such a separation of humanity from nature more alarming than it is today. All those who call themselves "advanced people," including white supremacists who think that a Blessed Holy God is a white man, are the very same people who have destroyed God's world.

Thirty years back, I strolled with the most progressive individuals on the planet, who lived in total balance with the world we live in. The Australian government thought about them as the flora and fauna of this country. The European pioneers didn't regard them as human beings and considered them primitive, but they were the most advanced society, unquestionably more developed than the savages who originated from Europe.

Europeans colonised this country and played out the most offensive violations against the most excellent ancient people. I had the honour to live among them and to love them in my lifetime. Those people turned into my kin in the days I walked among them. I found Kurrawurra, flying with his wings spread across the sky, as I lay under, looking up at the bird that became my Dreamtime.

I told Story Man that I had to make a trip to Darwin. I had a feeling that I'd heard my mother in my sleep. I listened to her voice, and my heart was aching to see them again; something was not right. I had been living for almost two years away from the white man's world, and I began to fear my return to that world. It had become alien to me, and I wondered if I could ever adjust to it again.

Darwin looked alien to me; it did not excite me at all. First, I went down to the Victoria Tavern. I did not want to drink any alcoholic beverages. I had some lunch and felt very Aboriginal; it was a weird feeling. I was experiencing the world I left, now from the perspective of an ancient, advanced species of a bushman. I felt I'd swung 180 degrees the other way around. For the first time in my life, I realised the city I'd left almost two years before had become pointless and irrelevant to the way life was meant to be. People are disconnected from the world in cities, caught in human frameworks, like captives to a lifestyle. We, as a whole, have come to be known as advanced people. I was so lost—separated and frozen to be among them. My heart yearned to be back with the people of my Dreamtimes.

I picked up the phone and called my mom and dad in India. It was going to be a long phone call. I heard my dad cry, my mother was in tears, and my siblings all gathered around the phone as I spoke to them. I was in a telephone booth weeping and talking to them all at once.

My mother was very sick, and she begged me to come home to see her. I promised her I would go as soon as I could. My dad, weeping, was equally painful. I was so upset with myself. I had put my parents through so much pain, and now they were so overjoyed just to hear my voice.

I stood in that phone booth and wept. A truth flashed across my mind: if those crocodiles had seen me in that marsh, I would have never been making this phone call this day.

I decided to get myself an Australian passport that day. I filled out forms, changed my name, and got the necessary documents attested and signed by authorities. I did not consider what was wrong or right. I had to see my mother, who was in poor health. I desperately wanted to see her. I was so overwhelmed with emotions. I was surprised at how easy it was for me to become someone else.

I submitted all the papers to the office and returned on the appointed day to receive my Australian passport. I did not need an article to tell me I was Australian. I was more Australian than any European who ever colonised this red land. I was Kurrawurra, and I needed to fly.

PART TWO

CHAPTER 13

BEAUTIFUL CHILDREN WITH UNGODLY WOMEN

I never realised that I'd feel torn from both sides; leaving Belyuen was no easy, natural choice, either. The only consolation I had going was knowing I could come back—all of a sudden, a wanderer of the Outback for many years. One blue book with my photo and a different name gave me the freedom to fly like an eagle once more. It was so extraordinarily bizarre. I was not inclined to do this. I did not want another name, but my extraordinary love for my mother was overpowering. Who can win with reason against the love a son deeply feels for his mother? I had an Australian passport issued to me on a different name. I would come to regret this silly, emotional mistake in my life. I paid dearly for the mistakes of my youth.

I left my people in Belyuen that morning and suffered mixed emotions that day. I was leaving one family to go see another family I had left behind several years ago.

Living for several years in the Outback, I'd cultivated a deep appreciation for this fantastic landmass. Its sheer beauty and lonely expanses, the unique animals, reptiles, birds, and plants were mind-blowing treasures. I can remember an early morning walkabout in the open wilderness, a place known as Cue. I had a staff in my hand, walking on an early-morning hike. I climbed over this ridge to see the sunrise. There was early-morning fog; the cold desert night was lifting like smoke on the water as the rays of light hit the surface of the ground, commanding the freezing fog to scatter at the sheer magnitude at the appearance of the sun.

I sat on the ridge with the staff in my hand, mesmerised at the incredible beauty of the birth of a new day. The morning warmth can be a rapid process in the Outback, and the sun took hold of the land perhaps more quickly than I had anticipated. I saw big red kangaroos foraging in their early-morning awakening. I sat and watched the big red roos. Two big males were approaching each other; some rancour that existed stirred between the two rivals. As they stood facing each other, with the rising sun as the background, I was immediately transported in my mind to Madison Square Garden. As they boxed each other, every blow, kick, first jab, and uppercut they delivered resulted in red dust flying in the air. It was easy for me to mark the scorecards with accuracy in ratio to the earth that flew from each opponent, indicating a perfectly landed punch, considering I was the only honourable judge elected to preside over the most significant bout in the history of the Outback. It was the most distinguished sportsmanship and the most significant fight I'd ever seen. The brave challenger respectfully accepted his defeat and moved on, wounded, but with his dignity intact. Now, some humans do not fight this way; they are capable of despicable, vicious, long, drawn-out conflicts that can torment their feelings for eternity. They humiliate and relish the fall of an adversary. They deceive each other with a genuine desire to perpetrate torment and betray each other—to inflict pain that can last a lifetime—and to hold on to resentment to the bitter end; in that process, they slaughter the heart of a child.

I would come to remember the fight of the big red kangaroos of Cue once again. I was looking at a paradigm in front of me, sitting on the ridge that beautiful morning. Even animals are capable of a fair fight.

I made frequent calls back home to my mother and was relieved to know that, although her condition with her heart was precarious, she was making good progress with her recovery.

It was 10:00 a.m. at Darwin Airport, and I was getting ready to fly to Indonesia. I was scared, because, in my heart, I knew I had done something wrong; the passport in my hand was mine, but the name was not. I could not change what I had done, but I was afraid to go directly to India. I did not want to be trapped once again in the country that I had so desperately left several years ago.

So, I made plans to fly via Indonesia and Singapore, and then on to India.

Sitting next to me at the airport was a bald, young German girl, dressed in a sarong, rubber flip-flops on her feet and a small bag in her hand. Sitting next to her was a young Englishman in his early thirties, covered in a sarong, a T-shirt, and charms from different belief systems hanging around his neck, and holding a *didgeridoo* in his hand. They were wandering hippies scanning the world, searching for freedom on the endless horizons, finding something new of themselves at every journey and destination, in a relentless search starting over again at the beginning of a new adventure at the end of every trip.

I was exactly the opposite, dressed in jeans, boots, buckled belt, and my Akubra hat; we met like wanderers in time on the benches of the Darwin International Airport, heading to the same destination. On the shortest route between Australia and India lies the island of Kupang, likewise spelled Koepang, capital of East Nusa Tenggara and the biggest city of Timor Island, Indonesia. It is situated close to the southwestern tip of the island on Kupang Bay of the Savu Sea. Roads connect it with Soe in the area and Dili in East Timor; Kupang additionally has an air terminal and lies on the Java-Australia air course. It is an exchange and transhipment point; copra, cowhide, sandalwood, pearls, and fish are traded to Java, western (Indonesian) New Guinea, and Australia. Most of the populace is Papuan, with a mixture of Malayan and Polynesian people groups. Angling and painstaking work, including wood-cutting, basket-weaving, and calfskin-tanning, are significant. The Portuguese colonised the city during the 1530s but were ousted by the Dutch in 1613.

Colonisation has now become a filthy word in these countries. European supremacism sprang from the minds of European men who believed they had some unnatural, self-induced rights straightforwardly from their kings and queens. The Europeans colonised countries like Indonesia just for their one-of-a-kind, favourable position, but to the disservice of the local people who lived there. Regardless of this history, local people were genial individuals.

The young blond German girl had suffered an allergy in the tropical north of Australia, developing some blisters and sores on her scalp—some kind of issue with hair follicles. To aid her in ridding herself of this malady, she had shaved her blond hair and now was bald.

As we strolled through the lanes of this town, mobbed by a gathering of little kids tossing small pebblestones at us, sneering at the young German lady, prodding her and calling her *geela*. As entertaining as it appeared to the children, it was moderately irritating to the young German lady. Trying to shield her from this provocation, I undermined the children with signals of reprisals.

I didn't exactly comprehend the purpose behind it, yet glancing back at how the young German lady was dressed and appeared, she may have seemed unusual to the youngsters. Next to her was an odd, half-naked Englishman with a *didgeridoo*. He was a cattle rustler such as myself, wearing a hat and long hair. The following day, we meandered through the first town on this laid-back island. I went searching for a lexicon book for interpretation of the local language to English; having found a bookstore, I was astonished to locate a little book, a voyager's guide, an adjustment of expressions and words in an alien language. I asked the book retailer on the off chance that he would benevolently reveal to me the meaning of the word *geela*, and he chuckled.

"Crazy," he replied, "*geela* means *crazy*." I laughed with him. I began to tell him the story of the kids throwing stones at us in the town. I asked if he could explain to me the cause of this and the danger of being stoned again as our journey progressed. The German girl entered the tiny bookstore, and the man looked at me, surprised. "Is this your companion?" he asked me.

"Indeed," I answered, "We are voyaging together." Consciously motioning to me, he pulled me aside and stated, "My friend," he said, "when a lady has no hair on her head, it's a major issue on this island."

I chuckled. "*A significant issue*? What do you mean?"

He said, "She is *geela*, and the kids will throw stones at her." I understood the whole scenario. I burst out laughing. I called the German girl and explained to her what the man had told me.

Did she laugh and understand! We walked to find a place for her to buy a scarf so she could cover her baldness and avoid the risk of being harassed by local kids. Laughing at our situation, she inquired, "What else did he say?"

"Oh," I replied surprisingly, adding some of my humours into the fray of things. "Well," I answered with jocularity and said, "The stones get more prominent as we hop the islands. This is the world's largest archipelago. You see, travelling with you has serious consequences.

"I reckon we better get this scarf before we get ourselves killed." We laughed as we walked into a local clothes store. We left the shop with lifesaving scarves, prepared to proceed with our voyage. We ventured out on to the road, appearing to be unique and progressively sure about the new headgear, brandishing a grin of certainty like she could overcome every one of the islands on the route without getting slaughtered.

We spent a week on this island, hanging out along the coastline and boarding an old cargo ship that was making its way to the Flores Islands. We sailed in an old rust-bucket ship for three days, stopping at isolated places along the way. The captain offered some alcoholic drink that tasted like some exotic jungle juice, although it slipped down our throats like some tasty exotic fruit juice. We ended up like two sick parrots at the bow of the ship, supping our guts out, dry-retching in the bellows of our stomachs. I collapsed on the deck, feeling like I was going to die. I lay with the worst hangover I had ever experienced. I was unaware that fruit juice could almost kill you in Indonesia. I even imagined that they would probably give me a burial at sea if I did not make it out of there. I was wrecked and felt a great sense of relief when I disembarked from that ship of death. We landed in Flores alive.

Flores is east of Sumbawa and Komodo Islands and west of Lembata Island and the Alor Archipelago. Toward the southeast is Timor. In the south, over the Sumba Strait, is Sumba Island, and, toward the north, past the Flores Sea, is Sulawesi.

We wanted to visit the most well-known fascination, the tri-hued Kelimutu lake; at 1,690 metres elevation, it comprises three lakes, of shifting hues from one another, making them dreamlike and energising to view.

One of the lakes is Tiwu ata Mbupu (Lake of Old People) which is generally blue. While the other two lakes are Tiwu Nuwa Muri Koo Fai (Lake of Young Men and Maidens) and Tiwu Ata Polo (Bewitched or Enchanted Lake), the other two are green and red, respectively, separated by a crater wall.

It was an enjoyable hike, a rugged country with tremendous volcanic activity and the most beautiful oceans I had ever seen.

Hopping along the islands, I finally reached Bali. I called home to receive the good news that my mother had recovered and was making good progress. I felt relieved and joyful that she was out of danger. I hung around the backpackers hostels and met a Scottish bloke who advised me to go to Thailand.

I arrived in Bangkok in the night and wandered around Khaosan Road, looking for a place to stay. This area was full of Western tourists, a city that barely slept.

I met a German girl who was wandering the streets in a calm state of mind; she helped me to find lodgings for the night. The next day, I met a bunch of Western hippies who were "Mekonged," an expression among these groups who were partying and drinking rice whiskey. Being "Mekonged" meant the painful suffering of the hangover from the effects of getting drunk on rice whisky—nasty stuff. I got lost with these people. I ended up in a nightclub called the Hippodrome, in Bangkok, playing the guitar on stage with these hippie friends.

I saw her dancing among the crowd; she was wearing a dress that exposed her back. Her brown hair was swinging from side to side as she moved with the rhythm of her body, swaying in the neon lights of the nightclub. I was attracted to her; it was physical, a robust, driven desire to know her. Generally a shy person, my overwhelming human instincts were driven by incredible physical desires. I asked her if I could dance with her; she smiled. Her lips were beautiful, and her slender neck was exposed as she swung her hair to one side. I was fatally attracted to this Dutch girl. I danced with her and joined her for a drink. I was surprised; she did not drink alcohol. I was immediately impressed. I tried to take her back to my place, but she shrugged me off; remaining interested in me, she continued to be polite, but she never rejected me outright. She was playing hard to get.

My mother would be ashamed of me if she knew I was in Thailand dancing in a nightclub with a Dutch girl; it's not something she would have approved of. For a moment, her words resounded in my head, "A good woman you will find in the corridors of the house of God and not in the neon lights of a nightclub swinging her body around." I told myself, *She does not drink alcohol*, and all of my youthfulness was mesmerised by the sheer physical beauty of this Dutch girl. She did not come back to my place that night.

I slept the whole day in the hotel room recuperating from the night of drinking and dancing in the nightclubs of Bangkok. The sun set in the Bangkok skies, and we were back in the same nightclub once again doing the same thing as the night before. I met her again, and she told me her name was Tabitha. We sat together at a table chatting and eating some food while the Thai and Filipino bands were entertaining us with romantic tunes. It was a romantic night theme, and we danced together; as I held her in my arms, my desire for her only got worse. I took her through the corridor; holding her against me, I kissed her. We danced together for the rest of the night together, and I took her back to my hotel room.

I was surprised by the sudden change of thought process that went through my mind. My shyness returned to me in an instant. I felt shy and was not going to take advantage of this girl. We lay in bed together sharing my earphones listening to some music, falling asleep in each other's arms like two kids.

I awoke the next morning, looking at her sleeping in my arms in her pink T-shirt and jeans. I moved my fingers through her hair, and I was glad we did not have any sexual encounter, although there was desire between us. I did not think it was moral for me to take advantage of her. After all, she was vulnerable; she trusted me. She came back with me because she liked me the way I wanted her.

In reality, she was a stranger to me. I felt she was unloved. Holding her in my arms as she slept, I knew that I liked her an awful lot. She looked beautiful. I kissed her. She smiled in her sleep and then cuddled up against me like a kitten. We went back to sleep till midday.

We spent the next two days together in Bangkok, falling in love with each other in the brief moment that stood between us. She was leaving to Amsterdam, and I wished that she would not go. I found it strangely hard to say goodbye; so much had changed between us in the three days we'd spent together. She looked sad; even though she tried to put on a brave face, two strangers had fallen in love in Bangkok.

She was gone, and I felt awful. I did not go to nightclubs anymore and did not want to meet any girls. I felt lost in Bangkok; I needed to divert my mind and get a ticket to fly to India to see my mother. I made a call home and spoke to my mother. She was doing very well, and it pleased me to know that she had recovered and was hoping to see me again.

I went to the travel agent and made inquiries for a flight ticket to India. But something caught my eye. *The Bridge on the River Kwai*. I had seen this Second World War movie, about the railway to Rangoon, Burma; How could the perpetraors of terrible atrocities not be guilty of the war crimes against humanity?

I requested the travel agent to book a five-day trip to this part of Thailand and organised a flight for India on hold. There was political unrest stirring in the city of Bangkok, a violent political cocktail of turmoil. And so, I got out of the town and decided to walk down the paths of history.

The Burma-Thailand railroad, however its popularity, will probably be remembered more as the inspiration of an anecdotal film than for its centrality in World War II. The Burma-Thailand Railway traverses the River Kwae Yai in Kanchanaburi; the scaffold was built in 1942–43 by British detainees of war based at Tha Markam. It comprised eleven steel ranges on solid columns. The materials were sourced from Java, and this was the primary steel connect worked by the Japanese in Thailand. The acclaim of the extension is because of the 1957 film by David Lean, *The Bridge on the River Kwai*. Based on a 1952 French tale by Pierre Boulle, the film includes an unhinged British POW administrator, Captain Nicholson (Alec Guinness), who takes such pride in specialised British mastery that he coordinates with the Japanese authority Saito in building a transcending wooden scaffold. At the point when an Allied commando strategist (played by William Holden) attempts to disrupt the structure, Nicholson nearly thwarts them. The structure, at long last wrecked, as Nicholson, injured in the shoot-out between the Japanese and the commandos, falls onto the detonator. The ensuing explosion brings the extension down—as well as the train crossing it—falling directly into the waterway.

The plot is altogether anecdotal. However, Nicholson put it together concerning the British colonel at Tha Markam. The extension in the film likewise looks not at all like the steel connect at Kanchanaburi. There were no scaffolds worked over the River Kwae during World War II. The stretch of waterway that *The Bridge on the River Kwai* ranges is known as the Mae Klong (Mae Khlaung). Nonetheless, the film was such a global achievement—it won seven Oscars—that sightseers came rushing to Thailand looking for the Bridge on the River Kwai. The town of Kanchanaburi changed its name from the

Mae Klong waterway in the region of the extension to the Kwae Yai (or Greater Tributary).

Therefore, the *Bridge on the River Kwai* was made. One hundred metres downstream, there was a second scaffold during World War II. This wooden extension could convey light diesel rail trucks shipping development materials while the first deck was being manufactured. The two extensions were frequently shelled by Allied flying machines from December 1944 to June 1945. A few ranges of the steel connect were annihilated—the wooden extension, which could be fixed without much of a stretch, filled the hole somewhat.

Although this was the historical backdrop of the spot, and there was no uncertainty that the POWs endured, the photos I found in the exhibition hall portrayed the horrendous conditions they endured. Hollywood has a method for composing history in the feeling of purposeful publicity, a legitimisation for the dropping of the nuclear bomb, a case to be made for one horrendous, unspeakable atrocity.

Maybe the scaffold on the River Kwai was a depiction of the horrible, severe Japanese, a defence for consummation of the war with Japan with the dropping of the atomic bomb and legitimisation of completion of the war. Man is fit for awful wrongdoings against everything, including his sort. I was moved by such musings visiting places that showed the uglier side of humankind.

I returned to my hotel and lay down to rest. I was tired; when I put my hand around my waist, the worst feeling in the world just shook me up. I was without my waist pouch, with four thousand dollars in it that I was carrying with me. I remembered taking it for a moment, but I could not remember where I left it. I desperately went to the receptionist and asked for help, and I felt so angry with myself. I would be lucky to find it. The tuk-tuk three-wheeler cab driver drove me frantically back to all the places I had visited earlier, during the day. My money was gone due to my carelessness. Luckily, my passport and thousand dollars were still hidden, kept in my suitcase. I went back to Australia and cancelled my trip to India.

I had an old bank account with a passbook and had no access to any money abroad. I flew back to Darwin and never got to see my mother because of my stupidity. I called her and told her about my tragic, pathetic story. I felt awful.

I felt horrendous. Instead of apologising to her, I selfishly made her feel sorry for me. I felt miserable. I had let her down. I got sidetracked and fell in love with a Dutch girl. I went back to Belyuen, returning to the only family I had among the native people. I felt torn up leaving this beautiful place and people where I always had a home, a belonging. Yet I was caught between two different worlds. I wish I'd never left this place and the people. Even when I eventually did, this place and the people never left my spirit.

CHAPTER 14

THE LOWLANDS OF EUROPE

My friend Tony Bartle got ahold of me, complaining about a Dutch girl who was trying to locate me. I had given her his number because I was not sure where I was going to be when I returned. He further stated that she called him at odd hours and left her phone number with him. "Get her off my back," he joked. "Is she a good-looking sheila?"

"Yeah," I replied, "she is a pretty thing."

"I reckon this girl is in love with you, mate," he said, "and she has called me up several times looking for you."

I called her up the next day; she was relieved and spontaneously happy to hear from me. I could feel her joy as she spoke. She asked me to come to Europe and spend time with her; it was very tempting, and I felt something tug at the strings of my heart.

I decided to go to Europe and take her to India for a holiday—well, at least that was the plan in my head. Three months later, I left Belyuen once again for Europe. I was excited and apprehensive at the same time. Travelling on my new identity, I left Australian shores once again, for the love of a woman from the advanced tribe.

In 1992, an Israeli freight aircraft crashed into a high-rise building, minutes after its pilot revealed motor issues on takeoff. Many individuals were killed in the ensuing crash—250 passengers died. The El Al Boeing 747 struck the high-rise, and blazing destruction dispersed over a vast region of a thickly populated area, close to the

Schiphol air terminal. City hall leader Ed Van Thijn, of the suburb of Duivendrecht, said that the burst had gutted fifty condos. Occupants scanned for relatives. The Amsterdam Medical Center emergency clinic said it treated around twenty unfortunate casualties. Yisrael Cherbin, load director for El Al in Amsterdam, said the plane's commander revealed issues with two motors soon after departure and requested to come back to the air terminal.

She talked about this terrible crash that happened a few blocks away from her; she rode the local metro train that evening when a massive exploding sound echoed, shaking the ground as the 747 cargo plane slammed into the building.

"I am lucky to be alive," she said. "It could have been my building, and if it had been fifteen minutes later, I could have been in my apartment, and it could have crashed into me—it was that close."

This was one of the many conversations we had in the months that led me to get on the flight to Amsterdam. Life is excessively short, and if you don't go, you would never know; I accepted that. The morning light streamed into the windows in European skies. it was a long flight, and I was beginning to feel energised that I was going to see her once more. The final two hours on the plane went by as I peered out the window at the morning skies. I was moving into new skylines, and I had a feeling of pining to go home to Belyuen, even before I landed. I had mixed emotions.

I walked out of the Schiphol Airport into the waiting hall, and it was a cold winter day; she was dressed in a long coat. She had a Dutch scarf around her neck, looking pretty, smiling at me. I walked towards her as she hugged me; she was excited and nervous. I held her hand, squeezed it, and said, "I can't believe I am here."

She smiled and said, "Thank you for coming. Let's get some coffee." We walked to the coffee bar; she got me a croissant and a coffee, got herself something, and, then, in her nervous state, she spilled the coffee all over the table. "Oh my god—I am so sorry," she apologised, as she rushed off to get the cleaner to clean up the mess.

I held her hand, pulled her close, and kissed her. I said, "Calm down, mate! Relax." I made her sit down while I got her a new cup of coffee; we sat there together, joking and laughing as all her nervousness disappeared.

We walked towards the parking lot, heading to a Fiat Panda. "Are you serious?" I said. "Is this a car? Oh, my, it's small."

She laughed. "It's my mother's car. The streets are narrow in this country, and soon you will know that this is the right car for Amsterdam."

I held her hand as we drove towards Ganzhof, in the southeast of Amsterdam. Here in this residential labyrinth of high-rise buildings, it was a cold winter day, and I had arrived on November 18, three days before her birthday. I was surprised by the neighbourhood. I saw many people hanging around this European ghetto; it looked dismal and run-down—graffiti all over the walls, black art, men hanging around the fireplace, a drum where stuff was burning, keeping these homeless souls warm.

On the left-hand side was a picture of a destroyed building, cordoned off by steel fencing. It was an L-shaped structure about eleven floors tall. The Israeli 747 cargo had ripped right through the ninety-degree angle of the building, blasting its way through and wiping out the structure in the middle down to the first floor. This had been a massive explosion.

She said it had been more than two years since the accident and that the investigations were still ongoing. We decided to visit the site the next day on foot. We parked the car and went up to apartment 987 on the ninth floor. She lived in a one-bedroom apartment.

The next two months were magical; we had fallen in love with each other. Something special had happened between us.

I had the opportunity to meet her family. You know, there is a saying, "First impressions are best impressions." I found them to be a strange family, nosey people; she had half-brothers and half-sisters from every side. There were some key persons missing from the family. Her biological father was never talked about. He happened to live ten blocks away from her mother's house with his new wife and a string of children, another set of half-brothers and -sisters whom she did not know or have any contact with.

Although they seemed very keen to meet me, I quickly learned that her family was slightly complicated; she had a stepfather who had four children from his previous marriage. It seemed like everyone was divorced and remarried a few times. These family ties, emotional connections, were all weird, strange, and friendly at the same time. Like the anchorwoman on TV, everyone was keeping up appearances.

Sometimes, when you meet some people, you know that something just ain't right. Her stepfather was a peculiar man, and I was not sure whether he liked me behind what seemed a fake smile; he had some kind of strange sense of humour.

He considered my actions strange that I would want to travel across the globe for a girl, and he joked about it with a dry sense of humour. It was weird because I did not know if he was joking or serious.

Besides all these family complications that seemed to have existed, there were a lot of dark shadows in the details of these families that I did not get myself involved in. Tabitha never spoke about her biological father; she never wanted to talk about the story of her parents' divorce.

She was happy that she had found me; it was her opportunity to move on in life and be satisfied. A woman's heart can hold many secrets, and I was twenty-four years old, lived in the Outback, and came from a family where divorce was never considered an option. It was a taboo to break up your family.

My Dutch girlfriend was from a complex society, a mixed-up family. In her heart and mind, she was born into this not by her choice. Her mother had been married for the third time, so she inherited three so-called "brothers." Not half-brothers but sons from her stepfather, who had children from a previous marriage. It is complicated enough just thinking about it. They were like Dutch hillbillies; there were a lot of unanswered questions. There were things about this family that were not simple, but I did not pay any attention to it because I was interested only in her. Neither was I inclined to get involved in the history of this family. We both lived in Amsterdam and met up with them for birthdays and particular family get-togethers.

Another fact that struck me about my Dutch girlfriend's family is that they were atheists; they were nonbelievers. I learned that my girlfriend had left her mother's home when she was eighteen years and moved to Israel for a year, working in a kibbutz. Many hidden complications existed, but for now, these things did not matter anymore.

We were the happiest couple—we had found each other, and our romance was powerfully intense. A beautiful passion existed between us, and, for the first time in her life, she had genuinely fallen in love. I told her my story. I told her about the change in my name. I told her about my whole life; it was important that she knew my journey in life, and we spent many evenings together, talking about each other's history and current situation. She struggled to speak about her life and instead chose to keep certain things covered and untouched, buried, and forgotten.

One day, lying in my arms on the couch, she just burst into tears. I asked her what was wrong; she looked at me with tears flowing down her face and said, "I did not think I would ever be as happy as I feel now. You have made me special. You came from Australia for me. Nobody has ever done that for me." I kissed her and held her close and wiped her tears. We were deeply in love. In a short while, we had become intensive in our relationship.

Surprises can unsettle you unawares; it can throw you into a turmoil in a jiffy. I was now very involved with a beautiful complex girl, but living in the Netherlands was not a natural choice for me. I was starting to get homesick and wanted to go back to Australia—take her with me back to never-never land.

She went to work, and I was at home alone. I decided to write some letters to some mates back home in Australia, so I went into the bedroom looking in the cupboards to find something to write on—a notebook or writing pad. I pulled a drawer and found a bunch of photographs tied together; I could have just left them, but curiosity got the better of me. As I began to look at the pictures, I went into shock; they were pornographic in nature. Here was my girlfriend dressed in lace, in sexual intercourse with two white men, while a third was taking photos of her. Shocked and surprised, I put them back in place. I went into the living room, sat on the couch, put my head on my hand. I remained in a state of upset; the beautiful girl had some hidden secrets. My initial instinct told me to pack my bags and leave.

At first, I didn't feel angry with her but rather felt disappointed about seeing her naked in those pictures. I was mad at the perverted men—and the sick, unhealthy, unclean, evil sexual immorality that was perpetrated on her. I was baffled why a girl would put herself in such an awful situation. Suddenly my relationship was in utter turmoil, and I could easily just walk away. I did not know what I was going to do.

The neighbour next door came knocking on my door; he asked me if I wanted to accompany him to the airport and go to the pub later on. I was glad to get away and clear my mind. I was baffled; my emotions felt like they had just been ripped from my heart and thrown into the raging sea. I sat on the bench at the airport. I felt betrayed and angry at those men. I didn't know what I was going to tell her; I didn't know how to confront these emotions with her. I could not understand why she'd kept those photographs. Knowing that I was coming to visit her, why would she jeopardise us? I wish she had gotten rid of them before I arrived. What you don't know can't hurt you, but you can't hide it forever—that's why it is always good to talk. People like to push things under the carpet and pretend like the bad things they'd done never happened. Maybe it was too painful to talk about it, but those toxic emotions remained within. I was going to have to confront her.

I went to the telephone booth and called her at the office. She was delighted to hear my voice, but I was compelled to tell her over the phone. I said to her, "I am so sorry. I did not mean to make this phone call. I don't even know whether it is the right thing for me to do, but I'm at the airport with the neighbour, and I am in such a mess."

She sweetly replied, "What's the matter, honey? What's the issue?"

I struggled to tell her, "I was feeling homesick. Augh, I was looking for a writing pad. Sorry—I did not mean to go snooping around your stuff like that. I opened a drawer. I found some photographs tied in a bundle. I know. I am sorry. Pictures of you," I stuttered. "You know the ones I am talking about." She went silent.

I spoke, "I am so confused. I don't know where this relationship is right now. I just feel like getting on a plane and going back home to Australia. I am so confused. I am sorry." I put the phone back on the holder. I felt so miserable.

Sincerely, I had ended up in a troublesome circumstance; seeing your sweetheart bare-naked in pictures, sexual perversion with two men, while a third individual was taking photos—it was all too painful a truth to manage, something I had never faced. Anglo-Indian families were moderate, old-fashioned, unlike the liberal Dutch.

I came from a conventional family foundation. A girl's respect of her family was valuable. Anglo-Indian mothers had Irish Catholic origins, and a decent spouse was significant for their children. Grow up, become an adult, locate an appropriate accomplice, take parental endorsement and counsel, a life partner with good character, a God-fearing woman. I realised my mom could never endorse this relationship. I returned home later that evening feeling disappointed and emotionally confused. I just wanted to go back to the primitive Outback of Belyuen, where life in the bush was simply beautiful.

She sat on the sofa crying. I said nothing to her.

I found a heap of photos that she had burnt up in the shower. I was confounded and did not know what to do, so I stayed silent. She was all the while sitting on the love seat, crying. So I strolled over to her, sat on the opposite lounge chair, and said, "I am so heartbroken."

Sobbing, she said, "It's all right if you want to leave."

I replied to her tears, "I don't accuse you on feeling the need to go. I am so sorry. I am baffled. I am not angry with you. I am simply hurt, distraught with those individuals who mishandled you. You are a beautiful girl; you are someone I love, so it's difficult for me to see pictures of you in a situation being abused and violated in this manner."

I could see that she'd endured abuse; it's the defenceless years in a young girl's life when fathers and siblings should secure them. I comprehended that there were a few issues that she had kept restrained inside her humble heart. I understood that I had to show more empathy rather than pursue my need to know the truth. I requested that she require some time to think and converse with me about it, so that we could figure out how to defeat the past. She was only a casualty of circumstances and bad choices. So, I put my arms around her, held her, and said to her, "We, as a whole, commit errors in life—all of us; we merit chances. I won't leave you. I am not moving, even though I truly miss home. I feel a pining to go home. I don't care for the Netherlands. I believe it's an empty place. There is something about this nation that is so unfilled that I think it resembles a shadow. There is no otherworldliness in this land. I am here as a result of you. I won't leave you. Everyone made you an unfortunate casualty. However, I will remain by you."

I lived with her for just about five months in the Netherlands, and we defeated the past because we discovered love with one another.

I discovered that one of her stepbrothers sexually abused her when she was sixteen years of age, while she lived with her mother and stepfather. She left the Netherlands at the age of eighteen for Israel, to live in a kibbutz. She just wanted to escape and find herself.

In her constant feeling of uncertainty, and bearing her mom's divorces, she'd had no contact with her natural dad, and he dwelled on the same street. When they split up, she was nine years old. All connection with her father ceased.

She would stroll past his home and never at any point thought about the fact that he existed. There were profound, mentally upsetting chronicles of severe family fights. I felt that it was all decidedly an excessive amount to deal with, yet I realised the more she was with me, the more delight filled her life. Presently, she could feel free to be content with the man she had discovered to be the greatest love in her life. In our little condo, with the snow falling outside, we moved to the music, upbeat and strongly obsessed with one another. We had discovered one another; there were no insider facts. She knew my story, and I knew hers. These were the happy years, when we abandoned the world around us and saw each other in the profundity of our eyes, grinning at one another as our lips met with the kiss of a beautiful love that we had discovered together in a topsy-turvy world. Our winter love had endured the coldness, and it bloomed with the early spring in April. We were happy with each other. One day she returned from work early, feeling nauseated; she told me she was going to see the doctor. I had to go to Amsterdam to meet some people to discuss a possible job. I had come with a fair bit of money, but I wanted to get a job in this new country.

I returned home later that evening; my sweetheart cooked dinner, and she was sitting in the couch waiting for me. She was smiling sitting there, glowing; she looked so happy. There was something about her face, something that looked different. I wanted to sweep her into my arms; she looked so beautiful, and her happiness shined like the glowing candle on that tiny table for two.

I sat down to have dinner with my love, and she looked grateful. I asked her, "What's up, babe? You look so different, so beautiful. You are glowing."

She smiled and said, "It's because of you." She went on further, "If I tell you something, will you get angry with me?"

"Of course not. There is nothing you can say to me now that can upset me—even with the way you are looking across from me." I took a sip of the red wine and said, "Go on, try me."

"I went to the doctor today. Are you sure you won't get angry with me? I am pregnant," she said.

I looked at her. "Are you kidding?"

She smiled again. "No, I am not, *Daddy*."

I hugged her, kissed her. I exclaimed. I lifted her in my arms and kissed her again.

After three days, I went into shock. It was all happening so quickly. Despite everything, I didn't figure my folks would support this. Having children out of wedlock goes against every value of my culture and upbringing. I needed to assume liability for my actions. I needed to propose to my love. I was too youthful to even think about getting hitched, yet my obligation to her and this child was my prerogative. I bought some delicate flowers, placed them on the table, placed postcards with profound written words in strategic locations.

I placed on the table a ring with diamonds and sapphires. I put a letter in the letterbox, and then I fixed a note on the door to the entrance of the apartment. I placed a bunch of flowers on the table with a card in between the flowers; written on it was my proposal to marry her. I put the ring in a box and placed it on the table. I left the house and called her at work and told her to check the postbox when she got home; I told her I would be back later that evening.

When I walked inside, she wrapped her arms around me and said, "Yes, you are a dream come true," and then she cried. "I love you so much—you have made my life complete." We got married when she was seven months pregnant. It was the most beautiful time of our lives together. She looked beautiful standing next to me near a windmill, as we took photos. We drove to the historic building in the town of Edam, along ancient cobbled streets to the entrance. A broad stone stairway led into the hallway behind an artistic green door, decorated with traditional Dutch carvings.

Standing there to greet us was the government minister, dressed in conventional Dutch apparel, with a coat of arms of the city embossed on his traditional dress. Turning left with my bride in my hand, I entered a beautifully decorated hall covered with Dutch paintings. I never imagined I would have married a girl from this old cheese town.

It was a beautiful day, and I missed my mom and dad.

Despite everything, I needed to get married in a holy congregation however, the Netherlands didn't correctly perceive church marriages. I chose to continue believing that God was essential in relationships. Nevertheless, I was in an area, in a certain time, among individuals who gave almost no significance to my sort of spiritual reasoning; this was a liberal nation, liberal with all things but the right things.

I was married now. My life had changed, and I hoped I could take her back home to Australia. A part of my heart remained wandering in the red dust. I hoped for the best for us together and was confident that we had already overcome many things, enabling us to get this far. We found love, and it was inside her womb—a symbol of our love for each other. A baby was coming to us soon. A son was born to us, a beautiful baby boy. I named him Sean Patrick. It was customary in the Netherlands for her to have the baby born at home. It was a profoundly emotional time in our lives together, having a baby born in front of my eyes; I held her in my arms while the midwife helped deliver the child. As I cut the umbilical cord and grasped this child, I was profoundly moved to tears. Impulses of parenthood overpowered me; my feelings relocated my spirit to encounter the most significant love I had ever felt in my life—a dad's love for his son. We both sobbed as we held this child in our arms; so much had changed so quickly. Our joy was looking at us with little eyes, and fingers were pointing in heavenly directions of otherworldly messages, transferring to us the supernatural occurrence of life itself. Who is this Holy God, who made this supernatural occurrence of life, that, despite everything, He enables the magnificence of a child to be conceived in these wonders of life? Did we cry in each other's arms? It overpowered me beyond any words I would ever discover in this life span to express what I had—a feeling that I felt the day I first held Sean Patrick in my arms.

I soon found a job in a steel-producing company; it was not the most excellent place to work on the planet. It looked like a depressing concentration camp in the miserable cold weather, but it provided me employment, and I could put food on the table for my young family. My joy was my wife and my son, and I could endure anything for them. My life had changed. In two years, I had gone from Outback Australia to working at a steel plant in the Netherlands. I'd endured a problematic, complicated transition, simply because the people around me were awkward—little-disapproved-of supremacist individuals. I encountered a great deal of small-mindedness in a nation of an alternate language. To talk it, I needed to build up some uncommon sort of throat disease initially. Disregarding the test, I endeavoured to attempt to speak it. Yet, I was disparaged by these little-disapproved (polder) village individuals that this nation famously produced. I don't think Europeans thought about the evil impacts of prejudice. I started to comprehend the entire idea of colonisation; it most likely began in the polders of these nations. What amazed me is that they didn't take in anything from their histories. All the evilness of supremacists slaughtered such a significant number of individuals in the numerous world wars that seethed in this European continent. I had seen this revolting European philosophy play out this equivalent evilness in the Outback of Australia. I missed Belyuen and my native people. I missed Australia. These Dutch individuals had no idea of the intelligence that existed in my psyche. This world was my oyster.

A great many people were proud and discourteous; swearing in the Netherlands has a level of pernicious insidiousness. Individuals append terrible malady when they swear and curse individuals. I didn't care for the individuals I worked with; tragically, I needed to endure them for a few hours every day. Small-minded village people sometimes passed some racial slurs at me, playfully, leaving me bewildered, to think about whether they implied it genuinely or not. Was it a joke? Such demeanours ordinarily have shrouded thought processes by making it sound like a joke but then saying something that shows their mean, treacherous spirits. I was blessed to have two excellent companions. Ron and Peter, who worked with me, were progressive and aware; getting connected to me, they turned out to be great family companions. It made my job much more comfortable because two individuals were excellent and kindhearted.

I figured out how to appreciate the beneficial things of this nation and its customs, the cheddar showcase, angling for eel and smoking it, the yearly carnivals where individuals stayed in a condition of consistent intoxication for three days. Unable to endure such aftereffects, I appreciated being the soberest individual among the senseless inebriation. The entertainment was fun.

Amid my challenges trying to get accustomed to a different culture, language, and country, the joy of my life was my wife and my son. I always hoped that I would be able to take them back to Australia someday. That someday could not come soon enough for me. Then came good news; she was pregnant again, and we were going to have another son. I worked long hours at work, in a society that was designed for families to function on two incomes. Hence, pregnancies and having children is economically tough—so much for family values in European countries. I had to work more hours and put in overtime to make ends meet and was taxed more for my efforts of being a hardworking, honest citizen. Even back then, we were starting to see the truth of living as European citizens—that life was determined by our governments, who were as crooked as they ever were. She stayed at home and decided not to work for a while; she wanted to stay home and raise the children. I made up the income by indulging in more overtime working in the Hoogovens steel plant. Driving through its gates made me feel I'd driven through a Second World War disaster; it was a dismal place, and I endured it for the love of my wife and children.

If any refugees coming across the Mediterranean Sea were risking their lives, there is a partial truth that a refugee was better off than a European citizen. For the refugee will be taken care of until he is put back into a system where he is given employment—and then he became like me: working hard, paying endless taxes, imprisoned in the ancient Roman order of government and taxes, and becoming a slave to the system, like I was in this nation.

We had an Iranian couple with a female child, refugee neighbours who lived next door to us. They were beautiful people who were kept in a dilemma and anguish for four years and put through a legal process created by the state; the people suffered court hearing after court hearing, several appeals. Every morning I would hear the woman next door play beautiful piano, a really remarkable talent; she went to the local school. She requested if she could volunteer as a music teacher and offered free piano lessons to Dutch children. She was told that she could not do any such thing like that until she received her *verblijfsvergunning* (permit to live in the Netherlands). They expressed their deep sadness and anguish at waiting for this most-inhumane process, which took years. Three years later, I would see my depressed neighbours torn down, with broken spirits, smoking marijuana from the three plants they grew in their backyard, which was legal in the Netherlands—a medicine to combat their inhumane process.

The city council provided them with cash to buy plants and have a great garden because they were refugees. I once jokingly told them that the Dutch city council never gave me seeds to plant in my garden, but posted endless bills taxing me for the air that I was breathing. We reckoned that a day would come in which they would tax us for the sun that shines on us in the name of the environment. It is such a bizarre world we live in, doused in hypocrisy. Human rights are violated by the very people in governments who write them. What a travesty! They are sometimes not worth the paper they have been written on.

One day, I spat the dummy at work. I was getting tired of the same slurs and remarks about my skills in speaking the Dutch language. I looked at the village morons and stood up and spoke in almost perfect Dutch. I gave them a lecture. "Recall the Second World War. Let me tell you folks something on the off chance that you go for a stroll down to the burial grounds of the war memorials around your nation. You may see gravestones of many dead soldiers from England, America, Canada, Australia, and New Zealand—men who died battling for your freedom, English-speaking individuals. Now, you bunch of jackasses, suppose we never did that. Let me remind you that, if we hadn't freed you individuals from the Germans, you would not be requesting that I talk in Dutch. In any case, we as a whole would be communicating in German here. Presently, shut up. I have had enough of your supremacist frames of mind and comments over the past two years I've been working here. Get yourselves a proper education."

Quiet fell, and everyone shut up. My dear companion Peter De Ruiter stood up and told his compatriots that they ought to be embarrassed about their behaviour and disapproved of their conduct. Putting his hand on my shoulder, he said, "My Australian companion here is a thoughtful individual and further developed than you lot. Your entire lives you have been driving from your small-minded villages to this depressing steel-manufacturing plant. This young man has ventured to the far corners of the planet and wedded a young Dutch lady, and he isn't here because he jumps at the chance to come every day and stay close to your sorry village arses. A little regard will go far around here." That was the finish of the dramatization. They all got further criticism from the chief of the contracting organisation that we all worked for. Prejudice and nasty comments ended that day.

My wife suggested that we leave Amsterdam and move to the town of Edam, a historic cheese village with 850 years of history; her mother and stepfather lived here. In fact, she'd been born there; she came from this place. I was a little bit reluctant to move; although it was a beautiful town, I preferred to be a little away from family. Small-minded cities and people were not my cups of tea. I didn't have a clue that, behind the scenes, it was her mother and stepfather who were authors of the idea. It was more convenient for her to have their grandchildren. My son was the first grandchild in the family, and there were a lot of claims of ownership starting to develop.

We moved to the town of Edam and into a three-bedroom duplex house a few streets away from her mother and stepfather's home.

CHAPTER 15

SEAN PATRICK AND JOSHUA AARON

Joshua Aaron was born on February 16, 1995; his elder brother, Sean Patrick, was the most energised kid about his new baby brother. He often lay down next to him and admired his baby brother. There was a unique bond between them. Sean was blond, and Joshua developed curly black hair. These two boys were the most precious gifts ever bestowed upon my life.

Fatherhood was something I'd never contemplated; in truth, I was not keen on having children, so planning for them did not exist in my inner self. Perhaps a wanderer like me would find it hard to settle down. My father called me "a rolling stone that gathers no moss," and I argued that a rolling stone is the perfect shape and becomes polished as it rolls along.

When fatherhood came, I was the happiest man on the planet, blessed with two awesome boys, the strength of my youth. I envisaged dreams of growing up with these boys, walking the journey of life with them. I dreamt of taking them to the Outback and having some great adventures with them.

Returning home from work each day was a joy, in spite of how crappy or good the day had turned out at work; the smiling faces of two boys waiting at the door for me to return were the greatest joy in my life. I could carry the whole world on my shoulders for these children.

I was not considered a typical father. You would find me rolling with them spontaneously in the snow on a winter's day. According to my spouse, we were supposed to walk along the boundary walls of the city of Edam and be decent and respectful, as most people usually do with their kids in this town.

I could always see inside the eyes of the boys and knew the mischievousness in them. I could see myself inside of them, and I knew they wanted to slide down the slope in the snow and get messed up and have fun. So it was unconventional in this town to see a big, grown-up man rolling in the snow with his two sons. According to the rules in Dutch country, it is considered better to take your kids to the ice-skating rink and play with them, but rolling down the slopes was not something most parents did. The only problem with these rules is that I was not Dutch and did not come from this town. So, we laughed and played in the snow, rolling down the slopes laughing; we got all messed up and had heaps of fun. A trip to the local baker, warm sausage rolls, raisin buns, were the treats waiting for them after all the fun. As for the wife, she just stood there smiling and shaking her head; she had three men in her life to take care of her. Happiness showed on her face; she was fearsomely protective of her children.

We lived in a typical Dutch town famous for its cheese, and it was an historical place—cobblestone streets, local shops that had a long history of family ownership, greengrocer, local butchery and bakery, home-based businesses rich in history. This was before the invention of corporate companies and supermarkets that rose and destroyed these unique cultural assets and drove them into oblivion in the competition of greed for more significant shares in the market.

Next to our town of Edam was a Dutch fishing village called Volendam. It was a strange place, because the people were tightly knit. Five surnames dominated the community, and it was well-known that the people bred between themselves, reducing the size of the gene pool and making the children born look similar to each other. The accent was distinctively different, to the point that people from Edam did not always understand everything the people from Volendam said. The fishing village was ignorantly racist, but on the contrary, it was the friendliest place for tourists to visit. It had no clear desire to like the tourists genuinely, but rather, they liked the dollar signs and had commercial love for black money that this fishing village was well-known to possess.

A genetic population isolated in the Netherlands displays an extensive haplotype sharing and great regions of homozygosity, on top of their previous history of geographic separation and strict endogamy. And, as of now, one of the most elevated fruitfulness rates in the Netherlands was giving indications of hereditary disengagement. The geographic withdrawal of this populace, joined with fast population development, has brought about a hereditary disconnect with an incredibly potential incentive for future genetic examinations.

According to the "Journal of Deaf Studies and Deaf Education," in a report titled "Hereditary Deafness in a Former Fishing Village on the Dutch Coast," by the author Victoria A. S. Nyst, in communities with an increased prevalence of hereditary deafness, social and linguistic adaptations are found in response. Aulbers (1995) describes a high prevalence of deafness in a fishing village on the Dutch coast: Katwijk aan Zee. This article aims to assess the current prevalence of deafness in Katwijk, as well as the current sign-language situation there. To this end, data were collected from various sources, including governmental studies on public health, archives, a genealogical database, and interviews with deaf inhabitants of Katwijk. The various types of data confirmed the presence of a higher prevalence of deafness in Katwijk that continues to date. Linguistic and anthropological research is needed to further establish the extent to which this has affected the experience and position of deaf people and their sign-language usage in Katwijk (Nyst 2015).

Fifty years back, Aulbers (1959) found a high pervasiveness of genetic deafness in Katwijk aan Zee, a Protestant fishing village on the Dutch coast, situated in the territory of Zuid-Holland (South-Holland). He recorded 20 individuals with genetic deafness in 12 families in Katwijk. Just a single family in this gathering was not identified with different families, having progenitors from outside of Katwijk. On the related families, Aulbers (1959: 76) noticed that:

"Genealogical research built up that these families are firmly related. Likewise, everyone except one of the guardians of the probands of these families is family of one another. Just the father of one family isn't from Katwijk. However, the mother is; she is additionally identified as genetically connected to one of the 12 families in this study of "Hereditary Deafness in Katwijk aan Zee families."

You may wonder why I have decided to diverge from my story and talk about genetics and inbreeding. This is the result of racism and white-supremacy ideology. My wife was not from this village, but she came from the opposite end of the spectrum. Edam was a town that was more open to other kinds of people. These close-knit communities were very secular people, not inclined to accept the teachings of the Bible. Many such communities live in the apostasy of atheism and are being lost. To receive God's blessing, one must be humble to open minds to perceive His great glory and receive. An open vessel can contain more than its capacity. It can contain the infinite and the unending, but a closed vessel is limited to know only what they know. It cannot go beyond its humanness to perceive something far greater than itself.

Hence, when you have two children with a diverse gene pool, they are usually adorable and become unique; they get the best of both worlds, and the mix was a good one because the children were different and uncharacteristic. The grandchildren became everyone's favourites, and the grandparents were obsessed; my wife's mother and stepfather had a profound influence over her. They started to become possessive about the children and influencing our family life in ways that made me uncomfortable. My wife's mother and stepfather deeply resented my good intentions to bring healing between my wife and her biological father. I'd opened a can of worms—the bitterness of the past that existed from the divorce feuds of these families.

Now, I had walked into the fire of the past, into the embers of bitterness that raged in the hearts of these people. For all my good intentions, I was secretly despised by my wife's stepfather. I often heard him pass sarcastic comments towards me at family get-togethers.

I slowly and gradually disconnected from her family and focused on my life with my wife and the kids. I wanted to move away from the town and even considered moving to Ireland or the United Kingdom. My wife did not wish to hear such suggestions; the influences and emotional blackmail of having the grandchildren always close to her mother was heavily burdensome on her heart. These ridiculous family dramas started to raise the ugly heads of past antipathies. There is one underlying reality for each person, and that will be that we all, in one form or another, be a part of a family. This experience is different for everybody. Our histories and cultures shape our lives together and how we respect and value each other in these relationships. My wife's stepfather had narcissistic ideas of control.

My wife's biological father visited us on a few occasions. He genuinely made attempts to rebuild his relationship with his daughter from the fragments of the past, and I truly believed that it was vital for her to build a relationship with her father and find peace and love in her life. I also thought that it was important for my children to also have a good relationship with their biological grandfather and extended family member in this complicated-labyrinth family. The biggest problem with these families is that they were mostly atheists, and I don't believe they were capable of forgiveness or ever searched for peaceful resolutions in life. There was also a cultural trait of terrible family breakdowns that seems to have plagued the Dutch society. Families matter, and the test around family breakdown has sweeping outcomes. In the Netherlands, there were issues of father nonattendance, youthful parenthood, and the decrease of marriage constituted a social decay, the developing number of complex families in these networks, and the effect it had on youngsters. My wife was a product of this society.

Family breakdown is likewise intimately connected with unfortunate results for kids. Kids who experience family breakdown are bound to encounter conduct issues; perform less well in school; need treatment progressively; leave school and home prior; become explicitly dynamic, pregnant, or a parent at an early age; and report progressively burdensome side effects and more significant levels of smoking, drinking, and other medication use during youthfulness and adulthood.

The Anglo-Indian family never considered separation; the social characteristics were the opposite of the Dutch condition. In any event, Anglo-Indian families stayed together, working through these difficulties. The divorce was a surprising result of a marriage breakdown. There was an idiom: the making up was considered the best part of the marriage in Anglo-Indian society.

With these different foundations, we had two excellent kids; our relationship was groundbreaking and significantly moving. Our issues possibly began when we drew nearer to her mom and stepfather. The harsh family fights and mental wars began to raise their ugly heads. Like Romeo and Juliet, our relationship started to experience some unnecessary worries between us—the firm claims the grandparents had on the grandkids and my significant other were unfortunate and profoundly upsetting. Clashes emerged among us, and my disappointments began to develop. I was known to have a temper. I didn't know that I should discover some approach to control this. I needed to resist the urge to panic, to wander my musings from the antagonism that was structured around my family life. I began to get progressively engaged with my children, and my parental consideration was truly surprising. On the weekends, I usually woke up early with my two sons, gave them showers, dress them up, eat breakfast, and take a walk together. My better half, on the other hand, remained in bed till 11:00 a.m. on weekends. I accept that she was experiencing some discouragement, and it was negatively affecting her.

Notwithstanding these numerous difficulties, her younger brother lived with us, up in the attic; his weekends would see him getting drunk with his companions and returning home at late hours. He never helped around the house while my better half thoroughly took care of him. These family complexities began to crawl into my home and marriage. I sometimes looked at her and all the changes that had happened between us since we moved to Edam, and it would make me sad. I longed for the times when we lived together in Amsterdam, slightly away from her family, when it was just us—and when things were beautiful without these family dramas. I began to feel desperately homesick and missed the Outback. I was going through an emotional crisis of my own, and it's hard to comprehend now how these difficulties played out. Like some unclean demons of the past, her family issues came back to haunt her, and it affected me as well. She became distant and cold as the arguments of her parents' interferences created conflicts between us, leaving a bitter taste in our mouths. I always believed that I'd still have to make up. I would buy her flowers, take her out for dinner, and work extra hours for the extra money to keep her happy. I began to miss her romance, passion, and affection she always had for me. Now, she was growing cold towards me, and there were some dark influences of past demons invading my home when I was gone to work.

Twisted mind games started to emerge that drove my frustrations even deeper. My wife began to use her body as a weapon against me; she would dress beautifully and flirt with me during the day, but at night, she would reject my affection for her. She would not talk about what was going on in her mind, but it started to get all weird and deeply confusing. My frustrations with her family got worse. I felt their influences on her, and my children were narcissistic and controlling by nature; I felt something unhealthy about them. In my frustration with her, I expressed the view that we should go to Australia and leave all the crap in the Netherlands behind. "*The family* now means you, the boys, and me." I genuinely missed Belyuen, when I lived a happy life in the Outback, and I would sometimes cry, as I felt hurt and confused.

I took my paintbrush and my acrylic paints and started painting all the Aboriginal art that I had learned from Story Man and the Aboriginal kids. I wanted to reconnect my spirit to a time when I was happy and carefree. I spent time with my sons teaching them to paint the ancient form of art. My joy was my two sons; they gave me the strength to carry on, and I was always hoping for the best. I never had a deep attachment to the Netherlands. It was a human-made, very controlled way of life, and there were rules for almost everything.

It was three o'clock in the morning, and I was asleep when the eagle returned to my dream; *Kurrawurra*, the wedge-tailed eagle from the Outback, invaded my thoughts. I felt joy at seeing him; like some spirit ghost of the past, he awoke me in my dream. I spread my two arms and lifted myself into the sky. I was flying by his side; his sharp beak and piercing eyes were looking at me like he was asking me what had happened to me. I started to weep in my sleep, and I saw that the eagle was crying, too. He was like a heavenly spirit that had come from a faraway place to wake me up, to visit me, to stir something again in my soul. I awoke from my dream, sweating on my forehead. I was inspired, like some power had returned to me, to lift me from my sadness.

It was the Aboriginal painting that I was indulging my spirit in for the past few weeks; that old memory of my people awakened ancient dreams to return. I woke up and tiptoed down the stairway from the first floor and went to the living room. I took my paintbrushes and painted *Eagle Dreaming*. The brushstrokes were rapid and intense. I was painting intensively, as it powerfully moved inside of me like a raging storm of emotions, cascading like wings spread across the thermal-uplift winds of life. My painting had three eagles—my two sons and me. I did not know why I did not paint any symbol of their mother; something else moved inside of me to paint three eagles in an ancient symbolic form of Aboriginal art. I took my pen and wrote a poem that Kurrawurra gave me in my dream. The plight of my people came back to haunt me in my pain.

KURRAWURRA DREAMING

If I could fly like an eagle and touch the blue sky
I would leave the world behind me with a heavy sigh
I'd soar among the clouds' blankets of white
And the earth below me a faraway sight
I look down below and smirch all the cities they have created
The hustle and bustle of the human species
Then sadness engulfed me as I soared high above
Because I saw the foolish mess it all is
They came to my land and invaded my shores
Desperate they were and numb in the toes
I saw them coming from a perch high on a tree
These band of white convicts on this land were set free
They have changed the natives, and they have changed the scene
The years have passed us by, and the ragamuffins have just got meaner
They built their cities with fortification
Now my never-never land has become a different nation
Two hundred years have passed me by, and two hundred years I'm asking why
Don't change my land, don't change its course.
Take it for what it is, and please hold it close
She has been my mother who always soothes my cry
Stop, think, and ask yourself, "Why?"
Kurrawurra invades my dreams with tears in his eye

—(Lyndon Berchy 1997)

Coming to the Netherlands was a big mistake. I had beautiful children but from ungodly women, and I was an ox yoked with a mule because I was not wise enough to read and follow the Word and wisdom of our Holy God in the Bible.

CHAPTER 16

MISE EN ABYME

There was a donkey in the field tied to a tree, and an insidious devil came and set the creature free. The jackass entered the area of a rancher and started eating the harvests the rancher was developing. The rancher's wife, alarmed at the donkey annihilating the plants, took a rifle and killed the jackass.

The jackass's owner saw the dead jackass and, in his fierceness, came back with his rifle to the rancher's farms and shot her. The rancher came back and discovered his wife dead; then, in his rage, he killed the jackass's owner. The raging children of the owner consumed the fields and murdered the rancher and all his relatives.

The general public, frightened at this catastrophe, summoned the devil in the courts of law, now that he was the suspect. They asked him what he had done. "I didn't do anything," answered the demon, "I just released a jackass in the field." The evil devil that rules the darkness in the world has no power in the presence of light. Perhaps a little evil thing that he does triggers the harshness and abhorrent purpose that stays in the hearts of individuals, to hurt and obliterate one another. They look for retribution and scrutinise past indecencies. Individuals who have never learned absolution live their entire lives in the sharpness of the past—people who don't have the foggiest idea about the love of a Holy God. The villain needs only to release one jackass in their lives.

My marriage was encountering the complexities of life; adverse events continued tormenting my home. Unable to break away from these strongholds, I attempted to find spiritual strength. In a town where most people had never lived meaningful Christian lives, I struggled to find a community or church for wisdom and solace.

I took my son to a church one morning, riding on a bicycle through the centre of Edam; there was a main street that had a canal next to it that flowed in the middle of the town. There was a little white church, a Lutheran denomination. There were hardly any people in the church, just about nine older adults bent over in age and in the last stages of life, trying to reconcile with a God they barely seem to have known their whole life. There were no families, teenagers, or children visible among the congregation. On the far end of the bench was a bent-over old lady, weeping and wiping her eyes and nose with a rose-printed handkerchief; she sobbed in the church.

My three-year-old child was worried about the crying older woman; clutching my neck with two hands, he murmured in my ears that the more-established lady was sad and she was crying. I asked my little son whether he might want to embrace the older woman and assure her that everything would be all right. He readily agreed. We approached the older woman when the service was over. Her eyes lit up as my child embraced her. The little child inquired, "For what reason were you crying, and for what reason are you so sad?"

The fragile old lady disclosed to him that all her relatives were dead and gone; she was the only one who was still living, and she was desolate.

My child gave her another embrace and said, "Don't cry. God is there for us all."

Tears tumbled down the old lady's eyes, and a couple of tears flowed from the sides of my eyes. The adoration for my child, the magnificence of a youngster's heart, lent euphoria to an old woman's heart. It made her day very special.

I felt lost and desolate; my lone delight was my kids, and the distance between my wife and me had gone cold and remote. It shuddered into an impasse. The "silent treatment" is more complicated than a verbal discussion that drives out damages and agonies. But it is still a hard bargain to accomplish when you have an outgoing individual attempting to get a contemplative person to talk.

I needed to get away for a while. I had some friends in Ireland. So, I took a break and went to Dublin for a week. I figured she'd miss me and realise that I did not have to put up with her country or this culture of interference that troubled me. I did not want to isolate her from her parents, or my children from their grandparents. I just wanted space for my wife and me to live our lives and to get on with it. I wanted our decisions and choices to be our own and not be influenced by deep emotional blackmail, selfishness, and the narcissistic control of this complicated family with whom I found myself associated. There was a troubled history and turmoil that existed in this family, and I wanted to put some distance between it and me. My wife called me when I was in Dublin; she spoke to me in tears. She was concerned that I was leaving, and she was fearful that I would not return. I told her that I loved her but that the distance between us was hurtful and deeply painful. I had never thought that I would end up in such complications, and it was only she and our children keeping me in the Netherlands. She promised to get closer to me again and find that joy we'd always had together. I was happy when I put the phone down. I could not wait to go back home and just hug her and my two sons.

I was a dedicated spouse and adored my wife and two children profoundly, and I was troubled that I was managing this unforgiving coldness between us. I stood up to her folks and her stepfather. I told them to back off from their control, communicating to them that I didn't welcome these meddlings and the division they had caused between my wife and me. They obtusely revealed to me that she was their daughter also. Unfortunately, as much as I tried to find a suitable solution, I left their home with a sour taste in my mouth. In my endeavour to address the issue, I may have exacerbated it, since some individuals are a peculiar kind. It could take you an entire lifetime of attempts to please them. It doesn't take a lot to trigger contempt or hatred—human instinct balances on the edges of good and evil tendencies, the precipices of human relationships.

I returned home with hope, and I looked forward to making up, as well as to the renewal of the emotional and physical bonds between us. We went out for dinner at her biological father's house for a birthday party. When we returned home later that evening, I put the kids to bed and sat together with her on the couch to watch a movie. Something happened in the short time that I went upstairs to put the kids to bed and returned; there was a phone call, and she answered. I think it was her mother, and moods shifted, attitudes changed. I went to bed lonely and sad once again. I could not sleep. I lay there next to her coldness once again. The hurt and pain were too much to bear; it had been more than six months since I'd shared intimate moments with her; I was hurting, and her coldness was cruel and mind-twisting.

I implored her to converse with me. "If it's not too much trouble, tell me what is happening. Was that your mom? Is it accurate to say that she was annoyed with us that we went to your biological dad's home for supper?"

"Go to sleep" was the resonating answer I got. I felt dismissed and hurt; it was my inability to deal with the hurt that made me troubled. I pleaded that we talk about this. I'd been pushed beyond my limits. I lay there next to her in tears while she turned away from me in the coldness of her heart and the confusions of her mind. I implored her, "Please talk to me." It was extremely painful. I felt frustration building up inside of me. I felt angry with the people who had come between my wife and me. I lay there and thought that she was so silly to be so cold to me. I lay there feeling hopeless and unable to change this situation. We were a passionate couple and blessed with a beautiful family; feelings of hurt exploded in my heart. I was lying on my back, and, like a nightmare, I just wanted her to go. I had no more control over myself, like some darkness was engulfing my heart. I swung my hand in front me and screamed, "Why me? Why! Why!" My left hand turned over and landed across her face. I cried, in frustration, "Leave me alone; go away."

I sat up in my bed and turned on the bedroom light. It was like a terrible dream. I looked at her swollen cheeks. I shouted in disbelief, "Oh, no! Oh, my god!" I ran downstairs and went to the fridge. I came back running with four blocks of ice and a towel. I was crying, "Oh, my god! I am so sorry." I was crying, "Oh, god! What is happening to you? Oh, no! I am sorry."

I put the ice on her face; we were both in shock. She was afraid, and I hated myself almost immediately. I cried, "What are we doing to each other?" She did not want me near her; our situation only got worse. I went downstairs and was deeply distressed. I hit my head against the wall, angry with myself. My blood pressure may have shot through the roof. I felt a shooting torment in my mind; the weight of the circumstance was so extreme that I felt bleary-eyed. I was in tears; it was a most exceedingly awful, bad dream. The only time I'd ever felt this way in my life was when I was a child and witnessed the fights of my parents. I lay on the couch and squirmed and rolled up like a terrified anteater into a ball of fear and sadness.

I went to the attic, crawled on the wooden floor, and lay there breathing and weeping like a child into exhaustion. If I died that night, I was not going to notice it. I collapsed into a valley of tears and fell asleep from being depleted by the awful event.

I awoke at 10:00 a.m. I was still on the wooden floor in the attic; it was the most debilitating and distressing morning of my entire life. *What am I going to do? Why did I snap? Why did I not just stay in Ireland and not come back? Why did I believe it would all change? Why did I love her so much, and why did I not just go and have affairs with other women if she was not willing to be a wife to me? Why was I not patient? Why am I not seeking a godly life? Why am I married to a girl who does not believe in God? Why?* My terrible *Why?* morning!

I came down the famous narrow Dutch death-trap staircase. I did not mind if I fell down the damn thing and died in a terrible accident. I felt utterly miserable as I descended to the first floor. The house was empty. I went to the bedroom; she was gone. I ran to the children's bedroom; the boys were gone. I ran down to the ground floor, hoping they were there, but they were gone. I looked out the window, and my car was gone. I was so mentally exhausted that I never heard them leave while I lay there, almost dying, on the wooden floor of the attic. It was the worst day of my life; it was a day I could just lie down and die.

I went to her mother's house and knocked on the door; they opened it and quickly slammed it in my face, telling me not to come there anymore. I returned home distressed. I called her biological father, who came to visit me. I told him what had happened as I sat there in tears telling him about the conflicts I had been having with her mother and stepfather.

I even told him that, in my attempts to reunify him with his daughter, I faced much opposition. He told me to stay calm but to expect that, from his experience, the interference was about control of the grandchildren. It was a profoundly distressing family history that was repeating itself. He felt responsible for his daughter's life and assured me he would try to contact her, but he had little hope for that because he feared that she would be brainwashed by her mother as she had been ever since the time they'd gotten divorced.

I just sat there and realised that I had gotten mixed up in a terrible family history and the generational curses of divorce that were embedded in the DNA of these people. What a complex mess I'd gotten myself into in spite of all my good intentions! After he left the house, I lay there with my eyes closed and wished I was back in time, back in Belyuen, and back among my people in the Outback once again. I wished I could just wake up and realise that all of this was not real but just a bad dream. It was like a terrible re-experiencing of my childhood.

I packed my suitcase; emotionally, I was in a mess and greatly confused. I just wanted to go away. I remembered the time when I found the dirty pictures of her and wanted to leave then yet decided to go against that emotion. I remembered that, out of fairness, I had decided to give her a second chance, and I did. I was doubting the wisdom of that decision this day. What shocked me was how something you take so long to build up could crash down upon you so rapidly. The attack of the enemy of this world is a swift one; hiding in darkness, the attack came and destroyed us.

Then I thought about Sean and Joshua, and it just ripped my heart in two. I was weeping and packing my suitcase with a million tears. I had never felt sadder in my entire life. I sobbed bitterly. I left the house and headed off to the airport. I was going to England and then return to Australia. I just wanted to go back to Belyuen, disappear into the Outback once again, and live once more with my peaceful Aboriginal people.

I sat at the airport, sobbing tears, crying for my children; it was deeply distressing. As I felt my heart pounding in my chest, I knew that I would never see them again if I left. My distress did not go unnoticed as a lady came and sat near me. Out of kindness, she asked me if she could help me. I cried and told her about my situation and that I did not know what I was going to do. The lady felt distressed hearing my plight; she even had a tear in her eye. She gave me her advice. "Listen to your heart," she said. "Think of your children, and give it some time." I thanked her and went back home to a broken, lonely house that night.

It was around 3:00 a.m., and somebody was at the door, ringing the doorbell. I awoke, startled, and looked out the window from the bedroom above on the first floor. There were two police officers outside. I answered the door; they checked my ID, turned me around, and put me in handcuffs. They told me I was under arrest for attempted murder, threatening my brother-in-law, and assaulting my spouse.

I was crushed and broken. I could barely handle it. I was put into a vehicle, while the cops bolted my home and took my keys. They came back to my house and searched it, with no authorisation or warrant, took me to a town called Purmerend, secured me in a jail cell, and surrendered me to a virus solid square concrete block in a prison cell.

My distress was profound. I began shouting and sobbing for my kids. I was crying in anguish. I was protesting. *This is all about the children—they want to take my children away from me.* I grew even more anguished, so the police moved me into an alternate cell with cameras to screen me. It was cold, and it was winter. I lay there for three days, and I felt dead. The police would pass by my cell. I would hear the clattering of keys and would be eased, trusting that they would give me a chance to go out for some fresh outdoor air. However, it was just a ploy; they were playing with my mind. The clanking would stop, and the cop would be gone. He would return and again jingle his keys. It troubled me profoundly. I had never been in a jail cell in all my years. It was such a dismal place to be—to be deprived of one's freedom. Three days later, they released me, and I returned to find an empty home. My wife's mother and family had come and emptied my house, leaving only a washing machine and a bed, simply because those were the only two things that were too heavy to move in a short time. I did not even find a spoon or a cup to make myself a cup of tea. I could not believe that people would sink to such low levels in their life. I was lost. I felt alone and miserable. I was interviewed by the probation officer (*reclassering* in Dutch). I broke down and gave him the true story, from my heart, about all the challenges I had faced with my marriage and her family. In my heart, there was truth, pain, and sorrow.

Peter De Ruiter, an old friend, came to visit me, and he told me that the police had contacted him. He'd given a statement about me, the years he had been acquainted with me from a professional and personal view. He'd also given a detailed explanation to the correctional board. I had no clue about these systems then and how they worked. My friend Peter also told me that my wife's family had painted an utterly different version of events to the same office, which indicated a lot of racism and hatred her stepfather had for me. It was all slightly sinister and evil from their views.

The judge, the prison system or the public prosecutor orders the probation service to issue an opinion about a suspect or convicted person. Based on our advice, they can make informed choices about the punishment or the granting of liberties. A probation officer usually writes a report or gives oral information.

For this purpose, the probation officer reviews the data known about the person in the judicial system, listens to his or her story, and conducts conversations with people from his or her environment. Based on all information, they issue advice to the judiciary. For example, they can advise on community service, probation supervision, behavioural intervention, ankle band, or treatment. Probation advice is always tailor-made.

Doing what is needed

The probation service advises the judiciary based on a thorough analysis of a perpetrator or suspect. We look at things like the crime, the causes, relationships, attitude. and behaviour. We then prepare a recommendation. The advice states which actions are necessary to ensure that someone does not go wrong again. This advice is a guideline for the type of punishment.

"Doing what is necessary" for a crime-free life is leading in our advice. This can be an area ban, or a means ban, but also resolving debts, following a behavioural intervention or tackling relationship problems. We also look at positive things in someone's life that can contribute to a life without crime.

Estimate risks

To better view the chances of specific crime groups, Probation Netherlands uses the risk assessment and advice instrument RISC. Their advice is always a combination of professional judgment and risk-assessment tools.

On a scientific basis, their advice to the judiciary is concrete, feasible, and factually justified. They are also clear about how conclusions are reached. The work is scientifically substantiated. The paragraphs above come from https://www.reclassering.nl/over-de-reclassering/wat-wij-doen (2020) Dutch Probation Service : What we do, available at: https://www.reclassering.nl/over-de-reclassering/wat-wij-doen (Accessed: 27th January 2020).

I am now aware of how the reclassering system in the Netherlands works, but back then, I had no clue about the system that I went through.

I was in a terrible state of mind. I knew deep in my heart that all my wife's family wanted was to see the end of me. They were the most vicious people I had ever met; pure atheists are like a representation of the devil because they don't have any spirit of goodness, compassion, forgiveness, understanding, or humanity in them. They are earthly people who have not known the kindness that can exist if they have known love. It's all about possession, and my children were their grandchildren—and, therefore, their possessions. They believed it was perfectly alright for the kids to have to do without their father. Considering the family had similar cultures and histories of divorces and separations over the course of their whole lifetime, these people were prepared to take such bitterness with them to the grave. I began to understand that World War II had changed these societies in Europe to such coldness of heart and separation of themselves from God. I began to understand the evil of the murder of six million Jews. Dutch society were no angels; many betrayed their Jewish neighbours during the Second World War; people betrayed each other, and they lost the trust that they had with one another back then. Wars alter society one way or another. I was now amid a terrible hatred that was directed towards my alienation and destruction.

I broke down and turned back to Yeshua HaMashiach. I crawled on my knees and turned back to God. I had not walked in the way my mother had taught me. I was not as prayerful as I use to be as a child. I was so caught up in the world that I had lived it like an atheist. I was in a world and a society that was different from my childhood upbringing. Like a prodigal son, I crawled back on my knees, weeping and praying to the Lord Jesus to rescue me once again. Once again, from this terrible condition, I had to find myself again. I opened my Bible and started to find some peace and strength once again through prayer. My deepest pain was over my children. I struggled to get back on my feet financially; she had taken my car, and I had no means to go to work without one. I borrowed a van from my friend Peter De Ruiter until I was able to get a small loan from my company and buy myself a small car. I returned home each day hoping that she would make contact with me and that we could find a way through all of these family dramas. I tried to remember the happy days, when we were comfortable, the memories of the birth of our children, and the moments when life was content with just us. I would break down in tears on my way back from work. Babyface singing, "Nobody Knows It but Me" ripped me apart as it became a hit song on FM radio. The damn song—I could not get away from it. I drove on the A2 Highway, my face soaking wet with tears; my pain was real, and it was devastating me to the core. I wanted to become hard-hearted, but I just could not do it. How was I to feel different when I was feeling the way I was? My mind could not convince me to become hard because it was hurting me so deeply.

I returned home to find a letter from her lawyer; my wife wanted a divorce and complete custody of the children. My hopes were all dashed, and my devastation only grew deeper. Although I did not want a divorce, I was going to have one. I did not want to deal with lawyers, but I had to go and face one. I had to pay for one, too. The court case still pending, I went through six months of mental torture as I was summoned to appear before a court regarding the charges they laid upon me. I was portrayed as a terrible man by her mother and stepfather. All I had in my defence was my broken heart, my true love for her and my sons, my cries and my prayers to an unseen God, whom I trusted. I wept many nights, calling the holy name of Jesus for my forgiveness. My cries were to rescue me from terrible, vicious enemies that were all out to destroy me.

CHAPTER 17

THE COURT CASES

My friends Ron, Peter, and Monica accompanied me to the court; it was the day of judgement. It looked like I was going to go to prison for six months. I handed the keys of my broken home to my friends, not that there was much of it left after my ex and her mother had ransacked it. They were trying to cheer me up with a typically Dutch dry sense of humour—dark humour in times of terrible consequences. "Prison can be like a six-month holiday in Holland." I was just grateful that I had my friends with me.

I stood in front of the judge as the prosecution laid out their case before me. It was very sinister, the views of the mother's and stepfather's statement. The case progressed for the next thirty minutes, and my lawyer spoke. I sat in my chair, and my heart was utterly ripped to shreds by the pain I felt. I stood in my defence and prayed to the Lord to speak for me. I had no evil in me, and I had only a pure-but-broken heart. I had no hatred against anyone, I merely expressed in interviews and written statements my pain, sufferings, and the difficulties I had struggled with in this Dutch society. The probation officer from the *reclassering* spoke in Dutch, and I could hardly understand the language thoroughly.

The judge finally spoke to me her verdict. She talked to me in English. "Mr. Berchy, whatever happened between you and your wife is indeed an unfortunate story. You found love with each other in distant shores, and I know you did not expect it to end up in this court. Although what happened may not be correct from a legal point of view, the court takes into consideration the neutral opinions of people who have known you and your wife. The court dismisses the statements of her family because they are biased and show some form of hatred or dislike between you and them. Hence, such statements do not paint an accurate picture of you.

"What the court sees is a broken person who went through a challenging time adjusting to this society and culture, and it understands the humanness of your condition and that, eventually, you exploded out of frustration and hurt. Although the court does not agree with your actions on how you dealt with your spouse, the court simply understands the circumstances of the prolonged agony you went through. Furthermore, the court recognises that humans at some stage are likely to snap into an outburst of some kind. There is no record of a history of abuse or any evidence to indicate you are that type of person. Although the prosecution aims to portray a different picture of you, this court does not see it that way.

"The court does not see it necessary to punish you in any way, and the court believes that this case is worthy of being dismissed without any charges levied against you. Mr. Berchy is free to go."

I left the courthouse completely devastated and hurt, so saddened that her family was brainwashing her again; my children were in a place hidden from me. I was shocked to read the statements of her mother and especially her stepfather.

The whole family was waiting for this case to end in my incarceration, as they intended evil against me; my God delivered me from the wicked plans of wicked people. Fear came upon those wicked people; they put up curtains and blocked the view of their living room. They came to know that their nefarious plans to take me out of the equation had not succeeded, and they became fearful of me. But, in reality, they were afraid because they had evil, wicked intentions to destroy me and keep my children to themselves.

A new court case for the divorce went ahead, and I was employing Dutch lawyers left, right, and centre. I was engaged and earning a salary scale that did not entitle me for legal aid, so I had to pay for lawyers even if I did not want to employ them.

The mother of my children was now hiding among her mother's family somewhere east of the country. She was provided with a family lawyer who was a friend of the family. Hence, my chances of even talking to her were remote. My kids had been kidnapped and kept away from me, and my only chance of seeing them again was through the courts.

A thought went through my mind: if I, as a man, took my kids and hid them among my family and did not allow the other parent to see the children, I am sure they would have come and arrested me and put me in prison for kidnapping. Nevertheless, it's legal for a woman to do this to her children and the father. Here is injustice, standing right in front of you, laughing in your face.

I was walking on eggshells, but I couldn't be upset. I was not allowed to show any outbursts of my emotions; I had to die to all of my human feelings because I was walking on eggshells in this society. One wrong move or one outburst of frustration against the civil legal procedure to see my children again would cost me all my chances of seeing my children ever again.

I waited for six months to see the two boys once again; it was like I died each day. My hope was all I had; my lawyer was able to negotiate a meeting for one hour with my sons at a McDonald's in a place called Hoorn. According to the arrangement, my ex-brother-in-law would bring the two boys, drop them at the McDonald's, and pick them up after one hour.

It was like life returned to me that day. I went with my friends Ron and Helma as witnesses, because I was so unsure what these people would say or do to jeopardise my visitations with the children.

I arrived early at the McDonald's, and my heart was aching. I was upset with myself because I had put my innocent children through this evil, inhumane, terrible drama. I wished I would never have to put a child through this. All these thoughts were rushing through my mind, like some kind of correction to my spirit and soul, to be caught up in this white man's world of terrible, awful, inhumane family drama. I was standing there waiting for them when I suddenly felt a sense of déjà vu about the old Aboriginal woman in Belyuen, Australia. This poor woman had lost her son to the white missionaries, and her life had stood still for forty years before she saw him again. When she did, she rejected him; she asked instead for the baby these white missionaries took away from her for all those years.

I shook my head in disbelief; almost a decade later I was experiencing the same thing once again, but this time, it was me, and my wife's white Dutch family were trying to keep my children away from me. History repeating itself. How bizarre.

Then they appeared. I was standing with my friends Ron and Helma; they put their hand on my shoulder to hold me up. It was emotionally breaking me up. I just wanted to hug them and cry, but I had to be healthy for them. I had no conversation with my ex-brother-in-law.

I took the two boys and sat down with them at the table. I got them some food, and I was excited and happy to see them. My heart was thumping inside my rib cage. Joshua was eighteen months old, so he did not know what was going on. My eldest son was looking at me, trying hard to remember; he was a child and was unable to ask me, "What happened to us, Dad?" It was that expression on his face and his inability to ask me that question—I could see him searching for it. Then suddenly, he wrapped his hand around my neck like he remembered and said, "Papa, Papa, Papa." My heart exploded in pain at his struggle to remember me; six months is a long time in a child's life. I was upset that the people in this society did not have a clue as to what they were doing to my innocent children and me.

I just hugged him as he gave me tremendous strength when he called me "Papa." Who can steal a son from his father? Only one person can do that—his mother. The hour flew past like a minute, and I stood there watching two innocent victims driving away in a car. My flesh and blood was being destroyed at the hands of evil people and society. I was going to fight for my sons. I wept as my friend consoled me.

The arrangements for visitations stalled once again, as the mother was very disturbed after the first encounter that took place between the children and me; she claimed it was emotionally traumatising for the kids. It would be good to wait for a month for a new date for visitations. (The family lawyer did all the talking; these were inhumane forces, people with evil inclinations and demons of their past evils, bitter because of their long history of family divorces, like dark clouds descending on my life and those of my children.)

I lay on my couch and wished I had never met this girl in Thailand. How could she be so cruel? What kind of dark evil of her family and her past childhood dramas were playing out? I lay there a bit longer and contemplated my actions. Where did this anger come from? Why did I burst out this way? Why could I have not walked away in silence? Why did I swing my hands in frustration at her? Why did I do something I hated watching my father do to my mother? It was not the same as my dad but the outburst of my pain. I did hurt myself, her, and my two sons.

I felt so wretched and repented sincerely. I was trying to put my finger on it and examining myself. I wept once again, and a dark voice appeared in my head. "End your life, and all this pain will end." It was the first time I'd ever heard it. It was scary. I was shaking. I lay on the couch and moaned for my sons. My cries were painfully and deeply mournful. They were coming from the bellows of my stomach. I was in deep agony. I walked around in the darkness of my house weeping and calling their names. I went into their bedrooms that I had so beautifully decorated. I screamed their names. "Forgive me, my sons." I wept uncontrollably till I heard someone ringing my doorbell and knocking at my door. I dragged myself mournfully from my pain, wiped my swollen, painful face, and crawled down the steps to answer the door. It was my neighbour, an Iraqi refugee. He said, "My brother, please don't cry. My wife and I can hear your cries, and it reminds us of the pain we cried in Iraq. Please let me help you, but do not cry—it's excruciating." I bowed my head repentantly and said I was sorry. I lay on the couch and fell asleep.

I waited for a month and received a letter from my lawyer, saying that I would be able to meet my children and my wife, at a restaurant in Arnhem in the presence of her mother and stepfather. I could not believe this, but I did not protest at anything. I would bend over backwards to do anything to see my children. I had no more say, no more rights, and no more influence in anything. I was humbled to my knees; my love for my sons was more significant than all the humiliation I was to experience in this lifetime. Maybe this was a ploy or a provocation to test me once again, so I just took a deep breath and told myself, "Look at the two boys, and stay focused on that." A voice and a spirit were always guiding me.

I struggled to find this place as I drove around in the city of Arnhem, looking for it. I did not want to be late, and it was lucky that I had left early. I saw my wife for the first time in seven months. I tried to hug her, as I felt love for her like I always did. She looked confused and was not herself. I felt unfortunate for her. I just wished I could heal all this unnecessary pain and go back to a place and time when all this had never happened and we were happy together.

As much as I did not like her mother and stepfather around, I had no choice. I was aware of all the lies these ungodly people had told. I knew their malicious intentions to destroy me, and the lies they told remained irreparable. They stood there with brass necks, pretending like they'd never done anything. I was in no position to show or tell my wife the terrible things her mother and stepfather did against me. It was not time for me to talk about these things. I stayed focused on the kids and played with the two boys in the park. I had to walk together with her while her mother and stepfather followed behind us. My wife looked lost, confused, and brainwashed.

One year had passed us since our home had been broken, and I was allowed to see the children once every two weeks—according to *her* wishes and always at a location of *her* choosing. I never missed an opportunity to meet them. It was all too delicate and very complicated; we had received a letter from the court, giving us six weeks to decide on a final divorce settlement. I begged her to come and have dinner with me so that we could, at least, have an opportunity to talk about reunification before the six-week deadline was up. I took her to the Argentinian restaurant at Rembrandtplein, 1017 CT, Amsterdam, Netherlands. We'd often come to this restaurant in a place and time when love and romance made us so happy. We sat down to have dinner, but it felt so weird; she was as cold as ice. She looked very brainwashed, still confused, and reconciliation was not something I could see on her face. On the other hand, I was on the other side of this human-drama spectrum. I wanted to save this marriage.

I ordered two glasses of Malbec wine and sirloin steak, grilled asparagus, smoked mayonnaise, pea shoots cured in egg yolk, and some salad. As I waited for the food, I asked her if it was okay to talk about the divorce. She nodded her head approvingly, and I requested that she cancel the divorce. I told her to consider coming back and moving out to a new place so we could be us again. It was emotional for me as my eyes welled up with tears; she remained cold as ice, emotionless. She looked at me as if she were feeling embarrassed by my heartfelt tears, these tears that naturally built up in my eyes, because, as a human being, I had a heart that was attached to the tear ducts of my eyes.

She said, "Please, no tears. I want to get a divorce. We can continue to work on our relationship in this way, and if there is a consistent improvement, then we can get married once again." I honestly did not understand this concept at all. I smiled because I felt like I was being treated like some kind of fool.

I replied to her, "We are married, and we can make this work out for you and me and these two boys. There is no way I am going to get married twice to the same woman."

Well, she was arrogant; tossing her hair to one side, she said, "Marriage—it's only a piece of paper. I don't see the problem in getting divorced and remarried to the same person."

I shook my head in disbelief. "Am I a piece of paper? Are our children a piece of paper? Are all the sacrifices we have made to be together a piece of paper? Is giving each other second chances, as I did with you, also just a piece of paper? Please, come on. Let's be real, Tabitha."

She stood up; she was upset. She took her bag and said, "I cannot have this dinner with you tonight."

I said, "Oh, please—don't do this." She walked away. I could not stop her or even hold her hand (she might say I tried to assault her again). I felt so helpless and so let down. I saw her walking away like she was going to take a trip back to the Arctic coldness of her mind and heart. I did not know this woman anymore. She was not the same person; some kind of evil darkness had beguiled her heart. I knew my divorce was sealed, and I could not prevent it because I'd married an atheist.

Three weeks later, the police came to my house once more; they arrested me and took me; they kept me locked up for three days. It was about my name and my identification. My ex-wife and her lawyer informed them about the change of name.

Further, she, in cooperation with Mr. Visser, was waiting for this investigation to lead to an end in my arrest. My wife knew everything about me. I never hid anything from her; nothing was a problem when we were married, but now it was an aim and goal to alienate me from my children. The agenda of this family was to get rid of me one way or another. This is called "the Delilah spirit" in a woman. I was like Samson; my long hair locks were cut, and I was betrayed once again.

The police detective threatened me at the police station and promised me that he would make sure that I was removed from this country. I looked at him and said, "I hope you are recording this. If this country gave me my children, I would gladly leave this country and never return to this godless society." I was summoned every day from my cell to the police officer and forced to make some kind of statement. I refused to do this.

I had started studying laws and the European Convention on Human Rights. I did not want to be ignorant about my rights, like most people are. I gently told the police officer that under the convention of European law, I had a right to remain silent, I had a right to have a translator and legal representation, and that he was violating all those rights. The detective was furious with me, threatened to throw me out of the country, and further stated that he knew everything about me because he had his sources. I gently smiled at him and said, "You have a close relationship with my ex-wife and her stepfather." Then he threw me back into the cell, annoyed and angry at me for my knowledge of human-rights law.

The next morning, I was summoned yet again; there was an Irish-Dutch translator available. I was allowed to talk to an unknown lawyer on the phone who I could not trust. I sat in the office with a video camera and an audio recording operating to record all my statements.

I was pressured once again to make a statement. I told the police officer that I had a right to remain silent and would talk only to my legal representative. Forcing me to make a statement was a violation of my right to remain silent. He was frustrated with me, but I had no intention of trying to defeat the man. I was now educated and knew my rights; police don't like people who know their rights because they cannot bully them. They asked for my Australian passport, and I told them it was with my lawyer and with the court. The arrangement was for me to surrender my passport so that I'd be able to see my kids. The truth was my children were hidden away from me in a place and address that I never knew. I asked the question, "Who kidnapped the kids? The ones who are claiming security. I am innocent, and I am still here only because of my kids."

They threw me back in the cell and told me to think about it for another hour. I sat in the cell silently; an hour and a half later, a police officer coaxed me into making a statement so that I would be able to go home. I went back up to the summons room, and the Irish-Dutch translator was sitting there translating Dutch to English. I was getting tired of this harassment about making a statement, so I did a Bill Clinton on them.

I raised my hand looking to the camera. I said, "I swear I never had an affair with Monica Lewinsky." The police officer went mad, probably cursing me or saying something in Dutch; they took me back and threw me into the cell. I thought that I had the right to remain silent.

The next day, they released me and pressed charges against me for fraud; a week later, I received a letter stating that I would not be able to see my children. I had to file for a case for hearing in the court in Zutphen.

My lawyer bill increased. I was still not entitled to any legal aid because I was a working man. Now I worked for the government and employed expensive Dutch lawyers. I had become a slave to the evil that existed in this society. I found it so hard to like these people; sadness and bitterness started to fall like a shadow over my life. I held on to pray, but there were days when even prayer slipped away. Evil had cast a net over me; the people I'd once loved and cared for were the ones who now sought my destruction. Once again, I had two court cases, entangled in a system that made me feel like I was descending into an endless abyss.

A few months went by, and, finally, I had a court hearing about my children. I was praying outside the courthouse. I asked the Lord to give me words to speak, to give me strength not to hate the evilness in the people seeking the destruction of my life. I entered the courtroom and sat there amid the ugliness of a human-made system. It was a circus, and I was the clown in the middle of it, employing the lawyers and paying the taxes for the upkeep of this circus. I was merely a father fighting for his rights and dignity to see his two sons and to maintain a social relationship among all the inhumanity that surrounded me that day.

The honourable judge J. J. Oostveen was presiding over the case, and we were in session. The lawyer stood up; she looked mean and cruel; feminist blood poured through her veins. She was forty-four years old, a face covered with indentation marks of a severe attack of measles she must have suffered as a child. Unmarried, female feminist lawyers are lethal women. As the poison poured out, I had to listen to my terrible crime over and over again. All about the night I'd lost control of my anger, and in my frustration, unintentionally struck her. It was never-ending, and I accepted the divorce. I regretted my stupid mistake in a valley of tears every day of my life. My ex-wife was sobbing to the point of exaggerating her suffering. Eighteen months had passed since the divorce, and this was all made to sound very dramatic by the lawyer. I did not understand it back then, but looking back now, it was a well-rehearsed coaching and plan initiated by a terrible, ugly lawyer. My soul sensed that the evil enemy was my wife's feminist, obnoxious lawyer—a man-hater. I sat there silent, feeling sad. The notorious Raad Van De Kinderberscheming (Child Protection Agency) now stepped up on to the podium and began a speech on the importance of protecting the best interest of the children. They were trying to influence the court for the authority to step into the case and make it more complicated.

I closed my eyes and prayed for wisdom among all the evil that was closing in around me. The judge looked at me and asked me what I wanted to tell the court.

I whispered to my soul, *Lord, be my guide.* "Your Honour." I felt a lump in my throat. I coughed and drank some water. I excused myself. "Your Honour," I began once more, "this is a sad and challenging time. When I met my wife in Thailand, it was a beautiful day, and we were happy, so I never imagined I would be in a courthouse feeling torn and broken. I have broken memories and sadness because I saw two sons born at home and held them in my arms, and it's for them my heart breaks. When they ask me for bread, I do not give them a stone, and if they ask me for a fish, I don't place a serpent in their hands. I may not have been the man she wanted in her life, but I am the dad my children have, and I am so sad to hear the pain, but I'm distressed at the hate against me. We all have suffered enough pain already, and I don't want to leave this place feeling hate. I am here because I promised my sons that I would be there for them." I stopped and sat down. I held myself and whispered to my soul, *Thank You, Lord. Forgive us for our sins.*

The judge spoke. "Mrs. De Bie, it's unfortunate that you and your husband could not overcome your relationship problems. The court has to deal with such sad realities in this society. Nevertheless, in all your statements and throughout this difficult time, there is not a shred of evidence that this man here is not a good father. In all your previous comments, it was proven that you had a very kind, hardworking husband. Many good things about this man have been spoken. Today, some contradictions have come from you that don't add up. The court has already established that his children adore him. He has been a good father. The court further does not see it necessary for the Child Protection Agency to step in because there are no risks that warrant any interference. The court does not find it necessary for this at this stage. What the court recognises is that you don't want your children to see their father. The court sympathises with both the parents about the breakup of their marriage. It is in the record that your husband made an appeal to the court requesting that he did not want a divorce. The court gave you both a year to think about it. I believe you did not see any possibility for a reunification.

"Nevertheless, today, we are not here to talk about your divorce and the sad things about them. I see a good father in front of me. You have said he is a good father for his children, and the children adore him. Now, I see a bitterness that you don't want your children to have contact with their father. This court upholds the rights of visitations between the father and his sons. Furthermore, the court imposes a fine of two hundred and fifty guilders every two weeks, a penalty on the mother if she fails to comply with the visitations between the children and their father." The court closed the session.

My ex-wife refused to oblige the court order and was in contempt of the judgement of the court. The feminist, man-hater lawyer with the jezebel spirit that accompanied her had found a different court with a female judge to preside over the case for an appeal.

I was back again in court, the only man sitting in the company of women in a court session. It amazed me how different the atmosphere was and how incredibly a well-made judgement by Justice J. J. Oostveen was now in the hands of a feminist-sympathetic female judge, where this judgement might be reversed. The multimillion-dollar question: in the best interest of the children? The circus at the court went against the clown and his children.

The court ruled that the visitations between the children and father must be investigated by the notorious Raad van de Kinderberscheming (Child Protection Agency), a report to be submitted to the court within six months; a determination of the visitations would then be made. I was not able to see my children until these agencies made the necessary arrangements. I spent days and months waiting to see my sons again.

I was in the zone of the living dead. I lost weight, and my face withdrew within itself. I was living in a godforsaken society, and everything around me was cold. I was numb with pain, and I hated the inhumane Dutch system of justice. I was reduced to a status worse than a refugee. A refugee gets legal aid. There was still the matter of my identification. I was now dealing with the notorious Dutch immigration department and overburdened with all the legal expenses. I employed more lawyers and went to work each day to pay this government and this inhumane system of justice.

I felt profoundly depressed, and my world around me was darkened; demons of destruction had surrounded me. I hid at home and closed myself off from the immoral society I saw around me. I did not contact my parents because I did not want them to know about my darkness; it would pain them and put them through severe distress in their old age. I was unable to function at work, and my doctor prescribed me antidepressant medications.

I lay on my couch like a vegetable as I withdrew from society—my heart in pain, a mind numb to emotions, and a soul dying in self-pity. The voice returned, and I heard it. "It's not worth living this life, and this pain will not end. Only you can complete it." I fell asleep tired and exhausted.

The next day, the voice returned; as the antidepressants popped in my flesh, the sound surrounded my soul. I did not pray anymore. I did not cry to God anymore.

Another voice came along. "Seek revenge," it said. "Kill these evil people." I was more scared of this voice because it was more sinister. I was afraid; I shook violently on my couch and shouted, "Get away! Get away!" I crumbled and crouched like a scared rabbit.

I did not find any solution, and I had no one in this country; my friends were tired of my misery, and I understood that it was too much. They did not shun me, but rather my darkness and suffering were so intense that it affected them if I was around. I felt sad for them because they liked me. So, I avoided them for a while and was all alone in a cold, godless, atheist society. When you entertain a demonic voice long enough, it becomes compelling. I started to make plans to end it all.

I went to the attic and walked around my children's bedrooms. I still had a few of their clothes, and I would hold them up to my nose and smell the clothes. I would always catch the baby smells of my sons. I would weep and feel sad. I apologised to them and asked forgiveness.

The voice got stronger and more attractive, and I went to the attic and tied the rope on a wooden beam. I was a good fisherman, and the hangman's noose was now firmly tied to the beam. I placed a small stool under the rope, stood, and watched the picture in front of me. It looked pleasant to my darkened mind.

A few days on my dead man's couch, I was on sick leave. I could not function anymore. I was unable to work anymore. My mind had been destroyed by the system of injustice and my struggles to see my children. I was banished, like a criminal, and my only crime was that I'd hurt myself more than anyone could have hurt anyone else. How can society, a government, and a justice system punish a man who has already punished himself?

I woke up one morning, and I suddenly felt happy; the end had come, it felt perfect once more, a sudden feeling of happiness flooded my house. I started to listen to music that made me happy again. I even cooked a nice meal for myself.

It was a great day because the end of the misery had come, and I found the solution to my terrible state that I'd been reduced to by this western Dutch society. The sun set, and a cold feeling of gloom settled once again into my broken home. The mood had changed from happiness to relief as I walked up to the first floor. I looked at the bedroom of broken promises. I went to the bedroom of my sons and smelled their clothes for the last time. I pulled the ladder down and climbed into the attic. I precariously stood on the stool and put the hangman's noose around me; it was going to be quick. Suicide is a live act. I was ready. My legs moved, and the stool shifted. I closed my eyes, and I saw a boy running in the fields.

Flowers were all around him; he was running among the wildflowers with his hands spread, with his back facing me. It lasted forever as I watched him running. He stopped, turned, and looked at me. It was me; it was me looking back at myself as a young boy at a picnic among the wildflowers; I was so happy as a child when my mother taught me to pray. I started to shake and shiver on the stool as I watched. Then I fell on the wooden floor; the stool slipped from under my feet and stumbled across the wooden floor. I was screaming, "No!" I was on the floor crying and screaming, "No. Oh, my god, why have You forsaken me? Oh, my god, why, why, why?" I went into some kind of spasm. I could not remember anything anymore. I collapsed on the wood floor and passed out. I woke up the next day on my wooden floor in my attic, and I had no explanation for what had happened. I did put a rope around my neck. I tied an excellent knot on a strong quality rope. I did stand on the round barstool. I shook and shivered on it. I saw a movie in front of my eyes that lasted forever, and I have no explanation as to how or when I stepped away from the stool. I landed on a wooden floor crying and screaming, and I was alive.

I looked at the rope; the noose was closed, evidence that my neck was in it. I was terrified. I ran downstairs, came back up with a knife, cut that ghastly rope, took it down quickly, and threw it down. I was over my divorce, and I did not hate that woman at all. I came down the foldable attic stairs. I pulled the cord and closed the entrance of the attic behind me and promised myself I would never enter that dark place again in my life. Suicide is a demonic possession and the most significant lie the devil perpetrates against your soul to cut short your life and steal the destiny for which God has intended you. It's not a mental condition that can be treated by man or by medications, but a state that can be restored only by Christ alone. I cannot explain why I did not hang that night. I am unable to tell how I found myself lying on a cold wooden floor and still alive.

I could have died in Kambalda mine at level eight when I was lost in the darkness of a nickel mine. I could have died crossing the road getting hit by a car. I can't explain all the reasons I could have died, but I am here still alive telling you this true story of my life and its dark days. I am alive because I have learned to find my God again in my life, and no weapon formed against me can prosper; no one can pluck me out of His hands, and even my attempt to destroy myself proved to be unsuccessful.

Kramer vs. Kramer and *Mrs. Doubtfire* became my favourite movies.

I waited for six months; then, I made several calls to the Child Protection Agency. They bluntly told me that they were busy with several cases and that they would petition the court for extensions. Eighteen months passed, and I still did not get to see my children. I was sent from pillar to post by the Child Protection Agency. During the entire period, they never made even one attempt to establish any visitations between my children and me. They never supervised, arranged, or observed one meeting. The Child Protection Agency was perpetrating a gradual alienation between my two sons and me, protecting the mother and her agenda to keep the children away from their father.

I contacted the United Nations researcher Dr. Nancy Faulkner. I sought permission for me to present the report to the Dutch Court, considering that the Dutch Child Protection Agency had no experience or conducted such a detailed study as the UN had. Their mother kidnapped my children for eighteen months; she refused to pay the fines imposed by the court. She successfully moved the case to a different court with a more favourable female judge, stalled all the visitations, and, with the help of the notoriously inefficient Child Protection Agency, was able to use these authorities to alienate my sons successfully.

Dr. Nancy Faulkner's alienation report reads as follows:

> In light of the hurtful impacts on kids, parental hijacking has been portrayed as a type of child abuse" reports Patricia Hoff, Legal Director for the Parental Abduction Training and Dissemination Project, American Bar Association on Children and the Law. Hoff clarifies:
>
> "Kidnapped kids endure genuinely and once in a while physically on account of abductor-guardians. Numerous youngsters are told the other parent is dead or never again adores them. Alienated from loved ones, snatched kids regularly are given new names by their abductor-guardians and taught not to uncover their genuine names or where they lived previously." (Hoff, 1997). As an early pioneer in the moderately new field of parental kid kidnapping issues, Dr. Dorothy Huntington composed an article distributed in 1982, "Parental Kidnapping: A New Form of Child Abuse." Huntington finds that, from the perspective of the kid, [it is] "youngster taking his kid misuse." According to Huntington, "in kid-taking the kids are utilised as the two items and weapons in the battle between the guardians, which prompts the brutalisation of the kids mentally, explicitly annihilating their feeling of trust in their general surroundings." Because of the occasions encompassing parental kid kidnapping, Huntington accentuates that "we should reconceptualise kid-taking as kid maltreatment of the most glaring sort" (Huntington, 1982, p. 7).
>
> There is a deplorable and apparent scarcity of writing on parental youngster snatching. Naturally, during the previous two decades, Huntington (1982), Greif and Hegar (1993), and others have started tending to worries for youngsters hijacked by their parent abductors. With developing concerns for kidnapped youngsters, a few specialists have authored terms like

"Parental Alienation" to portray the potential negative effect on kids [who are] unfortunate casualties. Notwithstanding the particular terms intended to outline the impacts of parental youngster kidnapping, there is the general agreement that the kids are [suffering] the resultant setbacks.

HAZARD FACTORS

Post-separation [anxiety] from parental youngster-taking has been on the expansion since the mid-1970s, paralleling the rising separation rate and the heightening prosecution over kid authority (Huntington, 1986). As indicated by Hoff (1997), "The term 'parental hijacking' envelops the taking, maintenance, or disguise of a youngster by a parent, another relative, or their operator, in disparagement of the authority rights, including appearance rights, of another parent or relative."

The abductor parent may move to start with one state and then [move] onto the next, beginning another round of examination concerning the maltreatment with each move, obstructing intercession by kid-defensive administrations (Jones, Lund and Sullivan, 1996). Or, on the other hand, the abductor may escape to another nation, totally closing down any expectations of association by youngster-defensive administrations in the country of inception. The unavoidable situation is that the kidnapping guardian seeks refuge or moves past the locale of administering the law. "These kidnappings are astutely plotted and arranged and regularly include the help of relatives. The objective parent has no sending location or phone numbers." (Clawar and Rivlin, p. 115). (end of abstract report).

I was back in court once more. I'd almost met death by my failed suicide attempt; by an unexplainable divine intervention, I was still alive. Hatred and anger turned to hope and despair; my love for the mother of these two sons was almost dead inside of me. I struggled in a battle within myself between hate and forgiveness. I wanted to forgive her, but there was no repentance or an apology before me to find the strength to forgive. Revenge was a whole lot easier to shelter in my soul, but it made me feel only restless and troubled. I battled with the Holy Messiah Yeshua in my desperate prayers unto the Lord my God.

I found myself in a personal battle with the teaching of His holy concept of "love your enemy." It was hard to wrap my soul around the idea that a woman whom I married and with whom I'd had children was all out in collaboration with the ugliest lawyer, turning my beautiful life into the most acrid torment, inflicting the cruellest pain, a genocide, a kidnapping, and the alienation of a father's love for his two sons.

The case was now in the High Court of s'Hertogenbosch, a province in the south of the Netherlands. I had spent almost two years studying the law, reading case laws of the European Court of Human rights, the several cases of the violation of human rights under Article 8, Article 6, and Article 14 of the convention. The simple question I had raised in my wisdom: if the European Convention on Human Rights has guaranteed these rights, why am I standing here fighting for reasons that are guaranteed? I realised that laws are not written to ensure protection, but instead, they are written so you can fight for them against those who perpetrate them. And those who commit them are the same people who wrote such laws in the first place and took no responsibility for implementing them—the concept of human justice.

The following debate took place in the court. The Child Protection Agency declared the following statement: "It has been a difficult time for the mother and the children. And now they have managed to find a stable situation. In the best interest of the children, we recommend that contact with the father at this stage would be emotionally and physiologically upsetting. We recommend two years of no contact, after which a further investigation can be requested." Does that not sound a little too much like the German Gestapo? "We are sending you on a train of death, and you have nothing to say about it—justice in the Netherlands."

High Court of s'Hertogenbosch Judge asks, "Does the Child Protection Agency believe that it would be easier for the children to emotionally bond with the father, after two years of further separation that this protection agency is recommending? There has never been any evidence that the children are in danger in having contact with their father. Thirdly, the protection agency has not made any attempt to conduct the investigations with observation and communication between the children and their father. Also, the case has been prolonged because this agency did not meet its deadline and delayed the court proceeding by eighteen months. The court does not agree that this report is fair."

My lawyer requested for the court to hear the father of the children speak. As I stood up once again in my endless court appearances in this country, I whispered in my soul, *Lord, help me overcome these people and this evil. Help me, God.* I looked up and addressed the court, "Your Honour, justice delayed is justice denied, and justice denied is laws violated. I understand that I stand before you because I failed to keep this family and marriage together. I also know that I live in a country where two in three marriages end in a divorce, but where I come from, divorce is a taboo and a last resort. I have read almost every case law from the European Court on Human Rights, which I have quoted with my counsel and forwarded to the court. I do believe that this court has respect for the laws and the guarantee of human rights by the European Convention on Human Rights.

"I also forwarded the court the Parental Alienation Report by Dr. Nancy Faulkner and the United Nations to the court. The Child Protection Agency in the Netherlands has never funded such a profound research study on parental alienation. It is evident for the past three years that the mother of the children has tried desperately to alienate the children from me. This profoundly troubling behaviour springs from the fact that her mother estranged her from her biological father for several years. As you can see, this parental alienation continues to be perpetrated against my children. I would request the court to dismiss the unprofessional, discriminative ill-informed Child Protection Agency and charge them for supporting this alienation between my sons and me.

"Your Honour, losing a child because of kidnapping by the mother is far worse than death by a car accident. People have tragically lost their children in car accidents, and somehow, they have a place in a cemetery to visit to grieve their loss. I don't even have such grief; mine is felt far more in-depth. I did not know my children's whereabouts; I was unable to see them; I couldn't hear them speak; I cannot hug them, and many nights I have gone to bed in a pool of tears asking God to stop my heart in the middle of the night so that a new day would not come to me. You all have children in this courtroom. Let me then ask a question of humanity: how many of you have gone to bed for two years not knowing where and how your children are?

"When I had these children, I made that decision with my currently ex-wife. I expected she would have the dignity and integrity to honour the children and their rights. I do not have much respect for this racist, discriminative Child Protection Agency. I hope this court can correct these terrible human wrongs in this country."

The court requested the Child Protection Agency to return with a new report within six months with visitations conducted with the father and his sons. The court adjourned.

My spiritual journey and the soul debate with the Holy Yeshua HaMashiach about forgiving the enemy and questioning my Christian faith was another battle that raged inside my spirit. Seven months later, I was back in the same court, standing in front of the same judges, without any contact established between my sons and me. The circus continued, but there were new twists and turns. Four years and six months had passed since I'd last seen my children, as my life was being tossed around by European systems of justice made by the first world who boasts of fair procedures and advancement of democracy and human dignity. Yet, these nations were unable to implement a democratic process for a father desperately fighting for his children. I cannot express the enormous amount of discouragement and advice I received from my Dutch friends and the general public. Many Dutchmen told me, "Find a new woman, and forget about your kids; you have very little chance of winning anything within the Dutch system of justice." They also highlighted a weekly snippet inserted by a father for more than twenty years in the Dutch newspaper *De Telegraaf*, which reads in Dutch, *"Ik verdom de rechtssysteem van de Koning van Nederlands"* (I damn the justice system of the Kingdom of the Netherlands).

In spite of all of these odds, I pressed on because I wanted to do my best to change it for my children and for all children who have good fathers who love them preciously. Many men did not fight for this, and men were not willing to go through this terribly acrid torment to see their children. Hence, many children remain without contact with their fathers. Perhaps, society needed a Dutch TV reality show called *Vermist* (*Lost*), a program that searches, finds, and tries to bring lost children together with their biological parent. With all this baggage, pain and suffering, anger, and resentment, I honestly did not know where this inner strength came from. I did not know how I survived it all. I was financially depleted, emotionally violated, psychologically tormented, publicly humiliated, and the same was done to my children by their mother and the system of justice that was just as crooked and discriminatory. How amazing are the words of a woman to a man in love: "Honey, I would love to have your children." In a divorce, they become words of a canard tongue: "I do not want my children to have any contact with their father." Then they try to replace the father by a stepfather, and the utter misery of these societies continues generation to generation, and they are called "advanced" societies. How ironic and perplexing it is. I painted an Aboriginal graffiti at a bus station one night; it read, "You ain't much if you are Dutch. Evil people. They stole my kids away." I remembered the Aboriginal children the white people had stolen in my never-never land.

The following court proceeding at s'Hertengbosch proceeded with a report from the Child Protection Agency finally reporting that the mother was refusing to cooperate in any form of visitation between the father and the children. The court questioned the mother, and she declined bluntly in the court that she had no intention to cooperate with any visitation between my children and me.

The court asked me to speak, and I was now a highly educated lawyer, having earned my degree with honours in the court halls of this nation. I was expecting they would confer a purple heart on my distinguished fight for justice, for the great opportunity I was giving the system to change the evils that exist in this society.

I looked at the judges and said, "Give me leave to venture my conjecture on how justice for my sons and I may come to pass. Your Honours, there can be no doubt in the mind of this court, and for the heartbeat of the justice system. You can see that as long as my children remain in the custody of the mother, my rights, my children's rights, the European Convention on Human Rights, and every other Dutch law are at stake here in this honourable court. The question is, are we prepared to hold up this law and enforce it?

"Malicious people are the devil's nymphs, and I believe this court has an excellent opportunity to make the change that the society outside these walls of justice so desperately needs.

"Now, if I had a crystal ball and looked into it, if I noticed where it was leading me to, I would have never boarded that plane in Darwin and left my beloved Australia to be here and be married to Mrs. De Bie. I did not plan on becoming a father. She got pregnant because she wanted to and never asked me about it. I took responsibility and did the right thing and married the woman who was becoming the mother of my son. I loved her dearly, and I honoured my integrity and principles to be a husband and a father.

"Now I was battling the system and her bitterness for a human right to have visitation to see the most precious children." I spoke to the court and added, "I believe the court is now in a position to change the custody of the children to me because, by this change, the children will have a fair opportunity to see their mother and me. As long as they remain with her, every decent law and human right will be violated. The history of this case shows it. Her public denial to work in the best interest of the children continues this alienation because the systems and the court continue to support the separation indirectly."

There was panic in the room. I was putting forward a case requesting a ruling for a change of custody. I did not want visitations anymore; enough is enough with this silly circus of Dutch family law. The court requested all parties to take a recess, discuss the issue with the lawyers, and return to the court in the afternoon for a special sitting on this same day.

My lawyer and the ex-wife's ugly lawyer discussed. It was extraordinary. The high court understood my position well, and the court anticipated how far I was now willing to go with this case. The reputation of this court was being held hostage by one uncooperative, disturbed woman operating with severe psychological impediments. Hence, they arranged a special sitting on the same day in their attempt to find a resolution for justice in a system—the incongruity of trying to milk a bull.

At 2:00 p.m., the court reconvened once again in an exceptional sitting in the case of Mrs. Tabitha De Bie versus Lyndon Berchy. The court was under pressure to apply the law that was deliberately and repeatedly being flaunted.

So, the judge said to the damsel in distress, "Mrs. De Bie, I hope you had a good chat with your legal counsel and time to think of what is at stake over here. The court would like to have some reassurance from you about the visitations between your children and their father. How do you respond to this?"

She remained silent, and the judge looked uneasy. "Mrs. De Bie, the court is waiting for your response." She continued her silence; her lawyer was whispering to her, urging her forward.

She spoke, "Your Honour, I do not want to cooperate, and I don't want my children to have contact with the father." The court went into an uproar, and the judges were furious.

The judge spoke, "Mrs. De Bie, this court is ready to change the custody of your children to their father. Would you like for police officers to come to your house and take away your children? Do you want the court to do that?" Her lawyer, now in a panic, asked the court to excuse her.

The lawyer said, "My client is not in a state of mind to answer the court." They gave her water to drink; the woman was lost.

I watched her humiliation and her ignorance, and saw that she was a victim of her parents' history and divorce, the complicated, disturbed life. I suddenly felt this powerful compassion fill my heart at her plight. The dramatic court case ended with set dates for me to meet my children. A stark warning was issued in the judgement that criminal charges could be laid on her for any further noncooperation. Change of custody would be enforced if this case ever returned to the Dutch courts anywhere in the country. As I walked out of the courthouse in what my lawyer hailed a great victory, I did not see any success but good overcoming evil. I was deeply saddened that it took so long and so many lost years.

I walked past her and the lawyer, and suddenly I stopped. This great feeling of compassion fell upon me, and I was overpowered by it. I turned around and walked back towards the mother of my two sons. I was filled with tears. I extended my hand to her and called her by her name. "Tabitha, please." I felt choked, talking to her after so long—so many years of unnecessary bitterness and legal wrangling. I continued to speak, "I tried to hate you, but I could not do it. I suffered greatly. Know this always, and I forgive you for everything you have done. I forgive you for everything you have put these kids through."

My tears flowed forward like water from a burst dam, spilling down my face. I felt the muscles of my jaw tremble, like a little child whining in agony, and I looked toward the window, as if the light could relieve me. There was static deadness in my psyche once more—a response to this constant fear and lethal, soul-depleting pressure I'd survived. I hear my agonies, like a grieved youth, unrefined from inside. This uncalled-for fight in court had expelled everything passionate from me. I didn't understand I had nothing left to give; I was wholly purged. That is how it is then when the wickedness of people you once cherished is executed against you. It is a theft of the spirit and a physical pulverization no other individual can see, and it was legal for a woman to do this to a man in this Dutch society.

I felt unfortunate and sorry for her. I wanted to hug her and chase every beast of torment away from her, but she was so far lost and gone. It was so painful to watch what had become of her. It was terrible. It took so many years of wrangling and game-playing by the legal system and its accomplices of similar feministic attitudes within these organisations to empower a woman to effect a separation between my sons and me. Abruptly, a feeling sprung from inside, something I had contended with my Lord for a considerable length of time, about the idea of forgiveness. It was the point at which I comprehended that my suffering was insignificant in contrast with Jesus's. When I gave up myself and my human thinking, the best blessing fell upon me. Like a cloud blasting forward in a downpour, the beauty of absolution spilled out of my heart. I strolled over the rambling lobby and moved toward my ex-spouse. I connected my hands in fellowship and absolution. I investigated her eyes; however, she brought down her head; she had not anticipated such a signal. She was incapable of looking me in the eye. Bringing down such an extensive amount of unexplained bitterness had overpowered her. I softly cried out these words to facilitate her misery. "Tabitha, I attempted to abhor you, yet I proved unable for all that you put my children and me through. I forgive you for the entirety of this," I cried. I stifled and trembled. It was finished.

I turned and walked away from her with my tears. I went outside the courthouse. I stood on the giant entrance steps and took a deep breath of air. I gasped. I held my lawyer's hand; my friends watched me. I took a deep breath once more. Someone may have thought that I was about to have a heart attack. I exhaled. I could breathe again. I closed my eyes and saw the cross of Jesus in front of me. I whispered to my soul, *Forgive them, Father, for they do not know what they do.* There was no more hatred, no more anger—just sad regret; two children were victims of this terrible, evil world I lived in. I still find that hard to let go of. As parents, how could we harm a child?

It was November 29, 2001. I drove to the office of the Child Protection Agency to visit my children for the first time in five years. I met an educated lady who claimed to be an expert in child psychology; she advised me before meeting my children that it was in their best interest that I do not enter the room and straightaway hug my children. According to her, it would be disturbing for them; she said that reunification would be a gradual process. I told the lady that, as much as I respected her views, I saw the face of death in this legal battle and dealing with experts like her to have victory for my children. "This is about their success and not mine that I am here today." I wore my Australian Akubra and Driza-Bone clothing so that they would remember me somewhere in their childhood memories. I walked into a room, a child playroom; there were two boys—one was tall and thin, the other was playing with the Legos that were on the table. I stood there with bags of toys and gifts. I was trembling but steady. I put the bags down and said, "Hello, Sean. Hello, Joshua."

Sean looked at me, and I knelt on one knee; he walked and then swiftly came and clasped his hands around me and cried with the words, "Where have you been, Dad?" I hugged him and could smell him again. I found strength from him.

"I was always here," I replied.

"I thought you went back to Australia," he responded.

"Oh, no, I did not do that," I replied. "Remember? You asked me to promise you to always be here for you. Well," I said, "I still kept that promise."

My second son, Joshua, hardly remembered me; the little boy approached me. He had curly hair, a cute-looking boy; he smiled at me, and I wanted to hug him, but he had a few questions that needed answering first. "Are you my father?" he asked.

"Yes, I am," I replied.

"Okay," he said; then he looked at me once again and said, "Now I know why I have beautiful light-brown skin."

I smiled and held his hand. Then he looked confused for a five-year-old boy. "My mother told me that you died in a car accident." My heart almost burst into tears when he said that. We hugged each other. I spent the next three years of my life building my relationship with my children that I had lost. The damage was grave, the wounds were painful, and the lessons still have never been learnt over the years.

Sean and Joshua went fishing with me in the North Sea, and we sailed on a boat among the deep waters of sunken wrecks of the Second World War, casting fishing lines and hauling big codfish. We laughed once again and were healing wounds inflicted on us by their mother and the society that we lived in. With them, I had the opportunity to do my best to build the emotional bonds that existed—picking fragments that were smashed like a clay jar exploding against a concrete floor, picking up pieces of the tragedies of our lives and trying to put the vessel of love and being back in shape and repainting it with passion once again.

I filed a case in the European Court of Human Rights against the State of the Netherlands for the violation of human rights and dignity. I found it hard to respect this society, this government, and a legal system that so arbitrarily and systematically violated the rights of my sons and me. I always found it hard to give the country my hard-earned tax dollars because I never received an apology or any compensation for the inhumane treatment I experienced in this country. Godless nations have very little soul in them.

Four years of my life in courthouses, like circus animals, the show went on. Fighting for my sons left me deep emotional and spiritual scars, my soul reaching out for healing. It seemed like a bad dream; now and then it dawned on me that I had overcome an epic struggle. I did not know where I had found such incredible strength to go through so much stress and anxiety. I had employed lawyers and paid most of my earnings to legal fees, because, according to the evil systems of justice, hardworking people are penalised for fighting for their human rights in a fake modern country that portrays a system of justice and democratic values that are fake, sugar-coated benefits. It can be compared to biting into the cake of honourableness, only to find there is an awful bitterness you need to swallow. You are not allowed to spit out the cake they feed you. A sadistic systems ritual; you need to eat, and it gags you when it goes down your throat, poisoning your every human emotion, harming each feeling and living cell in your natural body.

It resembled forced-marching to ascend a precarious, misleading mountain, and to descend alive was not a decision or a choice you can take. It resembled walking into a chamber where you might die from the exertion you made getting inside the secret chamber of death, where systems made by governments planned your execution.

I had to reason with people who are secular and unable to fathom the reality of the pain of separation between a child and parent. Does it truly make a man a lesser parent than a woman, or perhaps even a better parent than a mother?

In the arson of justice that burnt my whole life down and reduced me to ashes, it remains much more a significant task for the one who has to rebuild than it is for a court and ex-wife. I had to deal with an acrid, poisonous child protection agency and a Dutch bureaucracy that had no regard or respect for the human cost and suffering of a father and two sons. I had never encountered anything more unpleasant and demonic in my life as I did in this process. It was a spiritual warfare designed to destroy my soul.

Everyone got paid. The judge got paid, the lawyers got paid, the Child Protection Agency workers got paid, the taxman got paid. The ex-wife received state-funded legal aid, and I was the slave who was paying them all in return for my human rights, and those of my children, violated in a democratic, civilised secular society that has minimal regard for the commandments of God and living actual Christian lives.

I lay on the couch watching sports TV with my two sons, as they cuddled next to me, healing scars and pain and rebuilding broken lives. My second son was emotionally damaged, and I had to make great efforts to repair the wounds and injuries the divorce had left. We were healed because love conquers all things; light always disperses darkness away, good always triumphs over evil, truth forever remains truth.

And Scripture says in Romans 12:21, "Be not overcome of evil, but overcome evil with good." In spite of all the terrible pain and suffering we'd endured, the bitterness of people who do evil deeds and have evil attitudes never changes. I have come to know the true meaning of scriptures that teach us that our warfare is not against flesh and blood (Ephesians 6:12).

THE IMMIGRATION ISSUE

While I was fighting for my human rights to see my sons, I also had to deal with an awful organisation, well-known for violation of human rights in the Netherlands.

The Immigration and Naturalisation Department's notoriously bureaucratic establishments that have carved and embossed policies embedded in the walls—walls on which they bounce soft human bodies against hard concrete. They have documents that they throw at each other, designed to drive people to the brink of insanity, policies that contradict and confuse every aspect of arriving at a swifter, more-human form of conflict resolution.

I endured further harassment from police detective Visser, a man who knew my wife's family; being Dutch, they looked after their interests. This police officer repeatedly threatened my removal from the Netherlands. I endured awful harassment from the police, who trying to frame me for drunk driving and a false case levied against me, a setup and a fake fact built against me to discredit me and portray me as a criminal—all because I had changed my name illegally.

I was always amazed at how a country and a system could go to such inhumane lengths to make the life of one man so bitter and difficult. As much as I felt frustrated by this system, I had to remain calm and think of the two boys who mattered most. The police refused to renew my pass. I had to drive without a licence for eight years and keep my job in spite of all the odds they'd stacked up against me. None of it conquered me. I know the Lord had saved me from hanging on a rope in a cold attic a few years before. A voice in my soul said, "Greater is He that is in me than he that is in the world." Who can stand against me when the Lord is my shepherd? No weapon formed against me can prosper. My battles were not with flesh and blood. I knew the enemy hidden in the systems and among people. I understood God had more significant plans for me, and, for this reason, I was persecuted.

For the drunk-driving case, I was acquitted as innocent, because the claim was so false that the judge threw it out of the court. I was a mirror that shined each day and reflected the blinding glare of the nation's controversy and idolatry of immorality that existed in their systems.

The Dutch immigration office sent me a letter: "Mr. Berchy does not see his children, has no form of contact with them, and it does not constitute a family life in the Netherlands, so he can leave this country." My response to them was "Return my sons or prove by a DNA test that they are not my sons, and I will leave your country and never return to be among you and this culture."

The European Court of Human Rights assumes an auxiliary job in the security of the rights and opportunities set out in the convention. To empower national specialists to play out their essential role, it is significant that the court offers adequate direction on the understanding of the convention. It has just been contended that the case law of the court on the privilege to regard for family life in immigration cases needs consistency as far as procedural and substantive assurances are concerned. The irregularity for the situation law is, for the most part, the case in the affirmation and regularisation of the case law.

Dutch legislation or implementation has poorly demonstrated how the CRC or the "interests of the child" must be respected in family immigration cases. The courts pathetically implemented the application of the ECHR convention.

I began to understand why there was such a lot of confusion about family life. I lived in a country where two in three marriages end in a divorce and where broken families and bitter disputes and separations, bitterness, and loss of contact between fathers and children, mostly perpetrated by feminists, is endemic. I had spent six years of legal battles with the Dutch immigration office fighting for human rights that were guaranteed by the European Convention on Human Rights, a system of justice that pretends to hold high morals of legitimacy. In truth, if these values were as good as the pieces of paper in a convention that they had been written on, you are left baffled to consider, "If the value of human rights comes so cheap to those governments who perpetrate them, then it's foolish to believe they would not try to violate them." If you enshrine such precious values of humanity in the system, then, I ask, why does a human being need to fight for a right that is protected and guaranteed by such a convention?

Perhaps it's a case of allowing the governments to abuse these rights in any case. Therefore, for a person to experience the European Court of Human Rights, two things need to happen. The human right has to be violated and abused. Secondly, one has to exhaust all local remedies in that state before he can even have the opportunity to file and qualify his case for admissibility in the European Court of Human Rights.

A simple, uneducated man on the street can tell you that the purpose of human rights is to protect people and prevent abuse from occurring, thus making it unnecessary for a person to come to court fighting for the very same reasons that were made and guaranteed to protect him. How bizarre is the European Convention on Human Rights in a world that is so immoral and ethically demoralised? That hypocrisy always haunted me, and it stirred up ancient wrongs, similar to the pains that resulted when European settlers inflicted the same mockery on Australian Aboriginal people's values of family life. Similarly, European white settlers came to the ancient world with their hypocrisy and draconian laws.

They were holding a Bible in their hands, violating the holy words of God and separating native children from their native parents. Perhaps it was because they never figured out their own family life, for whatever bizarre reason, that they had very little respect for mine.

I closed my eyes several times during this process, and I always had a picture of the old Aboriginal Australian woman in Belyuen who had waited her whole life for her baby to return. Forty years later, when he came back to her, a grown-up man, she rejected him and just wanted her baby, for her life had stood still since the day they took her child away from her.

To overcome the terrible atrocities of human suffering levied against me, I found strength in prayer and faith. During these years, I met some fantastic people who came into my life at a time and a place that I could not have designed myself. They were great people who I believe God had strategically placed in my life to help me overcome the evils I faced in the Netherlands. They brought laughter to my face, hope to my heart, and love to my life. Some left "love prints" forever.

I was often asked how I had the courage and endurance for such a terrible plight imposed on me, and other Dutch friends were appalled by the awful truth of a corrupted system of justice with family law—the systematic, institutionalised discrimination against fathers. I often said that I had a Holy God who was standing before and behind me, and no weapon against me could prosper. I further felt it was a privilege to pave the way for change in this society; through my suffering, I hoped that the judges, lawyers, and social workers would learn new lessons. Nevertheless, it's hard to teach arrogant secular people in secular societies.

I filed a case in the European Court of Human Rights to bring to the attention of the European body the inadequacies and blatant flogging the law gets from the Dutch government, which is riddled with double standards and hypocrisy to the highest degree in the modern world. No nation is perfect, and no government is holy—they all violate human rights one way or the other and pretend they are the guardians of human rights and dignity. It's a lie, and if you believe they are, then you are kidding yourself.

CHAPTER 18

KEN TORRES

He hailed from Long Island, Boston, Massachusetts, a short man with receding hair. Standing near the coffee machine, I could have sworn it was Danny DeVito, visiting the Samsung construction company office in Almere, Netherlands. I stood there slightly perplexed, unable to imagine why the actor would be attending this office. I walked over to the coffee machine and said, "Hello, Danny. I swear, I thought you were Danny DeVito standing here."

"Shit, yeah," he replied, "I do get that quite often. I am Ken Torres," he said and extended his hand to a friendship that was going to last a lifetime.

I shook his hand and said smilingly, "You've just shaken the hand that shook the world. Pleasure meeting you, mate. You and I are going to be working together, and I reckon it is going to be fun."

Ken Torres coloured the world; our friendship blossomed into a brotherhood, and the joy he brought into my life was extraordinarily filled with humour. He was quirky and quick-witted, highly intelligent, and peculiar to some people who did not understand his humour.

The Samsung-Volvo office where he worked was a vivacious place because of him. His outrageously funny comments would have even the sternest person blushing with a smile. The Dutch have a weird sense for naming themselves.

299

In 1811, the French, under Napoleon, ruled the Netherlands. They started a system of registration, with the end goal of tax collection, and constrained everybody to have a family name, which was not a typical practice for the Dutch.

The Dutch idea: this would be a brief measure, and, so, they took on entertaining- or hostile-sounding names as a reasonable joke on their French occupiers.

A few typical names are the following:

Borst (bosom)
Naaktgeboren (born stripped)
Poepjes (little poop)
Piest (to pee)
Rotmensen (rotten individuals)
Suikerbuik (sugar belly)
Spring in 't Veld (jump in the field)
Schooier (beggar)
Scheefnek (crooked neck)
Uiekruier (onion proclaimer)
Uittenbroek (out of his jeans)
Zeldenthuis (rarely at home)
Zondervan (without a surname)

I can envision the Dutch lining up to register and having a couple of giggles to the detriment of the French authorities, only to end up having the name stick to them like baby shit sticks on a blanket.

There were additionally a few names that are not disparaging but rather aggrandising.

De Groot (the great, the large one)
Lair Beste (the best)

So also, some were simple ones:

De Jonge (the more youthful)
Marcel Dodeman (deadman) was a downer. He rarely came to work with a smile on his face, and every day when he passed by Ken Torres, there was this exchange: Ken Torres: "Oh, good morning, Marcel.

Now who pissed in your cornflakes?"

Marcel Dodeman: "Ha, very funny, Torres de Tuinkabouter (Ken the Garden Gnome)."

This exchange went on for a few years.

Ken said he would keep greeting Marcel Dodeman till his depression left him for good. Then it changed one day, when Ken began to learn Dutch and understand surnames.

Ken Torres: "Oh, good morning, Marcel. Are you still alive?"

Marcel Dodeman: "Ha! Oh, you little shit, I am going to kill you before I am dead."

These exchanges became funnier, and Marcel Dodeman smiled a lot; at the end of the day, Ken Torres had coloured his life as well.

Then there was the cranky middle-aged Irish woman by the name of Joan, who was as miserable as they come. She argued with everyone—irrational, uncompromising, and irritated with most people. There were those moments when she suddenly exposed her humour, but it was only a glimpse of a previous personality that she may have lost in the struggles of life.

The iconic greeting of Ken Torres, every day, was his response to the question of how he was when people asked him. "I am grooving out to the atmosphere of love and happiness." He always smiled and always gave you the same reply anytime you asked him about his welfare.

Joan walked in, cranky as usual, and Ken Torres was busy working at his desk completing some tasks for our Korean boss, Peter Park. He went over to see Joan about some sales figures and projections when Miss Cranky barked at him and gave him her usual dose of sourness. Ken smiled at her and jokingly said to her in a low voice, "I think I understand your problem, Joan. Is it that you have not had any tender loving in a long while?" She went berserk; she stormed off, feeling upset with him, and he was taken aback at her reaction. Ken did not mean to offend her at all. He was funny and humorous but never mean or rude; this guy could not hurt a fly. This was a copy of Danny DeVito.

She escalated the issue with the managing director, Anton Tregear, charging Ken Torres for sexual harassment. The poor fellow was so distressed by the unfolding drama. This is a serious charge at any company these days. You have to walk on eggshells and be very careful of what you say, even in good humour, because some people get easily offended. The issue with Joan was the only time I ever saw Ken Torres sad; he felt terrible and ended up giving her a public apology, in the presence of everyone. In humility and humbleness with a contrite heart, he did it. Everyone in the office believed that the cranky Irish Joan had overreacted, and she became even more unpopular with the staff.

Six months later, there was a total transformation. Joan came to work a happier woman; she was cheerful, and her Irish humour, by some miracle, had been restored. She'd found herself once again, and her transformation was welcomed by everyone. Everyone except Ken Torres.

While I was working together with him one morning at his desk, helping him with the paperwork, finishing off specific tasks, meeting deadlines for the monthly sales targets, suddenly happy Joan came walking past, greeting us as she tossed her hair in the air. Ken smiled at me, and in a boyish tone, he whispered to me, "Have you figured it out?"

I replied, "Figured out what?"

"Joan," he answered.

"I don't know, Ken. Whatever it is, I guess everyone likes her better this way."

He smiled at me with a naughty smile, full of humour, and said, "I reckon she is getting love?"

"Shut up, Ken," I replied. "Don't go there, mate!"

He giggled at me and said, "Do you reckon I should ask her?"

"Shut up, Ken—you don't want a second humiliating public apology again, do you?" I replied.

He laughed as if to say, "Watch this. I am going to do it." He looked at Joan and said, "You look good, Joan."

"Oh, thanks," she responded.

He quickly asked, "Did ya?"

She smiled at him. "What?" She looked at him and was blushing.

"You know," he replied.

She blushed at him. "Oh, shut up—it's none of your business."

Ken said, "I know—that's why I groove out to the atmosphere of love and happiness every day."

They both laughed at each other, good friends now, and no one was offended.

I left his desk and went to get myself a coffee.

It was hilariously funny, and no one was offended.

He joined me later on, and I told him he was a cheeky little bugger.

A month passed, and we had the annual Volvo employees family day. Joan turned up with her new boyfriend. He was a bodybuilder, a younger man she had found.

Her cranky days were the result of a divorce she had gone through. Ken Torres was right about grooving out to the atmosphere of love and happiness. He looked at me and said in Aussie, "Fair dinkum, mate. I was right all along."

Ken was married to a crazy Dutch Jewish woman who had three children from a previous marriage she'd had in the U.S.; she moved back to the Netherlands for reasons I never discussed with Ken. The three kids and mother lived with Ken. He tried very hard to be a father figure to these children, but they were rude and unkind to him. In all reality, he was not treated well at home. Quite often, he got kicked out of bed because he suffered from sleep apnoea, or "lion snoring syndrome." It was bad.

Monday mornings at work, it was common for people to inquire how someone's weekend had been spent. Ken would laugh at his treatment and misery at home. So, his response always cracked me up. "Ineke was the rude witch," he would whisper to me, "yet he loved her and forgave her a million times for her unkind manners towards him."

"Hey, Ken. How was your weekend?"

"Oh, absolutely fabulous. I was grooving out to the atmosphere of love and happiness, and my wife, Ineke, was riding the broomstick." We would laugh together. Nothing anyone could do or say could steal or destroy the humour of Ken Torres.

The annual Volvo family party in 2000 was held at the Partycentrum in Amsterdam. The theme was a medieval European party; all the waiters and cooks were dressed in medieval costume.

There was a fire with a massive steel grill where Bertha the Pig was being roasted. Bock beer was being served in ancient clay pots and medieval bowls; the atmosphere was really inspiring. In the middle of the hall was an old medieval fire with a big earthen pot of soup being concocted by the witch, sitting on a stool stirring it with her freaky voice of laughter.

She had a black crow costume, scary long fingernails, and long hooknose; a pointed, sooty-black witch's hat adorned her head. She was mumbling her charms, making hysterical laughs as the witch added herbs and vegetables to the soup. With her broomstick next to her, she clasped it in between her thighs and ran around the giant black earthen pot of soup shrieking and laughing an eerie laugh. Then she jumped up on the stool to announce that the witch's soup was ready to be served, but first, there would be a song. As she stood there with the broom in her hand singing, Ken Torres (Danny DeVito) walked by in the hall, passing the witch; he was transfixed in amazement at her. Everyone watched in silence, perhaps anticipating a funny comment. Ken Torres stopped in front of the witch, took off his hat, bowed his head and said, "I am amazed—you even sound like my wife. You must be her sister." Everyone burst out laughing; we were in splits of laughter. He had not brought his wife to the party that night.

Making music and people laugh was his business, from being the DJ at the Amstelveen local radio, hosting an English radio show that he called Wood-Rock Radio. He taught me the art of quick-witted, spontaneous humour, a tool to combat the crap life throws at you.

We did many shows together. We trashed the governments and the justice system, we attacked injustices and companies that violated consumer rights, and we were relentless until we got wrongs corrected. He trashed my ex-wife and dedicated a show mixing incredible tracks of music that expressed the injustices. "Green Onions" was the starting and ending theme song, but for my ex-wife, he ended it with "Godzilla."

He showed me the ropes for becoming outrageously funny; he was fearless with words, and witty one-liners just flowed like a river through him. One day I told him to slow down or we would get arrested for the ridicule we levied against the Dutch government.

He said we would become famous if that happened and just kept on going. Ken Torres was a movie and music walking encyclopaedia. We drank beer and watched movie marathons together. Our favourite movie was *Blazing Saddles*. No matter how many times we watched the video, we laughed more the more we saw the movie. He made the public laugh, and the radio was an extension of himself out there, saying outrageous stuff and making people think and laugh. His choice of music and knowledge of it was incredible.

Lobster and beer were his favourite food; his email was Lobsterbeer@ yahoo.com. A master musician and a great drummer, he had a band called the Camel Soup Band in his younger days in the US. In the Netherlands, he teamed up with Leda Baker, daughter of Ginger Baker from the band Cream. They formed a band called the Quintessential

Sound; they wrote songs and produced an album in the Netherlands. He was indeed an excellent drummer. I spent a lot of time learning music and came to better appreciate jazz and other forms of music. He educated me in music, humour, and life.

His marriage ended in separation from Ineke, and it made him sad. He loved her but could not stay with her because of her eccentric, unkind behaviour. Now, living with a British flatmate in Amsterdam, he went through moments of sadness and loneliness. He was abused as a child and carried those burdens; none knew his grief but me. He made the world laugh and coloured it with rainbows even when his own world had dark clouds and gloom of abuse. Here was a man who could not hurt a fly.

One morning he called me.

> Ken: "I think she loves me."
> Me: "Ken, what are you talking about? Did you find a new girlfriend?"
> Ken: "I called this escort service, and they sent me a nice girl."
> Me: "Ken, are you crazy? It's not worth it, my friend. Why are you doing this?"
> Ken: "I just felt sad and lonely. I only wanted someone to talk to."
> Me: "You can call me if you want someone to talk to, Ken. I am always here for you."
> Ken: "I did not do anything with her; we just sat and talked for two hours, and then she finally asked me if I was going to have sex with her. I told her I enjoyed talking to her and was happier with that."
> Me: "What did the woman think of you, Ken? She must have liked that."
> Ken: "She kissed me and gave me a hug and said I was a lovely man. Now, I think she loves me."
> Me (laughing): "Oh, you silly bugger, you are a kind man. I am sure no one has been so kind with that woman as you may have been."
> Ken: "I felt sad for her. I told her she was too beautiful to be selling her body and violating herself this way. I am going to try and talk her out of prostitution."

Me. "Why did you call an escort service? It's not
something you would do."
Ken: "I did not mean to, but I felt sad and lonely. I
wanted to talk to a woman."

*****

Ken Torres crept into my heart and found in me a friend he could
trust more than anyone out there. In me was a true friendship and a
brotherly love that was unshakable. In the darkest years of my life,
he came and brightened my days. I am ever so grateful for the most
precious friend I've ever found in this life. I had a shoulder for him
where he could lay his head and shed a tear; in return, he gave me
more days of laughter than I gave him a shoulder to cry upon. We
were the best friends in the world.

It was January 26, 2001. I received a frantic call from Ken urging
me to meet him at the Amsterdam Centraal Station; it was a Friday
night, and I figured he had something special with his band. I met
him at the station, a small giant among the land of giants. He had
grown a beard and now looked like Danny the Garden Gnome. We
boarded the tram from the central station heading towards Leidseplein.
Tonight, this was a very unusual Ken Torres; he was silent and did
not say much, not his usual self. I had never seen him like this, so I
gave him an elbow dig, inquiring him what was wrong. He looked at
me, and there was a sadness in his eyes.

He said, "Do you see what I am seeing?"

I asked, "Ken, what are you seeing? I don't have a clue, mate.
What's going on?"

He said, "Do you notice all the people in this tram? There is not
a person here with a happy smile on their face. Now isn't this a sad
state this world is in?"

I looked back and examined all the faces of the people on the tram.
I took a good solid six minutes to see if I could catch a glimpse of
at least one person smiling. Not a soul, not a smile—not one person
was wearing a smile, and for a moment, I saw what Ken was seeing: a
sad world of people heading somewhere on a train, and no one really
knows their final destination. They were burdened people, enslaved
in a system like captives trapped in life; it was a dismal sight, and
you don't notice it until you stop and look with a different set of eyes.

I turned back and smiled at Ken. I said, "'Ninety-six FM, Perth, Australia,' as I'd heard the DJ often say. 'If you meet people without a smile, give them yours.'" So, like two nutters, we turned back and smiled and greeted all these depressed people a wonderful evening; some thought we were crazy; others never smiled back and wallowed in the sadness of life.

The train took a right turn and halted as we hopped off, heading to the Café Alto.

"Okay, Ken. What's happening tonight?" I asked.

He smiled. "We are playing a gig with Hans Dulfer. Some blues tonight. Leda Baker is playing bass. Let's get some Belgium beers first."

We drank a few beers with the Quintessential Sound band; we ate some dinner and laughed some more. The sadness of the train journey was behind us, and I loved to see Ken himself again. He was just a kind soul.

When he held drumsticks and played, he was the happiest, a picture that I always hold close to my heart. He would be sweating like rain pouring in a tropical storm, like a lotus in the middle of a torrential downpour, sitting there in the middle of the pond, the happiest thing you would see in the rain. Ken Torres the Lotus Drummer, smiling in ecstasy; and you knew that was the place that made him the happiest—holding two drumsticks behind a Pearl drum kit.

We had a fantastic night with the band; with many Belgium beers under his belt, we headed off back to the Centraal Station. The beer had had some effect on his emotions; amid all the laughter he gave others, he had pain and sadness in his own heart. I was his best friend, and he had a shoulder to cry on.

He sat there next to me, feeling drunk and all emotional about his life; he was sad. He just did not play the blues this night, he made you contact them. I put my arms around his shoulder and gave him a hug. "It's okay, Ken," I said, "I know how you feel."

He had a sad twinkle in his eye; it was deep inside, shining; I noticed it for the first time since I had known him. He sobbed, for his sadness was profound.

He looked at me and said, "I am from one end of the world, and you are from the other. Here we are, mate, in Amsterdam grooving out to the atmosphere of love and happiness, and yet we have both been betrayed by those we have loved the most." Tears fell down as he cried. "It hurts, mate, it hurts. People we love have let us down."

I still had my hands over his shoulder and hugged him.

He said, "Thank you for being such a good friend, mate. I appreciate it."

"No worries, mate. You know me—I am always here for you." I continued, "Ken, we have known each other for years, and we have talked about everything else, so let me ask this: do you know what the greatest love of all is?" He looked drunk and sad as he lifted his face to look at me. It was a poignant moment in time, and I said, "There is no greater love the world has ever known than the love on the cross—John 3:16—and then the prayer that says, 'Forgive them, Father, for they know not what they do.' It's the state of the world, Ken. It is the ultimate love."

We had never talked about our faith until that day. He was silent as the train stopped at the Centraal Station; we hopped off when I asked Ken if he would like to come back home.

My girlfriend was also very fond of him, and I had never met anyone who did not like Ken. He had friends from across the globe.

He loved staying at my place on the weekends and usually never refused the chance of hanging around at my home. This night was different.

He looked at me, had a smile on his face once again like he had finally found something already known but never realised, and now he knew once again something that was liberating. He smiled once back and said, "Yes, mate, that is the greatest love of all. Thanks, buddy. I love you, man, more than you know."

I replied, "Yep—sure love you heaps, mate. You are something else." He turned and walked away. "Hey," I shouted out, "that drumming was the best I have ever seen. Take care, see you later."

The next morning, I woke up around seven thirty, when the phone was ringing. I had Shaun on the phone. He was the flatmate who shared an apartment with Ken Torres. He was inquiring if I was busy and requested me to come to his place, as it was necessary. He hung up rather quickly, leaving me slightly confused.

I was in the kitchen, making myself some coffee; my girlfriend in the living room was getting bags ready for our weekend shopping, and so she ushered me about her planned program. I related to her the unexpected phone call I'd received from Shaun and how he'd acted strangely, requesting me to come to his place immediately. "Oh, no," she protested, "we have a weekend program, and we cannot go there." I went back to my coffee-brewing task, so she picked up the phone and called Shaun to find out more details. I was looking at my coffee brew coming to the end of its aromatic procedure; there was a low sound of music playing in the background and a conversation that I could not hear in its entirety. Then my girlfriend looked at me from across the room and called my name; she said in a loud voice, "Ooooh, no."

I spun around with the coffee cup, looked at her, and said, "What's wrong?"

"Oh, my god, Lyndon." Her hands clasping her face, she said, "Ken Torres is dead."

My cup dropped from my hand. I was upset and told her, "If this is a joke, then I am going to be extremely upset with you."

She shouted a little louder, "Oh, my god, Ken is dead." I was too numb and too shocked to even react.

I was in the car with her, driving on the A10 heading to his apartment. I walked into the studio, and Shaun the Brit was sitting there, in shock. Ken was gone; the police had taken his body. I was shaking and could not believe it; this was going to take a while.

Shaun looked at me and replayed the scenario. "I was working the night shift. I came home at 6:45 a.m. and walked into the house, and Ken was lying on the couch. I told him, 'Ken, why are you not sleeping in your room?' I went over to him and shook him, but he did not wake up. I felt his forehead, and he was still warm, but he was not breathing. I felt his pulse; there was no heartbeat, and he was dead. I was shocked. I am devastated, mate." And then he broke down and cried. I was in tears, and we stood there in shock.

I returned home with the most painful task, given to me because no one else was willing to do it. I picked up the phone and called Don Torres, Ken's dad, who lived in Rhode Island. Ken had introduced me to his father through video calls, and I had a title familiarly known as Ken's best friend in Holland.

Don Torres answered the phone; he sounded happy and glad to receive a surprise call from me. I was dying and struggling with a terrible lump in my throat—the job of a messenger who brings sad news is the most painful experience.

Don Torres: "Hey, Lyndon, what a pleasant surprise, pleasant for you to call. What's up?"

> Me (I was breathing heavy. I was stuck.): "Hi, Don.
>   I am sorry." (I was dying here.)
> Don Torres: "Are you okay, Lyndon? What is wrong?
>   Is everything okay in Holland?"
> Me (I was choking, and my heart was breaking. I had
>   this terrible feeling of sadness in me, and I was trying
>   to bring it out gently across.): "It's Ken." (The last
>   night we had the most fantastic night together. He
>   told me how much he loved me; tears were flooding
>   my face.) "Oh, Don, please forgive me. Ken passed
>   away in his sleep last night. I am so sorry." (I burst
>   into tears.) "I am sorry. I am so sorry."

I heard Don Torres heave a painful sigh. I felt a father's pain for his son. I felt connected in grief and his total silence. The phone went silent, and he put it down. I fell on the floor, and I wept like a child.

This is the way the world deals with death everywhere, and many years later, I was given this incredible wisdom and grace to see something that put all these mysteries together in my journey. Ken was a friend on this journey with me.

The Dutch government sent the ashes to the U.S. embassy in Den Haag, and Ken was reunited with his family on the shores of Maine; there was a memorial for him, and we had some lobsters and drank some beer in his memory.

Two years later, my memories of Ken remained very present with me. I inherited all his music and boxes of CDs, about seven hundred of them. A lifetime of the funniest sketches of his jokes. His expression "I am grooving out to the atmosphere of love and happiness" became mine and all the friends' who loved Ken. The void he'd left was a silent office, an empty place that could never be filled. A few people quit their jobs and never returned to the Volvo office; it was never the same again.

Don Torres called me one day and said this to me: "I have lost two sons, and the loss of Ken is the most significant." A few moments of silence followed, and I heard him sigh in pain, "Lyndon, I am calling to thank you. Thank you for being his best friend, while he was with you in this foreign land."

I held my tears and replied, "Don, the thank-yous are mine and mine alone. No, sir. I thank you for giving the world a wonderful son.

Gumshoe Ken Torres will always live in the hearts that he touched so dearly." We both wept together.

After this heart-wrenching experience and the event of the tragic loss and emptiness, I wondered where he was. Did he make it to a place where we talked about the night before his departure? A night when we laughed, cried together, hugged like real friends, and told each other about the brotherly love between us? A flash appeared in my memory as I closed my eyes. I saw his smile and that sparkle and that light I saw in his eyes that night on the tram in Amsterdam.

Then one night as I was asleep, he came back in a dream; it was more than a dream because it was as significant as life, and it was real.

THE DREAM

My dream started with my being in a strange place, working with friendly strangers I did not know very well. I was in unfamiliar territory and working among the people each day, a place that was so real and faces so amazingly peaceful and smiling with love. I felt so reassured by the people around me in my dream.

Then there was an announcement about the annual celebration of the company, and everyone was invited. They asked me, "Lyndon, are you coming for this fantastic celebration?"

"Sure," I replied, "but what is this celebration?"

They all smiled and said, "You will see."

I was feeling happy for the surprise that they all wanted me to attend; in my dream, I felt loved and comfortable with these lovely people around me, like a loving family that you always wanted. It just felt so real and so warm and so beautiful. My body may have been asleep, but this whole thing was more than real. I wish someone had videotaped me lying there on my bed while I was having this dream, because I would be curious to see how my body was reacting to these larger-than-life emotions running through me in my dream.

The day of the celebration had come, and I was excited; we had to first go to a beautiful chapel, where the ceremony was to beheld. As I walked in, I saw white walls with a slight pink tint; it was filled with flowers and golden lamps, and people were all standing all around. They were starting to sing. I stood there among them, and as the song echoed and their voices were lifted up on high, I began to weep. I was dying and felt choked. The song was about Ken meeting the Lord today. I looked at them next to me. I barely could speak. I shivered and stuttered at the men near me as the words trembled from my mouth and my lips were quivering. I asked them, "How do you all know Ken?"

"Oh, Lyndon." They smiled. "Happily, we all know Ken. Today he is going to be meeting the Lord Our God. You talked to him the night he left the world. This is the celebration, and that's why you are here."

I just broke down, and I was crying. I was shaking, and I could not speak.

Oh, my god. My dream ended, and I awoke in my bed, shaking, totally disoriented from my dream. I was crying profusely, and my girlfriend woke up, startled.

"What happened?" she exclaimed and was alarmed. "Oh, your pillow is wet. Why are you crying?" I could barely speak. I was choked, and I squeaked out the words, "Ken came back. Ken came back. He came back in my dream. Oh, my god, it's so real." I was shaking and said, "He came back to tell me his ending was the most beautiful beginning." I wept happy tears. My friend Ken came back to comfort me in my dream.

Twenty years have passed since Ken Torres went away from this world, and I am still alive, I am still here. It was a fleeting moment when it mattered most—not something we designed, but something that we belong to that is far higher than human. We encounter certain people in powerful spiritual journeys, exchanging the deepest secrets of life that can be lost by those lost in a world of vanity and make-believe.

I have wandered through forests with my dad, worked in treacherous, dark tunnels mining for material wealth and risking my life daily between two scenarios that play out every day in numerous ways in people's lives. The question is this: How much are you in the light? or: How much of the light is absent?

As we know, the darkness does not exist; the truth is, it appears dark only because of the absence of light. It's a fact.

Sitting around a campfire on a mountaintop in the Golan Heights in Israel recently, I was hiking on a journey from Mount Hermon to the Sea of Galilee. As we camped when the sun was setting, we cooked some food and roasted some meat around the fire. Suddenly we heard the competitive howling of two packs of wolves challenging each other for the remains of the food they could smell being cooked.

As the competition heated up between the two packs of wolves, I whipped out my flashlight and surveyed the forest in front of me. Red piercing eyes appeared all around me. I moved my view to the opposite side, and there was an equal number of red eyes peering at me from the other pack of wolves.

Now the scenario was scary; we could be attacked by the wolves as we slept, and one of two things could happen to us. We could possibly get killed or be seriously injured, end up in a hospital badly mauled, and maybe get a more severe infection and die from it.

Then as I tried to sleep in my tent, I heard something approaching in the darkness, maybe a lion or a razorback; again, it could mean that I'd get killed or severely attacked. The end result is I could get killed. These are real things and real scenarios. What about the rocks falling down and almost killing me and being lost on a level-eight Western mining site? Can you imagine someone finding my body lying on a pile of stones at the bottom of a 150-metre hole in the ground, in the darkness of the most bottomless grave in the world?

Then I thought back to my terrible attempt of trying to commit suicide as I faced the appalling separation between my two sons and me and the pangs of those awful divorce years. The family has been the most enormous pain and burden I have carried in this life; I entangled my life from an ungodly woman and having the most beautiful children, only to lose them to the wickedness of the world. I still bear the scars of that pain as I have lost contact with my sons in the Netherlands' inhumane system of justice.

All these scenarios have affected me, emotionally damaging me, attempting to destroy me as I went through them in my thoughts. I felt deeply traumatized by the intense cruelty.

These life-and-death scenarios play out every day in people's lives. Just driving a car through the mayhem of traffic is a life-or-death scenario.

Yet, if all of this ends in death in one way or the other, then the light of Ken's death changed my thoughts; twenty years later, I was in Israel searching for my Holy Messiah in the wilderness.

Society is living in a great deception of life, one which has always plagued the thoughts and aspirations of man. We are living in the darkness of life, in the age of vast knowledge that technology has shrouded in the shadow of the truth that is devoid of light. Let me put it together.

If all of the above scenarios lead to death, and they do, then if the ending is higher than the beginning, we are free at last. So, for a child of God who has come to the light of the knowledge in the full assortment of this glory, death is the beginning of something far more beautiful than the present journey that reaches this end—because everyone does end in this scenario.

The next scenario is "no pain, no hunger or sorrows; anxieties, sickness, fears, and rejections are absent, in complete non-existence." So instead of focusing on the beginning of life, if man focused on the ending to the new beginning, he will escape the ordinary life he currently lives that ends in a scenario of dying.

There is, however, a terrible third scenario beyond this, and I pray you never go there—that is the death of the soul and the separation from God forever. For no matter who you are and what you believe or don't believe, you cannot say you don't think that death will not visit you one day. You know it will.

Yes, I am a born-again Christian. I never wrote this book to convert the world into Christianity. I have only shared my human journey of this life and my faith. I have only faith and good works. I pray for grace and mercy. A pathway was laid before me, even when I did not deserve the highway to glory. I could have died a long time ago, but my purpose had not been accomplished yet.

Ken Torres left the world because his ending was a great beginning. I believe that, on the night of his departure, there was a twinkle in his eye. His beautiful soul was pained and hurt by a fallen world, a deceiving world of vanity. When he heard something, he knew it was confirmed powerfully that night—a truth that shined a light in his soul and illuminated it to turn bright, like a chapel with golden lamps and a glorious orchestra of a choir of the reunification of his soul to heavenly places. Returning to me in a dream and showing me his remarkable peaceful state of heavenly bliss, he was a true friend, repaying me for my love for him.

The night he died, Ken looked at me and said, "You are right. I see it so clearly, the one who stretched out his arms and died on the cross gave the world a new ending to a broken and fallen beginning." With that twinkle in his eye, he said, "You are right. It is the greatest love of all."

Ken left that world as the soul who had found the bright light to the truth for those in Christ. Like the robber next to the Lord who never was baptised but looked unto the Lord and said, "Please remember me, Lord, in your kingdom." And Yeshua looked at him and said, "Tonight you will be with me in paradise." Ken was like that robber that night. He saw the light and his soul; he did not need to be in this fallen world anymore. Our ending is significantly greater than our beginning for those of us who walk in faith in Christ and find mercy, grace, and salvation.

CHAPTER 19

THE HOMECOMING

Time got away from me; like an eagle kept in a cage, all my freedom was gone for several years. Like the story in Gulliver's Travels, when Gulliver goes to Liliput, the land of the little people, I was a small man trapped in the land of the Dutch giants. I was torn and battered, bruised and beaten, kicked in the guts, and smacked across my knees. My legs were broken, locked by a system that caged me for many years. I left home for the West for a better life, and the words of my dad echoed in my ears, "The grass looks greener on the other side," a sentiment that haunted me.

Twenty years after when I'd said goodbye to my mom and dad, I was on a flight back home, returning as a foreigner. I was Dutch. My heart was filled with so many memories and emotions. I had let them down, my beloved parents. I had put them through many sleepless nights. I was gone for so many years and had indulged my life into so many selfish attributes. I felt so let down *by me*. I looked out the window into Indian airspace, and I cried with shame. Finally, I was going back home to see them again. Oh, what a wretched, cruel human being I was. How awful it was to put them through this separation. How terrible it was to put myself through this dreadful experience of the West.

When I left these shores, I was a boy who felt I could conquer the world, but now I was returning home, broken, ripped apart by divorces, and I was lucky to be alive. My mother's advice returned to

316

haunt me: "Blue eyes don't make an angel, son. Only a woman who truly loves the Lord will make a good wife." Beauty is vanity, and vanity cannot love with the truth.

When I left, I was a boy who loved the Lord Jesus; it was always within, it was still deep, and I believed that God had a plan for me, but I'd forgotten to keep the Lord at the centre of my life. My mother's words came back to me in a Biblical storm over my heart through these Bible verses. Although my mother blessed me no matter what choices I made, she always felt sad that her sons did not marry the right women in their lives.

Her words would always come back to haunt me and teach me the essence to seek God and his wisdom in all things. I had beautiful children with ungodly women; the women I married were atheists or unbelievers, and I failed to be a godly man in my youth. I hold myself responsible for being that lesser, ungodly man who was not able to live it and change the immoral women into godly ones. I was indeed an ox tied to a mule trying to plough a field. The instructions in the five books of Moses have the building blocks of a godly life. There was a good tradition in our Anglo-Indian culture that said it was the duty of the mother to find a nice girl for her son to marry. A mother has some unique gifts in discerning a bride for her son. I believe this to be a Jewish tradition.

I had become too Western to acknowledge these values of the past. Therefore, I married women my mother would not approve of. She was always wishing for the best and still praying for my family and me. She firmly stood by these words: "A godly woman who knows how to love the Lord in obedience will be a blessing to her family." Her advice is Biblical. I never applied it to my life. The Word of God gives results when applied to life. I learned it the hard way. There was no need for me to do it the hard way, but in my foolishness and lack of obedience, I did it my way, from highway to highway across the world.

10 Thou shalt not plough with an ox and an ass together. (Deuteronomy 22:10 KJV)

1 Now Samson went down to Timnah and saw a woman in Timnah of the daughters of the Philistines.

2 So he went up and told his Father and Mother, saying, "I have seen a woman in Timnah of the daughters of the Philistines; now, therefore, get her for me as a wife."

3 Then his Father and Mother said to him, "Is there no woman among the daughters of your brethren, or among all my people, that you must go and get a wife from the uncircumcised Philistines?" And Samson said to his Father, "Get her for me, for she pleases me well." (Judges 14:1–3)

1 And Abraham was old, and well stricken in age: and the Lord had blessed Abraham in all things.

2 And Abraham said unto his eldest servant of his house, that ruled over all that he had, Put, I pray thee, thy hand under my thigh:

3 And I will make thee swear by the Lord, the God of heaven, and the God of the earth, that thou shalt not take a wife unto my Son of the daughters of the Canaanites, among whom I dwell:

4 But thou shalt go unto my country, and to my kindred, and take a wife unto my Son Isaac.

5 And the servant said unto him, peradventure, the woman will not be willing to follow me unto this land: must I needs bring thy Son again unto the land from whence thou camest?

6 And Abraham said unto him, Beware thou that thou bring not my Son thither again. (Genesis 24:1–6)

The aircraft touched down at Begumpet Airport, Hyderabad, and my heart was racing. *How am I going to face these beautiful parents whom I had abandoned?* I was genuinely ashamed of myself because I had put them through so many years of agony.

I was dressed in a blue suit, wearing my Akubra hat and my cowboy boots, crocodile-skin belt, and metal kangaroo buckle. No matter what the passport I was holding said, in my heart, the burning fire of the Outback and the native people of Australia burned as a fierce fire in my soul, "Fair dinkum Aussie." I was going to feel this way forever.

I could have never come back the same boy who left. People at home were expecting the same boy who'd left to return, but although my heart was the same, I was aware that I had changed. I walked towards the exit; about forty people were waiting at the arrival section, so many waving hands in the air, in a joyous rhythm of love as I approached.

Their appearance struck me. My mom and dad had matured. Twenty years was quite a while. I acknowledged it when I saw them there crying and, with great enthusiasm, holding back to grasp me by and by. I kept walking towards loving arms. My heart was beating and pounding against my rib cage, blood pumped through every emotional cell and tissue, and I started to run towards them. In the middle of the crowd was a short woman with curly hair; a bald older man stood next to her. My mother reminded me of the native Aboriginal woman who I saw weeping, expecting a baby to return and not a grown-up man. Because for her, time had stood still. Even though the years passed them by, for my mother, time stood still the day I left.

I walked straight into my parents' arms and embraced them, and I was crying and shaking. I wept. I said, "I am sorry I put you through this—forgive me." I just held them and stayed there for a while. I had finally made it home alive.

I slept on a single bed with my mother opposite me in the other single bed, talking about the missing years. There was so much to hear and to tell. The morning sun had risen, and we had discussed the whole night through and still had so much more left to say in the morning.

My mother chuckled as we both went over to make some coffee. We laughed as I hugged her. Such a beautiful mother. This woman had been on bended knees each evening in her room with her prayer book. She prayed for me her whole life. We sat together drinking coffee, and she said to me, "Son, I have never done this with any of my children—talk so much through a whole night, especially when I usually tell people to talk less and listen more. All I had left once you were gone was to pray for you."

My mother is a golden, shining light of what a parent must be. Pray for your children every day of their lives and yours. Prayer is the key to keeping us safe.

I went to the master bedroom, and I saw my dad sleeping. I stood there looking at him. He was older now. He looked much weaker than I had known him twenty years ago. I'd left with unforgiveness toward my dad. There were so many things that I did not know about him. I felt it was time to heal these wounds.

I sat at the edge of his bed, lifted his feet, put them on my lap, and started to give him a foot massage. He woke up and felt embarrassed. "Oh, my son, you don't have to massage my feet. I am still very strong," he said.

I looked at him and replied, "I have missed you so much, Dad. All these years have gone by so fast. I know we have some healing to do together. I am concerned about your health; you look frail. You have been smoking for so many years, and Mum still keeps trying to get you to give it up." He woke up and sat at his bedside. I looked at him and said, "Dad, are you not afraid that smoking kills you and cuts your life short?"

He lifted his head, and his green eyes were welled up with tears. Holding back his emotions, he cleared the lump in his throat and said, "I am not afraid of death, my beloved son, for it comes to all of us someday." And then the first teardrop fell and then another; he lifted his head as the full face of his emotions appeared, like a little boy crying. He said, "Do you know what I was afraid of most the day I left you in that airport?" His face, now a full flood of tears and his lips quivering with emotion, he said, "I was afraid I would never see you again. That has been my greatest fear—even more than I could fear death. I am sorry for my brutality and anger and the violence I had shown you when you were a kid. I was not the greatest dad in those days."

I embraced my dad, and we stayed locked in each other's arms for a while, as we healed our pains, mistakes, hurtful words, destructive anger, and all things that had come from generational curses to break people apart.

The remaining years were the golden years with my parents. We healed in a million ways. I was blessed to become the centre of their lives. I visited my mum and dad more regularly, and I was with them always on the phone. I supported them emotionally, spiritually, and financially, by the grace of God, who brought much healing to all of us. I found myself ministering to both my parents; even though they were Catholic in their upbringing, they were in a denominational church. It was tradition rather than understanding and application of the Word of God in their lives.

I was a born-again Christian, and I would be preaching the Gospel to my parents, revealing to them the knowledge of the Word of God. My parents were people of tremendous faith, but the understanding of the Word of God was not preached very well in this denominational church.

I began to show them that the evil one that rules the world prefers people to go to a denominational church and be so trapped in a system of tradition and blindness that the Word of God is not revealed unto them with power and revelation.

My mother commented, "My son, you always wanted to become a priest, and you always fought with your siblings about fervent prayer, and you always loved to read the Bible. I thank God for you. I am so amazed to hear you speak, and I am mesmerised at your passion for the Word and how well you speak it."

This spiritual journey continued for the remaining part of their years; my relationship with my parents became the most beautiful gift of love in my life.

I saw my dad fall on his knees and repent and ask the Lord to forgive him as he said the sinner's prayer. I blessed him, put my hands over his head, and prayed for him. The evil one of this world had ravaged my father throughout his life. He did not know the enemy, and he did not know how to fight the unseen enemy. He did not understand the spiritual battles we all have to fight. He lived in the flesh, and his knowledge of the Word of God was limited. Yet, in spite of all these deficiencies in his spiritual battles, his faith in the mercy and grace in Christ Jesus was unshakeable.

I know the Lord preserved us through the years. I could have died so many times, and by his precious mercy and grace, I returned to these days and this healing with my father. I walked the journey with them for the rest of their lives. The Lord had restored me to be there for them when they needed it the most.

My mother was a truly blessed woman, and there was a lot of hurt and pain that did not show in her face because she did not dwell on them; there was not a wrinkle on her face at the age of seventy-seven—and not because she used any special anti-ageing creams. The only reason she never aged in her face is because she wore the cream of forgiveness all day, every day of her life since she had married my dad. I know this truth: no woman in this world could have endured what she endured with my dad. My mother was his saving grace. She was from a time and an age when women were made exclusive. My mother prayed every day, and my dad left the door open for the devil to come into the house and destroy everything.

My mother endured those onslaughts of anger, violence, hurt, and affliction by prayer, hope, and faith. Yes, indeed, no matter how many times she was broken and wounded, she was found on her knees, hoping and praying. She was blessed with many happy days in her life. But it did not take much for my dad to wreck those sunny days.

The enemy was attacking him with the generational curses he'd inherited from his own father. As I began to see this in my dad, I realised these generational curses came to haunt me as well. I saw how the evil one accuses each of us before God. The war is real, and the enemy is crafty. I began to share such knowledge with my mom and dad and show them that the enemy is not flesh and blood. The knowledge of the Word of God is available to every man who comes seeking for it. And it's not by an intellectual means but by grace and mercy when you hear the Holy Spirit, who teaches you all things.

My return to their lives was like a gift, a gift they received for praying for me for all the years that I was absent. My days with my parents were the most precious memories of my life. The enormous significance was the power of the Gospel that we shared in the last years of their lives. Grace and mercy had found us.

CHAPTER 20

FINAL GOODBYES

My mother fell one day when she was alone at home. When my dad returned from church, he found her lying on the floor; she had suffered a stroke as an artery burst in her brain, causing bleeding, and, due to her weakness, they were unable to operate on her. She was now confined to a bed by the stroke, partially paralyzed on the left side. Unable to speak or recognise anyone, she was silent. A woman who liked to talk less and hear more was now quiet.

I took time off from work to be there for my mother. When I heard the news from my siblings, they sounded so desperate and hopeless. I fell on my knees and began to pray. I listened to a voice that guided me: "Go and show them some miracles. I am with you." My siblings are all Catholic, so they are very traditional in their beliefs, and the same differences I'd had with them from childhood remain until this day.

I took a flight home, armed with the Word of God, the Bible, in my hand. I went home to my mother. When I walked into the house, there was an eerie silence in the home, and hopelessness had filled their hearts. My dad's face lit up at my coming; he felt secure. He clasped me in an embrace the moment he saw me.

I hugged him and said, "You are going to see the power of God before your eyes."

He said, "I thank the Lord for you."

323

I walked into the room where my mother was lying; she was staring blankly at the small TV screen. I sat next to her and called her name; she looked at me but could not speak. She was unable to express anything, and her brain was slowly dying. It was painful. Therefore, I went to work.

I rallied all the grandchildren that evening and made an appointment with them to show up every evening at their grandmother's place. I instructed them to gargle their throats with ginger-infused green tea and honey in order for angelic voices to come out of their hearts.

We all gathered around her bed every day, and we sang Gospel songs praising the Lord for their wonderful grandmother. I changed the atmosphere from doom and gloom to one of praise and worship. It was terrific to see the power of prayer. We stood around her as I led them into prayer and worship. I proclaimed the Word of God on this house and rebuked every unclean spirit to depart in the name of Jesus.

My mother was fed by two tubes inserted in her nose down into her stomach. It was truly awful to see her in this plight. Yet, one morning she sat up on her bed, and, signalling to me, she asked me to get rid of them.

I told her that she must promise to eat some food as I warned her that the people with little faith might come back and reinsert them if she did not eat. She signalled to me that she was going to eat food but hated the tubes down her nose.

My elder sister was protesting that we should not remove the tubes and walked away, feeling angry and upset.

I asked her, "Where is your faith?" She stormed off, upset.

My mom ate her first bowl of soup after seven days from the time we'd started to praise the Lord and sing and give Him thanks.

In the evening, I led the family and the grandchildren into prayer and prophesied unto them: "You will hear her speak; you will see her smile and remember these days. You all will see these miracles, and then the Lord will take her away forever into His glory."

All these things came to pass. My mother even remembered people she had not seen in three years. I saw miracles before my eyes. I saw a dying mother come back to say her final farewell.

I sat next to her one morning, reading from John 14, as she lay in her bed listening. Then she looked at me and said, "Thank you, my son." Her voice was soft like a whisper; she smiled even though her face had suffered a stroke. My heart was filled with tears, but I held them inside. I knew she was thankful and was getting ready to go.

I looked at her, and my eyes filled with tears. I kissed her and whispered to her, "Do not be afraid, Momma, for He said, 'I will never leave or forsake you.' He has mansions for us, Momma. I will miss you forever, Momma."

Then she whispered, "My son, He is waiting for me."

I kissed my mother once again and said, "Goodbye, Momma. You are the jewel in my crown." My mother left this world on January 21, 2014.

My dad was utterly lost without her; he wept and moaned at her departure. He felt wretched, and the accuser rose again to torment him. I was ready and armed with the Word of God to defend my dad. With the passing of my mother, my concerns for Dad increased. I went into a protective mode. I had to shield my dad from the attack of the enemy.

I was always on the phone or Skyping him, praying with him, reading scriptures, and exposing the darkness and lies of the devil. It was, indeed, a remarkable journey with Dad. His love for me was immense. I had become his best friend, and we found strength in the Word of God to endure and smile once again. He still missed my mother more than ever. "I did not deserve that woman in my life, but God has been merciful to me even when I did not deserve such grace. Oh, my son, why do we learn lessons so late in life?" he would cry.

I would find solace and comfort in the Word of God and teach my dad also to find support in them. My dad's sight was failing him, and he was now unable to read the Word of God. He remarked to me, "How foolish we humans are. When we have the opportunity to read the Word of God, we do not take time. Now that I am old and my eyes are failing, I am unable to read the Word of God that I long to hear in my soul in my old age. Surely I have been a foolish man, my son, but I thank God for you." I shared scriptures like this and opened up a more significant understanding of the Word. I heard the voice in my soul and asked the Lord to instruct me as I spoke to my dad.

4 For whatsoever is born of God overcometh the world: and this is the victory that overcometh the world, even our faith. (1 John 5:4 KJV)

In 2016, at the age of eighty-five, my dad made a trip to Australia to visit all his family. He was the only one among his family who had decided to remain in India. While every one of his family had left for Australian shores decades ago, he stayed in India because he loved the country of his youth.

My dad wanted to go and preach to his family about the Lord and tell them to turn back to God. I smiled in my heart when he said he wanted to evangelise. I had a feeling that, on his return to India from his trip, my dad would not last much longer. I quit my job and went and spent three months with my dad. I was the most fortunate son in the world, and I learned to love and honour my mom and dad, to be there for them, and to walk a journey of faith with them. I held them close to my heart, and I miss them so much even now.

I came to comprehend everything about my mom and dad; my relationship with them was an extraordinary one. I found out about their adolescence; I knew the sentimental story of their lives; they never stayed discreet with me. They imparted to me their wrongdoings and, together, discovered forgiveness. I walked an excursion with my folks as no other child could. I realized their lives so well. I was significantly honored to have such elegance to honor my parents in this life. However, I am still left continuously with the inclination that I could have accomplished more for them. Even when they expressed that I do a lot, I had some sense of feeling they would be gone, and I would never get another opportunity to be there for them.

I was not there when my dad breathed his last, sitting on a rocking chair. He had been asking about me for a week. He imagined I was around him as he become slightly disoriented; he kept calling my name even until the last day of his life. I was on the phone with him all the time talking to him, but he wanted me to be next to him. I was at work and could not get the time to be with him immediately. I was on my way, but it was too late. He had all his children around him, and he loved them all, but he wanted me to be there, only me. I did not make it to his funeral because they could not wait for me to arrive. It was a sad day. I knew he wanted me to be the one to bury him. I knelt and wept. I was afraid I would miss my dad a lot the day he left. I felt like an orphan the day he was gone. The two best people in my life had gone.

I stood at his unfinished grave as the people rebuilt it. I supervised the rebuilding of the cemetery. My dad wanted to be buried in his father's grave. He loved his parents, and even though he found himself torn between them, he was the one who'd brought healing to his father and mother. History was repeating itself once again. I placed this scripture on his tombstone:

I have fought a good fight, I have finished my course, I have kept the faith.

—(2 Timothy 4:7 KJV)

I stood there, bowed my head, and remembered all the words that he had shared with me. I knew the man I buried, the man I called my dad. I honoured my parents, and I thank the Lord for them. I miss them always and still feel like an orphan without them because we do get orphaned when they go.

I put those words on his gravestone. I believe they particularly fit him. If he had known how to fight a better fight, he would have; but in his last days, when his life was fading, he was willing to put up a fight against the evil one who comes to destroy the world with lies and darkness. My dad knew that God was forgiving, and he was not afraid to go. I played a part in his journey of faith and redemption. I thank the Lord for this. Amen.

I walked away from the grave, closed my eyes, and praised the name of Yeshua HaMashiach, the Holy Messiah, the first fruit that rose from the grave, and the love of God, who gave us a great hope in a fallen world. I saw a vision in my soul of a father in heaven who dressed them in skin clothes when they fell, made provision for a redemption and a return to the tree of life from the beginning of time. Our ending is the beginning of the greatest gift of life in Christ Jesus.

It is the glory of God to conceal a thing: but the honour of kings is to search out a matter. (Proverbs 25:2)

12 For as the body is one, and hath many members, and all the members of that one body, being many, are one body: so also, is Christ
13 For by one Spirit are we all baptized into one body, whether we be Jews or Gentiles, whether we be bond or free; and have been all made to drink into one Spirit. (Corinthians 12:12–13)

PART THREE

CHAPTER 21

FINDING YESHUA HAMASHIACH

THE CALL OF ISRAEL

The year 2016 was dawning to the calling of a childhood dream of going to Israel. The same passion that burned in the heart of my wife and mine was now a reality. We both made up our minds to make it happen, yet, it was not our will and desire alone that got us there. It was the thirsting of the soul within us to see the home of our Lord Jesus Christ, an earthly home that He walked on to bring salvation to a fallen man. The Emmanuel—*God with us*.

Joanne was my first love, so when you think you have had enough and given up on relationships after failed marriages, something good happens. Here was a woman who loved the Lord, with prayer and worship a way of life. A girl I first loved and wanted to marry so long ago appeared before me. She helped me find the Jesus of my heart once again.

I have had a book that the Lord was writing and living inside of me for all my life and realised it would be selfish on my part to leave the world without writing about it. I knew that there might be a big audience who would love to read what I have left behind. Twenty-seven years later, you unintentionally meet the girl you wanted to marry and love first, before them all. Is this an ironic twist of fate? Are you telling me this is not the grace of God? We both came from Christian backgrounds and had been raised by beautiful parents. Therefore, we

331

both had similar childhood dreams. One of them was going to the Holy Land. However, I believe God prepares you to come to His Holy Land at a time when it is right.

All those early childhood stories of Abraham, Isaac, and Jacob, and the most captivating story of betrayal and forgiveness was the one of Joseph, and I remember weeping like a child for Joseph as he was led away with his hands bound to a life of slavery into Egypt. These lifetime classic tales of the Bible were now embedded into the innocent pureness of this childhood heart. No one can snatch away what belongs to God. No matter where I went, and no matter how many times I lost myself in the world and all of its vanity, my heart always belonged to God. Now, my life was going to be His forever. I had to get to Israel first and find my angels.

Although I knew of this angel in some way, the trip was made possible by my wife, Joanne. As destiny would have it, I had survived two divorces before I finally met up with her. Awkwardly, we had grown up in different cultures, and, despite twenty-seven years apart, the history and ancient culture of the Anglo-Indian had bound us together. The common bond between our parents and the memory of innocence and sincere hearts held us together in a universe that had devastated our faith in the world and people. We are all bound to be betrayed, to be tied up in bondage in some way, by the circumstance of our lives, and sold into slavery into the Egypt of our lives, into the systems of labour and taxes, debt and greed, our lives controlled by governments and regimes that bind you and leave you with a feeling of having no choice. We are still in Egypt, waiting for the final exodus to salvation and eternal life.

Somehow grace locates us by an incredible power and mercy of God when the human being starts to go through a process of correction (*tikkum*). A man must be able to understand the matter of modes of his behaviour that conflict with each other. In the beginning, when God formed man, he was made only from the dust of the earth. It was the spirit of Holiness that God—"Blessed be His Holy Name"—breathed into the nostrils of Adam life, giving him a life of Holiness—This man in the image of God was a holy creation until, at the Tree of Knowledge, the sin of evil fell upon him by the act of disobedience perpetrated by the serpent and the woman. The man was now bound up in a fight for survival. The conduct of survival and sustenance of humanity has passed from the system of holiness to the method of the "other forces" (of evil—*sitra ahra*) as a result of the wound of the "will to receive" for himself alone, that became attached to humanity as a result of the eating from the Tree of Knowledge. This eating brought about separation, resistance, and even hate between the bodily structures of humankind in this world.

When, as a consequence of this fact, the system of holiness was no longer able to maintain and sustain them from its table on high, to ensure that existence would not be destroyed and that their proper functioning in the future would be guaranteed, this man and woman were handed over for the receiving of all abundance that is necessary for survival—which consists of 288 sparks—to the system of the "other forces" (of evil, *sitra ahra*). This system was then to sustain all humanity throughout their "correction" (*tikkum*). Thus, the order of the world came to be very confused, for, "bad results from bad," and whatever way one considers it inadequate must result as a consequence of this transference. If the "other forces of evil" (*sitra ahra*) give only a small supply to the world, the apparent result is destruction and suffering. Whereas if they provide ample supply, they increase the "force of separation" for those who receive it.

My life was on a path of separation from the God of my childhood, and I had suffered broken marriages. I was only emotionally attached to God and only cried for His help all my life. I had become accustomed to being the cry-baby man. I would pour my heart out to God in a pool of tears, and somehow He obliged me with undeserved mercy and lifted me several times. Now it was over.

God was not going to have any of this nonsense anymore; the man in me had to rise and finally get serious with the Lord. My two marriages were like a bull tied to an ass trying to plough a field for a fruitful harvest. The mule always left with a burnt-out farm and fields lying in the ashes of his dust from where God had formed this man. The enemy used these women unknown to their self-awareness and lack of knowledge of God in their lives. They did not have any deep, meaningful relationships with God, and I was saddled like an ox ploughing a field with a stubborn mule. Not that it's the fault of the mule, but the mule does not realise that it has been given the undeserved grace of having an excellent, strong, God-fearing ox tied to it. The enemy is not flesh and blood, as the Bible says. By His grace,

I learned to find this tremendous power of forgiveness and break the stronghold of the enemy that tried to hold me in that bondage of Egyptian hate that I never accepted. I cut those chains.

If a man has one hundred coins, he desires two hundred; and if he has two hundred, he wants three hundred. We can compare this desirous behaviour to an example of a cancerous part of the body that is separate and distinct, and the relief the organism gets when it is separated and cured of this ailment. For the more pleasure that is received, the higher is the separation. And the less the separation from cancer, the more severe the disease grows inside the man. Thus, love of self becomes stronger in those receiving this supply from the "other forces," and each man swallows his companion alive. The lifetime of the body also becomes shorter, for the increasing amount that is received brings one even earlier to the final drop of bitterness that is at the end of it all.

Before a man prays for the Holy Word of God in the Holy Bible and the Torah to enter into his body, he should pray that pleasures do not come to his body. My prayer started to be different, and I was now praying for God to cleanse me from all the filth that lodged inside of me. I wanted to be saved, to become pure and holy; my heart was yearning and thirsty. The inner light in me was turned on, and the darkness of my soul was illuminated by the false pleasures of this life that I had allowed to enter into me. I wanted all of this out, but this was no ordinary desire or wish. I would need to work hard at this for a long time. Now on the long road to my salvation, I needed help, and I had to surrender all of life's pleasures. I first had to deal with what I'd become. The current state of my soul was caught in the form of receiving self alone—which is the opposite of holiness. I had grown proportionately larger in proportion to the pleasure that the body gets.

My current condition: how is it possible to receive the light of the Word of God and "the Gospel of Yeshua HaMashiach" when I, the man now separated from holiness, was employing opposite forms? "For a tremendous mutual aversion exists between these two forces, found in the case of all alternate extremes. They loathe one another and can't be placed in a collocation." It is, therefore, evident that a person must first pray that pleasures and delights should not enter his body. Then, by grace and means of high activity and preoccupation with the Holy Word of God in His holy book, the Bible, the Torah, and the *mitzvoth*, a man will gradually come to transform his "form of receiving" into receiving to impart. He will thus make his form similar to that of the system of holiness, and there will be similarity and love between the two of them as there was before the sin of the eating from the tree of knowledge. He will attain the light of the Holy Word of God and enter into the orbit of the holy, blessed, one Almighty Father in heaven, through the Gospel and blood of Christ, the wonderful saving grace upon us all, Jesus, who knew and taught us how to receive it entirely by His Word and His life that He gave us. All this knowledge and grace came to me later, and I imparted this to you toward the start of this chapter with the goal that you may acknowledge how I got to this knowledge and revelation of the reality about our lives. It's an adventure, and I need you to join me on it with the goal that it might assist you with getting to that realm that the Lord needs you to be in.

For now, I had an early-morning plane to catch from Dubai International Airport. Joanne and I were excited as we met other members of the tour group. The group was predominately Asian Catholic people, and their natural enthusiasm and talkative nature ensured that we were among a lively bunch of happy, excited people.

Then there was a particular Filipino family that consisted of aged parents with their daughters and sons-in-law who seemed very religious and faithful. Yet, everyone else was on a similar journey. We landed in Bahrain and then went on to Amman, the capital of Jordan. After going through the immigration checks and the head counts, we were greeted by our tour guide and driver and escorted onto a brown bus.

The road was a dusty one across Jordan as we made our way to ancient lands; it was indeed a feeling of joy and excitement. As we sang songs of worship and the classic Catholic rituals of prayer, our journey was starting to take on the purpose of a spiritual pilgrimage. We had a young Indian Catholic priest in our midst and a Goan tour guide.

As we left the valleys below us and ascended into the higher elevations, our first stop was Mount Nebo; the landscape captured the essence of the books of Exodus, Leviticus, and Deuteronomy. The greatest prophet, Moses, led them from bondage into an exodus to the promised land. It was desert, parched and thirsty; as you gazed into the labyrinth of the valleys below, it made sense how easy it was to get lost and wander for forty years, even when you are still close to the destination of the promised land. Yet, only two made it from the original group—Joshua and Caleb. It captured my very soul as Joanna and I gazed across the Holy Land from a distance. En Gedi, the Dead Sea, Jerusalem; my heart was lifted with tremendous joy as the whole childhood dream of coming here was now alive. I hugged Joanne, my wife and friend, and said, "Thank you." She was not so vocal as I am, but there in her silence, she squeezed my hands, and it expressed her emotions of joy. Here was a woman who loves Jesus Christ with all her heart, a woman who had been through some painful experiences of loss and betrayal; here next to her stood a man who was crushed and broken by divorces, failures, and disappointments. It's incredible how the brokenhearted seek the face of God by faith and works. The world tears their lives, and yet God is the one who restores all things. Children of an exodus, we seek to escape from the world we live in and go on the exodus of the heavenly realms that Jesus spoke of in John 14. Our real hope and saviour is our Messiah, Christ Yeshua.

We walked up to the monastery on the hill, and the Scriptures started to come alive. It was the most fantastic sight that greeted our eyes; my wife and I looked across the land of the hills and valleys below us. In the distance was the Dead Sea.

Serpents raised on two poles at the edge of the hill where we stood, two twisted-iron serpents facing each other—the *caduceus*—the symbol that you see for medical service on some ambulances, a reminder of Moses raising them to heal the sickness of the people. Gazing upon the deadly serpents, they were healed. A paradigm was playing out, for the true salvation that was to come to all nations. For now, the story of Moses was the story of one country.

I wept as I saw the cross in front of me, the Holy Messiah nailed to the cross for the healing of all nations. A foreshadowing of his coming played out here in the wilderness.

I was already overwhelmed at the first stop as we began to pray and realise the power of God and His presence in our lives. The Catholic group celebrated a mass in the monastery managed by the Franciscan monks, and the journey into the Holy Land had come into our very heart and soul.

We departed from Mount Nebo and drove across Jordan into the border crossing into Israel. The security at the border was a poignant reminder that we were entering a nation that was heavily protected by its inhabitants. As I gazed across the Jewish soldiers, I was living the scriptures of Joshua and Caleb at the walls of Jericho inside my head. They had to fight to get to the promised land, and with that pillar of fire and the spirit of God upon them, they were fearless because they had seen His power, His anger, His commandments; they ate manna in the desert and perished in it. A stiff-necked people were ungrateful towards a God who was writing His laws and commandments in their hearts for the world to behold His holy nation—the glory of the one, true God that man was to bow down before, the Holy God of Abraham, Isaac, and Israel, the Yehudim, the Hebrews, the Crossover.

We were informed that one of the Filipino girls had an Iranian stamp in her passport, and we were going to be delayed indefinitely. This process took forever as the Israeli authorities at the border crossing interrogated her relentlessly about her visit to a hostile nation that vows to destroy the state of Israel. You are always going to have one person in your group who is not educated enough to be in touch with the times in which we live. On the other hand, maybe she desired to visit the Holy Land, and so she never mentioned to the tour operator that she had visited Iran two years ago for employment as a nurse.

There was a spirit of Christianity among the whole group as our young priest assisted the authorities with their enquiry about the tour group and the troublesome individual with the Iranian stamp on her passport. Israel takes their security seriously, and when you have so many enemies who hate you because you are Jewish, I understood the measures implemented in this tiny nation. To hate is evil, and to love is holy. "For God so loved this world that He gave His only begotten Son that whosoever believed in Him shall never perish" (John 3:16). These kinds of thoughts went through my mind as I began to see the faces of people, the Arabs and Muslim people crossing into the Jewish nation. I was amazed that the truth of the Gospel had not yet captured those closest to the Holy Land, like this fantastic revelation and joy of salvation and truth had done us, who had come from faraway lands more than it ever did to those who were so close to it all.

I was slightly perplexed and did not want to make any judgement of my own, but words of the Bible came into my head. I recall Jesus saying, "I came to My own, and My own have rejected me." Jesus was not only the rejected Messiah, but the King who had captured the nations from afar—amazing grace unto the Gentiles. These thoughts overwhelmed me.

We finally were set free into the Holy Land, and we headed straight to our hotel for a shower, dinner, and a good night's rest. It was all so overwhelming as Joanne and I slept like two babies on our first night in the Holy Land.

We awoke each day with a spirit of prayer and joy of visiting every holy place, every footstep where the Lord had trod; my childhood love for the Messiah returned to me, this saviour and redeemer who had saved us and secured forgiveness for our sins. There is an emotional attachment to Jesus that was born within us as children. And now we were getting to see the holy places on high, places from where we looked in our childhood imagination during our prayers my mother taught me, places we imagined miracles and healing manifested, places where we hoped prayer would be heard, and the many miracles we had experienced and witnessed in our own lives. The tragedies and the unanswered prayers were all wrapped up in a tapestry of faith— an emotional attachment to the suffering, death, and crucifixion of Jesus Christ.

Our journey took us on a pilgrimage of prayer and mass at every holy site. From Bethlehem to Nazareth, and then on to Tabgha and Capernaum, we were on a boat singing Hebrew songs as we sailed across on the Sea of Galilee. Jesus walked upon the water, and Peter was sinking with doubt; Mark 5 in the Bible came to mind as the storm arose. Why was He going across to the other side of the sea? Jesus calmed the sea. But why was He going to the other side? Who was that troubled man in the tombs cutting himself with stones? Who was he, and why did a man so possessed by evil spirits fall and shout out loud, "Oh, Son of the Highest God, I adjure thee, do not torment me"? "What is your name?" He said, "Legion—a troop—a troop shall overcome Him, but in the end, He will overcome." Was this a fulfilment of Jacob's prophecy to his son Gad? Was this man a descendant of Gad? Did Jesus come across to fulfil this prophecy?

People on the boat told us that the Sea of Galilee was known to throw up some unexpected storms. We passed along the way as the stories of the Bible we loved so much kept coming alive because of the faith we had in this pure, humble gentile heart. Faith does not need intelligence for someone to possess it, and faith needs humble hearts of children to believe the stories, miracles, and wonders of Jesus Christ and the humble faith that does it. Wisdom about this faith was to come later. Humbleness ought to come first.

We rested in a hotel on the outskirts of Jerusalem later that evening, and our next day was the Holy City that had captivated our hearts. As we slept in our hotel room, around 3:00 a.m., I heard a cock crow. I went to my window and pulled back the curtain; the town was asleep as I looked at the lights of Jerusalem in the distance. I heard the cock's crow again; and there was a small farm-house located about 150 metres away from us. The cock's crow sounded again, and I started to cry. I remembered the apostle Peter as he denied Jesus Christ three times. I was now weeping, as I had done the same as Peter—denied Jesus Christ by the way I had lived my life. I looked out the window when a soft hand touched my shoulder; it was my wife, Joanne, holding me from behind.

I whispered, "Did you hear the cock crow?"

"Yes, I did," she replied.

I felt she'd responded like she precisely knew my tears and emotions. Peter denied Him not because he did not love the Lord, but because he was afraid for his life. She had put my heart to rest almost immediately with her words of comfort. We all love God deeply, but we have never given Him our lives entirely; we are easily caught up in the worldly life that we have all denied Him in some way or another. Intentionally or unintentionally, it has happened. As we held each other and looked out through the window towards the city of Jerusalem, I was so thankful that I had this precious woman next to me, a true friend of old.

The next morning, we entered Jerusalem, the Holy City on the Hill. The Catholic homage was to perform the stations of the Cross to the Church of the Holy Sepulchre. The Via Dolorosa took us from the sentencing and the place where He was handed His cross. This event is a weekly routine on Friday in Jerusalem. There is a Muslim school on an elevated level to the street below that you can get to if you get a chance to go there by offering twenty shekels to the Muslim man. Who is the corrupted watchman of the school? You may get an opportunity to visit the premises of the school, and on the lookout from three windows, looking into a garden of olive trees, you have a perfect view of the Rock of the Dome. However, if you know of the image it harbours inside its walls, you would put your twenty shekels to better use than to view that place. Of all the places opened freely to the public of all nations, this Dome of the Rock is the only place in Jerusalem that has restrictions not only to non-Muslims, but even Muslims who don't know to recite a particular prayer may be rejected from entering. Every other place is open to visiting except for security checks at the Wailing Wall of the temple of Solomon.

When Adam and Eve sinned in the Garden of Eden, the Bible tells us that they hid from God. When God walked in the Garden and called out to Adam, he revealed that he was afraid and naked. I did not have to be highly intelligent to realise that, when something is unclean and evil, it surely must hide in fear of its uncleanliness. Thus, I did not attempt to go anywhere to a place that was so restricted, especially when I had so many other places of more profound significance to go to than the Dome of the Rock; let them keep it hidden from people; if it's as holy as they claim it to be, then holiness is for everyone. It's not to be protected and restricted.

As we walked up the Muslim quarters of the city of Jerusalem, I noticed all the shops were selling everything related to Jesus Christ. Even though many of these people denied the Messiah, they were sure making a living from His story right here in the city of Jerusalem.

I smiled to myself and remembered *Kesade* grace—undeserved grace, for He makes the sun shine on the good and the bad equally. His ways are not ours, and for these much-higher illuminations of love from God, far beyond man's imagination or experience of love, God is far above the ways of man because he is the epitome of love. I was going through these kinds of thought processes in my mind. I walked along with the group of pilgrims on the journey to the place of my Lord's final hours.

What would our final hours be like, and what can the wicked and evil say to a Holy God on their day of judgment? The devil is an accuser, and he can bring only accusations of unfairness and illuminations of lies and darkness, so, in the light of God, no one could ever say that His judgement is not fair. Because He made the sun shine on the good and evil and their mortal lives, their earthly lives were filled with every opportunity to turn back to Him, for their hope of salvation was hung up on a cross. The paradigm came to life as Moses raised an object of hope and healing to the sick and the dying out in the wilderness. Here I knelt, my head bowed to the ground at the site of the crucifixion. God had raised Him on a wooden cross on a hill in Jerusalem, this hill of Moriah, the very mountain where Abraham was asked to sacrifice his son Isaac. This paradigm was now in water and blood raised on a cross for the healing of every soul and nation and for every tongue and every knee that bows at this cross and confesses that He is the way, the truth, and the life—Jesus Christ, Holy Messiah.

I prayed for the forgiveness of my sins and my ignorance of His great sacrifice for the atonement of my sinful life. "Oh, God, forgive me." I wept at the holy sanctuary. "Cleanse me and make me whole and complete. Bring holiness into my life, O God!" I lamented in my heart. I was here at the foot of the cross, and my heart was overwhelmed by a Holy God. I came undone and saw the unworthiness of the flesh and felt the thirst for the spirit within me.

As I went to the Jewish Quarter of Jerusalem, the whole atmosphere was completely different. There was more order, more peacefulness, and no one hounded you to buy anything. Unlike the Muslim Quarter, where people lured you into their shops by saying words like "I have a gift for you; come inside." It was so corny and deceitful. Opportunists and tricky places—one can surely find them in the Muslim Quarter. There was always a sense of hidden hatred in the atmosphere when you walked among the people there. I wish it were not that way and that I don't have to write it and describe it the way I experienced it, nor do I want to sound racist or discriminatory in any way; but for the truth to be spoken, I write what I have seen, experienced, and felt.

As I walked towards the Wailing Wall, I was greeted by an American Jew who told me the direct telephone line to the Almighty God is right there at the wall of the temple of Solomon.

I understood very well what he was telling me and what happened when Solomon built the temple and the smoke that had filled the place as the spirit of God descended into the holy of holies. God promised the people His everlasting presence at His temple. I fell to my knees at the wall and poured my heart out in prayer to the Lord that day. I put into the wall the wrapped-up prayers of my children, my friends, and my own. As my legs trembled in this place, I knew and felt the presence of God in this holy ground.

Jerusalem had captivated my very soul and human existence. I felt the urgency and need for my life to be changed. To be renewed and rectified, I wanted to offer myself once again to my Holy Saviour. I wanted to do it right and with power, with no weakness but with a firm resolve; a desire to become worthy of Him was born in my soul that day. I had no clue as to how it was all going to happen, but I realised that it was going to be a tough road with many rocks and stumbling blocks thrown at me. I had just made a U-turn in my life, and I knew the dark ruler of this world was the most disappointed that day. I was going back home to my Saviour.

We climbed the Mount of Olives and found a church that was built to look like a teardrop. It was at this place Jesus looked at Jerusalem and wept for it. I recalled a verse in the Bible in the book of Genesis 6:5–8, which reads as follows: "Then the Lord God saw the wickedness of man was great in the earth and that every intent of the thoughts of his heart was only evil continually. And the Lord God grieved in His heart that He made them, So the Lord said, "I will destroy man whom I have created from the face of the earth, both man and beast, creeping things and birds of the air, for I am sorry that I have made them. But Noah found grace in the eyes of the Lord."

I connected to this verse, and as I looked from the small window, I could see Jerusalem and the Dome of the Rock. My eyes filled with tears. I felt the presence of the pain of God in my heart; as I looked, I could see the desolation of the abomination that stood on that mountaintop—the Seventy Weeks Prophecy of the prophet Daniel in chapter 9. God will always bring His righteous to reign in His time. I knelt and prayed.

My journey in the Holy Land was significantly extraordinary because I had someone special to share it with. Joanne was right next to me all along, and I could not have asked for a better friend and companion. She was a woman of faith, a woman of endurance, of values and decency. She had cleaved to the Messiah all her life through the darkest days of her beautiful experience, and she had witnessed His saving grace, His mercy, and hope of salvation. Meeting her was a turning point in my life; it was all there, right in front and next to me. So why did God give you gaps in your fingers? So that someone special would come along and fill them up by holding your hand as you walked together across the fields of gold. You cannot plough the land with an ox tied to an ass. Wisdom also knows how to choose and find a woman who loves God before she loves you. Such understanding came late to me; even when I did not deserve it because of my foolish ways, grace had found her for me. I squeezed her hand, for she did not know the thoughts that were going through my mind as we smiled at each other.

We arrived at a location where the stream of water from the Jordan River flows into the Dead Sea. Dressed in white robes, we entered the water to be baptised, to announce our surrender of repentance to God. There were two Israeli soldiers, a Catholic priest, and our group, but no priest to baptise the born-again Christians. We were not sure about the location and expected that there would be a priest or a holy man who would be baptising people.

There were two men from Eretria in the water; one was baptising the other in a cleansing ritual. The man tapped him hard on the head with his hand every time he submerged and reappeared out of the water. It was like hitting out every unclean spirit out of the man; the desire of being clean and holy was the same in every one of us. Seven times he did this as I watched the baptism of the men at the river. The four girls and my wife looked at me and said, "You can baptise us all since there is no priest over here." I was overwhelmed by such a request. I had come to be baptised and not to baptise. As I held them in my hand, I asked them if they renounced Satan and the world and all of its evil deception, if they accepted salvation and forgiveness for their sins through the blood of Jesus Christ. I submerged them into the water of the Jordan and baptised them in the name of Jesus Christ. Amen.

Then those who I had baptised now baptised me in return, and the five of us walked out of the water feeling blessed. In our journey to the Holy Land, we experienced a miracle that occurred later on that night.

We journeyed through the Dead Sea, an experience of floating on the waters of no life. I had never stepped into any water so corrosive and salty as the Dead Sea. A few drops hit my eyes, and I had to shut them, as it felt they were on fire. I recovered from this experience and floated on the sea with my eyes closed. I prayed for every unclean sin, impure thought, unclean spirit, anger, disappointment, hurt, and betrayal I had experienced to die in that water. I floated away into the distance with my eyes shut and my heart praying for death to sin in my life. I opened my eyes, and the blue sky shone above. I prayed again and asked the Lord to clean me forever.

I looked towards the shore, and Joanne was a far distance off; she was waving at me to come back, as I had drifted far away from her. I slowly made my way again, careful not to splash any water into my eyes. The Dead Sea was the lowest point in the world and sinking even lower; it was a mystery, and I could not figure it out. It was dead, and nothing living could live in that most corrosive water. Yet, the shop En Gedi made the most amazing beauty products from the minerals of the Dead Sea. *How ironic*, I thought. *From that which is dead comes products to beautify our mortal bodies. How strange.*

We returned later that evening to our hotel accommodations tired and exhausted from our Dead Sea experience. Then that night, we heard sirens of an ambulance at our hotel premises and did not know what was going on.

Our tiredness had overtaken us as we soon fell asleep. We understood that whatever the matter was, it was under control, as help had arrived. We were tired and barely could stay awake. The next morning, as we got into our bus, I was greeted by the middle-aged Filipino couple who had sat at the front seats throughout the whole journey. However, this morning they looked more thankful. This was the family who travelled with their daughters and sons-in-law.

"The Lord be praised" was my usual greeting.

The man looked at me and said, "God is good, and glorify Him forever." He had tears in his eyes. "Last night, she left me," he said, looking at his wife.

"What do you mean?" I inquired.

"Did you hear the ambulance?" he asked.

"I did," I replied. "Forgive me," I quickly added, "I was so tired, I could barely stay awake."

The man's tears filled his eyes. I held his hand and hers. "What happened?" I asked.

Then one of the daughters stepped into the conversation and explained that their mother had had a heart attack and had stopped breathing; she had breathed her last. And as they gathered around her crying, "Mommy, not now, not here, not like this," the ambulance arrived and revived her. I stood dumbfounded as I looked at the lady; she smiled at me. I was speechless.

Her husband said, emotionally, "She is beautiful, and God gave us a miracle last night."

We held each other's hands and gave thanks, and I praised God that morning; this was a profoundly moving testimony, as every person in that group was filled with gratitude, worship, and praise as this event unfolded in their presence right here in God's Holy Land. We sang joyfully in the bus praising and thanking the Lord. It was truly a spirit-filled day.

We made our way to Mount Tabor, to the place where the transfiguration of Jesus along with Moses and Elijah had taken place, in the presence of Peter, John, and James. As we went to worship in this sacred place, we also visited the two small chapels on either side. Joanne knelt and opened her heart out to the most beautiful prayers. As we knelt, it was a powerful and moving experience. Then a flash occurred, and a revelation took place in my mind.

Moses led the people up to the Holy Land, and the Bible tells us that this great prophet of God never entered the Holy Land himself. Neither was the body of Moses ever located.

In the book of Jude in verse 9, Michael the Archangel simply rebuked the devil when he disputed about the body of Moses. As I pondered on this verse, I understood that God had reserved the visit of Moses into the Holy Land to appear in this transfiguration with the Holy Messiah Yeshua and Elijah—prophets of God raptured from Earth into heavenly places in the realms of holiness in the kingdom of the everlasting.

Our journey into the Holy Land was coming to an end, and the beginning of a transformation of our lives was about to take place. We now knew that we had been very blessed and that we had received all these blessings of our visit to this Holy Land, this childhood dream, this vision of truth unfolding before our eyes. Life surely must get better with all this grace and blessings received. Now, you may not realise it, but you have been given the power to fight the war that is to unfold in your life, the battle with the darkness and the evil one who beguiled your life with lies and deception.

Now you are back on the side where you always belonged, on the team with Jesus Christ, and your life will never be the same again. For now you are in a war fighting for your soul and its journey towards holiness. Not by your merit or grace earned or deserved, but by the word of God spoken by Jesus in John 17 and 18, when he prayed for us and asked the Almighty Father that none of us should be lost in this world, none who was given to Him. As I bowed my head at these verses, I realised that we were predestined and called unto Him to be the bride for Christ, His church.

We were on the bus back in Jordan, heading towards the airport and our journey back to Dubai. The whole experience of being in the Holy Land was beyond what I had imagined it to be in my childhood dreams. Now, this wish had come to pass, for the Lord had appointed this time and age for us to visit a place—Jerusalem, closest to my heart.

I had this feeling inside my heart, and I knew I would come back. I needed to come back. I did not know when, but I knew I would.

So many things have changed since I visited Jerusalem in 2016. Life was never the same, and it was more blessed, more robust than before, and my thirst for the *binah* (intelligence), *hokhmah* (wisdom), the *ze'eir anpin* (small face), *malkhut* (kingdom) has never ceased ever since.

I found myself awake at early hours of the morning, reading my Bible and finding all kinds of treasures in the Word of God. It became honey to my soul, dripping honey on my soul. It has become a treasure trove, a place where I find amazing treasures in His Word that connects me and my spirit to other places in the Scripture where these treasures are found in the heavenly realms. I remembered a scene in the life of Jesus when the Pharisees asked him the question about divorce, and the explanation that the Lord gave. He said to them, "In the beginning, it was not so." I captured that and knew He was telling me to go and understand the beginning. One day as I was reading and exploring the beginning with the Holy Spirit of God, I found myself in a flood of tears, and for that moment, I felt the tears of God. I could see His two children, Adam and Eve, who had fallen from holiness, and He gave them His judgement. "Unto Adam also and to his wife did the LORD God make coats of skins, and clothed them" (Genesis 3:21).

As I closed my eyes and held them shut, they burst into tears. I saw a father dressing His children who had become corrupted and knew evil and good, and He stood there watching His children leave His home of eternal life that He made to keep them close to Him. Tears begin to flow like a rushing river from two tiny tear ducts. How can so many tears be held in such small vessels? I thought for a second. A father's pain is deep. How do you think God felt to see them go? He dressed them and did not send them out naked. I tell my daughters, "Place that thought of who you are when you dress and go out in the world as women. Dress up like God dressed your mother Eve and covered her so that that desire and beauty may be protected." He made them male and female, and He allowed their passions to now be a part of their life in holy union of marriage. When I look at the world and see the endless divorces in the Western world and the tearing down of families, suffragettes who put each other down, my heart breaks, for we have all lost our way, and everyone is hurting with sin.

I wasted so much life missing out on the true joy of His Word, such resounding, everlasting joy that has filled my life with inexpressible gratitude for the grace and joy of the hope and love that has been placed inside my heart and soul—undeserved grace. A crown of salvation and everlasting peace, *shalom aleichem*—the ultimate blessing, the final *shalom* (order) after the price of atonement was paid by blood and water on that holy cross. We did not deserve one drop of His holy blood, but He is God, and we are His creation in His image, He is the creator, and we His creation. Only He could save us, for we who were lost have been found again. *Amazing grace, how sweet the sound that saved a wretch like me. I once was lost, and now I am found. I was blind, but now I see.* I fall to the floor as I write such things, and I shake, and my hands are folded, clasped together. "Thank You, Lord, for all You have done for us." Life has changed indeed. I prayed for the one who threw my Bible at me and said, "Take your God and leave." It's sad, so sad.

There is a strange sense of feeling these days. I could not be bothered anymore about my career in the oil and gas industry. My CV and my job prospects are of no interest to me anymore. I am not a part of the system of man and their taxes. I wish I could tell them to collect it at the mouth of the fish near the sea. I must admit I am apprehensive about my money sometimes and wonder where the funding will all come from. My heart desires more to find a job with the Lord if he requires me to work for Him. I could not ask for a better employer. The world has become vainer, and I am interested only in those who are interested in Christ. I am happy to testify to the unbeliever or speak of the Word of God to the ones who listen. I can handle people who reject me and call me a "Jesus Freak." I am humbled by such accusations. For, I know who is behind them. I learned not to wage war with flesh and blood, and forgiveness comes easy for me to those who have betrayed and harmed me. It's harder when those you love reject your knowledge of the Word of God in you. Yet, in the peace of the evening, as the sun sets, you realise that all Jewish celebrations start with the setting sun. So, the mystery is complete, and our lives go from the darkness into the light; we move from sinful pasts to a life of holiness, from sickness into health, from sorrow into joy. I have become a person of the Shabbat. For the Shabbat is the prayer of the Jews. The politicians can keep their world. I am not a part of that which comes to an end.

The Lord is my provider. He is my hope and my shelter. His words are a lamp unto my feet, and His promises are forever. I can do all things in Christ who strengthens me. Then I hear the words of the apostle Paul—in life or death, I belong to Christ. Amen.

The great mystery of the relationship between men and women was opened up to me by the Scriptures. I came to grips with the failed relationships of my life. As I looked at the world around me, I realised that there was not a man or woman unaffected by these endless failures of relationships between men and women. In the West, where I grew up and lived the condition of family life, the devastating lawlessness among people have destroyed the very essence and fabric of society, the family. It's all fallen apart and hanging on fine threads. I prayed that God would enlighten me more to understand these days of our lives.

So, therefore, come and let us see the amount we ought to value the Word of God and the individuals who instruct it to us and sparkle their sacred lights on us. Those genuine godly men in the Bible forfeited their lives so as to advance the condition of our spirits, which are balanced precisely in the centre between, on one hand, the way of misery and torment, and, on the other, the idea of forgiveness and restoration. They save us from the bottomless pit that is more regrettable than death itself. They educate and train us to go after the heavens of joy, to the statures of joy and loveliness, which is our rightful lot through Christ Jesus and which have been set up for us. What's more, it has been waiting for us from the beginning of time. Truth be told, it is a general principle that, from a similar spot, an astute man determines the wellspring of his astuteness; the fool additionally extrapolates his silliness.

I should hence prefer to alert my readers in this part in my book and caution the readers that I have not endeavoured for the individuals who need to see reality from the well-being of a triple-coated glass window at a sheltered separation. However, for the individuals who love the Word of the Lord, it is valuable and significantly precious and gifted up with knowledge, for the individuals who love to pursue the Lord all the days of their lives and receive His goodness to accomplish the purpose for which we were made.

Proverbs 8:17 says, "I love them that love me, and those that seek me earnestly shall find me." In the book of Deuteronomy, chapter 6, verse 13, it says, "The Lord your God shall you fear and He shall you serve." The Hebrew word for "you shall fear" includes all the *mitzvoth* that prohibit action—whether by the mouth or by the heart or any bodily action; and this is the first level from which one ascends to the service of the Almighty, which then includes all the positive *mitzvoth*. These come to cling to the Almighty; it was for this reason that man was created. He was not made to aggregate riches or to manufacture monstrous structures. He should, thus, search out all that will carry him to love the Almighty, to learn wisdom, and to look for the faith with the good works of his life. At that point, the Lord will be in debt to him and open up the eyes of his heart, and He will make once more in him a new soul, and after that, he will wind up adored by his Creator in his lifetime. The Word of God is in this way given to men with hearts. Keep in mind Moses. God coaxed him out of Egypt for a long time to provide him with a heart for the Lord God Almighty.

Jesus was perfect in life and in death—a heart of obedience and filled with pure love, obedience unto death on a cross, the most genuine heart for God in total submission and obedience for the ultimate victory of salvation.

One thing can be learnt from these men with hearts for God—man is obliged to search out the purpose for which he was created. This he defines as a close attachment to the Almighty. A man is compelled to seek by all means that heart that will bring him to love the Almighty Holy God deeply, to find and study His wisdom and to search for the faith until such time when he shall be worthy that the Almighty will open up the eyes of his heart and that he will become the beloved of God in his lifetime, to become wisehearted.

Having two failed marriages is no ordinary feat; it's a disgrace for a man who says he loves God. I must admit that I had married an atheist woman, and I aimed to please her. So, I did not talk much about God with her, nor did we have a deep spiritual connection. It was a human connection without the spiritual binding of two souls. It did not surprise me that it ended in utter bitterness and a total evil path with the ultimate aim to annihilate me. It was dark and sinister. I had survived a self-practised suicide attempt on my life, and I had survived sixteen years of a second marriage that ended in unfaithfulness and defiled the marriage in adultery. No one is safe from this enemy; it is real, and sin is like a roaring lion. Such failures have been painfully awkward in my life, so I had to seek the wisdom of the Word of God to understand them. I could be still saved by His grace and become a person who imparts wisdom to others despite the foolishness of my past.

I have regrets in my life, and the ones that are the most profound are the ones of my youth, when I failed to seek the wisdom of the Lord in all my decisions I made emotionally. So, I had to go back to the beginning—to the Tree of Knowledge of Good and Evil.

I turned to the book of Genesis 2:25. "And they were both naked, the man and his wife, and they were not ashamed." This reference to clothing is a reference to the "outer vessels." So, to explain it, the man and woman, from the aspect of their formation, were without outer vessels. But they constituted only from the aspect of the "inner vessels," which extend from the system of holiness. And therefore, they were not ashamed; that is to say, they did not feel their deficiency, for shame is a matter of feeling deficiency. In Psalm 66, the Bible teaches us the reason for the sin of the Tree of Knowledge. The verse "Come and see the works of God: For man was first made by God and Adam was made Holy." He was constituted from only the aspect of the "inner vessel," which extended from the holiness of God. They were not ashamed. Adam was the handiwork of the Holy One. Blessed be He Almighty God. But because of the cry of loneliness, Adam spoke to God and said that there was no one suitable to be his helper. As for Eve, God apportioned to her even more intelligence than the man (Genesis 2:22). The Bible says, "And the Lord constructed the rib" (*vayiven*, the Hebrew word for *constructed*, which is close to the Hebrew word *binah*, meaning "intelligence"). So, He made the helper more intelligent so that she would be a suitable helper.

How then did the serpent beguile the woman? Did she suddenly become a fool? Did she not know that they should be wary of the cunning serpent? This story becomes difficult to understand from another angle. "He was more cunning than all the beasts of the field" (Genesis 3:1). Was this cunningness enough for the serpent to beguile the intelligent helper first? After all, it seems the target for the serpent was the holy man that God made in His own image. So, the helper accepted this utter stupidity that, if they ate from the Tree of Knowledge, they should become gods. Further, the passage in *Genesis* adds later that they did not eat from the Tree of Knowledge out of a desire to become gods, but simply because the tree was good for food, and it was a delight to the eyes (Genesis 3:6). This, at first sight, seems to be a simple, basic animal desire.

I wanted to go deeper to pray for more understanding about this, so I felt it was necessary to examine the two discriminatory senses—one that allows human beings to distinguish between good and evil, and one that allows us to distinguish between true and false. The Almighty, blessed be His holy name, planted in all creatures the first discriminatory sense, a physical sense that helps a person recognize when something is bitter or sweet. A person usually rejects something that has a bitter form or taste and is more disposed to that which has a pleasing form. However, in the human species, this is on a higher level because the Almighty had implanted in human beings a mental force, namely the ability to reject matters of falsehood and vanity with absolute abhorrence and bring ourselves nearer to Him with real-life matters of truth and benefit. This ability to distinguish between truth and falsehood is not found in any other species—only in man. Man attained this second ability as a result of the advice of the serpent. For at his formation, man possessed only the first discriminatory sense—the power to distinguish between good and evil, which was sufficient for all his needs at the time.

Now let's be rational and understand this more practically with an example. If a righteous man was rewarded according to his good works in this world and wicked men were punished for their wicked evil deeds in the world, then holiness would be clearly defined to us in terms of the existence of "sweet" and "good," whereas the "other forces"—of evil—would be clearly defined to us in terms of the existence of "bitter" and "evil." If this were the case, then the discriminatory sense of choosing, with which God commanded us, has reached us by His word in Deuteronomy 31.

One can see from the beginning of time that the Word of God and His commandments were a shield of protection against the evil that existed in the world: *Do not eat of the fruit of the Tree of Knowledge, for you will surely die.* It was the Word of God, and where His Word was kept, His Spirit of guidance was present in His Word, and that Spirit was in the man. The woman was created by God to be his intelligent helper and for the loneliness that Adam had experienced for which he cried out to his Creator.

It all changed when the serpent entered the garden, so let's examine this more closely in Genesis 3:1. This force of evil (*sitra ahra*) began by saying, "Has God said that you might not eat of any tree of the garden?" The understanding I get from this passage is that the serpent started talking to the woman because the Holy Almighty had not directly commanded her, but it was Adam who'd received the commandment.

So, the cunning serpent asked her, by way of clarification, how she knew the Tree of Knowledge had been forbidden.

Maybe all the fruits in the garden were forbidden. And the woman said unto the serpent, "Of the fruit of the garden we may eat; but of the fruit of the tree which is in the midst of the garden, God has said; You shall not eat it, neither shall you touch it, lest you die."

There are two precise points here to be noted in this passage; first of all, "touching "had never been forbidden, so why did the woman add on this extra prohibition? And secondly, she cast some doubt on the words of the Almighty, heaven forbid. For the Almighty said, "You shall surely die" (Genesis 2:17), whereas the woman said, "Lest you die." Is it possible that she did not believe in the word of the Lord, heaven forbid, even before the sin of the actual eating of the forbidden fruit had taken place?

Nevertheless, we must perceive that the answer of the woman was directed to the question of the serpent. First, she knew well what the Lord had forbidden. All the trees of the garden were sweet, pleasant, fit to eat, except for this tree in the middle of the garden, which she had come close to touching, and she felt that its taste was more bitter than death itself. And so, she had proved to herself, through her own powers of discrimination, that there was a danger of death even from touching. She therefore adduced an additional prohibition to that which she had heard from her husband, for none is as wise as a person who has knowledge from personal experience. And, thus, she said, "Lest you die," and made this depend on mere touching. She was apparently of the opinion that this answer should be sufficient, for who can contradict the sense of taste of another person? Yet the serpent contradicted her and said, "You shall surely not die: for God knows that in the day you eat from it, then your eyes shall be opened and you shall be as God knowing good and evil" (Genesis 3:4, 5, and 6). One may be precise here and ask, what is the relevance of the "opening of eyes" here? Nevertheless, the serpent was letting her know of something new and enlightening; he was proving to her that it was foolishness to think that the Lord had created something evil and harmful in His world. Quite clearly, according to the serpent, it was not evil or harmful.

However, the bitterness that you taste even when you come within touching distance is something that comes only from you. This eating will take place on your true high levels. You are, therefore, in need of extra holiness at the time of the action of eating, so that your full attention to obedience remains intact, so that you will still be able to give pleasure to the Almighty by your obedience to his commandments for your good.

The fruit appears to you as evil and harmful only in order that you should understand that extra holiness is required of you. This should be interpreted to mean that, if the action of eating will be performed in righteousness and in purity, then "you shall be as gods knowing good and evil." In other words, God made all things good, so Adam was created good, and evil was not supposed to be his portion. God implanted in us the power of discrimination so that we should recognise by ourselves that which benefits us and keeps us from harm.

In these scriptures, they cast doubts of what the serpent was saying, for the Almighty Himself did not inform the serpent of these facts. But the serpent anticipated this objection and said, "For God knows that on the day you eat of it, your eyes will be opened." By this the serpent meant to say, "It was superfluous for the Almighty to inform you of this fact because He knows that if you are careful to eat of the fruit in an aspect of holiness, then your eyes will be opened by yourselves, so as to understand the elevation that is contained in this action. For you will be aware that the fruit will be amazingly sweet and delicious. There was therefore no need for the Almighty to inform you of this, for it was this reason He implanted in you the power of discrimination so that you should know what can harm you (disobedience)."

Almost immediately the Bible says, "As the woman saw that the tree was good for food, and that it was a delight to the eyes, and the tree was desired to make one wise, so she took of the fruit of it and did eat; and she gave also to her husband with her, and he did eat." This is to say that she did not rely on the words of the serpent but went and investigated for herself with her own knowledge and understanding. It further became clear to her that "the fruit was to be desired to make one wise." That is to say, this tree has in its power to give delight and desire from a distance much more than any other tree in the garden, which is the meaning of "to make one wise." And it was for the sake of performing this action of eating that they were created. It was, in fact, their whole purpose in life, as the serpent beguiled and disclosed this to her. She did eat and also gave to her husband, and he did eat with her. The Biblical verse is precise in its usage of the words "with her"; that is to say, with the same pure intention as hers, namely only in order to impart and not for his own needs. The verse indicates this by saying that she gave to her husband "with her," that is to say, with her in holiness.

We may now come to understand the deep meaning of the whole of this story, avoiding mistakes that are deduced through a superficial reading of the Bible. For this Tree of Knowledge of Good and Evil was constituted from the aspect of the "empty vacuum." All of Adam extended from the system of holiness, whose objective is to impart. As described in the *Zohar*, Adam, the first man, never attached to him anything of this world. It was for this reason that the Tree of Knowledge was forbidden to him just as it was to his source and to the whole system of holiness. For he was separated from the "other force" of evil (*sitra ahra*) because of their "difference of form," which was a separation made when God formed him from the dust and made him in His image in holiness. Thus, Adam was also commanded against it and warned against becoming joined to it. For he would then be separated through it from his holy source, and he would die just as the "other forces" of evil (*sitra ahra*), and the shells are dead because of their being opposed to and separated from the system of holiness and eternal life. Now we know Satan, who is the poison of death and also the angel of death—clothed himself in the serpent and went down and seduced Eve with untrue words, saying, "You will surely not die." You might wonder: *How did this serpent beguile the woman?*

Now you well know that a lie will not be believed unless some truth is attached to the beginning of it, so the serpent, first of all, told her that the whole purpose of the creation was "to correct this tree"; that is to say, to transform the large vessels of "receiving" into "imparting," for man would in the future transform the form from receiving instructions into imparting them. This is a true statement; thus, the serpent was fortunate in claiming matters that were true, and as a result, the woman came to believe him. Then she was preparing herself to receive the enjoyment only in order to impart it, and it happened: automatically, the evil flew out of the Tree of Knowledge of Good and Evil, and it became only a tree of knowledge of good.

Let me try to explain this to you in a practical way of edification. A person who vows to refrain from a certain lust *before* he tastes it and becomes accustomed to it is not similar to a person who vows to refrain from a certain lust *after* he has tasted it and becomes attached to it. Thereby, the first person can obviously abstain himself from his desire once and forever, which is not the case for the second person, who needs extra effort in order to withdraw gradually from his craving, until he is entirely free of it. Our example here is very similar. For when the woman had not tasted the fruit of the Tree of Knowledge of Good and Evil, and she was totally in the state of imparting, it was easy for her to eat the first bite with the intention of revealing pleasure in a state of absolute holiness. But after she tasted it, she became bound by an intense craving for the fruit of the Tree of Knowledge. She was unable to withdraw any more from this craving, for it was already out of her control.

Whoever marries his childless dead brother's wife in a levirate marriage for the sake of her beauty or for the purpose of physical enjoyment, it is as if he was committing a sexual crime. And they made a decree forbidding the first act of sexual intercourse as well, in case it led to the second act of intercourse, and as in the statement of Adam, "I did eat, and I am still eating." This is to say that even at the time of eating the fruit, he could hear that the Almighty was angry at him for this. For he was no longer able to stop eating of the fruit since he had become attached to it with a strong desire. Thus, the first eating of the fruit took place when they were in the state of holiness, but their second eating was in great depravity.

We may now comprehend the severity of the punishment from eating from the Tree of Knowledge, on account of which all humanity was destined to die. The Almighty Holy God, blessed be his name, had warned Adam, "On the day you shall eat of it, you shall surely die" (Genesis 2:17). The reason for this was that the great amount of receiving became drawn into his body from the "empty vacuum," and the "upper light" could no longer exist together with it after the "contraction" had taken place. As a result of the eternal breath of life, mentioned in Genesis 2:7, as man became a living being, *nefesh* was compelled to leave his body, and his existence became dependent on crusts of bread. This life was no longer eternal as it had been previously when it was totally for himself; now, it was similar to a drop of the sweat of the eternal life. That is to say, life became divided up into many drops in such a way that every drop was a part of a previous life. These drops are the sparks of the soul that were divided out and distributed to all the descendants of Adam, so that his descendants from all the world, throughout history until the last generation, will complete the purpose of this creation.

All form one chain of existence in a way that works of Almighty God have not changed at all as a result of Adam's sin of eating from the Tree of Knowledge. But this light of life, which was to be found concentrated in one mass all at the same time in Adam, the first man, became extended and lengthened into a great chain that revolved through a wheel of change and differing form until the completion of the "correction," without any break in it at all. For, the work of the Lord must continue to endure and exist and "in holiness one ascends, and one does not descend." It's essential to understand this well.

What happened to man also happened to all creatures as well. They all descended from the aspect of eternity through the wheel of change and differing form, just like the man. For man and the rest of the world have both an inner and outer aspect, and the outer aspect continually ascends and descends in accordance with the inner dimension: the flesh man and the spirit man.

This is the meaning of the verse Genesis 3:19, "Through the sweat of your face shall you eat bread." That is to say, in place of the previous "breath" (*neshamah*) of life that the Lord had breathed into his nostrils, there was now the "sweat" of life in his nostrils.

The first murderer the creation had seen was Satan, for, by his deception and lies, he committed murder. He killed what had made for eternal, everlasting life. Adam, the first human—made in the image and utter holiness of God—was now destroyed by death. Cain was of an evil seed, and from the beginning of time, there have been two kinds of seed in this world. For, in his arrogance, when God questioned Cain about his brother Abel, he responded with utter contempt, "Am I my brother's keeper?" The second murderer was Cain. The world is filled with good and evil seed.

Jesus reveals this fact in the exchange with the discussion of Abraham's seed and Satan's seed.

> Why do you not understand My speech? Because you are not able to listen to My word. You are of your father the devil, and the desires of your father you want to do. He was a murderer from the beginning and did not stand in the truth because there is no truth in him. When he speaks a lie, he speaks from his resources. For he is a liar and the father of it. But because I tell you the truth, you do not believe me. He who is of God

hears God's Word: therefore, you do not understand, because you are not of God.

—(John 8:43–47)

Today, the world is in the grip of the old sin; many men, women, kings and queens, princesses and princes, presidents and prime ministers have all sinned in sexual immorality. The world is plagued by it, and the sacredness of marriage is still being ripped apart in a fallen world among stiff-necked people who lack the knowledge of the Holy Word of God. The enemy is laughing at the world; it's time for the world to rise and answer the call of holiness and the glorious kingdom of God to correct it forever.

If you know that your ending is far-more-significantly greater, more holy, everlasting, and, above all, sinless, you would want to run towards it and get away from the world.

Jesus saith unto him, I am the way, the truth, and the life: no man cometh unto the Father, but by me.

—(John 14:6 KJV)

We have come a whole circle, and here in this passage, Jesus tells us this: You do not hear, because you are not of God. Obedience to the Word of God and repentance are the first steps to salvation and redemption, first steps towards the pathway to a Holy Almighty God, blessed be His holy name.

CHAPTER 22

THE RETURN TO ISRAEL

I returned in May 2019 to Israel. Now I had a backpack, a tent, and hiking boots, and I was ready to walk this Holy Land on foot once more. I knew the Lord would call me back to teach me some things that I ought to know. Now, from becoming a man who was intensely learning the Word of God, I was to become a man who would impart to others. Tel Aviv has something missing about it, so I did not stay there for more than two days. I boarded a bus and went to Kyrat Shimon to meet up with a trail from the north of Israel that would lead me to the Sea of Galilee. I had read about the Yarden, the Descender, in one of Johnathan Cahn's books. It was an excellent inspiration (Ephesians 4:8–10, Philippians 2:3–9, James 4:10), so the idea of my journey was to get as close as possible to Mount Hermon in the Golan Heights and make my way hiking through the wilderness of this Holy Land. I wanted to follow the Yarden from the highest place to the lowest place in the world, the Dead Sea. My spirit wanted to experience a humbling of my body to lift my soul to a level of ascent. Ever since my baptism in 2016 and my surrender to the Lord, I found the strength to stop my addiction to smoking tobacco, something I never thought possible; my desire to become transformed continues to evoke my spirit each day. I find myself trembling in fear at the thought of my judgment. I find myself asking the Lord to wash me clean—my thoughts, my actions; it's like a relentless desire to be standing in holiness in front of Him. They never stop, these desires of becoming holy. There is a fire that is raging, and it's a good fire in my soul.

The biggest challenge I faced was trying to get Map 1 for the hiking trail. I had visited every bookshop, army store, and the outdoor shops in the famous Dizengoff shopping malls of Tel Aviv. I met an American Jewish woman who was on the same quest as myself. We could not get Map 1 in Israel, period. I even called the publisher of the trail maps, only to be told that they were out of stock. The Jewish lady said to me, "You'd better get used to Israel." I smiled and wished her all the best. "So long." I waved at her saying, "Who knows? I may even catch you up on the trail." It never happened because God had other plans for me, and I was going to go without a map or any navigation device. I always had the trail signs and was sure to meet up with someone along the way.

I arrived by bus at the town called Kyrat Shimon. My Swedish backpack weighed around seventeen kilograms, way too heavy for a hike. I had become complicated. I had packed too much stuff for such a long journey. I was slightly overweight and apprehensive of my journey and my fitness. I always knew I was strong, but when you are fifty years old and back on the trail after twenty years of family life, a lot of survival skills need to be learned anew.

I had lived among my native Aboriginal people in Australia and learned many Outback survival skills. I always knew those instincts would still kick in in times of peril; those of a native origin are forever embedded inside of you. However, I was not genuinely relying on those skills. I was walking now as a man of faith, a man of God, and Jesus was my provider for all things.

I had survived many things in my life, many setbacks, and I had accomplished many things at personal sacrifice. I was not without fault and didn't consider myself a perfect man. Still, I never gave in to falsehood, and I never held a job just to advance my career. I never stepped back when it came to speaking the truth. I never clambered over people to promote myself. I had a natural-born desire to be close to God. I was not a perfect man because I could not contain my anger against injustices I had seen in the world. I could not stand false and fake people. I disliked fakery. I spoke the truth and was cut down because of it. I stood against governments and states, held steadfast in courts fighting for human rights and the rights to see my children, who'd been stolen from me by ungodly women and the evil systems of a sinful world. As I raged inside against such unclean things, I sometimes forgot that God was always in control of my life, even when I had made a mess of it and married women who were atheists. I was trying to plough a family field like an ox tied to an ass. I learned that the Scripture was true; women were the smarter ones because they were able to think ten steps ahead of the man, and they held the fruit of desire.

I was now much older and wiser from it all; it did not interest me anymore, the fruit of desire, and I was to learn some powerful things on this journey that God had put in my spirit to undertake. So, yes—I was now a man walking on faith.

As I approached the central bus stop in Kyrat Shimon, I noticed two young couples sitting on a bench with a muzzled dog that was ready to bite at anything and anyone who came close to them. I passed them by with a smile as I went inside to make inquiries about the bus I had to catch to get to the trail. Unable to speak Hebrew, I walked back to the other hikers as my source of information. Dannie was a charming Jewish girl who greeted me with a smile; her boyfriend was a delightful person, and as we shook hands, the vicious dog with the muzzle pounced on me. I had forgotten about the dog sitting under the table. The other young couple held the dog back, and I was glad he was muzzled.

Looking at the dog, I inquired, "Has this dog been abused by people?" Sure enough, the response I got from them was they had rescued the dog from terrible abuse. The dog had no faith in strangers, had become fearful, and had no confidence in man or its surroundings.

"Are you going to join us on the trail?" they inquired. I explained to them I was travelling alone; I had no map or navigation tools but relied only on trail signs and was walking on faith.

"Now, I meet you lovely people, and that is the blessing. However, may I suggest, can I bribe your dog with food? Because, if there is one thing I need to do right away, it is to gain the confidence of this dog. He must know I am a friend and not a threat. Food is the key to building this relationship. A dog desires food."

We all laughed as I had found four new Jewish friends to accompany me on my journey across the Holy Land for a while. I, therefore, set out to make friends with the muzzled dog, as I had no intention to be mauled by a dog on the start of my journey. This vegan thing among people had become popular with dogs as well, because this dog was vegan; he ate cucumber. As I attempted to feed him pieces of cucumbers through his muzzle, it was proving to be rather tricky, because each time he snapped at the food, I felt he was going to bite my fingers off. And I decided that he'd had enough veganism forced on his life by his new owners. Dogs chew bones—give me a break. I was slowly getting the hang of it, feeding him through his muzzle, and our trust was starting to develop, but an abused dog is a mentally traumatised animal, and he could turn the tables at any time. It made me sad to see what humans can inflict on one of God's creatures by the evilness of abuse. We don't realise it, but violence has no goodness attached to it; it victimises both.

Soon we loaded our gear on the bus, but we were stopped; the driver did not accept it—no dangerous dogs muzzled on this bus. He protested in Hebrew, but to no avail. The couple with the dog unloaded their gear and said they would find another way to get to the trail. So now there were just the three of us. In the hurry of matters at hand, we all parted, and as fate would have it, I did not have to worry about a dog made dangerous by human beings.

We made our way to Tel Dan and found the start of the trail from north to the south. It was not the trail I had intended, yet I just allowed God to be in control of my journey and knew He had a purpose in everything. We started the walk on the trail, and it was a hot, humid afternoon. Dannie and Ehud were a delightful pair, very friendly and accommodating, hailing from the West Bank of Israel. I was glad to find such excellent people to accompany me along my way; as a matter of fact, I had been meeting charming people in Israel since my arrival—people who went out of their way to help a stranger. Outspoken and friendly, they always want to know if you like Israel and its people.

I always responded truthfully that the stories of the Bible, of Abraham, Jacob, Moses, and King David are as close to my heart as they are to them. And I noticed a surprise when I started telling them, "I am Jewish because my God is the God of Israel." I received only smiles and help from these beautiful people I met along the way to the hiking trail.

Now I had two new friends, Dannie and her boyfriend, Ehud. Jewish people have come from every other nation as they were exiled and dispersed away from the Holy Land. Dannie had an Argentinian background, while Ehud had a Russian Jewish history. They have some lovely women in this tiny nation; Dannie was a pretty girl, and as I was walking behind them, I heard her humming and singing a jazzy song. There was a voice there, a powerful jazz voice. I had to tell her what I thought of it sometimes along the way.

It was hot and humid as we walked through the trail, and on the left-hand side of the landscape, I could see the snow-capped Mount Hermon. I had my shofar with me and wanted to blow it at the start of my journey but was embarrassed by what my Jewish friends would think of it. I did not want to offend anyone here, so I decided I would find a quiet place to pray in the evening and blow my shofar and praise God for his mercy and goodness in my life. I soon learned that my Jewish friends were not firm believers and had some issues with the religion. I would later find out more about how they felt about it. I also realised they were young at heart and that spiritual maturity was a process.

We found a cluster of trees, a wooden table, and two benches in the shade of a tree near a beautiful stream of water. Down went the backpacks as we ducked into the inviting shade and the coolness of the beautiful water stream. It was such a beautiful sight. Across us was a field with cows, and we were in prime farmlands. "Now, you may not know the traditions of being an Aussie swagman," I announced. "Still, I am just that type of guy, and I never go to the bush without my billy (kettle)." I had bought myself a lightweight aluminium billy before starting my journey. I did not know that Jewish people had anything in common with an Aussie swagman, but we were soon going to find out. I dug into my backpack and whipped out my billy. I looked at my new friends and said, "Now, are you ready for a tasty brew of coffee?"

"OMG." Their faces lit up like sunrise. "Oh, you made my day," Ehud exclaimed. He was ecstatic and excited. "Oh, man," he exclaimed, "you just made my day. We boil our coffee in Israel, and that is the best thing ever." I corrected him almost immediately.

"My friend, this is not a 'kettle'; it's called a 'billy' back home in Oz. So, we are going to stick to calling it a 'billy.' It's more personal because it's a friend to an Aussie swagman. Two things are your friends out in the Outback: a fire is one, and a billy is the other, mate," I replied.

He sweetly embraced my billy and said, "A billy it is, indeed." We lit up a fire. I ate the rest of my sandwich that I had preserved from Kyrat Shimon and sat down to brew ourselves an excellent cup of coffee.

We turned on some music and grooved out to the atmosphere of love and happiness. It was turning out to be an excellent time together.

Soon we were back on the trail again, feeling refreshed and getting used to walking in the heat of the warm summer Israeli sun. As we made our way, we suddenly saw two people appear from among the bushes, a young Jewish chap with a Dutch girl who had joined the trail from a different direction. Now there were five of us once again. As we started chatting to the new people, it soon branched off into two separate languages. I spoke Dutch, having lived in the Netherlands. The system of justice so educated me in everything Dutch, and I could even talk about the style of Dutch lawyers. After all, I had seen it all and was thoroughly integrated with it.

I had employed so many lawyers in my lifetime in that nation that all the income I ever earned, I gave back to the oppressive system—every cent of it back to the system that demanded it from me. Oh, yes. I am all Dutch now. We chatted away in Dutch and walked a few miles till we all reached a new stream of water near a bridge across a highway road. Across the street was a small shopping mall, a fuel station, a McDonald's, and a few other shops; it was weird. For a moment we were back among the civilised, with a feeling of being disappointed. About five hundred metres ahead, there was a camping site where you had to pay a small fee to pitch your tent and make use of the facilities.

We unloaded our gear near the big tree that stood on the banks of a beautiful stream of water. There were warning signs posted, restricting us from swimming in that inviting cold water that was flowing from the mountaintops. I was feeling sweaty and sticky and would have done anything just to get into that water to cool down. The Dutch girl insisted that she was not going to have anything to do with buying food in any of the shops. And she was annoyed at the sight of the McDonald's across the road. She was not keen to pitch her tent under the big tree just across the street and requested her Jewish friend that she'd met along the way if he could find a place where she could get away from it all and sleep under the stars. I exactly knew where she was coming from and that this was not her idea of camping for the night.

As for my mates, we just went with the flow. We walked across the highway, got a nice cold bottle of Coke, a couple of falafel sandwiches, sat at the tables, and got stuck into that and a few good laughs. I knew we would be back in the wilderness the next day, so "Enjoy it while you still can" was our attitude. Nevertheless, I must say that nothing beats the taste of cold water on a hiking trail down a warm country road. You appreciate the least the greatest.

The group decided to stay put and sleep under the big tree next to the highway; it was rocky ground, and I knew it was going to be a rough night ahead. I had an excellent twilight tent from Mammoth, so in a few minutes, I had it up and ready for the night. I took my shofar and my *tallit* (Jewish prayer shawl), and slowly disappeared, walking back up the trail into the wilderness. I knelt and prayed for all my friends, for members of the church. I prayed for Joanne and my children. I prayed for my new friends, and I prayed for myself.

I stood up, and, looking at Mount Hermon in the near distance, I blew the shofar and gave thanks to our Holy God Almighty. Blessed be His holy name.

I returned to my tent and retired for the rest of the night. The stones and rocks under my tent were not making it a comfortable night. Still, I had no choice. I was hoping my tiredness would take over, and I would be asleep, but it did not happen, As I kept tossing and turning, trying to sleep, a speeding truck would pass by, and I felt like it was going to go right through my tent and kill me instantly. It was not a good idea to camp so close to a highway. The highway was never silent as cars and trucks kept passing by. This ruckus went on for the next two hours, and then the traffic became less frequent. As I lay awake to the much-needed silence, most of the people around me were asleep. Later in the silence of the night, I heard a beautiful sound of a hooting owl on the tree above me. It was such a cute sound, and I assumed that this was not a big owl, but it had to be a small one, a different species of owl, perhaps native to Israel. I would love to have a view of it, for the sound of his hoot was a sequence of the sweetest melody. I reached for my phone and started to record his perfect sequence of hooting. I listened carefully; three whistling hoots, a ten-second break, and then three courses of a different rumbling sound. Then there was a silence for a while, and then the sequence of hoots and three series of that different sound—all in perfect timing and consistently the same. Wow. I recorded my little wise friend, and in my prayerful spirit of the night, I gave thanks to our Holy Creator, blessed be His holy name. I marvelled at His tiny feathered creation singing above my tree. I soon fell asleep.

Early the next morning, we moved out of the location, as everyone was eager to get back into the wilderness. It was a beautiful day, and an early start would allow us to cover some distance before that midday sun beat down on us like a furnace. The weather was getting warmer, as the hot summer months was not the best time to hike towards the southern part of the Judean desert. I was going to make my way to the Sea of Galilee and then walk the Jesus Trail from Nazareth to Capernaum. This journey for me was not just an adventure but a spiritual walk that connected me to God and the revelation of His Word in the Holy Land of His glory. I kept looking at the beauty of the snow-capped Mount Hermon in the distance as we kept moving away from it, walking towards the south.

Now, most of the time, travellers in this group were twenty-five years younger than me, so they were tuned to a different degree on how they viewed life. Nevertheless, I could understand when young Europeans told me they were atheists, but I did not quite expect that would be the case of young Jewish people. The conversation began when the young Jewish traveller told me that he used to be an Orthodox Jew, but the religion did not interest him anymore. He moved away from Israel and lived most of his time in Canada. He was still very much connected with Israel and his Jewish roots, but he had some opinions of his own. We never got deeply into this conversation as we walked along the way. They all knew I was a Christian, but they did not get to grips when I mentioned that I was a born-again Christian. So, everyone was curious about what the difference was. It suddenly amazed me. I was witnessing my faith to four young people who did not know Christ.

I turned to Mount Hermon and began to speak the mystery of the river Jordan. Yes, the Jordan River flows from one end of Zion to the other end, and as it flows, it gives life to the land of Israel. It begins its course in the north at Mount Hermon and flows down to Galilee; then it makes its way through the Jordan Valley and into the wilderness of Judea. And finally, into the Dead Sea, where it comes to its end. In Hebrew, looking at my young Jewish friends, I said, "The Jordan is the *Yardena*."

I had everyone's attention now, and I was preaching, imparting, and realizing some things deep in my heart. The word *yarden* comes from *yarad*. *Yarad* means "to go down, to descend," so Jordan is the descender. All rivers descend, but no river descends like the Jordan. This river descends like no other river in the world. This river, my friends, descends to the lowest place in the world—the Dead Sea. "Do you see the amazing mystery?" I asked.

"Who is this descender? The God of Israel, who brought your ancestors from the land of Egypt into this promised land, is the great descender. God is the Yarden, and He humbled himself, descending from a very high place, and taking the form of man. And as the Jordan descends into the Sea of Galilee, it gives life to the land of Israel. The Sea of Galilee receives this life-giving water, and giving out what it receives, a small outlet flows into the Dead Sea. However, the Dead Sea, on the other hand, gives nothing out and is dead, without any life.

"Do you see it? Why this beautiful land so absorbs me!" I exclaimed. For those who receive Him, Yeshua the Messiah, like the Sea of Galilee, and give out the countenance of His light unto the world by living in the Word and commandments of the Living God of Israel will have life, that eternal life that Adam once had at the beginning of creation. Yet, those who receive it and give nothing out of what they received are as dead as that Dead Sea. God is love, and for this love of salvation to save us, He descended like the Yarden.

"God has a purpose, and it will always be accomplished, no matter whatever view we may have about it, my friends." I stopped talking and just kept walking.

Ehud looked at me and said, "You should meet my dad. He is deeply religious, but we are not. So, you think Yeshua is the Messiah?" he asked.

I replied, "Do you know of anyone else who conquered death and rose again?" There was a silence, and it was all too heavy for everyone to take in such a short time; that's what the revelation of the truth does to people—makes them think, perhaps uncomfortable. As for me, it's like finding a treasure trove; it fills me with joy, and I want to have more of such revelations of God's Holy Word.

We walked on, and Dannie turned on some music and changed the atmosphere from a profoundly spiritual one to one that says, "Let's have some fun along the way." The Dutch girl walked closer to me, speaking in Dutch, and she commented that she was not religious as a person, but she expected Jewish people to be; she was surprised that young Jewish people were not as religious as one would come to expect. What surprised her most was that not many people gave much importance to Jesus and that they did not believe in Him. I smiled at her and said, "You should read Isaiah chapter 53."

I was now the religious man in the group, and no one perhaps was going to talk about spiritual matters with me anymore. It was heavy, this sudden revelation, and it needed time for such words to sink into hearts. We walked on, listening to music as we made our way uphill and down into a valley where we met a beautiful stream of clear, cold water flowing into the land from the mountaintops. There is no getting away from the Word. This river and the many streams keep reminding me of the message delivered. Maybe God had planned it all along the way, and it was no coincidence that He chose these beautiful young people for me to witness to; as for me, I will speak His Word to the ends of the world.

As we all got into the water, it was the most refreshing swim in the world; the summer heat and the long walk made us appreciate the gift of water as the most precious thing in the world. I whipped out my billy to a smiling Ehud, and we brewed some coffee by the beautiful stream in Israel. What a pleasant land. I noticed a lot of Aussie gum trees and was informed by my Jewish friends that they were planted in these areas because they were very swampy in the past, and these eucalyptus trees were used to soak up the water and dry out the swamp. And so, it was true that the young saplings had come from Australia. I stood next to the massive eucalyptus tree, crushed a few leaves, and inhaled the smell of an old friend from back home. I felt connected.

We moved on, making tracks after a splendid refreshing swim and a tasty brew of coffee, and we made our way across the land for a few hours until we reached a vast cemetery that was an historic war-memorial stone structure. In front of the obelisk stood an impressive stone sculpture of a roaring lion. The cemetery was laid out in sound levels and neatly arranged. The stones were yellowish-white, like limestone, and the whole place was a masterpiece of construction. It blended so beautifully into the landscape, appearing as if it had been intrinsically woven into the land. It did not appear as a cemetery alone but more like a nation hugging its fallen sons—an excellent, fitting place to honour soldiers who gave their lives. I had a keen eye to look beyond what my eye was seeing. I was quite sure that the man who designed this place was talking to me in his spirit as I felt the energy of the site. You don't bury a solider. Still, you lovingly hug him as you lay him to rest and make a memory forever visible that can see beyond, by embedding him into the landscape of the nation for which he so willingly gave his life to protect—what a marvellous expression of honour.

I went to pay my respects to the dead and many a fallen soldier. The names of the soldiers who had given their lives in the Golan war were all written in Ancient Hebrew. The roaring lion reminded me of the Lion of Judah—the one who gave His life on the cross. As I gazed upon the sculptured lion, he was sitting on his four legs, with his head lifted and his mouth opened full, roaring towards the heavenly sky. What a beautiful message. I found a shady place under the trees from across the Roaring Lion with my friends Dannie and Ehud. I was thirsty, and the midday sun was beating hard on our backs. I was tired and losing weight.

I drank so much water, but it all seemed to evaporate from under my skin; the relentless thirst was a reminder that we had to fill up our water bottles for the remaining part of our journey. I truly enjoyed travelling with Dannie and Ehud; they were not in any rush to get anywhere by the end of each day. I loved it because it allowed us to be absorbed by the land and its magic at a leisurely pace. The Dutch girl and her Jewish friend wanted to push on and keep going. After they had rested and taken some group photographs, it was time for the group to split. As we hugged each other, our goodbyes done, the Dutch girl and her Jewish friend disappeared from view on the trail that led into the forest, uphill into the mountains. We left the cemetery and went into the small *Kafar* (village); finding a beautiful park and a shady tree, we unloaded our heavy backpacks and decided to cook some lunch and rest for a few hours.

We found a small shop where we bought some bread, fruits, a couple of beers, and a small bottle of wine. Dannie fired up the butane gas stove; chopping up some vegetables and cooking the rice, we prepared a delicious meal. I had picked up a box of cherry tomatoes, a kind I'd never seen before. I sliced them into halves and feather-dropped tiny grains of salt on them. I popped the first one in my mouth, and it exploded into a flavour of cherry tomatoes that I have never known before. My taste buds hit the roof of my palate; the last time I recall this happening to me was in Italy, when I had eaten a salad with black truffle olive oil dressing with a dash of lemon and parmesan cheese. Wow! Naturally grown food in Israel is the best agricultural produce I have ever tasted and known. Unlike the food we are forced to eat by the Dutch and Spanish growers of tomatoes in Europe—developed in the greenhouse, pumped with all kinds of additives, not to mention the genetically modified plants, where 90 percent of the vegetables are filled with water and have absolutely no flavour. All made for the profit and greed of the corporate companies that produce such crap food that makes people obese and sick. Here I was eating the most delicious food in the way it should be grown and consumed, just as nature gives it to us with love from the Creator. What has happened to the world? Greed? Corporate greed?

We had prepared a wonderful lunch with vegetables and rice, and it was bursting with flavour. I had consumed half the box of cherry tomatoes with Ehud, drank two glasses of wine, and it was the best lunch we'd had since we started on the trail. The wind was rustling in the leaves as we settled down for an afternoon nap under the shade of the trees, drifting off quickly into a blissful sleep of love and contentment—what an excellent place.

An afternoon nap under the shady trees with a steady wind blowing among the leaves is like sleeping in paradise. No hotel in the world can provide you with this kind of heavenly luxury as God can do when you sleep in the bosom of His marvellous creation. I woke up precisely with this thought and a thankful spirit in my soul. You see, the secret of happiness is to be thankful to God for everything in your life.

You guessed it: Ehud and I fired up the gas burner and put the billy on for a brew of coffee. It was 3:00 p.m., and we wanted to get moving by 3:30 p.m. We had eight kilometres of a steep uphill climb to our destination on the mountain ridge overlooking the town below. Soon we were on our way, but the sun was still up, and it was a scorching day. As we walked uphill, we came to a small pathway that led slightly uphill; there was also another path that led slightly downhill and a narrow way that went into the thick bushes. We could not see any trail markings; yes, indeed, there was a moment of confusion as Ehud and Dannie were looking at their Google maps app, trying to figure out which was the right way to go. Ehud insisted it was the path that would lead us slightly downhill. So, we took that path and walked the way downhill. The weather was unusually hot this day, and the weather prediction was that it was only going to get hotter for the rest of the week. We were thirsty and kept drinking water. We may have walked two kilometres downhill when we came to a fenced gate that led to a road. We stopped, and Dannie looked at Ehud. I knew we were on the wrong path. I could not see a trail marking.

As they looked at the Google maps and other applications, I knew we were lost; we now had to walk back up two kilometres uphill to where we'd started. It was hard going back up. As for me, I had a heavy backpack, while Dannie and Ehud shared their load between them. It was a tough slog up the hill. Our thirst was relentless. As I tried to drink less and preserve our dwindling water supply, my mouth got dry, my tongue got thicker, and I spoke no more. We walked back to where we got confused and took the other path that led uphill. We walked five hundred metres, and Dannie just dumped her backpack on to the ground. I knew it! Even this was the wrong path—no trail markings. She was now furious and angry at Ehud. She was giving him a real ticking off and holding him responsible for the mess we found ourselves in. I had only half a litre of water in my bottle and still seven kilometres of an uphill climb left. With this hot, humid weather, we were going to be in trouble if we did not make it by sunset. The atmosphere was tense, and a woman was exhausted and upset. I looked at both of them and suggested that we had two options: return to the cemetery, where we knew there was a water supply, sleep there for a night, and start again early in the morning. The second option was to move forward slowly and make it with the water we had and have faith that God is with us, and we would be fine. Apparently, I said the second part wrong.

Dannie flew into a rage; she exclaimed, "Lyndon, you have a staff in your hand, but you are not Moses. Come on, give me a break. You don't hit that rock with that staff, and water comes outpouring from it." I understood her point of view. "How much water do you have?"

"Half a litre," I replied. She was even more frustrated at my response. We had seven kilometres to go all steep uphill.

"I am not sleeping near a graveyard," she said. Ehud was silent because she had given him a verbal bashing.

I looked at Dannie and said, "Don't be upset. If you only knew my life and if you could only fathom what I have experienced and why I have this faith that I have in the God of Israel, you would not question it, young lady. Do we move forward or go back?"

We took the narrow pathway that led us into the thick bushes. And as we made our way through the thorny bushes that scraped our skins like surgical thorns, Ehud and I used our staffs to press the trees down so they did not scratch up this beautiful Jewish jazz singer in our midst. This girl had a beautiful voice.

We kept walking through the bush for about an hour, making our way through the forest, when suddenly I heard the sound of a vehicle. I moved forward, parting the grass in front of us, and, suddenly, it was there—driving straight at us was a white SUV pickup truck, a Toyota Hilux.

A man in a green uniform with a smile on his face stopped near us. I raised my hands, and we all smiled as he got out of his vehicle with the same happy smile. I asked him in English, "Do you have water?"

"How much water do you want?" he replied. He was a Druze police officer in charge of the forest area. As he talked to us in Hebrew and English, he said that he was planning on an inspection trip on the other side but had decided to change his plans and come in our direction instead. I just listened to his confession. He told me that he had family in Australia. He was the most delightful person and police officer I ever met in my life; this was a man with a heart of gold. I quenched my thirst with some of that cold water that he offered and told him that I was praying for the Lord to help us through this one, too.

Ehud told him about our ordeal of getting lost and the confusion that existed at the juncture of the three pathways in the forest. He reassured us that he would do something and inform the authorities who had marked these trails. I got my breath back and said to him, "I was praying Psalm 23 and Psalm 91 in my heart the whole way through. 'Even though I walk through the valley of the shadow of death, I will fear no evil, for your rod and your staff they comfort me.' Remember King David, a man after God's own heart." I said, "I was praying all along, and then you just show up here with that confession and cold water." I just hugged this water angel that God had sent our way. This man was the miracle of the day. God heard my prayer. The two young Jews looked at me as I smiled back at them and said, "Faith. This Holy Mighty God of Israel split the seas and brought your ancestors out of bondage."

He suggested we throw our bags on the back of his utility vehicle; he was going to drive us to the top. We did not even need to climb it up. When we reached the top and stepped out of the vehicle, we were greeted with the most beautiful sight on the plateau of the mountain ridge lookout. There was a range of mountains to the north. Mount Hermon looked majestic with its snow-capped mountaintop in the background. There were sweeping valleys down below, six artificial lakes filled with water, a small town and cars that appeared to be the size of matchboxes winding their way through the highway, a cableway that was redundant from the mountaintop to the valley down below. Yousef, the Druze policeman, informed us that the cable cars were not operational anymore and needed repairs. The organisation was looking for three million shekels' investment to get it back up and running, but it was a risky business, and nobody wanted to invest. So, the system was now lying idle. To see such views, you sure need to get on top of such places.

We had a photo session with our angel who had rescued us and made our day special; then he left us and drove away with that big happy smile on his face—what an awesome man.

We sat there looking at the scenery and smiling at each other. I dug into my backpack and pulled out my billy, lit a fire, and got the brew of coffee going. Dannie looked at me and said, "I am sorry for being so upset. I must say, you have an excellent staff."

I smiled at her and said, "You could say it's all a big coincidence, but you heard the man. He said he was actually going a different way but changed his mind and came our way instead. You see, my girl, faith and works get us to places when it seems impossible." She was a nice girl. She hugged Ehud and told him she was sorry. He just smiled at me and hugged his girl. I left them alone and walked away to a quiet place and turned on *Psalms* by Shane and Shane. I was singing Gospel songs and thanking the Lord for what He had done for us this day. Praising the Lord on mountaintops is an extraordinary thing, indeed. I watched the sun go down and the moon and stars come up. I was singing and praising His holy name. My whole being transformed into a different state of life. I bowed down and prayed as my heart was overwhelmed for what God had done for us. I prayed to the Holy Spirit of God to be ever present in our lives. I understood mountains that night, and I followed why men of God climbed mountains seeking the presence of the Lord. It's a platform, a higher elevation into a different heaven, one that brings you to a different realm in the spirit of the Lord.

I returned to where we were camped, found a mattress from the supply shed, dragged it on the floor, and slumped on it with my sleeping bag. The wind came blowing through the trees at different intervals, and you would hear it rustle in leaves of the trees ahead, and then it came blowing past you. A beautiful cold wind, and then it would stop. A few minutes later, you would hear the rustle again ahead of you before it hit you once again. I was gone—I fell asleep with the stars above me. There was no else on the mountaintop; it was just us.

I woke up in the morning, lit a fire, and got ourselves a brew of coffee going. Ehud was slumped on a mattress in the distance. Dannie was sitting on the wall looking all swollen up. Her lip was swollen, her eyes were swollen, and she was not happy. I went to my bag and got some anti-allergy pills that I had picked up from the pharmacy in Sweden before I'd departed to Israel. I gave her these pills and a glass of water. It was like some kind of magic potion. Within thirty minutes, the swelling disappeared, and she felt better again. I left her a strip of these pills. "Keep them," I said. "Next time you wake up and look like a beautiful Chinese girl, you know the medicines that makes you Jewish once again." We laughed.

"I was shocked," she said, "when I woke up looking like I had gone through plastic surgery."

A few more days together, and I knew we would part ways. I cannot explain everything that were coincidences, but somewhere in my soul, I hoped these young Jewish people would turn and see the image of Jesus Christ in their hearts. I never was going to impose my spiritual truths and views, but right here, if there was a testimony of Emmanuel—that amazing *God with us*—then He was right there with us on this mountaintop. Maybe this was the reason I ended up with these two lovely people, and I hoped the miracles we had seen along the way would illuminate their minds away from their religious confusion and just look up to the God of Israel with a big heart. As for me, I silently whispered, "You can use me, Lord, for I will walk across the world for You and confess Your love." We departed from the mountaintop and headed down on the trail to the valley below. The going was great because it was all downhill, so we made good time and covered a fair distance. We came across several groups from the opposite side who had started the deep trail south on their way north.

They all told me my backpack was way too heavy. I felt like a stubborn mule who was saddled with the heavy load as a punishment. I decided to get rid of stuff and lighten myself at different stops. I got rid of my winter jacket and hung it on a tree, for anyone who needed it on their winter trek up north. I got rid of some clothes and put them in a wooden box at a campsite where people leave all kinds of stuff, including books and maps for fellow travellers on the Israeli trail. I did not feel any difference, because my bag still felt the same—heavy.

I just kept going. The days were getting hotter, and I started to get darker. Many people don't realise that brown people also burn in the sun. We were lying under the shadow and shade of the trees taking a break when the red German woman walked past us in that burning midday sun. We asked her to take a break and join us, but she was on a regimental walk to her destination. "So long, my friend," I whispered.

We were not going anywhere till 3:30 p.m.; the mountain was on our right-hand side towards the west. That midday sun would soon slip behind the mountain, and this brown man was going to walk in the shadows of the hill with the sun behind the mountain. I had made this arrangement with Ehud earlier. We had it all figured out like two experts. Then we saw this sheila walking with her small backpack and the little guitar that she had strapped on her back. She stopped and looked at us. "Come on over," I called out to her. "Get out of that sun and play a beautiful tune for us, lady." She was Jewish British. She was a delightful character and was travelling alone, so she was happy to have some company. It seemed like she was a loner and had not spoken to many people on her journey. So, now there were four of us. We made sandwiches; tahini and hummus she had brought, along with some olive tapenade. It was a tasty little meal we shared. Coffee for the boys, and it was merely a blissful day. She played a few songs, and soon we all were singing together playing the little ukulele and grooving out to that atmosphere of love and happiness. She told me her name was Ava, and she kept talking a lot about her dad. She sounded very British, and she hated Swedish boys, despite the fact that she had a Swedish boyfriend. She said he was emotionally delinquent; she always talked about her dad. I did not hear her say much about her mom; it was all about Dad.

I looked at her and said, "Are your parents divorced?"

"No," she replied, "they are not divorced, but they don't always live together. They get along, and they don't—you know what I mean?"

I smiled. "Tell me about it. I have seen terrible divorces twice, not that I think it's some excellent achievement, but relationships are demanding these days because expectations are unrealistic with people. However, love conquers all, they say. It's all a perplexing mystery, this relationship between men and women. I can assure you, lady, I have been reading and learning so much about this mystery. With no disrespect to anyone, if a man can stay away from the need of having a woman in his life, he would be better off, but because it's almost impossible; he is better off finding himself a good one. Now that's the million-dollar question for women and men. It's all a significant risk these days because people are lost. The Bible says not to yoke an ox with a mule. If I understood all that and was obedient to the Word of God, I am sure I would have been a different man. Yet, God is holy and pure, unlike us, and because of who He is, we are rescued and saved.

"Forgive me," I said. "Oh, please don't listen to all my ramblings. Go ahead, fall in love. Sometimes it's better to love and lose than never to love at all." We played a few more songs and sang together; she gave me some of her dad's favourite one-liners, and I then popped her a question. "I see how much you appreciate your dad, and I am sure you miss him a lot, but when did you last look him in the eye and tell him that you love him and appreciate all these beautiful things you have said to me about your British dad?" She was shocked and had a tear in her eyes. Well, I tapped her on the shoulder and reassured her with a piece of good advice. "I lost my parents a few years ago. My mom and dad always appreciated whatever I did for them. I never missed an opportunity to tell them they meant the world to me. Now they are gone, and all I have is memories. Make happy memories, child—it's all you will have when they are gone. Tell them, even if they don't say it to you. It's a white thing, I guess. Many people say very little, and some are going to look at me and say, 'Lyndon, he sure meant a lot.' The secret of life is not how you meet people but how you leave them when you say goodbye. How will they remember you?"

"Oh, I like that," she replied.

We saw shadows appearing; the sun had dipped over the mountain. Our pathways were in the shade, and so we made tracks and headed off to a camping site and a water fountain the girls had talked about. In two days, it was Shabbat, and so they wanted to head off to a kibbutz. We were soon going to part ways.

I had mentioned some good lamb chops and beef steak on a barbecue that I would like to have; the last time we had cooked some food in the *Kafar* (village) a few days earlier, I had noticed some mountain goats and sheep grazing on the mountain and valleys in such natural pristine landscapes. There was so much unusual foliage of natural feed. I know such happy, healthy animals do make delicious, tasty lamb chops.

And I had forgotten to mention a beautiful Druze couple in a four-wheel drive who had stopped and given us some cold water and a packet of biscuits while we walked in the hot sun. You rarely refuse anyone who offers you water to top off your bottles along the way. No one says "No" to water. I had never met people who were called "Druze," but from what I had experienced this far, these are very kindhearted and friendly people. They have a peaceful manner about them, and they are kind and respectful. I liked these people in Israel.

We walked for three hours without any more breaks and reached the bitumen roads that led to the camping site. It was a beautiful site with many olive trees; one was the biggest olive tree I had ever seen, its branches spread out so vast that they had installed wooden supports. I could see smoke rising from behind the tree and the smell of food and a barbecue. A Druze extended family were having a picnic, and right there, I saw the same couple who had helped us with water and biscuits a few days back. I could not believe it. They smiled at us, and as I sat there across from them near the water tap, the man came with a plate, and two excellent grilled lamb chops were on it. I could not believe it. I just stood up and hugged that man, and I asked Ehud to translate for me. I just said, "Thank you," for I was too overwhelmed to say more.

Ehud looked at me and said, "There are your lamb chops." We all ate it, and it was so good. I kept that rib bone in my mouth for the taste to linger in my mouth forever. He offered us more, but out of respect for him and his family, we said we were okay; they were beautiful, kind people.

The more I travelled, the more overwhelming everything got. "Is it me, is it just me feeling this way?" I asked myself.

"Such lovely things keep happening to you," Dannie smiled at me and said.

"There is a God," I replied. "Those lamb chops were the best I had ever eaten. Do you suppose the good Lord heard us the other day?" I looked at them and said, "Tomorrow is the Shabbat, and I would love to celebrate it with you guys. It's like a dream come true." I offered the group two hundred shekels to buy the wine and the food for the Shabbat, and we all agreed to go to a place called Wadi the next day and celebrate the Shabbat in the evening over there. I also announced to the group that I would soon be leaving, the next day after the Shabbat.

We camped for the night, and I moved my tent under a tree a little distance away so that I could have a good night's sleep. It was around 2:30 a.m. when a flashlight was shining on my tent and a terrified woman was asking me to please help her. I was startled but calmly got out of my tent and asked her what the matter was.

"Jackals and wildcats are attacking me," she replied. "Look, see their red eyes?" She shined the torch in the direction she was camped.

"Don't panic," I replied as I picked up some stones and walked in the direction of the wild animals. I threw a few rocks at them, and they disappeared into the darkness. Spread out on the bench were all her clothes and shoes; she had no tent and was sleeping on the table. She had come sometime late in the night, walking the trail, and tried to sleep when she heard the terrifying cries of cats and laughing jackals.

I told her to sleep in my tent alone if she wanted or at the table next to my tent where she would be safe and not alone. She told me she was from Poland and that the whole trip had been a big mistake. I tried my best to calm her down, but she never trusted the cats and jackals, and she sure was not going to listen to me. She hurriedly packed her bags, stuffed her clothes and stinky socks, and I walked her to the road, where she was going to walk away in the darkness. I tried to make her stay and told her that, logically, she was safer in the camp than walking alone in the dark. She thanked me and walked away into the darkness.

There was not much I could do to convince her to stay. A wise person does not need advice, and a fool won't take any. I went back to my tent and lay there concerned for her and wishing I had done more to knock out that stubbornness in that woman. Feminist.

The next morning, I related the story to everyone, and they could not understand why she just did not stay. I smiled and said, "I reckon she may have been more afraid of me than she was of the jackals." Ehud laughed; Dannie smiled. The other one did not say a word; she was not a morning person. I added, "Man, she sure was a strange one—hiking without a tent, travelling alone, sleeping in the open, and having no one with her, and she cannot trust people or take good advice. I was once married to such a woman," I added and laughed to myself.

It was another beautiful day. The ladies went shopping; the men washed clothes and hung them out. We brewed some coffee, had a bath under the taps, an excellent shave, and it felt so good. Ehud and I climbed up that big, massive olive tree and just lay on the branches, reading a book, while Shane and Shane were singing *Psalms* on the JBL portable speaker. It was a perfect day to give thanks. Shabbat was soon approaching. We had an excellent ten days of hiking the northern mountains of Israel. God's chosen land. I was here right where He called me back. So many wonderful things had happened, and I was hoping that the Polish girl was safe, and maybe it was okay if I prayed for her instead.

Then Ehud told me about his family. His father was Jewish, but his mother was not; she had to prove that she was Jewish. They had come from Russia with almost nothing but suitcases. He struggled to be accepted as Jewish and explained the struggle he had to go through to become Jewish. He further related to me that his mother follows all the strict Jewish traditions, but she has to go to school at her age and learn all the scriptures and pass a rigorous program. Her wish is to marry her husband once again in the proper Jewish tradition. He told me that was why he did not like religion. "Further," he added, "I get confused when people ask me, 'What does it mean to be Jewish?' I don't know what it is to be Jewish."

I understood why he had issues with the religious system; it is easier for a child to be Jewish if the mother is Jewish but harder if she is not. I looked at Ehud and inquired once again, "Can I tell you what it is to be Jewish? I am a born-again Christian, and I am Jewish. My God is the God of Israel. Let me explain my knowledge and understanding of what it is to be Jewish, and I hope it may help you in some way, my friend." I began to explain the word in Hebrew for "the Jewish people" is *Yehudim*. "It comes from the Hebrew word for *praise, thanksgiving,* and *worship*. A Jew is one whose identity is based on praising God, giving thanks and worshipping the Almighty. A Jew is one whose very existence is praise and witness to the presence of God. It's a cruel world because it's an evil one," I said, "for the ones who were brought out of Egypt and chosen and born to praise God for all He had done for them that they should be the most hated people of the world who were cursed and warred against."

"What was that which was written over the Messiah's head—*King of the Yehudim*?"

"His life was the epitome of the word *Jew*. *His* life itself was a praise to God. Everything He did was to bless, to worship and glorify God. And the world crucified Him, whose life was a praise to God. And yet even in the crucifixion, He did not stop being the King of the Jews. He never succumbed to the evil of the world and overcame evil as He blessed those who cursed Him. See how many people from all over the world come to Israel? The place is filled even with Germans—those same people who burned six million Jews as a burnt offering, making a mockery of God. But yet the Jewish nation holds no grudge against them, nor does it restrict them from coming to Israel. See, we are the children of God, we are the praise and the *Yehudim* of God. I am a born-again Christian, and I am Jewish because I worship, I praise, and I give thanks to the God of Abraham, Isaac, Jacob, Moses, through Jesus the Messiah. This is what it is to be Jewish, my friend."

"You should meet my dad," he replied.

I looked at him and said, "I have met the Son." We shook hands under that olive tree and sealed our friendship.

The girls returned from their shopping expedition, and we soon packed our gear and got a ride hitching our way to a place called Wadi near the mountains. We then followed a trail that took us up into a hill and then downhill into a valley of rocks and a flowing stream that emptied itself into a lagoon that was like a huge bowl made of rock overflowing with water and flowing farther down the path we came. It was the same stream of water that we crossed earlier getting here, and so we were walking towards the direction of the water flow. We swam in the pool of blessed water. Israel has so many hidden treasures that you get to see them only if you walk this land on foot. It's a small nation, but it's immensely blessed. It's unique, and I truly loved every step of the way.

We walked back to the place called Wadi and followed the stream back from where we had come and crossed the road; we found a perfect campsite, with the stream flowing close by, so the sound of flowing water was our lullaby song for the night. Some Jewish farmers came and gave us lemons and oranges; they told us that there were wild pigs in the area but not to worry about them. I gathered some wood and started a fire; the sun was going down, and we were getting ready for the Shabbat. Three stars came out, and the moon rose, and we celebrated Shabbat. We prayed in Hebrew and gave thanks to God for His love and great mercy. We broke bread and ate it with salt. I was given the bread and salt first, being the oldest person in the group. Then we did the same with the wine, said more prayers, and sang Psalms 92, 94, 95, and 96. We sang songs of praise and brought the Shabbat home. We had meat and vegetables and cooked food on the barbecue and drank wine and ate a wonderful meal together. Then I heard the sound of laughing jackals on either side of the camp; they sure made a lot of noise. When I shined the flashlight in their direction, I could see a whole lot of red eyes in the darkness. I reckon it was the smell of the food. We kept the fire burning and sang songs until late in the night, hung up all the food in bags on the tree, crept into our tents, and went to sleep. *Shabbat shalom*, another perfect evening.

On the day of Shabbat, we just rested the whole day till around three o'clock in the afternoon. I was lucky to get a ride back to Kyrat Shimon. The time had come to say goodbye to my Jewish friends. As I mentioned earlier, it's not how you meet people, but how you leave them. We are all on the journey of life, and we are all going somewhere. Some people don't care where they are going, and some people are *hoping* they know where they are going. As for me, I rely on the Word of God, the Gospel of Jesus Christ the Messiah. I am going to the Lord.

> And the WORD became flesh and dwelt among us, and we beheld His glory, the glory as of the only begotten of the Father full of grace and truth. (John 2:14)

I hoped that my Jewish friends would remember me. I hoped I'd left them with love and that they would remember these few days we spent together—the wonders and miracles we saw along the way. When we were thirsty, He gave us water; when we were hungry and complained, we ate only manna. There were two pieces of the finest lamb chops on a plate served for us. I pray that they would find their way and not be lost in the world.

I thanked each one of them for the beautiful Shabbat meal. I hugged each of them, and Ehud and I walked to the road; we firmly shook hands. I hugged them. I said, "Shalom aleichem, my friend. So long. May God bless and keep you, and may the countenance of His light shine on you, and may He fill your life and give you His peace. *Shabbat shalom*." I drove off into the distance towards Kyrat Shimon. Now, I was in the company of another marvellous Jewish individual who was happy to give me a ride all the way to Kyrat Shimon. Another opportunity to spread love. *Shalom aleichem.*

I took a bus and went to Tiberius. It was a busy place at the central bus station. It was filled with many young soldiers, holding their automatic machineguns. Not for a moment did I feel uncomfortable, seeing so many armed young men and women. Many are conscripted to serve the army and protect this beautiful, tiny, holy nation. People are accommodating in Israel. They go out of their way to help you; if you ever hear a different opinion than the one that I just told you, then I am the lucky one. I met only good, amazing people—the ones I spoke to or asked a question or sought some help. I took a second bus that dropped me at a bus stop somewhere near Golani Junction, and I had to wait for a different bus company to get me to Nazareth. It was Saturday evening, and Shabbat was almost coming to a close; public transportation comes alive again. Finally, I arrived in this ancient city once again; the last time I had been here, three years before, on a "hop-on and hop-off" bus tour, it had all happened too quickly. This time around, I could explore the city with the privilege of taking my sweet time. But first I had to find the well-known ancient Fauzi Azar Inn. The Fauzi Azar Inn was once the home of the Azars, a wealthy family residing in the city of Nazareth. It was built in 1830 by Habib Azar, while the inn itself was named after one of his great-grandsons, Fauzi. The family remained in the area until the 1948 Arab-Israeli War, when they relocated to Syria. The nineteenth-century building built from stone has been preserved and restored over the years. The three-story building has original hand-painted ceilings, Turkish marble floors, and limestone arches. The house had been converted into a guesthouse to serve as a waypoint for hikers, travellers, and tourists.

As I inquired for the directions, two older men walked with me through the labyrinth of ancient narrow lanes that anyone would easily get lost in if they did not memorise markings. This ancient city was extraordinarily absorbing. I thanked the men in Arabic and went through the door, walking through history many people before me have passed by. I walked into a courtyard and a beautiful ancient building. It was kept very clean by the staff and had a real Arabic feel to it. I was expecting the smell of *oud* and some incense smoke burning in the corner of the house—a complete feeling of being in an age of time that had passed, where people had lived there so long ago.

I checked in with the staff and got my allocated bed in the eight-bedroom dormitory on the upper floor, next to the big dining room and kitchen. The place was teeming with a lot of Americans, and for the good fortune that had favoured me throughout this journey, I was glad to meet someone from back home in Australia. Mr. Kim Williamson. Now, this bloke was all crashed out on his bed, like he had been knocked out by a sledgehammer, exhausted from all the tours he undertakes each day; it's usually the case when you have a schedule and a time frame to see the Holy Land. The Americans had taken over the kitchen and the banqueting room, and there was an evangelic group with pastors and deacons and various members of a church; this was their night for the Arabic food-cooking training extravaganza (burlesque).

Mr. Kim Williamson was finally awake and was giving me his nod of disapproval at the noisy American club outside the bedroom door. He was in the same dormitory as me, sleeping on a bed from across where I was. "Gidday, mate, how you are going there!" He was astounded and replied, "Fair dinkum, mate. What a pleasant surprise. Fancy a half-caste Aboriginal fellow in these parts." I smiled back at him and said, "I've been on a walkabout for twenty-four years, mate, bugger! Wish I hadn't gone chasing after them silly Dutch sheilas. They have caused me only grief." We laughed together; our friendship was on.

The noise outside the bedroom got only louder, and Williams put his hand up and moved his four fingers towards his thumb as a sign language of the annoyance of the chirpy American crowd outside. We talked about our extraordinary journeys across the Holy Land. "I had come to recuperate in Nazareth before I undertook hiking the Jesus Trail." Kim Williamson looked amazed. "I wish I could do the same, mate," he remarked. "How exceptional that you have this zeal to do these things. My legs are getting too shaky for me to be going on hiking trails."

I smiled at him and said, "I met a bloke who was seventy-two years on the Israeli path just ten days ago. They were from a walking club. Fancy that, mate! I suppose all you need is the zeal and the purpose to do it. As for me," I commented, "I am doing it for the revelation, for the word and wisdom of the Lord. I am ready to wrestle with my angels for that blessing of eternity." Kim Williamson was a delightful bloke, and I was already glad that I'd met him. "I saw the reason we were here," I declared, "so the next three days, were going to be spot-on marvellous." Exhausted and tired from long journeys, I soon crashed out into a blissful slumber at the Fauzi Azar Inn in Nazareth.

My convalescence plan was to stay in bed all day and let every limb and muscle in my body remain motionless in the stillness of complete rest, hoping for the total revitalisation of the extreme power with which these legs carried the heavy backpack over the mountains and had brought me to this resting place in Nazareth. I woke up before midday and went strolling through the narrow streets of the ancient town, keenly observing the street markings and familiarizing myself so that I would not get lost coming back through the winding lattice of narrow streets that interweave with each other, forming a matrix of confusion. I stopped at the entrance of the old Anglican church across with its steps leading up. As I stood there, I met a lot of senior spiritual tourists who were visiting the Holy Land, and some of them for the first time. They were friendly and kind and pleasant to the eye; as I walked with a group of them, I had this sudden urge to impart something that would make their journey even more special. For, the revelation of Jesus Christ is the greatest joy to those who genuinely seek Him. And so, I boldly asked them, "Do you know why Jesus was born in Bethlehem?"

"Go on then," came the reply of this older man next to me.

I explained, "The word *beth* in Hebrew means *house*, and *lechem* means *bread*, so, *Beitlechem* means 'the house of bread.' Remember the Messiah said He is the bread of life. Still, even more importantly, the lambs raised for the sacrifice during the time of the temple did not come from everywhere. The temple lambs raised and appointed for the temple sacrifice came only from Bethlehem. These lambs needed to be close to the temple in Jerusalem.

"Jesse and his son David raised sheep in Bethlehem, and there was a prophecy from Isaiah that the Messiah would come from the seed of David. There was only one place where He could be born, and that was Bethlehem—not just in the place where lambs were born but in the area where *sacrificial* lambs were born. So, that's why the first to see him were shepherds, and then, again, not just any shepherds, but those shepherds who tend the flock at night during the lambing season. And *no*, he was not born in December, as the Romans say, who changed it for their deceptions of the truth. He was born in spring, in the month of Nisan, during the night, as shepherds tended their flock of sheep for the birthing of the lambs. That is the only time shepherds tend their flock, to help the ewes that have difficulty giving birth. It was March/April in the time of Nisan and the time the lambs were born. 'He was the Lamb of God who took away the sins of the world.' Our God is a God of perfection, and only He can do things like He does. It's all there, right from the beginning. In the Holy Book, read Micah 5:2, Luke 2:8–20, Isaiah 53. God is in total control of this world and our lives as He was in the perfection of the birthplace of Jesus Christ. He was the Lamb of God, the holy sacrifice that came from Bethlehem. Blessed be His holy name. Amen." Looking at them, I finished, "You people have a blessed day."

"Thank you," they replied. "That was so beautiful, and God bless you, too."

"Now, I may have said too much here!" There was a skinny lady from my own country, Australia, who happened to be the tour guide; she spoke Hebrew, and she made me well aware of that. I am not sure. Still, I think she did not like me talking to the tour group that she was in charge of. I love the Hebrew language, and so I praised her for her ability to speak Hebrew. I think she was Jewish, but she did not tell me that. She said that she'd lived in Israel for several years, and, looking at me, she said in a slightly annoyed manner, "You know what I think? He was born right here in Nazareth." I remained polite and decent; for a moment, I thought I should tell her about the Nazarene mystery (Zechariah 3:8, Isaiah 11:1–2, Matthew 2–23, and John 15:1–5). But I let my peace remain with me. "Shalom," I greeted her and went into the church for a service of prayer and worship.

When my mate Kim returned from his daily excursion tours, I was happy to eat a good meal and drink a glass of red wine and meet the Christian community that had filled the place. Guesthouses are places where all kinds of strange people are also found. Not everyone is on a spiritual journey, and some people are just there because it's interesting to be in an old place. Then there are others who are there because it's on a bucket list, a tick-off list. You have those who complain about everything and everyone, and then come the boasters, who say, "It's not like this where I come from." Then you have the Germans, who will be terrified to speak if anyone talks about the Second World War in Israel. Then you have the egalitarians who think women are a gift to man and that God made man to serve women. Then you have humble, simple, good-hearted people who are just simply lovely and pleasant. If you understand the spiritual, you will understand the realm in which people operate.

Kim Williamson returned from his daily tour looking annoyed and agitated. He told me about his encounter with an Australian woman on the journey who was rude and a nasty person, very self-opinionated, and that the audacity of the young woman was just awful. I listened to him explain the whole episode and smiled. "You are not alone. I have met one too," I replied. "Fair dinkum, Aussie as well." So, we exchanged our stories and laughed. He was still raging about the audacity of the woman he'd encountered. "Now, aren't you glad you are not married to her?" I said. We laughed some more.

I then proceeded to tell him of a funny incident that I experienced with a Dutch couple I knew in Sweden. I tried to bring some humour to calm him down, to bring about a spirit of fun and laughter. So, I continued, "There is this bloke called Gerard, and his wife is called Gerda." Kim started laughing.

"Is it a joke?" he inquired.

I replied, "No, it's a real incident." I continued, "So, they, for obvious reasons of being married for many years, have gotten used to not liking each other. You know how that goes with some marriages." We laughed some more. "So, they complain to others about themselves. They were invited for a barbecue at my place. Gerard was next to me drinking a beer while I was preparing the steak and sausages on the hot coals. Gerard utilises hearing-aid devices due to some deafness he suffers, according to his wife. His wife was approximately ten to twelve metres away from us, talking to other women, complaining about the deafness of her husband and how difficult it was for her with his hearing. I was standing next to him, thinking he probably couldn't hear a thing that his wife was complaining about him. Gerard looked at me and sipped on his red wine; Then he said, 'Now, she does not know this,' he whispered to me, 'every time I hear her whining and nagging, I slowly turn the volume of my hearing aid to zero, and then I don't hear a thing she says.' A burst of laughter. The curious women inquired, 'What was so funny?' I was embarrassed. I never told anyone this because it was the secret weapon of Gerard and his peace from a nagging wife. I was not going to take that away from him. Later on, that evening, he whispered, 'Gerda goes for therapy.' I realised he was serious about his trauma.

"So, Williamson, maybe we are blessed, after all. Spare a thought for Gerard and other men who are married to women who complain and whine and bellyache about their husbands. I reckon it all comes down to the lack of knowledge and knowing where each one has been placed in the spiritual realm of creation. Perhaps, creation has fallen, and it must get so bad before God takes action. Like the days of Noah, when the Bible says that every single creature was corrupted that it grieved the heart of the Lord God that He'd made them. Perhaps we live in an era when men have failed to be real, true men of God and leaders at home. Probably women have forgotten the values of Proverbs 31. The vows of marriage have descended into a string of complaints and blaming. Thankfulness and humbleness have left the hearts and spirits of men and women in the world today. It is truly a sad state we have in the world, with the relationships between men and women."

It comes down to being a thankful spirit and recognizing the miracle of multiplication. A few evangelical American Christian men joined us for the rest of the evening as we shared the Gospel at the balcony overlooking the city of Nazareth, with all its lights and ancient buildings in the background. What a marvellous way to spend an evening, to be among the company of men who were happy to share and learn from each other without distended pride.

The conversation later turned to me, and they asked, "*The miracle of multiplication.* You mean the feeding of the five thousand and the food of the four thousand?"

"Yes, indeed, there is an excellent revelation about that in the scripture. Did you know the feeding of the five thousand were the Jews, and the feeding of the four thousand were the Gentiles?" The men looked at me, surprised.

"I did not know it."

But there was a senior pastor in this American evangelic group sitting from across us, listening.

"No, I am not a pastor, I don't have a degree in theology, and I don't belong to any denominational church in the world. I am an avid listener to the ministry of William Marrion Branham. No one seemed to know much about his ministry in the 1960s. Nevertheless," I said, "the revelation is in the Word and the scriptures. So, we repeat the scriptures Matthew 14:14–21 and 1 Thessalonians 5:18." I read, "'And looking up to heaven, He gave thanks, broke them, and gave them to the disciples.' You see the picture?" I asked. "Jesus standing there breaking bread and fishes and kept giving and kept giving while it multiplied as they continued distributing the food to the people. The Lord is standing, and the food multiplied in His hands, and it happened with the giving of thanks. That is the revelation of this Word. To multiply your blessings, give thanks, never-ending thanks for one another, for your life. Your children—and ministry if you have one— for your blessings, for your food, clothing, and every other aspect of our lives. Yet, we forget so quickly and complain about many things. While we are standing here breathing and alive, we forget to give thanks, and many people don't multiply their true blessings because of giving no thanks for all He did for us to save us. Such fantastic grace and such undeserved favour over our fleeting lives. We must give Him everlasting thanks.

"I have two more days in this beautiful place with all you wonderful Christian men. Then I am off, walking the Jesus Trail. God has brought me this far with some amazing miracles that I have witnessed on the mountains of the north getting here. I have to meet my angels and wrestle with them and get my blessings before I leave this Holy Land. So, I am going to witness to you some more if you men don't mind?" I asked politely.

"Life is a wrestling bout with God, and you remember the story of Jacob when he wrestled with a man all night. He even got hurt in the process on his hip. The man asked him what his name was. He answered, 'Jacob,' and the man said to him, 'From today, you shall be called 'Israel,' and blessed him immensely. Jacob did not let go of that man, and he wrestled with him to complete exhaustion. So, it's all right to wrestle with God during your times of struggle and stagnation, when things don't always go well. Be willing to be like Jacob until you are exhausted of trying to figure it all out by yourself. You have finally exhausted your foolish self-thinking that you can do it all on your intellectual self. And all you have left is a little strength to hold on to that man—Jesus Christ—and say, 'I am not going to let You go, Lord, until You have blessed me,' spiritual blessings to live this life entirely for Him. That's the blessing we want—to let go of the failures, the past, the tragedies, the sinful, selfish lives we have lived, the desires and the endless greed and ingratitude, and the desires for success and material wealth. And yet, there's the uncertainty of what comes next—the loss of loved ones and the tragedies of sickness and death. And being caught up in the bitterness of it all because we don't know how to ask for blessings, and when we ask, we ask for the wrong things.

"When we have exhausted all, and all we have left is just that little strength in us to surrender ourselves finally and to cling to Him and say, 'I give up, Lord. I am holding on to You because I will not let You go until You bless me to have that breath of life that Adam received before he fell. Oh, my God, bless me with that Holy Spirit of Yours to be completely new and clothed in Your holy grace. Give me that grace, for it's all I ever need, my dear God,

Abba Father. I will never let You go.' You get your true blessing because you asked for something that God wants you to seek. Seek Him and His glory."

This covenant-keeping God does not make promises. He makes a covenant. His word in the Holy Scriptures demonstrates that He is a God of a covenant between Him and man. He created us in His image and made provision to save us by a holy blood sacrifice—blood because it is life. The Jesus covenant is no ordinary one, and this is the stairway to heaven that Jacob saw. This is the man that Jacob wrestled. This is the same Lord God who stood at the entrance of the stairwell while the angels ascended and descended from heaven. This is the man who walked on water, and this is the man who called Lazarus out from the dead. This man is the firstfruits of the one who rose from the dead and conquered the grave. All else may fail in your life, if every disappointment and betrayal has come across you; your wife betrayed you and ran off with another. Even though you gave your employer your very best, they used you and threw you out when they did not want you because you were too honest for their crooked ways, and you felt disappointed and betrayed. You toiled your whole life giving all your sweat and tears and your endless labour to your government, only to find that your pension moved closer to the grave so they hope you go into the grave before the state can release the retirement that you worked for. When you know all of it is vanity and deception, and you look with the eyes of your heart, this relationship with Jesus Christ is the most essential covenant in your life. This is everlasting life. He declared it and said it: "I hold the keys to heaven and hell, life and death." Live for Christ, and in the end, you will live with Christ, and the glory of heaven will be with you.

"I am astonished at the world every day because so many people are still not captivated by this covenant. What kind of blindness is this?"

We spent the next two days in a spirit of prayer and talking about the Word of God and exchanging our testimonies. On the third day, we all parted and left Nazareth. I felt ever so blessed with a new friend, Mr. Kim Williamson from Queensland, and we have been in touch ever since. I walked out the door of the Fauzi Azar Inn and stepped out on to the starting point of the Jesus Trail to my destination, Capernaum.

In Hebrew, "Capernaum" is *Kafar Nahum*. *Kafar* in Hebrew is a village, and there was never a record of any prophet who came from Galilee by the name of Nahum. However, the other meaning of *Nahum* in Hebrew is "a comfort." I was going to the village of comfort, Capernaum, where my Lord started His ministry, the ministry of comfort for all those who turn to Him. Glory, hallelujah.

CHAPTER 23

THE JESUS TRAIL

The Fauzi Azar Inn is the starting point of the Jesus Trail. I took the street to the right and followed the trail signs, which was an orange dot along the way. The ascent led me to steps that were a steep climb, leading me upwards like a stairway to heaven leaving Nazareth, 480 steps to the top. Now before I tell you about what happened to me along this journey, I believe I must share the Nazareth mystery before I move further with you on the Jesus Trail. I stood exhausted by the climb, looking down at the city below me, and the mystery of the city of Nazareth and the Lord Jesus, who lived in this place.

The Bible says that He came and dwelt in the place called Nazareth and what was spoken of the prophets was that "He shall be called a Nazarene." Here was not the prophecy of one prophet but a prophecy of prophets. It was a collective voice of the prophets. They spoke of him as a branch, that he would appear in the world in littleness, in weakness, growing up as a shoot, a sprout. He was born among us on the tree, the genealogy of humanity. His presence on Earth would grow greater and greater, bearing fruit to the world. In Hebrew, one of the words for *branch* is *netzer*. It is used by the prophet Isaiah in his prophecy of the Messiah as the branch that springs forth from the line of David. If you add an ending to the word *netzer*, it becomes *netzeret*, and this *Nazareth* is the name of the place I am standing at telling you my story "Nazareth." So, "Nazarene" speaks of the Messiah the Branch; in that light, what would "Nazareth" mean? The site of the branch. The location of the branching forth of the Messiah. In the most unknown and obscure place of His time, this town called Nazareth today.

So, here I am branching forth on to the Jesus Trail, in a similar way for the same reason God chooses the most unlikely of people like myself, and it's not about who we are, nor does it matter how known or unknown we are, how sinful or imperfect our lives have been. Only that we receive, for when we receive Him through this life, the presence of God will come. And from that life, He will branch out to the world, for we are each called to be His Nazareth (Zechariah 3:8, Isaiah 11:1–2, Isaiah 53, Matthew 2:23, and John 15:1–5).

The sharp rays of the sun were hitting my brown skin and turning it into a darker-chocolate colour, and I was already exhausted from the steep climb out of Nazareth. I needed to push on forward and get to Cana by the end of the day. I had followed the trail map and the signs that led to a place past the last grey house into a valley of shrubs and bushes and rocky terrain, and there were no more trail signs. It is possibly a human-nature thing to always take the easy way out, so I dumped my bag in the bush and walked down the path leading towards the valley below. In case it was the wrong way, I would not have to carry my heavy backpack back uphill. I did not find any trail signs, so I walked back to the grey house and saw a lady at the balcony. I waved at her and shouted out, "The Jesus Trail?" She pointed to the rocky outcrop and the thorny bushes. I thanked her and hopped around the rocks and found trail signs again. I followed them down the valley, and as they led me uphill, I took a break to drink some water. I noticed some cows and two bulls looking at me. Now I have been chased by some mean bulls before, but I had my Moses staff that I carried with me, and I would stop those bulls in their tracks if they made any attempt to charge me.

I was on my way, as the trail signs were more regular and more comfortable to locate. I was singing Gospel songs from some of my favourite artists—Joshua Aaron, Shane and Shane. I was praying and thanking the Lord for helping me find my way when I got lost. It was around noon, and that midday sun was belting down on me. I was now coming close to the Zippori National Park and ducking down under the shelter of pine trees. I took a rest for a while.

I sat there with my fine-grain Barmah squishy kangaroo-skin beautiful leather hat, covered over my face to keep the flies out. I was sweaty and had lost weight hiking this beautiful nation for the past two weeks. Now, of all the species of flies I have encountered, the Israeli flies are not that bad; they buzz around you. Still, they don't attack your earholes, nostrils, and are not persistent, and they don't have special suction pads on their legs or are such experts in somersaulting that, when you chase them away from your face, they somersault, do a flip, and go into your nostrils. These unique skills are found only in the flies that live in Australia. Now, when you hit an Aussie fly with your hand, even if you miss him, it has triggered in him an act of vengeance, where they disappear for a while and return with a whole bunch of mates to drive you insane.

I slept for an hour and then moved on to the Zippori forest. I crossed a stream of cold flowing water, so I stopped to wash and cool off with that water all over my head. It was hot and humid, and I was feeling tired. I saw a couple cross the stream and make their way towards me. Lovely, friendly people, they asked me, "Are you on the Jesus Trail?"

"Sure am," I replied. "Looks like I am the only one on the Jesus trail. I have not met anyone on it, and you are the first two people I have encountered today. *Shalom aleichem.*" They were interested to know if I loved Israel and where I was from, and we talked for a few minutes.

She took out a box of grapes and said, "These are grown by my neighbours; please have some—they are delicious." I took a bunch of them, and then she blessed me with words, "May God bless you. If you are making this trail in this heat, surely there is salvation for you at the end of the road."

What a beautiful thing to say, I thought. "Thank you. May the Lord then bless us with that salvation at the end of the road, too. *Shalom aleichem.*"

"*Aleichem shalom.*" We exchanged that greeting.

The grapes were sweet and truly very refreshing. I was just amazed at what these two people had just told me. I said a prayer for them and asked the Lord to guide them and to bless them for their kindness and for the powerful words they spoke and with which they glorified Him.

I kept walking in the heat of the day and entered the road that led into the Zippori National Park. I was walking on the road and could not see any trail signs, so I followed the map, knowing that I would soon encounter the security-gate entrance. Then I saw *it* lying on the ground—I think it was a brown viper; it had a swollen head that said,

"I have venom glands." It was dead. A vehicle had passed over its body and crushed it. I don't hate snakes, but I don't like them, either. No, I am not Crazy Steve from Australia. I stood there looking at the dead snake and saw a sign, and it was a sign for me; it was a message for me. I stood there and closed my eyes and read the sign, understood the message, and kept walking.

A big SUV stopped behind me as I pulled a little over the side of the road to give way when the driver asked me if he could give me a lift to the gate entrance of the national park. I was happy to get out of the heat for a little while, so I took the offer for the two-kilometre ride to the gate. They were American Jewish people and so kind. I briefly shared my journey details, thanked them, and left them with a blessing, *Shalom aleichem*, my favourite greeting in Hebrew.

I found the trail signs and flowed into the forest heading to Cana. It was around 4:30 p.m. I was approaching the town and walking on the bitumen road when I stopped to notice an old, dried-up, dead serpent. It had probably died a long time ago and became embedded in the bitumen like it was like a thin sheet of paper, a dried-up flat white sheet of paper; as I walked over it, I understood the sign. I realised the message. This was an old serpent that once tried to destroy my life when the darkest times descended on me. And I faced the cruellest people I had ever known, the worst divorce in the world, and the anguish I suffered fighting the horrendous system of human justice and dignity in the Netherlands, and I was driven to desperation by this old serpent to end my life. The people, the system, and people I fought were from those "other forces" (evil, *sitra ahar*), and it drove me to what would have been the most melancholy part of a life cut short. I tied a rope to the wooden beam and almost hung myself on it. Not because I was a coward but because I wanted the pain to stop. "They stole my sons away from me." Now, I saw that serpent of old, a thin sheet of dried, white-scaled paper, lying under my feet. "You shall tread upon the lion and the cobra, the young lion and serpent you shall trample underfoot" (Psalm 91:13). Only I know who saved me that night from that rope and beam. My God is an awesome, wonderful Father. Blessed be His holy name.

I walked downhill and came to the end of the entrance of the street that led to the Church of Cana. I walked past the church and went to the Cana guesthouse and booked myself for two hundred shekels for the night. I felt I was being overcharged, but I just wanted a shower, a bed, and a good night's sleep. The heat had worn me out, and I was tired. I later went to the Church of Cana and prayed for people and gave thanks to the Lord for teaching me the signs of the day. I was lost on the trail but found again.

The next morning, I awoke early, went to the church for a final visit, had some breakfast, and then started another uphill climb out of Cana into the wilderness towards kibbutz Levi. My daily walk on the Jesus Trail was filled with Gospel songs, psalms, and prayers; I would find myself just talking with the Lord. I had conversations with Him. I would stop on the trail and feel overwhelmed at times. I would just sit down or kneel and give thanks, and I found myself asking, "Only for one grace, to keep us holy, fill us with holiness, Lord." Then an old classic song, "Fill me, Lord, till I overflow. Fill me, Lord, till I overflow." Then it overwhelmed me, filled me with happy tears. My heart was filled with joy. I knew He walked with me, as I heard it in my soul, "Follow the signs, follow the signs, you will never be lost, read My Word, follow My signs. You will never be forgotten." It was all more than I could take; my heart was filled to the top. I just kept walking. I followed the trail that led me into an olive plantation, and I was lost once more. No more trail signs. So once again I dumped my bag under a tree and went looking for the signs. I heard the voice, so I looked for signs. After crisscrossing a few pathways in the olive grove, I found the trail sign once again and walked out of the olive grove into the forest leading to Levi kibbutz.

I crossed the road and the highways and lost the trail signs because there were none to be found. Still, I looked at the map and trusted the voice in my spirit that led me in the direction to the east. I came across the two fuel service stations and made my way to a camping park across this place called the Golani Junction. The park was filled with Arab boys and girls, and there was a massive party going on. There were youngsters on quads doing wheelies and tricks on them; prominent speakers were playing some live music while the girls were dancing on one side and the boys on the other, and then everyone was dancing as the music raged on. I kept a distance as I put my bag on the rock, wondering if it was a good idea to camp here for the night. My instincts told me it was better if I moved on. So, I asked three Muslim youths for some directions, but these were not nice guys; they pulled the staff out of my hand and said to me, "No speak English." I spoke to them in the little Arabic I knew. I calmly took my stick back and left in peace. I had enough courage to knock the guy out with my staff, but I came and went in peace. It was not a pleasant encounter, but I saw an evil spirit in these men. There was an unclean spirit of sinful ways right there in their eyes.

As I walked away, I met an old Muslim man in an old, beat-up car, so I asked him if he knew Levi kibbutz. He urged me into his vehicle, and my recent encounter had made me slightly sceptical, but the older man looked harmless and wanted genuinely to help. So, I took his offer, and he drove me across the road, down into a dirt road that leads east, and I saw the trail sign up ahead and a park with pine trees. So, I stopped the man and told him I wanted to get off at the trail sign. He told me that the kibbutz Levi was ahead, and he wanted to drop me there, but I failed to read the sign the older man was giving me. God was sending me to the right place for the night, but I was focused on the trail sign and not the sign from God. So, I did what I wanted to do—or thought was more logical. I thanked the older man as he sped off before I could give him something for his effort. He was gone—a missed opportunity to thank someone so kind and humble. I felt bad.

I found two pine trees close enough to each other, about fifty metres further, near a wooden table and benches that you find in camping/picnic areas. I decided to put up my hammock instead of the tent, so I hung up my blue neon hammock and tied it between these two pine trees. I wanted to sleep, get up early, and leave the place. There was a road opposite the site where I saw people walking in both directions, so it was a busy road as some people used it for walking their dogs; because it was busy, I felt it was safe enough. There were three wooden tables and benches in the camping area. I took out my boots and socks, tied my backpack to my hammock, and I ate some bread, canned fish, olives, and some pesto. I washed my face, drank some water, and slipped into my hammock. As soon as the sun had disappeared and the big moon started to appear in the shadows of the pine forest, I lay in my hammock for a while, said my prayers, and went to sleep.

I must have slept for a few hours cradled in my hammock when I awoke to the sound of voices approaching in the dark, and I was startled and alert; my sleep just snapped out of me in a flash. I lay in my hammock and remained silent. Then I heard them laugh, and it was the voices of two or three young women and two men; they were speaking in Arabic. I heard two different voices of two men, and I slowly tried to peek through the moonlit darkness, slightly moving with minimum disruption; my instincts told me that this was not a pleasant situation to be in. This could get ugly if I got up. So, I lay in silence. I was not far from the picnic table where they were sitting, and I was sure they could see a hammock hanging between two pine trees. I heard the girls giggling, and then it began. I listened to the sounds of sexual immorality approaching as I started to feel uncomfortable to be there. I lay there silently. I wished that I'd taken the advice of the older man who was willing to drive me further to kibbutz Levi.

Sin is such a filthy, evil thing. I wanted to peek and see what was going on, but a voice in my soul held me to silence. Then the sounds got worse, and they were all involved in the sexual activity as a group. I could hear the women were on the table and started to moan, and the men were slapping them on their rear ends. I put two fingers in my ears and pressed hard against them till I could feel my eardrum pop. I was screaming inside of me. I hated being there. I was screaming in silence, *Oh, my god, get these filthy people out of here, please*. It was utter agony, and I was fighting the devil and the spirits of lust that had surrounded my hammock. I had a demon trying to make me take a peek; another beast was trying to get me excited, and evil had surrounded me from all sides. The sexual lusts of these people were getting intense, and I shut my eyes and ears and screamed the loudest scream of anguish in the silent of the night. *Please take away these awful people away from me, O Lord*. My heart ripped into a realization of what the sin of fornication was. I understood the sin of the Tree of Knowledge of Good and Evil, and I realised why God hates sexual immorality and how the devil had perpetrated this sin that is so rampant in the world today. I was crying, and tears were flowing from my eyes. I felt terrible and started to pray Psalm 91 and Psalm 23. I became deaf to the sound around me as my mind was switched off from the disgusting, awful lust around me. I saw how people don't even have any sense of guilt for their sinful lives. I had no more inclination to be sexually aroused by the sexual immorality around me. I understood why God had given his commandments of laws in the book of Leviticus and the guidelines of His rules in the meaning of marriage. It was to keep us holy and protect us from the most potent sin, and that is the sin of desire. The crime of sexual lust, the sin in the Garden, the one biggest sin that is ever present and is being exploited till this day by that old serpent. *I curse you, Satan*, I screamed. *May you burn forever in the fires of hell. In the name of the Lord Jesus Christ, I rebuke you. I cover myself in the blood of Christ. I rebuke you in the name of the Lord.* I began to decree and declare power over myself. I began to confess my strength in the Lord, and I repeatedly rebuked the demons in the name of the Lord.

I lay in silence once again and removed my fingers from my hard-pressed ears, and I heard them laughing, and then it sounded like they were leaving. I was praying in my heart, *Get out of here, you filthy, stupid demons of sin deceiving the world.* Then they left. I heard them walking away. I slowly peeked and saw the lights of two cars as they opened their doors. After a few minutes, and the engines roared to life, and they drove away into the darkness of the night. I got up from my hammock and got myself some water to drink. I was crying. I saw and heard the deception of sin in a garden this night. I felt sad for the world that I lived in. I had survived a sinful night, and I felt exhausted and tired from this awful experience. I lay in my hammock and prayed and talked with the Lord. I understood the power of sin and the blindness that it brings to the soul. And I heard the voice of the Lord say, "He who is born of the flesh is born of the flesh, and he who is born of spirit is born of the spirit." This is the sin of fornication, and it has plagued the world. I lay there in my hammock for a while.

I could not believe it when I heard the sounds of a man and woman talking and approaching in the dark once again. *Not again*, I screamed in silence. I just lay there in my hammock, and nothing these people could do or say would affect me. I just shut my eyes, my ears closed, and I went to sleep. I woke up early the next morning, packed my bags, left that awful place, and walked to the Levi kibbutz located about two kilometres down the road. Again, I was foolish to have not listened to the signs; the older man in the old beat-up car was taking me to a safer place. It was a lesson learnt: follow the signs, and you will see that God is protecting you all the time; stay connected to the spiritual realm all the time. This life is a constant war against the "other forces" (evil forces, *sitra ahar*). Satan cannot be everywhere at the same time, but demons assist him. They cause people to sin and then make accusations against you. People don't even understand why God, in His commandments, told us not to eat unclean food. You are what you eat, they say; how true is that. I left this awful place and walked towards kibbutz Levi. It would have been better to have slept in a field in the wilderness or closer to a graveyard than to have slept among the living.

I found a Jewish graveyard near the kibbutz Levi where many of the Holocaust victims from the Second World War had their remains returned and buried in their ancestral homeland. What awful sins the world and people in power have committed against God's people. The Jews have been hated for no reason except as a testimony that God exists, because so much evil exists in the world today.

I sat there near the water taps and washed my head, my hands, and my feet. I wanted to have a bath and wash my whole body clean, like take a shower. I put some stones on the Jewish graves and said a prayer and honoured those poor souls who'd been lost in the Holocaust.

I heard a voice in my soul. I heard a voice say a word, "*Yardenit*. Go to Yardenit." I did not have a clue as to how I would get there. I did not know in which direction I would find it, but I just said, "Okay, Lord God Most High, blessed be Your holy name. I am going to this place You are telling me to go." I put on my backpack, filled up all my bottles with water, and walked nonstop for a few hours through the fields. I got lost again as I had missed the signs and had to walk back a kilometre through the thorny bush to find the trail signs. I started singing my favourite Gospel songs in the fields as I climbed the hills and could see the valleys below and the Sea of Galilee in the distance. I never met one person on the Jesus Trail. I stopped at the hills of Hattin and said, "Lord God, I have met a lot of unbelieving Jews. I have seen the Orthodox Jews. I have seen many young people on the Israeli trail. Angels have rescued me on these trails with my prayers. You used me to show my Jewish friends the question of faith on that Golan trail. My Lord God, thank You, for my heart and soul belong to You. But dear Lord, on the path that bears Your name, I have met only two people who blessed me and gave me the most delicious grapes with words of encouragement. Yet, not many people are walking Your trail today." I fell to my knees, lifted up my hands, and prayed to Jesus for the world.

I didn't see or meet even one person as I was walking the Jesus Trail. I was on it all alone, by myself, with the spirit of the Lord right there at my side. I was now going to this holy place called the Yardenit. I just kept walking on. That was a revelation of the state of the world—no one is walking the Jesus Trail. I thought I was walking the trail because I was a Christian. Until I discovered that, I'd been misleading myself, as I had been on the wrong trail most of my life.

I stood on an ancient ground where Joshua, the son of Nun, had won some battles near Nebi Shu'eib and the Horns of Hattin, and I could see the area of Wadi Hamam from across Kafar Zeitim. I climbed the hill at the Horns of Hattin and was attacked by some most persistent midge flies that harassed me like crazy. It was blistering hot, and I knew I would have to get out of that sun soon. From the hill, I could see a highway, so I broke off from the Jesus Trail and went to the road to see if I could make my way to Yardenit in obedience of the voice in my soul. I stood there near the highway, trying to get a ride and some directions to this place when a small Toyota car stopped for me. It was an amiable Jewish man who asked me where I was going. I explained to him the voice of my heart and the place that I needed to go but did not know how to get there. He volunteered to drive me to a bus stop near a service station where there was a bus that could take me down there in approximately twenty minutes.

The Jewish man was a schoolteacher, a father of twins, and there were two baby seats fitted in the rear; he was on his way to pick up his wife, and he still had time to drop me off at a location that took twenty minutes of driving to get there. Honestly, I was just overwhelmed with gratitude and knew that this was another blessing sent to me along the way—what a delightful, beautiful soul. I thanked him and blessed him and his family and offered to pray for him. *Shalom aleichem.* I shook his hand and thanked God for such people in the world. I got myself some cold drinks at the gas service station and walked to the bus stop to go to Yardenit. My heart was filled with thoughts of what I had experienced this time, and as I realised my journey, I'd gotten lost three times; I did not see or missed the signs. I began to realise that it was also three times that I had backslid in my spiritual life. Three times I failed to heed the warnings and the signs in my life. It set me on a course that reversed me away from my calling and the very purpose of what the Lord wanted me to be in my life and what I did not become. I sat at the bus stop and put my face in my hands as I went through the fifty years of my life, like a flash of recollections from my childhood heart and love for the Lord and what I wanted to be when I was a young boy. I was twelve years old and in boarding school, and I told my parents that I wanted to become a priest and serve God. My parents came from a denominational Catholic church, and being a priest meant that I would have been celibate. When I was seventeen years old and began to find girls interesting, the whole idea of becoming a priest flew out the window, and I knew that I would fail entirely and miserably and do dishonour to God. So, I did not become a priest. However, they did not tell me I could be a pastor.

Now, I look at the state of the Roman Catholic Church, and it's so naked, it's so immoral, like every other denominational church made by men. The Bride of Christ is not a denomination; it's a church where people have come to complete *repentance*; there is a *tikkum*. It's a transformation of hearts and souls and a desire to be washed clean and walk in holiness, to be dressed in beautiful clothes and washed-pure souls, dressed as the most beautiful bride for the most amazing Prince of Peace to come and take His bride home in a rapture. It's the sanctified temple of God in the hearts of the people who genuinely love the Messiah Jesus Christ, Son of the Most High Living God, blessed be His holy name. It's the temple of our souls and the *menorah* of the seven lampstands that we have lit in our hearts and souls for Christ; it's the repentance of our souls and the correction (*tikkum*) of this generation. It's the revelation of the Holy Word of God and the seeking of His wisdom and excellency, His majesty. It's walking away from a life of sin and into the freedom of salvation and forgiveness. It's the clinging and cleaving to Christ. It's the desire to wake up and seek His holy word and act on it and apply it in our lives. It's the giving and not the taking and walking up to those who hurt you and betrayed you and still in your humbleness finding forgiveness and putting things in vessels of peace. It's the daily defeat of Satan and his lies and his deception, this angel of death that descends to cause you to sin and ascends to make accusations against your soul and then returns to take the soul. All this sin was generated from eating that fruit of desire from the Tree of Knowledge of Good and Evil, so when the disobedience took place, evil flew out of that tree; only good was left, and death came to man.

There was our Holy God saying to Adam, the first man, "What have you done?" God made us holy and gave us eternal, everlasting life. Now, having been seduced to eat the fruit of desire and filling his body with it, Adam fell into a vessel of receiving from the "empty vacuum." This occurred as a result of a clash between the light of eternal life that the Lord had breathed into Adam's nostrils and Adam's physical body. Pride derives from the vessel of receiving from the "empty vacuum" from which the "upper light" had become separated from the time of contraction onwards.

God loves us even more today by the forgiveness of our sins by the holy blood of Christ. And I did not meet one person, not one fellow traveller, on the Jesus Trail; it was only me—all alone—on this trail. I sat there at the bus station with all these thoughts flooding my mind, and I started to weep. I was crying for the world I lived in.

The Jews were still waiting for the Messiah to come when he had already been born. Then those denominational churches took the Gospel of Jesus and made a religion of the church while people remained unholy and walked in unholiness. Where is that *tikkun*, that correction, that change? How can it come when there is no presence of the Holy Ghost? There is no Comforter, no Holy Spirit of God to dwell in us without the correction (*tikkun*), no comfort in us to gain the power to live it by His holy wisdom, for the Word and Spirit are as one. I prayed while waiting for a bus that took a while to come.

I looked at my own silly life, filled with ignorance from the past—the unchanged soul and the foolishness of my pride and living it all for myself, the emptiness and vanity of it all. How could I be so blind not to see it all? Oh, God, may I never backslide, may I never go there again ever, may I now just live for You, and may my life and whatever that is remaining of it be entirely Yours. My soul was filled with these prayers and these thoughts. Then the bus arrived.

I threw my backpack in the hold and boarded the bus to my destination. I got off the bus and walked to a beautiful building that said "Yardenit, the Baptismal Site of Jesus Christ." I walked into the reception area and made an inquiry; the young man looked at me and said, "You are a pastor." I was perplexed and said, "I am?" He was gone before I could say anything more. He returned with a white robe and told me that he was not going to charge me anything because I was a man of God. I was dumbstruck because it happened all so fast. He gave me further instructions; I went into the changing room and dressed in white robes.

I walked barefoot on the burning concrete and made my way to the river down below. There was a group of American evangelic Christians and some pastors baptising people from their group, and I joined them as the last one in the line. I briefly told them my name and my journey from Mount Hermon to this river of cleansing and rebirth. I was baptised in the name of our Lord Jesus Christ. I would never be the same again. Some fish swam past my feet rubbing me as my face disappeared into the water, and an orange-green light hit my eyes and flashed across my face as I was lifted out of the water. I was born again into a new creation—glory to God. Hallelujah. The voice sent me here.

I came out of the water and stood there in the crowd; I honestly had no control over myself. I started preaching because I was moved by some power in me to tell these people something special this day. So, I began by telling them my name. "I have walked from Mount Hermon from the fort of the highest mountain in Israel where the River Jordan starts to flow into the Sea of Galilee. The Jordan descends from the highest place and enters to this Sea of Galilee, and this sea had an entrance and an outlet that further flows into the Dead Sea, the lowest point in the world. There is life in the Sea of Galilee. Still, there is no life in the Dead Sea. Do you see the revelation?" I cried out to the crowd that gathered in front of me. "Jesus came from the highest holy place. His life flowed throughout this land. He brought with Him life and forgiveness. He descended from on top, and we, who receive Him entirely and make an outlet for that light of His revelation by our lives, living it for Him, are like this Sea of Galilee. Those who reject Him and only receive the message of His Gospel but do nothing with it, ignore it, and live in the world only for themselves in the acrid waters of sin and bitterness are as dead as the Dead Sea they swim in. There is hatred towards holiness in people, for the forces of evil, *sitra ahra*, have plagued them, and the system of righteousness is not able to maintain and support man and the creatures of the world. Hatred arises between holiness and vessels of the 'empty vacuum,' according to the law that governs the two forces acting against each other. Now, you see it, and there had to be a holy sacrifice, a pathway for the Lord declared here in this holy land, in the Gospel of John.

"I am the way, the truth, and the life. Jesus Christ is the way, the truth, and the life. Live for Him so that you will live with Him forever. This is His message of salvation, His peace, His *shalom*. It was the only time recorded that He said these words when He saw the apostles again after rising from that grave. *Shalom aleichem*. The last greeting of peace was now yours and mine because now atonement had been made, and the price for us was paid. God bless you all for listening."

I was standing there wet in white robes and bold enough to speak my heart, which was filled by a burning fire for the Lord. Some women came and blessed me. "Thank you, brother; such beautiful words of power. The Holy Spirit is in you—praise God." I hugged them, shook hands, and then made my way to the showers to get changed. I felt so blessed and humbled in my heart at the prospect of all those people down there wanting the same holiness that we seek in our lives through Christ.

I needed to get back on the Jesus Trail to complete my journey and then go to Jerusalem before the Shabbat, so I took a bus that headed to Migdal and decided to get on the trail from there. Migdal is the place Mary Magdalene lived in. I arrived on top of the hill in a small Jewish town just above Migdal. I sat at a small supermarket and pizza place and ate a slice of a very delicious homemade pizza. The owner was a delightful, kind man, and he did not want any money for the pizza slice, but I insisted that he take the money. I saw he was hardworking and generous, but I also realised he was running a business. He gave me a bottle of cold water for free and told me the directions to get on the Jesus Trail. I sat there for a while, eating my pizza and taking a break. An elderly lady passed me by, and I greeted her in Hebrew.

She smiled at me and asked me, "Is the pizza all right?"

I replied, "It's excellent. The owner is a wonderful, good, kind-hearted man—that's why the pizza is so good."

She replied, "Because he is a good man, I let him marry my daughter."

Such a joy to be in the company of such lovely people. I thanked them and made my way downhill. I saw a mulberry tree and two Jewish girls collecting the black mulberries from the tree, so I stopped to get a few for myself. I hadn't eaten mulberries in forty years. I had a flashback, a déjà vu; I was the same age as these kids the last time I ate mulberries; they are not a common fruit that you can find in supermarkets. The girls gave me some, as they had already picked the choicest ones from the tree. I thanked those beautiful kids and went down the hill to join up with the Jesus Trail.

I walked along the dirt road leading me into the fields when I saw a young woman riding on a horse without any saddle. Her back was towards me as I approached.

I said, "The last time I rode a brumby horse bareback without a saddle was in a cattle ranch called Victoria River Downs in Australia."

"Hi," she said and smiled. "My name is Kelly, and I am from the U.S." I stopped to talk to her as she told me that she'd moved to Israel a few years ago. She had tawny hair; she was slim, well-built, and athletic. She had a few tiny freckles on her face and a friendly smile. She was a pretty woman. She looked beautiful up there on that horse. I stood looking up at her while her horse was nibbling at the flowers and grass at the side of the road. She was an equestrian horse-riding champion, and she still rode horses in Israel.

"I don't suppose you miss the U.S.?" I asked.

"Not at all," she replied. "Although it's tougher out here in Israel, it's a lot better than being in America. I just miss some of my friends." She added, "And for the girl you see riding without a saddle, it's because someone stole all my best seats from my stall that I had locked up, and I am so sad about that." I sympathised with her; it was awful.

"I am so sorry to hear that. I sure know how that feels. A few years ago, some young delinquents broke into my house in Sweden and stole a lot of my stuff. It's awful because you feel so violated." She was adorable and offered me some advice and any help I needed. I told her I was looking for a place to camp for the night, and she pointed me to a fenced camping site with a beautiful stream of water flowing through it. She said that it was a great spot to stay but advised me to stay close to my things as a precaution because of her own experience of having stuff stolen.

"I can store things for you inside my house if you'd like me to, but don't leave your stuff lying around your tent if you leave to go somewhere."

She was adorable. I thanked her and headed off to the campsite slightly downhill. Finding a sweet spot of grass near the water's edge, I put up my tent and took a bath in the cold stream of water. I had settled down on one of the benches and gotten myself a burger from a run-down shed restaurant above my camping site. A film crew arrived—two guys and two girls. They were making a video of a Hebrew song as the beautiful girl stood in the water singing the song while the crew filmed her. I sat on the bench and watched it all. Later they all left, and the evening shadows started to appear with the setting sun. I lay in my tent peacefully, with the sound of a flowing stream to keep me company, and then the frogs started croaking, and I went to sleep.

Early the next morning, I heard a group of young Orthodox Jewish lads come over to the water stream; the morning was hot and humid as these guys got into the water one after the other. They all took a bath in the flowing water, and an hour later, they were gone. They spoke to me in Hebrew, but I did not understand everything they asked me. So, our conversation was limited. I made breakfast, packed my gear, and walked down the road past Kelly's place. She was outside with her mom and two horses, so I stopped by to thank them and wished them blessings for a good life; they were charming people. I moved on to the road that led me to several banana plantations all along the coast of the Sea of Galilee. I kept walking past the camping ground that the trail led us to and up into a small hill, and then winding slightly to the right. It went down into the valley; the trail followed the highway to Tabgha, the place of the feeding of the five thousand with the five loaves and two fishes. I visited the holy locations, the mount of the beatitudes, and the house of Peter.

I was now close to the end of my journey; Kafar Nahum, or Capernaum, was not more than 3.5 km away. I was feeling hungry and kept walking on the trail; then I stopped at a mulberry tree filled with fruit that was easily reachable. I climbed on the slope of the hill to grab hold of the branches and pick the choicest black mulberries on the tree. I ate as many as I could find. Maybe I'd have to wait another forty years to eat such beautiful mulberries again, so I ate the best of it.

The Lord is my provider, whom shall I fear? I was singing this song by Shane and Shane as I made my way to Kafar Nahum. I never met a single soul on the Jesus Trail. I walked on it all by myself and saw the days of our times. Few people of the many billions that inherit this Earth are eager to walk the trail to salvation in the world. Are the words of the Messiah right, then? Jesus said to His disciples, "Broad is the road that leads to hell, narrow the road that leads to heaven, and few find it." "O, God," I lamented, "put us on the road to salvation," I prayed, "I am holding on to the Lord. I will never let go." This was one of the many "conversations of the heart" I had along the way.

Now, *Kafar* in Hebrew means "a village," and *Nachum* is a Hebrew name, as in the case of Nahum the Prophet. In the Bible, there is a book named after this prophet. So Kafar Nachum could mean "the village of the prophet." Nevertheless, there is no evidence or historical fact ever recorded that any prophet by the name of Nahum came out of these parts of Galilee. The excellent mystery of the Hebrew language is that it is ancient and that it has a purpose, so that the mysteries of God had to be hidden and revealed in their appointed time. You must go deep; *kafar* also means *shelter* in Hebrew, and it comes from the root word *kaphar*, which also implies "atonement, reconciliation, mercy, and forgiveness." And the word *Nachum* in Hebrew means "the comfort of the atonement, the consoling of God's mercy, the comfort of His forgiveness," and, so, Kafar Nachum means "the village of His comfort, the shelter of consolation."

I had two hundred metres to go to drop my baggage at the security gate, and I walked to the place of discovery of the oldest known synagogue in Israel. This was the place where the Lord started His ministry of comfort to the world. I walked to the synagogue, put my arms around one of its pillars, hugged it, and kissed it. I made it to the end of the Jesus Trail—in Capernaum, the village of His comfort. Praise God, I had made it home safe—tired and exhausted, scratched, pierced, and wounded by sharp thorns, burnt by the sun, and worn by the travails and trials of the world. I'd made it home. Now, I had to celebrate in the Holy City of Jerusalem.

I had to walk back to Tabgha and then walk another kilometre uphill to get a bus that would take me to Tiberius, to connect me to my journey to Jerusalem, to the city of my heart. I tried to get a ride from Capernaum, but no one would stop for this man in a hat. So, I walked in the heat of the sun uphill to that bus stop on top of the hill. Joy is a powerful, long-lasting gift when you find it in your heart. It's a power that transforms you from the inside out.

JERUSALEM

Central Bus Station, Jerusalem, is an active place; as you step out on to the street, this city captivates you. I crossed the road across the tramway and made an inquiry for directions to the Abraham Hostel at Davidka Square. I walked along the way following the tram. I struck up a conversation with an American Jewish man who kept me company right up to the square. I checked into the hostel where I had a booking in a four-bed dormitory. I met a grey-haired, middle-aged man, an American Jewish man from Arizona, about five feet five. He wore glasses, and he was a kind, respectful man. I recognised the type of man he was because, in life, for some unexplainable reason, you meet people who have possibly been through what you have been through. There is an energy that exists that is hard to describe and sometimes impossible to explain, but you just know that you are bound to become friends. His name was Bernie.

Bernie was a messianic Jewish American who says this about himself (let me do it like you can imagine me say it): "Hello, my name is Bernie. I am a believer first, and I am Jewish next, from Arizona in the United States. I have been in Israel for more than one hundred days, and I don't know what I will be doing next." Then he warned me about the other Jewish man from New York, whom he described as a crafty chap and one who does not believe that Jesus Christ is the Messiah. "I have been trying to talk some sense into him, but this fellow is a hard nut to crack, and he is crafty." Looking at me, he said, "Maybe you will be able to succeed more than me, considering the journey you have made getting here. Perhaps you might make a difference in that fellow. His name is Richard." I took an instant liking to this man; we had a pleasant conversation, getting to know each other. I agreed to meet up with him for lunch at the Church of Christ in the Old City, opposite the tower of King David.

I took a much-needed shower and went down into the new city to the famous market square of Jerusalem to get something to eat. My heart feels joy when I am in Jerusalem. There is no place on earth like Jerusalem. One word describes it—love, the ultimate love, the perfect love, underserved love, mercy love, the epitome of love, the Jesus Christ love, the "Emmanuel *God with us*" love. I returned to my hostel and put on my breathing-aid device in my nose, and I did not want to snore too loud, which happens when I am exhausted. So, I warned the two Jewish men to put in earplugs to avoid any uncomfortable disturbance. I met Richard, the crafty fellow, and he seemed slightly odd, and I understood Bernie's scepticism. Now Bernie had not put anything wrong in my mind, but it was true; this Richard fellow looked a little crafty. He was about five feet eleven, bald, had a long nose, a big belly, grey hair around the rim of his head, like a decoration for craftiness around his head; he was a wheeler-dealer businessman looking for opportunity and did not like spending money. He was not the kind of guy who would offer you a drink or buy you a sandwich.

I went to bed and stayed awake to allow the two older men to sleep. The crafty fellow started to snore, and he was louder than I have ever been; I know this for a fact because my woman had recorded me on her phone. I saw Bernie tossing and turning on the other side, and he did not put in his earplugs. The truth was Bernie did not like Richard because they'd had a few words of disagreement before my arrival.

So, I heard Bernie say to him, "Stop snoring, for God's sake." Now, I was not going to sleep because I knew for sure that I would breathe even if I did not want to snore. Richard kept snoring, and Bernie now and then protested.

I heard Richard wake up and say to Bernie, "Goddamn you, take your damn mattress and walk on the damn roof, you old fool. Find a place on the balcony outside somewhere, and sleep there."

"I am snoring, so stop disturbing me and go to sleep."

Richard was snoring again, and I heard Bernie say, "You inconsiderate son of a bitch. Stop your damn snoring—you're scaring the pigs away." I had to step in because the crafty one did not give a damn. I put on my light and talked some sense into both men.

I gave Bernie some earplugs and said, "Gentlemen, you are in a holy city of love. Even if you don't like each other, we all must sleep in this room together. I also snore—not because I want to snore—but if we all put in earplugs, the problem is easily solved." I diffused the situation and turned off my light. I saw Bernie signal to me with some gestures that he appreciated my support and signalled his dislike of Richard with his hands, pointing at the crafty one. It was rather funny. I diffused the situation, and we went to sleep and unfortunately joined the crafty one with the snoring bit for the night. My heart was sympathetic to Bernie as he lay there with earplugs, resting silently.

The next day, Bernie was the first one to leave, followed by Richard; they were trying to avoid each other. After Bernie left, I heard Richard mumble and grumble about Bernie. When I awoke, he complained about Bernie's attempts to persuade him about Jesus Christ, protesting, "I am not interested one tiny bit about all the religious stuff. I don't want to know his views and opinions." I did not respond to his rantings and just let my peace remain with me. I told him to have a beautiful day, and I left the room and headed to the old city of Jerusalem.

There was a Cain, and there was an Abel. There was an Esau, and there was a Jacob. There was an Egyptian Pharaoh, and there was a Moses. There was a Jesus, and there was a Judas. Even unto the last moment of His death on that cross, there were two robbers; one humbly begged to be remembered and was promised paradise that night, and there was one who did not want to know and ridiculed the Lord Jesus Christ Messiah. I walked through the Jaffa Gate into the city of Jerusalem with joy in my heart. I walked the streets just happy to be there.

I could spend weeks, even months, in this city because it's so captivating and so beyond leaving; it's like you could wait here forever and see the coming glory. It's a city that does not leave you. It has such opposing people; it has love and peace with antagonism and resentment; it has believers and unbelievers; it has good, and it has evil; it has the truthful and benevolent and the swashbucklers and circuitous. A Palestinian man who sold bread at the Jaffa Gate, had been requested several times by the Israeli authorities to apply for his licence, which they are happy to give him so that he can sell his bread at the Jaffa Gate. The man refused to bend to the rules. The authorities have fined him a few times. However, he still refused to pay the fine required by the Israeli authorities, like every other trader in the city does. After several attempts, the Israeli authorities did not do anything more to persuade him to follow the norms. If you are at the Jaffa Gate, stop by and ask the man how many years he has been selling bread at the Jaffa Gate; he will proudly tell you, "Forty-two years." In all these years selling bread, he has never paid any tax to the state of Israel or the city of Jerusalem. In 2017, when Donald Trump visited Israel and Jerusalem, he was one of the first persons to put up a more prominent banner of protest against the persecution of the Palestinian people.

I was never a tourist but a traveller. I get into the heart, into the contentious issues, the searching for the truth and the language of it and the admission of it. And yet in the same city, a ruler and a governor once asked the same question: what is the truth? I would love you to capture this.

> Pilate, therefore, said to Him. "Are you a king then?"
> Jesus answered: "You say rightly that I am a king, for this cause I was born, and for this cause I have come into the world that I should bear witness to the truth. Everyone who is of the truth hears my voice."
> Pilate said to Him "What is the truth?" And when he had said this, he went out again unto the Jews and said unto them "I find no fault in Him at all."
>
> —(John 18:37–38)

At this point, whenever I read this scripture, I always wondered why the Lord never said anything to Pilate when he asked Him the question about the truth. He only defended the question about Him being a king because He was a king; He answered that question, but when Pilate asked Him what the truth is, the Lord chose to be silent.

My search for the wisdom of the Word of God, by his Spirit, revealed this to me in the following verse, answering my inquiring soul. I hope it captivates you as it has me.

Be still and know that I am God; I will be exalted among the nations; I will be exalted in the earth.

—(Psalm 46:10)

What did the holy one do, blessed be His holy name? He took the truth and cast it on the earth (Daniel 8:12). If the lips of truth speak truly, how could the angels of mercy and righteousness agree to the creation of a world that is all lies? For what reason did the truth deserve such a severe punishment of being cast down to the earth and into the earth? How could truth describe here all of the human race as being lies? Surely there is never a generation that does not have men like Abraham, Isaac, and Jacob.

There is the truth. He was a man, a perfectly obedient man. A son, the Holy Anointed One of Israel, a redeemer and saviour of the world. He was clothed in complete holiness, a perfect Adam, untouched and undefiled by the evil of the world. In the sacrifice of Atonement, He was standing there in flesh and blood; He was going to the cross to become the Prince of Peace. He was the prophecy of Isaiah 53 come true. He was the name above all names, the darling of heaven—the Emmanuel *God with us*—the Lamb of God and the Lion of Judah. He was the light of the world, the pillar of fire (*Amud Anan*) that brought them out of Egypt. He was the Messiah who would be cut off in Daniel 9:26. He will be "a covenant for the people" (Isaiah 42:6). "I will give you…to be my salvation to the ends of the earth" (Isaiah 49:6 NKJV). This Messiah is the one who will bring the new covenant in which the problem of sin is dealt with (Jeremiah 31:31). His sacrifice will be the foundation of this new covenant. What is the truth?

The prophets also speak of this correction (*tikkun*). "All the Prophets prophesied only for the days of the Messiah." The days of the Messiah will see the restoration of the methods of the survival of the world by means of divine providence, which is as it was before the sin of eating from the Tree of Knowledge. But as for the world to come, which is the absolute end, when the form will be similar to its Creator—"The eye has not seen a God besides You" (Isaiah 64:3). Whereas in the messianic era: "And it shall be that whosoever of the families of the earth does not go up to Jerusalem to worship the King, the Lord of hosts, upon them there shall be no rain. And if the family of Egypt go not up and worship not, they shall have no overflow" (Zechariah 14:17–18). These verses indicate that a distinction will still be made between good and evil.

This is the reason Jesus answered the question of Pilate when he asked Him, "Are you a king?"

I understand people who don't know "what the truth is" because they did not go seeking for it and continued to live in the flesh. You cannot be in the light if you are in the darkness, and you cannot be in the Spirit if you are trapped in a denomination. Your heart and soul need to become a blank sheet of paper—no thoughts or education, no ideas, no theories, no corruption, just an empty vessel that stands in front of God so He can fill you with His holiness and truth.

The joy of being in Jerusalem filled me with the Word of God, and I felt so blessed just walking around and exploring the ancient city. I walked through the Armenian sector, one of the smallest; the Armenians were the first nation to accept Christianity, in the early fourth century. They have been living in Jerusalem since the Byzantine period, and this quarter has an active monastery that is home to a secular population and makes it the most unique in the world. In the heart of the quarter is the dome of the St. James Cathedral. James was the half-brother of Jesus. According to tradition, the body of James is buried in western Spain, in the Church of Santiago de Compostela. I walked through the streets, watching the artists work on their pottery pieces, with Christian paintings, with great skill and talent.

I went on to the Jewish Quarter with its prominent white dome of the Hurva Synagogue rebuilt in the early 2000s. The Jewish Quarter has been around for six hundred years, but before that, it was on Mount Zion near King David's Tomb, and even before that, it was located in other areas of the city. After the Six-Day War, the Israeli government started rebuilding the Jewish Quarter, and today it is once more found bustling with life and echoing Biblical scriptures. "And the broad places of the city shall be full of boys and girls playing in the broad places thereof" (Zechariah 8:5).

I stood on the walls of Jerusalem, walking the Old City's Ramparts Walk on the southern side. I could see the Dome of the Rock on the Temple Mount. I saw the Western Wall, the holiest place in the world of Judaism and the third most sacred place in Islam. On the southern side of the Temple Mount, above the south wall, I could see the grey dome of the Al-Aqsa Mosque, which commemorates the story of

Mohammed's nighttime journey from Mecca to Jerusalem, according to Muslim tradition.

I went to the Wailing Wall and prayed with my Jewish people, walking down the road from the gate that would lead me to the City of David, in a deep valley at the foot of its hill. On this hill, the City of David was established near the Gihon spring as early as the Middle Bronze Age, some, 3,800 years ago. During the time of King Solomon, Jerusalem expanded to include the Temple Mount, and only at the time of King Hezekiah, in the eighth century BC, did the city spread to the Western Hill on which I was now standing. The valley between the City of David and me was called the Tyropaeon (the Valley of the Cheesemakers). The whole experience is deeply absorbing: there many centuries of history represented; so many people have lived through it all, and there, in the midst of it all, the City that bears the name of a man who after God's own heart, the author of the book of Psalms, King David. And there are many more things in the Scriptures that the Tanakh reveals to us about the Messiah.

- He will be a descendant of David (Jeremiah 23:5–6)
- He will be born in Bethlehem (Micah 5:2)
- He will reveal Himself in Galilee (Isaiah 9:1–2)
- He will have an earthly as well as an eternal origin, and He will be human as well as divine (Micha 5:2, Jeremiah 23:5–6, Isaiah 9:6–7)
- He will be rejected and despised by His own people (Psalm 22:6, Isaiah 49:7 and 53:3)
- He will suffer terribly and be laid in the dust of death, but God will raise Him up. Because of this, many Gentiles will turn to God (Psalm 22)
- He will die but live again (Isaiah 53:8–10 and Psalm 16:10)
- He will be cut off (die) before the destruction of the second temple, that is, before 70 CE (Daniel 9:26)

Here was a man who stood silent when he was asked by the Roman governor, "What is the truth?" The hope of Israel and the whole world, Yeshua of Nazareth. Here stood a sacrifice not far from the place where Abraham learned the need for a substitute sacrifice.

You now may come to understand the deep meaning of the whole of this story, avoiding the mistake that is deduced through a superficial reading of it. For the Tree of Knowledge of Good and Evil also arose from aspects of the "empty vacuum"—that is to say, from the form of the enormous amount of receiving, upon which the "contraction" (*tzimtzum*) occurred, from which the "upper light" separated itself.

Adam, the first man, did not possess in him the form of the enormous amount of receiving that extends from the "empty vacuum," but all of him extended from the system of holiness whose objective is to "impart." And as it is written in the Zohar (Kedoshim, p. 83a), Adam, the first man, never attached to him anything of this world. It was for this reason the Tree of Knowledge was forbidden for him, just as it was to his source and the whole system of holiness. For these were separated from the "other forces" (of evil, *sitra ahra*) because of their "differences of the form," which is a matter of separation. Thus, Adam was also commanded against it and warned against becoming joined to it. For he would then die, just as the "other forces" (of evil, *sitra ahar*) and the shells (*kelipot*) are dead because of their being opposed to and separated from the system of holiness and the eternal life.

Here stood a man, the Son of the Living God of Israel, Yeshua Messiah, the Holy Anointed One; the new covenant scriptures testify about Him.

- Look, the Lamb of God who takes away the sins of the world (John 1:29)
- God presented the Messiah as a sacrifice of atonement through the shedding of His blood—to be received by faith (Romans 3:25)
- I am the way, the truth, and the life. No one comes to the Father except through Me (John 14:6)
- For God so loved the world that He gave His only begotten Son that whoever believes in Him should not perish but have everlasting life

There stood on this hill this Holy City, Jerusalem, the correction (*tikkun olam*), the atonement, the glory of God, the love of God—put to the cross and lifted up high on a holy hill for the healing of the whole world.

But there are still people walking in darkness asking the same silly question, "What is the truth? I don't believe in religion, and I don't believe in God. I believe in the Big Bang Theory." You are in darkness, my friend, with the "other forces" (the evil, *sitra ahar*). No one is judging you now, but there will be a judgement because of the separation that you have inflicted on yourself. Jesus condemned no one, so must we not condemn people, but we must condemn the darkness that lives in the world. The Lord came to save the world, not condemn it. This condemnation is reserved for the judgement day; until then, we have the opportunity to turn back even now and receive this grace to live in holiness, for all of your past is washed away even in this hour. There is no condemnation in Christ.

As I walked in the streets of the City of David, the joy of faith, my best companion, was with me. All the scriptures come flooding in upon me like a rushing wind, and the love of God filled around me. O, Jerusalem, how I love you. I could wander in your streets and sing with joy every day.

I returned to the Church of Christ, opposite the Tower of David, the Oldest Protestant Anglican Church in the Middle East—what a beautiful place indeed; there is an excellent café with many books to read, free Wi-Fi—and they make a wonderful lunch for just under sixty shekels. I met my old friend Bernie. I was a little late because of my indulgence in the joy of Jerusalem; my timing was a slight setback, but we still had lunch and talked about the various praise and worship programs scheduled in the church that we planned to attend.

Bernie told me that he was moving out of the hostel and coming to the accommodations at the church premises; he did not want to have his heart filled with those bad feelings he had with the crafty fellow Richard. Looking at me, he said, "All I did was try to talk to him about the Lord, and he rudely discarded my goodness with utter contempt and rudeness."

I responded, "Today you will pray for him, that the veil of darkness will lift from his eyes; that's all we can do. Jesus is still rejected in this day because the darkness is the absence of light. The eyes of the heart need to open, and we can pray for people with love." He approved of my view with a smile, and I left him at the church and offered to move his stuff the next day if he wanted.

I went down the steps from the dining hall to the café with a door leading onto the street, when the smell of coffee caught the tips of those tiny, thin hairs on my nostrils, which triggered a desire for a cup of coffee. What a terrible thing desire is. So, I got my cappuccino and went outside to sit at the few tables outside on the terrace. I could have just passed through, but there were two men at the table with big smiles who invited me to sit at their table. They were from Sydney, Australia, home country. It was just brilliant; we drank a few more cups of coffee and talked about the Lord Jesus Christ in our lives. It was amazing to hear the testimonies of both the men; Steve was just ecstatic and so filled with joy. He told me that he was originally from the UK but had lived in Australia for more than twenty-two years. He told me his entire story of how he was saved and became a believer, a born-again Christian, and his joy was infectious. I shared some revelations of the scriptures, and we three men sat there for the rest of the afternoon just sharing our stories and wisdom of the Word of God.

How marvellous are such days! How amazing are the heavenly connections that the Lord prepares among the believers and the saved. I could feel a spirit of the apostles Peter, John, Andrew, James—when they had discovered the Messiah. I remembered that amazing story of Nathanael under the fig tree when Phillip told him that they had found the one about whom Moses had written about in the law and about whom the prophets also wrote—Yeshua of Nazareth, the son of Joseph. Nathanael was given a revelation by the Lord when he approached the Holy Anointed One—blessed be His holy name.

Here we were sitting together in this ancient city, filled with joy, talking about the same Jesus Christ and how amazing it is when you believe. I spent the next three days in the company of these men and introduced my friend Bernie to the group. We also had an Ethiopian Jew in the group by the name of James, who worked in the church, so we often had the pleasure of his company as well. It was a time of sharing and reminding ourselves of the obligation to the common sense of the Gospel of Jesus Christ. It was an electric environment that I found to be extraordinarily spiritually stimulating—almost like a fire, like a rushing wind, blowing past us, as we shared our experiences and the changing grace that drew us back to Christ Jesus. We shared our testimonies, the togetherness of faith, and the burning need to impart the Word of God to one another, almost like building up one another for the Maranatha. We shared the look on every face, the smiles and the hope of that salvation and redemption, the thirst for the holiness of God Almighty—blessed be His holy name.

We continued to explore the city of Jerusalem together each day, and I could not have asked for anything better than being in the company of men who love the Lord. We spent our last evening with a dinner together, sitting around like apostles, asking each other those special moments of this journey; certain events occurred that were most memorable. When it came time to say goodbye, I declared, "One of the greatest secrets of life is not how you meet people but how you leave them when you say goodbye." We shook hands, and we hugged; we said goodbye.

The next morning, I was walking to the central station in Jerusalem; as I crossed the road from Davidka Square, I followed the trail on the left-hand side next to the tramline and the side of the famous market in Jerusalem. I walked for a few hundred metres, and on my left side, there was a stone wall parallel to the pedestrian pavement. There was a man with a white beard, well-built, muscular and strong, maybe in his early forties, well-dressed, and with a small backpack, a fantastic face, with a glowing smile towards me.

I greeted him, "*Shalom aleichem.*"

He repeated it in reverse, "*Aleichem shalom.* I have a silver ring that says that on my hand."

I extended my hand to shake his. "I have a silver ring, too, with Hebrew inscriptions of blessings like yours."

"How wonderful."

"I am heading off for Haifa," I replied.

He looked at me and said, "Are you going to Mount Carmel and Elijah's cave? It's a powerful place. When you get there, take your time, and spend it in silence; wait, and don't go past quickly but wait in silence. It's a holy place for Jews, and if you wait, you will feel the spirit of Elijah."

I shook his hand; it was warm. "Thank you—I will remember this well, and I will remember you."

"My name is Michael," he said. I told him mine. "Shalom, Lyndon. God be with you always, my friend."

I walked on, stopped after about fifty metres, and turned back. He was there; for a moment I was struck by it. I turned after another ten metres, looking back; he was there. When I reached the end of the street and turned back one last time, he had left. *How incredible is this encounter,* I thought. The smile and the glow of his happy face were remarkable. I boarded a bus and made my way to Haifa.

Taxi drivers are the same in most countries, and there are some professions in the world that require a certain degree of craftiness or crookedness: lawyers, car salesmen, bank managers, bankers, government officials, and taxi drivers are some of them. I asked the taxi driver a question as a person from a different country, but I have read a lot about where I was going and what landmarks I needed to watch for. Whenever you display your knowledge to a taxi driver, he will pretend like he does not know what you are talking about to throw out some confusion because he knows you are not from Israel.

At very least, this taxi driver won again; he took me on a small detour to the place. I wanted to go where there was a shorter way and a quick bus to get me there from the taxi stand. Nevertheless, it worked out better for me even when he did what he did. I was on top of a hill at a beautiful monastery and took some rest under a shady tree. I visited the monastery and got all the directions from a nice lady and walked down the pathway on this mountaintop to the Cave of Elijah. It was beautiful scenery—limestone mountains, cliffs, pine forests, and a blue sea in front of your eyes make Haifa a magnificent city. It's a much better city than Tel Aviv.

I slowly made my way down the mountain pathway and found a wooden bench, so I sat there in silence for a long time with my eyes closed and praying. I was contemplating the whole life of the prophet Elijah as I'd read it in the Bible. He was raptured in a chariot of fire—how remarkable. I loved the part when the ravens brought him food when he stayed away from that evil Jezebel.

I was alone in the forest, so I sang songs of praise and made my way down, praising the life of this remarkable prophet of God. I did feel a wonderful sense of peace; what I learned was the sea wind rustled in the leaves; blowing across to me was love and trust God, for He makes all things happen according to His time and will—walk in faith. I remember that fantastic scripture that speaks about the seven times Elijah sent Elisha to see what he could see; then the cloud appeared, and then came the rain.

The cave was a holy shrine where there were many men and women present. There were branches of hyssop, myrtle, a table of dry fruits, and all kinds of nuts, and there was prayer and worship as I was allowed to join the Jewish tradition. I sat on the wooden bench absorbing all of it; there were two distinct prayer divisions for the men and women, young and older people singing in ancient languages. Then they sprinkled with the leaves and offered me some dates and nuts; the women were covered in traditional Jewish clothes and veils, and the atmosphere inside the cave was holy. On the right-hand side, the wooden board of separation had many scriptures, ancient writings, and all kinds of religious pictured scripts, Holy Words, and books. At the end of the cave, there was a dark-blue-purple veil that people went behind, touched the Holy Scriptures, and prayed. So, I paid my respects to the spirit of Elijah and prayed. On the right-hand corner of the cave was a single step that led to a square corner, where people tied up their scarfs to the ceiling. I assisted an elderly lady and tied her veil for her. I did not want to leave any stone unturned, so I tied my bandana as well on the ceiling. I spent some more time in the cave in silence.

This was the cave that the prophet Elijah was believed to have rested in before he took on the prophets of Baal during the time of King Ahab and the evil Queen Jezebel. If you truly understand the times of this prophet, you know that it was no small feat. He stood against tremendous adversity, against an establishment, a foolish king, and an incredibly evil queen; Elijah was one man who stood for God amid the killing of all the prophets at the time of high paganism and offering of children as a sacrifice to the evil, pagan idol of Baal. I felt the power of this prophet as I left the cave. I went to sit in the forest alone, in the tranquillity of the silence and the spirit of ancient days of the life of Elijah.

I prayed to the Lord to be with us in the days of our lives, and I prayed for family and friends and the world. I thanked God for the encounter with Michael and prayed for him. I left Haifa and took a bus to Tel Aviv.

The next day, I went to Eilat, Israel, a particular place called the Home Shelter, to meet some Christian friends and spend time with them in prayer, thanksgiving, and worship. I sat in the last rear seat of the bus on my trip to Eilat, travelling across the Judean Desert. It was only the most fantastic scenery, and I would need many words to describe it—its limestone dry mountains and valleys are simply beautiful. Deserts are truly spectacular the world over, but this one was breathtakingly awesome. Other passengers with me were a young Israeli warrior, armed with his machine gun and two young Jewish students. In the second half of my journey, I was involved in a deep intellectual conversation with the Jewish students, who were incredibly curious about my faith as a born-again Christian. They were keen for me to explain by scriptures why I believed Jesus Christ was the Messiah. So, this led us to look through scriptures and cross-check them with the Hebrew versions. It was, indeed, a pleasant exchange. I left those Jewish boys with a lot to think about. *What is the truth?*

I arrived at Eilat around 4:30 p.m. The heat wave hit me like walking into a boiler room while someone opens the furnace door. This is a scorching place in summer and has the most beautiful beaches of the Red Sea, an amazing place. I walked over to the Home Shelter and stayed with my friends for five days. It was a wonderful time of being among God-fearing people who don't just say or pray the Word, but they do their very best to live it and share it with everyone who comes through their door. Now, there you are: that's the mission for life. I wanted to go back to Jerusalem, so I did.

At the Jaffa Gate, just before you enter the gate, on the right-hand corner of the stone wall, there is a cylindrical metallic object and a second one at the second entrance gate that leads you into the courtyard of the Old City of Jerusalem. It's a custom for Jewish people to touch those metal objects whenever they enter the Holy City. A second thing I noticed during my first visit was a man with a beard who wears sackcloth and sits in a square carved out of the section on the entrance wall, like the balcony of a large window. He spends the whole day sitting on that wall. People were too busy passing by to stop and talk to him. So, I did.

His name was Elijah Nevis. He said to me, "Most people just pass by, and only a few stop to notice me. I am here almost every day. Do you know why I wear these sack clothes? I am waiting at the gates of Jerusalem because I saw a vision and a dream. Shall I tell you?" he asked.

CHAPTER 25

THE DREAM OF ELIJAH

Elijah Nevis told me, "I had a big house where I lived with my father, and one day my father announced that he had sold the house and that we needed to prepare the house for the new owners. I got busy packing stuff from our beautiful house and putting them together, but I was so tired that I fell asleep. The next morning, when I woke up, the house was larger, and the work was more and never-ending. I got busy again and was exhausted at the increased workload on me. Painstakingly, I packed all the precious stuff our house had. I was tired and fell asleep again. The next morning, I awoke to yet a larger house than the previous day. My father came, and I asked him, 'Father, do you think these new owners who are coming will take care of all the stuff we are leaving?' My father said, 'They couldn't care less about all the stuff we cared for so much; they may even trash most of it. It's too late now to think of these things. Let's go, for the new owners are almost here.' My father and I left."

I offered to buy him some lunch, and we prayed together; he placed his hand on my head and said a beautiful prayer of preservation over my life. I thanked him for his words. "Most people don't stop to notice me," he said, "but you took time to come over, so you are blessed."

I don't have all the answers as to why some things panned out the way they did, or why I came back to Jerusalem to spend another five days. Still, I know this: I have become wiser by my ability to see signs,

421

to hear the voice more clearly, to follow instructions and command-ments, to be more connected to my soul, to be a blessing to others, and to take my blessings and meet angels along the way.

I had only a few days left in Israel, and the Shabbat was soon approaching; with issues of public transportation on a Saturday, it was better for me to stay in Tel Aviv. I did not want to miss my flights. I boarded a bus and left Jerusalem.

I checked into a brand-new hostel on the northern part of the coast called the Spot Hostel; it was a good value for the money, in a good location close to shops, cafes, and the beach. Mine was an eight-bed-room dormitory filled with one girl and six young boys, who went out to party all night and slept till late in the day. The breakfast area was a great open dining place with a lot of space, and there were added terraces outside with trees and a small stream that flowed towards the sea; it was a new place, so the staff were trying their best to get their act together.

I sat to eat my breakfast and was joined by Dr. Jack Leitner, from Boston. He was a delightful man, about seventy-two years old, and he was a fascinating, friendly, and intelligent man, an American Jewish doctor who had a brother living in Israel for the past fifty-two years. He had come to visit his family and was staying in the hostel in a single room. People like Dr. Jack fit the profile of my meaning of the word—intelligent, exciting people. I thoroughly enjoyed his company as we talked for a few hours over breakfast. He attempted to call a Brazilian Belgian girl he had made friends with and introduced her to me because she was as deeply spiritual as I was. She was also living in the hostel, but we could not get ahold of her because her phone number was incorrect; he may have written it wrong. We agreed to catch up again sometime.

I went walking with Benny, a Serbian guy I met in Jerusalem when I gave him a guided tour of the city that I'd come to know so well, and we caught up in Tel Aviv, as he was also in the same hostel. We walked for hours along the coast to the old city of Jaffa. The beach was packed with people, kids, dogs, an active place, bursting with life—the beautiful Mediterranean coast, with some gentle waves and mild surf. Benny was impressed at the beautiful, half-naked women at the beach and commented that he had never realised how beautiful Jewish women were. It's because they had spread out to all the nations of the world, and the gene pool had mixed so well. Israel had some beautiful-looking sheilas on the beach. I smiled and said, "Beauty is in the eye of the beholder, my friend; it all depends on where you find that beauty and how you perceive beauty to be." We walked for miles exploring the coastline and the inland streets and cafes. We decided to stay out late into the night. Tel Aviv is very absorbing; it has a lot of contrasts, a bustling city of life. You could ask, "What kind of life?" Just like many coastal cities of the world, the "sea, sand, beach" combination makes them a hub of activity the world over.

We ended up in a square somewhere and sitting on some chairs and benches. We watched the world and the city pass us by; a young girl was lying on the seat opposite us, accompanied by two young boys on bikes; they were friends, joking and horse-playing around. There was an Eritrean man with an old bike sitting opposite us, trying to start a conversation, but we could not communicate with him because he did not know English. So, we talked in sign language of hands, facial movements, and expressions; it was funny. About twenty metres behind us was a homeless man, a drunk man lying on the bench, trying to sleep. Then he sat up, urinated on the street, and went back to sleep on the bench. I wanted to leave but saw an older hunched-up white woman with plastic shopping bags and a rolled-up handmade cigarette; she came walking towards us with a smile. She was wearing black trousers and a brown top, with a pattern of printed flowers on the fabric; her face was slightly wrinkled, and she looked worn and tired. She looked sad and lonely and wanted to talk to someone, and, as she smoked her cigarette, she asked us where we were from and introduced herself as "Naomi."

"A beautiful name from the Bible, and a wonderful woman too," I commented. She was very friendly, and I realised the poor woman was lonely. I felt sad for her. I immediately realised that, in her younger days, she must have been a real beauty. So began our long conversation; even Benny stopped admiring the half-naked Jewish girls on the street and shifted his attention to the story unfolding as she began to relate to us her life story.

She started by saying, "I messed up my life. You are right about me being a beautiful woman. I was beautiful, all right. My husband was from the U.S., and he was Jewish. He lived with me in Israel for many years."

I instinctually asked her, "Do you have any children?" You wouldn't think that such a question would be a wrong question to ask, but it was the most painful question I had just asked this lonely woman. I felt so ashamed that it was a painful reminder of her barenness.

"Oh, god! I wished you wouldn't have asked me that question," she responded almost instantly. "My heart falls apart when I think of my life." She lit up another cigarette. She began to draw on it, took a pause, and then she spoke again. "My husband used to work with me in the kibbutz, but he had a habit of smoking marijuana. Sometimes he would get his hands on hashish. The Jewish elders at the kibbutz told me that if he did not stop this drug habit, we would have to leave the kibbutz. I tried to talk to him several times. Still, he could not stop his practice. We eventually had to leave the kibbutz. We lived in the south of Tel Aviv. Then he started drinking as well. Soon the problem became worse, and then our marriage was over. He went back to the U.S. About a year later, we tried to get back together. Still, it never worked out. I went from one man to another and screwed my life up. Now I live in the north of Tel Aviv by myself, and it's much more peaceful and silent than this part. I come here sometimes, as I have a lot of memories in the south."

I was broken inside as I heard her story; my heart was torn apart. I wished I could take her and keep her with me for the rest of her life and make her happy and bring a smile on her face. (As I write this story, I am all tears, and I am praying and asking the Lord to take care of her, wherever she is.)

I stood up from my seat and said, "Naomi, please—would you allow me to embrace you?" She was so fragile and sensitive, a rose among the thistle shrubberies. I tenderly embraced her since I was reluctant to hug her like I genuinely wanted to. I was lost for words, and I couldn't find words of comfort for the story of her life. What could I say to her, when, shortly, I would leave her and lead my own life and its challenges? She was somebody's child once, somebody's better half, somebody's sister—but now desolate, without children, and forlorn, strolling the boulevards of Tel Aviv. She was not searching for any cash or sustenance to eat; she was simply desolate. I discovered it challenging to leave her there, wretched and defenceless. I hugged her once more and told her that I would always pray for her. I told her, "Trust God and seek His forgiveness. Jesus Christ has secured for us a home in heaven, and if you read John chapter 14, verses 18 and 19, you will have great hope. I want to leave you with faith and hope tonight, and I wish I could spend more time with you—a few weeks perhaps, sharing the good news of the Lord. Wherever I am, I will pray for you. May God bless you and keep you."

She smiled, thanked us, apologised for the sad story, and, in her humility, this rose among the thornbushes walked away into the streets and towards a bus stop. Benny and I got a shared taxi and made our way back to the hostel. Naomi was still on my mind.

We returned to the Spot Hostel and decided to walk around the beach and coast around the area of the north. Benny was keener to check out the night scene, and so I kept him company. There were bars and nightclubs on the beach, women dressed in short pants and revealing clothes, drunk men and neon lights, and music blaring out of loudspeakers. As we walked farther down the beach, there were more clubs and more of the same. We stopped to watch over the fence a group of young women in short pants, dancing to the most vulgar song and lyrics that said words like "f**k me like a whore, I like it when you f**k me like a whore"; the boys were dancing. The girls were moving their booties in sinful movements, like of Sodom and Gomorrah, or maybe even worse than those evil days. It was way too much for my eyes. Women have become more vulgar than men—this was not a place for a man like me. I don't get impressed with locations where evil lurks; my heart was already filled with the story of Naomi, and this filth was not my cup of tea. I told Benny I'd had enough for one night; we terminated our night and went back to the Spot Hostel.

The next morning, I met up with Dr. Jack Leitner and we had breakfast together. I briefly told him about our trip and a summary of my encounter with Naomi. Dr. Jack looked at me and said, "I think she must have been a lonely woman." We spent a while chatting, and he asked me if I wanted to go to the synagogue with him.

"I would love that," I replied. "I even have Jewish clothes."

"You do?" He looked surprised. "Are you Jewish?" he asked.

"My God is the God of Israel. Jesus is Jewish. Dr. Jack, does that make me Jewish? I am a Yehudim." I said, "I praise and worship the God of Abraham, Isaac, and Jacob. I believe in the Messiah our Lord Jesus Christ and the Holy Scriptures and commandments of God. I am willing to face any persecution, just as the Jews have to show the world. God does exist; the end is drawing near, and the world will see His glory."

"Are you circumcised?" he asked.

"Ha, ha," I laughed. "Do I have to show you that, too, Dr. Jack?" We laughed some more.

Then he said to me, "From today, you are Moshe from Akron in Yemen. I cannot tell them you are from Russia or Argentina. You are a brown man, you see, and you are not blond either, and there were never many Jews in Scandinavia. So, I am going to take you to my brother's house and introduce you as Moshe, and then we will go to the synagogue and worship and pray like a Yehudim."

I read signs, you see. I have been wrestling angels along the way for my blessings, and here a Jewish man was giving me a blessing: "And from today you shall be called Moshe." Dr. Jack had no idea what he had just declared unto me. But I knew exactly what was going on. So, my evening was all planned out, and I was looking forward to the prayer and worship in the synagogue.

Benny and I spent the day at the beach and walked back to the old city of Jaffa; I was hoping to meet Naomi and take her out for lunch. I knew the chances of meeting her would be slim, but one can hope, can't he? The beach was more crowded than the previous day, as it was a Friday. I did not like Tel Aviv that much; it was okay for a few days, but when you are in the Holy Land, Tel Aviv feels odd to me. Maybe I read the signs of our times ahead in the world I live in.

I noticed rainbow flags all over the city fluttering in the wind and announcing the arrival of the gay, lesbian, confused-gender parade. I am not judging, so don't kill me for my expression. Concerning the issue of the rainbow flag, "the judgement is for the Lord." Like I said earlier, I read signs. So, I boldly want to share this admission of truth. It says in the Bible, in the book of Genesis, chapter 6, that, after the sin of eating the fruit of the Tree of Knowledge and the separation of man from a vessel of holiness and eternal life, sin was introduced into the world—of sexual intercourse, the fruit of desire; it was the curse that fell on Adam and Eve and perpetrated by Satan—other forces (evil sin, *sitra ahar*). The Word of God says this:

> Now it came to pass that man began to multiply on the face of the earth and daughters were born to them. That the sons of God saw the daughters of men, that they looked beautiful, and they took wives for themselves of all whom they chose.
>
> And the Lord said, "My Spirit shall not strive with man forever, for his is indeed flesh; yet his days shall be one hundred

and twenty years. There were giants on the earth in those days, and also afterwards when the sons of God came into the daughters of men, and they bore *children* to them. Those were the mighty men of renown.

Then the Lord saw that the wickedness of man was great in the earth and that every intent of the thoughts of his heart was only evil continually. And the Lord was sorry that He had made man on the earth, and He was grieved in His heart. So, the Lord said, "I will destroy man whom I have created from the face of the earth, both man and beast, creeping thing and birds of the air, for I am sorry that I have made them. But Noah found grace in the eyes of the Lord.

—(Genesis 6:1–8)

In Genesis 9:15–17, God made a covenant with Noah, and the rainbow is the sign of that covenant.

And God said to Noah, "This is the sign of the covenant which I have established between Me and all flesh that is on the earth."

I want to show a contrast here that is as painful to me as it is to my Jewish brothers. The Second World War was Satan's mockery of God. Satan had used man from the day he was created to mock God and His holy creation. It was the same thing in the Second World War. Let me explain. Adolf Hitler was a profoundly evil man, the son of Satan. He built altars in Nuremberg based on the altars of the temple of Pergamon, which was described as the seat of Satan in the book of Revelation 2:12–14. Albert Speer, the architect of these altars that he built for that evil man Hitler, took those very ideas from the temple of Pergamon. With great deception and mockery, Hitler appeared in Europe like a messiah—an evil, false messiah—received God's chosen people, and offered them as a burnt offering, a tithe, one-tenth of all who died, 6 million precious souls of God's people. A total of 60 million people perished in that war, and it was a mockery and the greatest evil crime against humanity. So, as a man of God, I must speak even if people want to stone me for it. I do not judge but share my wisdom. Sexual immorality and sexual desire are potent forces that continue to plague our world, just as they did the ancient. After the fall of Adam and Eve, every other creature became the same. Yet, animals have a season for it; they mate only during seasons and then depart from each other. It's the law of nature and pure instinct. Yet, the creature that walks on two legs is of a higher level and can think more profound evil things because of the separation from holiness. God allowed it and sanctified it in the law of Moses and the Torah with the marriage of a man and woman in holy matrimony. Animals reproduce in competition and pure instinct. Humans are capable of very evil deeds with the act of sexual immorality, and we are at a crisis in the world with these values.

The next thing I experienced on the beach in Tel Aviv may drive home my message even more as I saw the signs in front of me. The apostasy of our times and humanity in crisis is because the rainbow flags that fluttered out on the streets of Tel Aviv played out with the dogs on the beach.

My companion Benny needed to take a dip in the sea, so I kept an eye on all his stuff for him on the shore. The shoreline was packed and dynamic, with a lot of things going on. I remained on the asphalt and sat on the wall with the water taps below me. I watched individuals having a ball while Benny was catching a few waves. There were seven male pooches on the shoreline strolling behind the weakest male in the pack, all attempting to mate with it. It was a hot day, and this canine drama was happening on the coastline. When the male canine plunked down on the sand, attempting to shield his backside from being infiltrated by the other male dogs that hounded it, one male mounted on his nose, and another climbed him on his side, and the canine tumbled down on the sand while every one of the dogs sniffed him. The furore deteriorated. I began to feel upset for the pooch since he was in a wrong position; these dogs were very much bolstered with muscle and bone and desperate to mate. When the pooch stood up, a steady progression continued, assaulting him from the back, attempting to mate with this male dog. I'd never observed anything like this in my life. I have seen male pooches mate with female canines; however, this was a gay motorcade directly before me performed by mutts. The canine was depleted, and I began to yell for assistance since it was getting extremely genuine. Individuals were snickering at the scene, uninformed in their obliviousness that the canine was experiencing weariness.

I asked some odd Jewish folks to enable me to safeguard the canine, yet I was stunned and deadened at their reaction: "If the owners of the pooches don't mind, it's okay."

I looked at them and stated, "Are you out of your mind? Can't you see it's six male pooches attempting to mate with the weakest male canine in the gathering? Come on, folks!" I began to yell for assistance and make a clamour so that the reprobate owners would deal with their mutts and put them on a leash and salvage the pooch. "What isn't right with you individuals? Can't you see what the heck is going on?" I yelled again.

The two strange Jewish fools looked at me and stated, "No judgement, man." These men had tattoos; they were around thirty years of age and looked like ordinary dopeheads.

No judgement—I shook my head disapprovingly and said, "You all are simply miserable and have no clue, man!" I was yelling for help on the shoreline, and the two owners began to isolate the canines. It was somewhat troubling as we were hauling hounds off of one another. The owner of the "weakest male" canine put that poor creature under the taps and began to cool him down. One specific Labrador canine was exceptionally solid and robust. He was hauling his proprietor to the taps and still attempting to mate with the other male pooch. At that point, all of a sudden, it collapsed and was struggling to breathe; it was either exhausted to death or having a heart attack. Some people attempted to pour water on him and salvage it; the canine lay there gasping for breath with a horde of individuals pouring water over its body and giving it some water to drink.

The owner of the "weakest male" canine drove his pooch away and left the shoreline. Individuals were on the telephone calling animal rescue since it looked like the Labrador was not going to make it, as it had collapsed from complete depletion from its compelling impulse to mate with another male pooch. I was so bothered by the absence of responsibility in reprobate individuals who own dogs. I have been a canine owner, and if you are not going to breed your pooches or offer them the chance to mate, you can castrate the creature and put him out of his misery. Indeed, even the canines turned out to be gay on the shoreline. Those two delinquent fools with their reprobate responses, those silly women laughing in giggles, almost butt naked on the beach, at the sight of the crisis at hand, were irresponsible people who don't know how to control their dogs and leave them on the beach unattended.

People see a terrible thing and think it's okay, and they take a good thing and say it's awful. I was viewed as the fool who was making a big deal about silly mutts, when, in fact, it was the humans that were reprobate, with all their gay parades and sexual immorality. Even the dogs were displaying the same behaviour. Creation has fallen to a new low, and I could see the days of Noah before me in signs of our times and the abandonment of indecency surrounding me. I needed to leave, and leave I did. I felt so distressed by the experience of it all. What is wrong with human beings?

The rainbow was a holy covenant that God made with Noah, and now they take the same colours, flag it up on poles, and make a mockery of God. In the darkness of their mind, they have gone astray. "No judgement," but there is a separation, and there is a judgement at the end. It's written, and it's the Word of God (Luke 10).

We are living in a time when humankind is presently considering the most befuddling cluster of emergencies it has ever gone up against. There is a population emergency, an energy crisis, and a financial emergency, and there is a crisis in morals and values, a crisis of lack of faith and good deeds. There is a crisis in the environment, there is a crisis in ethics and values, there are confusion and crisis in sex perplexity, a crisis in education, and we additionally have an emergency with plastic. You don't see it, however, there are two spots in the seas: one in the Indian sea and the other in the Pacific, where vast amounts of plastic are beating around in currents of the sea. Since you live ashore and will never get the opportunity to see it, because nobody is going to take you out there, yet if you do go out there to see it, it's more than an emergency you will see. There is a political emergency, government emergency, an EU emergency, an Iran crisis, and there are many who have contended that the inability to determine the urgency being referred to implies the extinction of human civilisation. Now is the ideal opportunity for a basic revaluation of the monster size and nature of the emergency with which the world is confronted.

What's more, with the ways by which they cogitate, they may have a shot at settling them. The issues may go further; be that as it may, such specialists have the ability. Maybe the problems are embedded in the traditional process of decision-making itself.

The events of the day overwhelmed me, and Tel Aviv made me tired and depleted, so I went and took a shower and put on my Jewish clothes, my *tzitzit*, black trousers. I did not have any white shirts, so Dr. Jack Leitner gave me one of his shirts and a Jewish hat. It was the day of the Shabbat, and I could not wait to place myself in a holy sanctuary. Outfitted with a lovely name, Moshe, I walked with my dear friend Dr. Jack Leitner down the boulevard towards his brother's house. Along the way, I got a crash course on Jewish traditions, but I was well versed in them already. I have read so much of scriptures these last years; I had read the book of Leviticus thoroughly.

Jack remarked to me, "And you sometimes know more about the scriptures than the average Jew. Are you sure you have no Jewish ancestry?"

"Well," I replied, "I couldn't say for sure, Jack, but my family is such a mix—they came from all over the world."

We got to the house and went upstairs. I was introduced to his sister-in-law, who was setting up the table and lights for the Shabbat dinner. Jack's elder brother came down, and I was introduced to the family as Moshe, whose family had come from Akron in Yemen. These were lovely people. My stay was brief, and we talked about our favourite musician, Van Morrison; everyone in this house adored his music, and so did I. I love it. We walked down the road together, chatting, to the synagogue. I sat between the two tall men—a brown Jewish man with the most beautiful name ever: Moshe.

I was given a praying book in English and Hebrew, and celebrated all the Jewish prayers with pure joy from my heart. I loved the psalms and the traditional prayer of the Torah, as the Rabbi read, and the men and women were separated by a screen but their faces were still visible; they were singing in Hebrew and declaring the glory of God. I loved the way people dressed—the women in traditional Jewish clothing. It was a solemn, significant, powerful revelation when I understood the colossal awakening when the whole congregation turned to face the entrance to greet the bridegroom. I was delighted when I realised that the Shabbat was a wedding of the bridegroom with His bride, a day of rest and peace for the world. I closed my eyes, and my eyes filled with a million tears that I'd suppressed. The grace of God fell like a billion stars from the sky, like fish scales falling off the eyes of Rabbi Paul when He saw Jesus. It was the revelation of my life, right here in the Holy Land, Israel.

I did not join the family for dinner because I did not want to inconvenience them; they had already been too kind to me. I shook the hand of my dear friend Jack. I already loved him for what he had done for me; he was another angel that I had met on my last day. I had wrestled for a blessing walking down from Mount Hermon and travelling on that Jesus Trail all alone with thorns and tears; now I felt like a small Jacob who had just received a new name and a blessing.

I was leaving Israel in the evening the next day, and as much as I did not like Tel Aviv, Dr. Jack, my angel from Boston, made it a special place for me. So onwards I marched on with this blessing; this is the story of my life, and I hope the Lord, blessed be His holy name, will give me a long and fruitful life. I thank him for the downfalls and troubles in my life because, all along, He was drawing me back to Him. I don't have enough words in my heart to thank Him for undeserved grace, so I look to King David for the psalms. For the instructions of my life, I look at the Book of Life, the Holy Bible. When I look for wisdom and the love of the bridegroom for His bride, I turn to King Solomon. When I seek the revelation of the secrets of the Messiah, I pray to the Holy Spirit of God Almighty. When I visited the Jewish Quarter, the prophet Zechariah came to my mind; the prophecies of the boys and girls playing on the streets of the old city—I saw them before my eyes. When I open my Bible, and the four Gospels— Matthew, Mark, Luke, and John—tell me all about the Messiah, Yeshua HaMashiach, the name above all names, this captivates my very soul and heart. When I read the letters of saints—Paul, Peter, James, Jude, John, Philemon, Timothy, Titus—I know my purpose in my life. When I turn to the book of Revelation, I tremble in fear, for it's the testimony of our Lord and Saviour Jesus Christ. I know that He is the way, the truth, and the life. There is a judgement, and there is a separation.

I walked these trails in a physical form but in a more profound sense of spiritually seeking the spirit and wisdom of God. I cannot read His Word superficially anymore, because the eyes on my heart and the enlivening of my spirit were activated to the "upper light." So, you may ask, what does one do to ensure you make it back home, where you belong—in the bosom of His creation and eternal life? The Word of God says faith and works.

Ought ye not to know that the LORD God of Israel gave the kingdom over Israel to David forever, even to him and to his sons by a covenant of salt?

—(2 Chronicles 13:5)

And every meal-offering of thine shalt thou season with salt; neither shalt thou suffer the salt of the covenant of thy God to be lacking from thy meal-offering; with all thy offerings thou shalt offer salt.

—(Leviticus 2:13)

The Lord has called me, and I have answered His calling. He has promised us an everlasting reign in the glory of his holiness. I follow His voice, His commandments, and His signs.

Recently, I was in the state of Washington. I was given instructional signs to go, and so I went. My spirit moved me to pray for America, to pray for a revival in this nation.

We assembled on Mount Rainier, and some of my Christian friends were unaware of the covenant of salt.

The hardest difference two individuals can have is when both accept they are in the will of God. How would you know which one was correct? Absalom felt God was favouring him and attempted to persuade everybody. David realised it was anything but a matter of convincing everybody what was true. David and Absalom both had a daily commitment to God in prayer.

In old times, each individual in Israel carried a little pack of salt. The word for *salt* in Greek is *salarium* and means "compensation." Salt was utilised to pay officers and preserve meat. It was valuable. However, there was substantially more to it than merely this capacity. At the point when two individuals guaranteed each other something, they took a touch of salt and traded it in each other's sack and shook it up. Presently their lives were inherently fortified together. It was known as the "covenant of salt."

On Mount Rainer, we petitioned God for a pledge of salt, our lives to be saved and preserved in holiness. We appealed to God for America. We blew the shofar to stir the sleeping spirits in this nation.

A cloud appeared and descended, a circular rainbow showed up, and an eagle lifted in the air and orbited us. The name of God was carved on the wooden log we were sitting on. These signs were genuine, and they were captured. It astounded everybody, and I was lowered to my knees in worship and prayer. These events took place in August 2019 on the Mount Rainer as we gathered to pray. I believed there was a shift coming and I did not know what it was precisely. The photographs are the evidence of these events. By the end of the year the Covid19 plague came into the world.

FINAL WORDS

Let me then share with you a final scripture that came to me:

2 For if Abraham were justified by works, he hath whereof to glory; but not before God.

3 For what saith the scripture? Abraham believed God, and it was counted unto him for Righteousness.

4 Now to him that worketh is the reward not reckoned of grace, but of debt.

5 But to him that worketh not, but believeth on him that justified the ungodly, his Faith is counted for Righteousness. (Romans 4:2–6 KJV)

It is a simple truth: faith is counted to us as righteousness, because the angel of righteousness agreed with the Creator during the creation and formation of man. The Word of God teaches us this:

26, And God said, Let us make man in our image, after our likeness: and let them have dominion over the fish of the sea, and over the fowl of the air, and over the cattle, and over all the earth, and over every creeping thing that creepeth upon the earth. (Genesis 1:26)

The creation of man was an agreement between angels and God; it says, "Let *us* make man in *our* image." This *us* means the council of holy angels with God Almighty—blessed be His holy name. Hence,

435

your faith counted to you as righteousness. But the Bible says faith without works is dead.

> *14 What does it profit, my brethren, if someone says he has Faith but does not have works? Can Faith save him? 15 If a brother or sister is naked and destitute of daily food, 16 and one of you says to them, "Depart in peace, be warmed and filled," but you do not give them the things which are needed for the body, what does it profit? 17 Thus also Faith by itself, if it does not have works, is dead.*

—(James 2:14–14 KJV)

> *Now to him that worketh is the reward not reckoned of grace, but of debt.*

—(Romans 4:4)

There it is—when you live the Christian life by your daily works of holiness, righteousness, mercy, love, forgiveness, charity, generosity, and every godly aspect of the "upper light," God and all the angels say it is counted to you as debt. Can you imagine that heaven is in debt to you and counted unto you as debt? Your rewards are that you will be called the sons of God. Your name is counted in the Tree of Life. You don't want to miss heaven.

I pray my little, imperfect life will inspire and illuminate you to find your peace with the Prince of Peace. I am back in orbit and positioned with my creator like never before—to function once again in perfection—and I found my calling to serve the Lord. I surrendered everything in the world because everything in this world is nothing. I like nothing because He created the world when it was nothing, empty and void. Only with His word did He speak existence into it. God's love for us is real; it had no beginning, and it has no end. Jesus is real, and His love is everlasting. He loved us first—but not because we are appealing or beautiful in our character.

He loves us because He is the epitome of love. God does not like us *because* Jesus died for us, but Jesus died for us, so that God *could* love us once again and bring us into His Holy presence through the blood of Christ—the correction of creation when a man walked with him in the garden in the cool of the day.

Glory to God. Hallelujah.

Yeshua HaMashiach
Shalom Aleichem

BIBLIOGRAPHY

1. "Anglo-Indians: Is Their Culture Dying out?" *BBC News*. BBC, January 4, 2013. https://www.bbc.com/news/magazine-20857969.
2. "Nizam of Hyderabad: Fifth on the *Forbes* 'All Time Wealthiest'." HelloJi, April 12, 2008. https://helloji.word-press.com/2008/04/11/nizam-of-hyderabad-fifth-on-the-forbes-all-time-wealthiest/
3. In the BBC program "Anglo-Indians: Is Their Culture Dying Out?" https://www.bbc.com/news/magazine-20857969., 2013
4. "Floral Emblems—Australian Plant Information." South Australia—Floral Emblems—Australian Plant Information. Accessed February 15, 2020. https://www.anbg.gov.au/emblems/sa.emblem.html.
5. "Convicts and the Colonisation of Australia, 1788–1868." The Digital Panopticon. Accessed February 15, 2020. https://www.digitalpanopticon.org/Convicts_and_the_Colonisation_of_Australia,_1788-1868.
6. "Our Culture: Sections." Share Our Pride. Accessed February 15, 2020. http://shareourpride.reconciliation.org.au/sections/our-culture/.
7. Tracy, Jessica and Robins, Richard. (2007). "The Psychological Structure of Pride: A Tale of Two Facets." *Journal of Personality and Social Psychology*. 92. 506-25. 10.1037/0022-3514.92.3.506.
8. Bedells, S. J. (2010). "Incarcerating Indigenous People of the Wongatha Lands in the Eastern Goldfields of Western Australia: Indigenous Leaders' Perspectives." https://ro.ecu.edu.au/theses/137

9. Wikipedia contributors, "Teredo navalis," *Wikipedia, The Free Encyclopedia*. Accessed February 17, 2020. https://en.wikipedia .org/w/index.php?title=Teredo_navalis&oldid=909237781

10. *Environmental Health Perspectives*. 116. No. 2c (Januaryhttps:// doi.org/10.1289/image.cehp.v116.ic

11. Blyton, G. (2020). *Health and History* on JSTOR [online].Jstor .org. Available at https://www.jstor.org/journal/of health [Accessed 24 Feb. 2020]

12. Chabad.org. 2020. Explanation Of 120 Forms Of Name Elokim; Explanation Of 288 Sparks That Fell In The Shattering Of Worlds Of Tohu – Letter No. 177:. [online] Available at: <https://www .chabad.org/therebbe/letters/default_cdo/aid/2282398/jewish/ Explanation-of-120-forms-of-name-Elokim-explanation-of- 288-sparks-that-fell-in-the-shattering-of-worlds-of-Tohu.htm> [Accessed 23 July 2020].

The Author and Christian friends experience rare events on Mount Rainer Washington USA August 2019 According to US Forest Rangers.
Unusual events in the sky, a descending cloud on the mountain , eagles circling as we blew the 'shofar' and prayed for a revival and mercy for America.

The miraculous rescue of the Author and friends on the Golan Trail in Israel May 2019.

ABOUT THE AUTHOR

Lyndon Berchy was born into an Anglo-Indian family and raised in the Outback of Australia. He worked across the globe in the oil and gas industry and became a global voice for speaking the truth to people across the world. His love for Aboriginal art and culture was deeply embedded in his experience of life in the Outback with the true people of Australia. Native art and storytelling, and literary development led him to study creative rhetoric writing at UCLA. He also holds an MBA from the Middlesex University London. He writes from the depths of his heart. He is an author who accepts that a decent book should be intensively lived to be told. Writing the story was deeply intense, a prophetic voice, a servant messenger for this age. The astonishing story is now presented to the world. He lives and travels the globe with the amazing *The Flight of Kurrawurra,* his debut book.